FALLING EAGLE

FALLING EAGLE

THE DECLINE OF BARCLAYS BANK

Martin Vander Weyer

Weidenfeld & Nicolson

LONDON

First published in Great Britain in 2000
by Weidenfeld & Nicolson

© 2000 Martin Vander Weyer

Second impression March 2000

A CIP catalogue record for this book
is available from the British Library.

ISBN 0 297 64406 8

Typeset by Selwood Systems, Midsomer Norton

Printed in Great Britain by
Butler & Tanner Ltd, Frome and London

Weidenfeld & Nicolson
The Orion Publishing Group Ltd
Orion House
5 Upper Saint Martin's Lane
London, WC2H 9EA

CONTENTS

List of Illustrations vii
Acknowledgements viii
Introduction 1

1 **Falling Star** 5
1998: Why Martin Taylor was unhappy – Problems with Russia –
Problems with LTCM – Problems with Sir Andrew Large – The
New York board meeting – Taylor's resignation – Sir Peter
Middleton's moment of destiny

2 **Origins** 26
1896–1966: The rise of joint-stock banking – The great
amalgamation – The Local Head Office system – The triumph of
Frederick Goodenough – The wisdom of Cuthbert Fitzherbert –
The rise of Deryk Vander Weyer

3 **Zenith** 45
1966–1979: The birth of Barclaycard – The partnership of Derek
Wilde and John Thomson – The discovery of marketing – The
acquisition of Martins Bank – The buying-in of Barclays DCO –
The global vision of Anthony Tuke – The Fringe Bank crisis –
Relations with the Labour government – The creation of Barclays
Merchant Bank – Barclays at its zenith

4 **Table Manners** 67
An interlude on Barclays' eating habits, architecture and uncles

5 **The Mood of the Eighties** 77
1980–1986: The impact of Thatcherism – The accession of Timothy
Bevan – The challenge of being Number One – Problems in New
York, Hong Kong and Milan – The departure of Deryk Vander
Weyer – Falling morale – NatWest takes the lead – How John
Quinton was chosen

6 **South Africa** 97
1925–1999: DCO's roots in South Africa – The rise of the anti-
Barclays protest movement – Barclays as the anti-apartheid bank –
The decision to withdraw – The difficulty of returning

7 **Biarritz to Tokyo**   107
1973–1986: An interlude in France – A series of job interviews –
Joining Barclays Merchant Bank – Cold calling in America –
Diplomacy in Malaysia – Guerrilla war in Tokyo

8 **The Birth of BZW**   128
1983–1991: Camoys' brainchild – Buying de Zoetes and Wedds –
The culture clash – Sir Martin Jacomb arrives – What autonomy
meant – Buxton steps in – Onwards and upwards – Sir Peter
Middleton takes over

9 **Boom and Bust**   148
1987–1992: Quinton makes his mark – An explosion of property
lending – An unpopular rights issue – The turn of the tide – The
Imry loan – Quinton's heart trouble – Too much restructuring –
Brian Pearse goes to Midland – Relationships break down – The
crowning of Andrew Buxton

10 **The Pig Ceremony**   169
1986–1992: Playing games with the Japanese Ministry of Finance –
Battling with Barclays in Tokyo – The crash of Black Monday –
The pleasures of Asia – A memorial service – The end of a short
career

11 **The Annual Show**   189
1993–1998: The dividend cut – Buxton splits his job – The
appointment of Martin Taylor – A mixed impression – The share
buy-backs – A turning-point for Taylor – Difficulties in pleasing
the customer – Barclays as seen from an agricultural show

12 **The Band Cocktail**   207
1988–1996: The man from J. P. Morgan and his appetites – The
peak of BZW's performance – The second Big Bang – The death
of David Band – Martin Taylor's doubts begin to show – Bill
Harrison arrives – Bob Diamond arrives first – Tenth birthday
celebrations

13 **BZW: The Last Ten Months**   226
1996–1997: Revolving doors at Ebbgate House – The move to
Canary Wharf – Reassurances from Martin Taylor – No deal with
Smith Barney – Breaking up BZW – The sale runs out of control –
A deal with CSFB

14 **A Sexier Future?**   246
1998–1999: No internal candidates – A bout of Californian flu –
The sexiest banker in Canada – Branch banking is going to look
different – And so to judgement

Bibliography   264
Index   267

ILLUSTRATIONS

Silvanus Bevan the Third
The premises of Barclay, Bevan, Tritton & Co (1864)
Francis Augustus Bevan
The board of Barclay & Co in 1900
Frederick Crauford Goodenough
A Barclays delegation in Kyoto (1975)
Deryk Vander Weyer
The board of Barclays Bank Limited in 1980
Sir Timothy Bevan, Deryk Vander Weyer and Margaret
    Thatcher (1982)
The first staff of BZW Tokyo (1985)
The opening party of BZW Tokyo (1985)
The senior management of Barclays in 1987
    (*Barclays Bank*)
BZW's Hong Kong equity dealing team (1988)
'The team taking BZW to the top' (*Nick Rogers*)
Martin Taylor (*Sue Adler*)
Sir Peter Middleton (*Fergus Wilkey*)
Martin Taylor and Andrew Buxton (*Popperfoto*)
Bill Harrison (*Financial Times syndications*)
Sir Andrew Large (*Dan Atkin*)
Matt Barrett with Anne-Marie Sten (*Toronto Sun*)

ACKNOWLEDGEMENTS

This book is the product of some fifty interviews with past and present Barclays group executives and other people with strong views on the subject. Several former colleagues have also taken the time to read and comment on sections of the manuscript. Many of those I talked to offered me generous hospitality and I should like to have thanked them here by name, but a large proportion asked not to be quoted directly in the text and it would be invidious merely to name those who spoke freely. So I thank everyone who has given me their time and express the hope that I have not misrepresented them, even anonymously. I must thank also Barclays Bank itself for its limited but enlightened co-operation.

I have made use of many informal conversations which took place long before I thought of writing this book. The corporate tittle-tattle of long ago is often impossible to check for accuracy and must be taken in that spirit. I have had particular difficulty in handling confidential information learned from my late father, but where it might have been gratuitously hurtful I have not used it, and I have not disguised his voice in anonymous quotations.

I salute all the City journalists whose coverage of Barclays has contributed to my source material: notably Andrew Lorenz, Kirstie Hamilton and John Jay of the *Sunday Times*, Neil Bennett of the *Sunday Telegraph*, Christopher Fildes and Helen Dunne of the *Daily Telegraph*, Paul Farrelly of the *Observer* and George Graham of the *Financial Times*. I am grateful to the *Telegraph*'s librarians for their help and to the *Spectator* for permission to reproduce the article which appears in Chapter 10. Finally I take this opportunity to thank three people who were particularly helpful to me during my banking career – Christopher Haviland, Nick Sibley and Kaye Squires – and four who encouraged me in my transition from banker to writer: Christopher Fildes again, Dominic Lawson of the *Sunday Telegraph* and two former BZW colleagues, Robert Cottrell of *The Economist* and Jo McBride of Asia Agenda International in Hong Kong.

Falling Eagle is affectionately dedicated to the memory of my father.

INTRODUCTION

Companies are not, and never have been, machines for making money, though management gurus sometimes tell us that they ought to be. Whether they operate corner shops, grand hotels or giant factories, companies are accumulations of human skill, hope and weakness, of individual and collective will-power, of accidents of history and advances of science. They are shaped by the times and places in which they operate. They have their own vocabulary, their own architecture, their own folklore.

Barclays Bank is, in all these senses, much more than a business, perhaps more even than is usually conveyed by the word 'institution'. As banks go, it has a remarkable and colourful heritage. To the thoughtful observer, it has as much in common with historic regiments, religious cults, primitive tribes and small countries as it does with its rivals along the British high street.

And it has significance, in different ways, for many millions of people, living and dead. A survey published in June 1999[1], when the bank had been suffering a run of atrocious publicity for the best part of two years, found the Barclays brand to be 'the most valuable in Britain', worth, according to expert calculations, almost three times as much as the names of Marks & Spencer, Tesco or Burger King. Barclays' 'spread eagle' symbol and turquoise-blue corporate colour are (or were, until they were interfered with recently to create a softer, more sophisticated image) instantly recognized by almost every British adult. Some ten million people belong to Barclays as customers and – though they may feel no warmth in the relationship and have long since ceased to have dealings with anyone resembling a traditional bank manager – they are still constrained by loyalty, caution and inertia from moving their business elsewhere. Some hundreds of thousands of people since the bank's modern foundation in 1896 have been tied to Barclays as

---

[1] The survey by Interbrand, a consultancy specializing in brand valuation, put a value of £5.3 billion on the Barclays name. Lloyds TSB was in second place at £3.7 billion.

employees and pensioners. Almost 130,000 people, as shareholders, feel that Barclays belongs to them today.

Outside Britain, most people in the developed world and a great many in the developing world, especially in black Africa, know roughly what Barclays is, and to the extent that they have any opinion about it, they probably think of Barclays as they think of our royal family: a little old-fashioned, perhaps, but reliably British, gently evolving with the times, always there. To the British traveller abroad, meanwhile, the advertising slogan last used a quarter of a century ago – 'If there isn't a Barclays, you're probably lost' – still has a certain resonance.

And yet Barclays itself has been lost for years. Like so much that seems reliably British, it has indeed evolved over the past twenty years, but not for the better. It is not what it was, but nor is it what it might have become. This is the story of how Barclays rose in the 1960s and 1970s to become one of the biggest, most profitable and most admired banks in the world, but how it fell in the late 1980s and the 1990s to the diminished state in which it found itself in mid-1999: leaderless, bereft of coherent strategy, trailing behind competitors to whom it would barely have tipped its hat a decade ago.

It is a story rich in irony. Until the mid-1980s, for example, Barclays retained an anti-egalitarian management system in which descendants of its founding families and their friends rose by an accelerated stream to the top of the bank, bypassing talented managers of humbler social origin. And yet the last period in which that system reigned unchallenged, under the chairmanship of Sir Anthony Tuke from 1973 to 1981, was also the zenith of Barclays' fortunes. In the 1980s a battle was joined between old forces and new ones: internally between meritocrats and hereditaries and between mercenary, fast-moving investment bankers and loyal, convention-bound clearing bankers; externally in high street competition and international capital markets. Barclays was never the same again.

It is ironic also that Barclays continues to make, in its basic branch banking business, a barely diminished river of profits. This is a bank whose last three chairmen – Sir Timothy Bevan, Sir John Quinton and Andrew Buxton, spanning eighteen years – have rarely attracted a kind word from financial commentators. It is a bank which in the winter of 1998–9 lost two chief executives – Martin Taylor, who left his job in a moment of high drama unprecedented in recent British corporate history, and Michael O'Neill, an American who never actually took up his post at all. It is a business which has destroyed well over a billion pounds a year for the past decade in unwise lending and in its investment banking and trading adventures. Yet Barclays managed to report operating profits of almost three and a half billion pounds for the turbulent eighteen month period from January 1998 to June 1999. At the operating level, it seems, Barclays can go on making satisfactory profits whatever its state of internal chaos. In that sense, and contrary to my opening gambit, it actually is a machine for making money. And like all machines it must face, eventually, the threat of obsolescence.

But this is not a business-school analysis of how banks ought to be run, and nor is it an official corporate history. It is unofficial, and it is also personal. My father, Deryk Vander Weyer, was an employee of Barclays from January 1941 until September 1988, rising from junior clerk to deputy chairman. By making him a central figure in the first half of this story, I do not intend to suggest that he was uniquely heroic, but merely that he was one of the prime movers in the events which shaped the bank in the sixties and seventies, as well as a role model for many people who followed him and an illustration of Barclays' unique social nuances. He had strong views on everything to do with Barclays, and he enjoyed being outspoken. He was 'arguably the outstanding commercial banker of his generation' (Nigel Lawson's words, not mine) but, arguably also, he was prevented by Barclays, at the final stage, from achieving his full potential. Yet he remained extremely loyal to Barclays, and proud of his career there. He died in 1990 long before I ever thought of writing this book, and I cannot know whether he would have approved of it.

I was also a Barclays employee myself from 1981 to 1992. The account of my own undistinguished career in the bank's investment banking arm in Chapters 7 and 11 may seem at first to lean towards the pointless and self-indulgent. But the reader will perhaps wonder whether I am using pointless self-indulgence as a literary device to illustrate the very nature of investment banking in the 1980s. I cannot claim to have made any personal difference at all to the bank's destiny, but I can claim to have been a witness to the struggles of that decade and to have known at close quarters most of the personalities who were to dominate the next one.

And my relationship with the organization goes back further and deeper. I was first interviewed by a Barclays branch manager in 1959, when I was caught as an unruly four-year-old playing in a cupboard in the machine room of the High Barnet branch, downstairs from the flat where we lived. I was first interviewed at the bank's head office in Lombard Street in 1968, for a scholarship funded by one of the grand Barclays families; and again in 1973 for a summer job in one of the

French branches. I first applied, unsuccessfully, for a permanent job in Barclays in 1976, and finally struck lucky, if that is the right phrase, five years later at Barclays Merchant Bank, which in due course became part of Barclays de Zoete Wedd (BZW), Barclays' ill-fated attempt to build a global investment bank. I became a director of BZW in 1987, set up several of its offices in Asia, helped to run its corporate finance division, and was sacked – abruptly but rather to my relief, and on relatively generous terms – in January 1992.

In the meantime, I have been a customer of Barclays for almost thirty years. I entrust my modest investments to the management of a very nice Barclays man in Peterborough. In due course, I look forward to collecting a BZW pension. Given this lifelong relationship, the most disloyal thing I could do to Barclays would be to take my accounts away, but that is not an option I have ever felt the need to consider. Merely to write about Barclays would not seem disloyal at all, if I thought of Barclays as merely a business. As it is, my conscience is troubled, but only a little. If this story is uncomfortable to read for some of those who were part of it, I hope it is also in a small way cathartic. I have returned to Barclays' historic corridors armed with prejudices which I had no intention of concealing. Some have been reinforced but others, happily, have been blunted or overturned in re-examination.

The developments of my father's era in Barclays and of mine contributed cumulatively to the circumstances of the 1990s, when internal faultlines suddenly combined with external market storms in a way which came close to blowing Barclays apart. Before we trace those fault lines back to the nineteenth century, let us remind ourselves how the story ends.

I

FALLING STAR

1998: Why Martin Taylor was unhappy – Problems with Russia –
Problems with LTCM – Problems with Sir Andrew Large –
The New York board meeting – Taylor's resignation – Sir Peter
Middleton's moment of destiny

Two things went terribly wrong for Martin Taylor in the summer of
1998. Stock markets and currencies across the globe were caught up in
a sudden bout of extreme turbulence which seemed briefly to threaten
the entire global financial system. And Sir Andrew Large joined Barclays
Bank.

Martin Taylor, chief executive of Barclays from 1 January 1994 until
his sudden resignation on 26 November 1998, has a very big part in
this book. Sir Andrew Large, who was executive deputy chairman of
Barclays from 1 May 1998 until 1 January 1999, has a much smaller one
and we shall return to him in a moment. To understand the tensions
of Barclays in the summer of 1998, it is the rise and fall of Taylor's star
that we have to follow.

We shall learn more about Taylor's personality and past career in
Chapter 11, but suffice it to say by way of introduction that when he
was hired from Courtaulds Textiles to become Barclays chief executive
at the age of only forty-two, he was heralded as one of Britain's cleverest
businessmen, an intellectual leader of his generation and a stunningly
good choice to be the agent of change in an organization desperately
lacking leadership. Having once been a brilliant financial journalist
himself, he commanded the respect and attention of the press. In his
first three years at Barclays, though he occasionally made unguarded
remarks, he rarely put a foot wrong in action. He brought refreshing
clarity to the question of whether Barclays' shareholders were getting
a decent return on their money, and if not, whether it would not be

better simply to give them some of it back. Internally, the same clarity was applied to the process of risk assessment in the bank's lending business, and to its management structures. As the British economy pulled itself out of recession, so the bank's lending performance and its relations with its customers steadily improved.

But from first to last Taylor had a problem in Barclays, and that was BZW. The investment banking side of the business had a certain fascination for Taylor, because – unlike the clearing bank – it employed clever people doing clever transactions. But it also carried dangerous risks without producing satisfactory returns; it represented, in Taylor's view, an enormous management distraction relative to its real importance in the group; it was in need of huge additional investment to give it the critical mass it needed to compete at the highest level, against the giants of Wall Street; and he had no personal empathy with most of its senior executives.

In exasperation, and in the teeth of powerful internal opposition, Taylor had decided in September 1997 to split BZW and sell off the parts he liked least: its equities and corporate finance divisions. The sale to Credit Suisse First Boston, completed two months later, turned out to be an acceptable solution for most of the BZW staff who moved there, but a fiasco for Barclays. The press which had once been so uncritical in its admiration for Taylor turned savagely against him. Within Barclays, his support drained away and his enemies rubbed their hands.

There might still have been a great face-saving deal for Taylor: in mid-November 1997, when the flak over the CSFB deal was at its most intense, there was also a resurgence of the rumours about merger talks between Barclays and its high street rival NatWest which had first circulated in the City in June. These became so concrete that it was reported Barclays had appointed J.P. Morgan to advise on the deal and LEK, a management consultancy, to work on the presentation of it to the competition authorities; NatWest was said to have appointed Lazards. It came to nothing, however. NatWest was not interested, having regained self-confidence after a long period of problems and begun to plot a path for its own recovery. And its directors were not keen to talk to Taylor, whom they blamed for stirring merger rumours in the summer in a way which they saw as intentionally destabilizing.

Three months later it all happened again but this time with Standard Chartered, a perennial marriage candidate for Barclays. In mid-February, Taylor dined at Chez Nico in Park Lane with Malcolm Williamson, Standard's chief executive and an ex-Barclays man himself.

Suddenly the newspapers were full of bid rumours. Had Taylor popped the question, the press wanted to know, or had Williamson? Either way, Williamson's chairman Patrick Gillam was against the deal, and nothing came of it. Nor did anything come of rumours that Taylor was talking to Halifax, Prudential, Norwich Union or Legal & General.

Perhaps that was because he was not talking to them, or perhaps it was because the damaged rating of Barclays shares made merger deals too unattractive to work. Either way, Barclays seemed to have entered a period of drift, and its 1997 year-end profits – hit by the £688 million cost, up to that point, of dismantling BZW – had been 25 per cent down on the previous year. The name of Barclays was diminished, and Taylor was taking the blame.

Taylor's confidence was shaken. He is not a man who likes to be challenged. He is acutely sensitive to criticism, and to his own media image. From the day he joined Barclays until the day he sold BZW, he had been allowed to do very much as he pleased by his chairman, Andrew Buxton, who was no match for him in intellect or clarity or drive; and he had rarely been troubled by the views of the bank's non-executive directors, with whom he had little rapport. Now, however, Buxton and his board were taking a closer and more sceptical interest in Taylor's plans and decisions. It was apparent that personal relations between Taylor and Buxton had deteriorated. Board meetings became tense and dysfunctional: there was 'an undercurrent of unpleasantness', as one director put it. Taylor began to feel not only that the board was against him, but that elements within it were actively undermining him by constant whispering to the press. He even went so far as to call in a specialist security company to trace the sources of suspected leaks.

His aim was to get the better of his opponents – real or imaginary – by proving them wrong. He believed the rump of BZW which Barclays had retained and rechristened Barclays Capital – dealing only in debt and bonds – would prove itself to be a better business than BZW as a whole had been. He was anxious to find a merger partner in the retail financial services sector but seemed determined to do so in secret, without leaks, using only his most trusted lieutenants within the bank. Meanwhile, he believed that the great machine that was the high street banking business of Barclays would gradually retune itself, under increasingly benign economic influences and his own skilled hand, to maximum efficiency and profitability.

It didn't quite work out that way. At the end of July 1998 another force turned against Taylor: the markets. After a strong run in the spring and early summer, US share prices suffered their biggest fall of the year in the first week of August, driven by fears that US companies' earnings would be squeezed by weak demand and strong competition from Asia and by rising wages at home. There were also deep fears about Japan, where the government seemed paralysed in the face of recession, rising unemployment, a collapsing banking sector and a rapidly sinking yen. By the second week of August, the FTSE 100 had followed Wall Street downwards, falling 12 per cent from its July peak. Commentators were arguing as to whether the bear market, long expected by some of them, had finally arrived.

That was the week in which Barclays announced its interim results: pre-tax profits were unchanged at £1.3 billion, much in line with analysts' expectations, but still the shares fell 50p on the news to around £16.40. That fall would become much steeper in the coming weeks, but its immediate significance was to thwart what may well have been Taylor's last hope of striking out in a bold new direction. He and his team, advised on this occasion by Flemings, were poised in that same week to launch a hostile take-over bid for Standard Chartered, where Malcolm Williamson (having fallen out with his chairman over the possibility of a friendly merger with Barclays) was about to retire, and where worries about Asian loan exposures had driven the share price down from a March high of £9 to around £6. Standard's own interim figures came out just before Barclays' and provoked mixed reactions from commentators; but after an initial dip, bullish opinions prevailed and Standard's share price rose. Both shares had moved in the wrong direction, as far as Barclays was concerned: the calculation behind the take-over bid no longer worked because it implied too much dilution for existing Barclays shareholders. The moment of opportunity passed.

Then the market doomsters' attention turned from Asia to Moscow. George Soros, the billionaire speculator and philanthropist, wrote in a letter to the *Financial Times* on 13 August that 'the meltdown in Russian financial markets has reached the terminal phase'. He recommended a swift devaluation of the rouble. Such was the weight attached to his pronouncement that the Russian currency immediately tumbled by 34 per cent – prompting debate as to whether Soros had inadvertently damaged his own and many other foreign investors' interests by the unexpected power of his opinions. Intervention by the IMF, linking bail-out loans to support the rouble to strict demands for budgetary discipline, looked hopelessly ineffective. By the end of the month, the entire Russian stock market had a capitalization smaller than that of J. Sainsbury, the British grocery chain.

This was the point at which the countdown to Taylor's departure from Barclays began. Looking pale and tired, he announced in the first week of September that:

> On 31 August 1998 Barclays had total Russian banking and net securities trading exposure of some £340 million, mostly held within Barclays Capital. The majority of this exposure was in the form of Russian government securities and financial institutions' counterparty credit. The situation within the country continues to be highly volatile. As of today, the Group would expect to make a charge, taking account of collateral held, of the order of £250 million during the second half of 1998 to cover potential losses. The net effect on the Group's 1998 profit attributable to shareholders after tax is expected to be some £150 million. The impact of the situation in Russia on markets in general has had an adverse effect on trading elsewhere in Barclays Capital. Initial indications are that in July and August Barclays Capital has lost approximately £75 million pre-tax in addition to the direct consequences of its Russian exposure.[1]

His audience was not impressed. What on earth was Barclays doing taking £300 million of proprietary trading exposure in Russia in the first place? Wasn't Barclays Capital, under the management of veteran American trader Bob Diamond, supposed to be the sensible, lower-risk end of the securities business? What was the point of Taylor focusing on 'shareholder value' if he let his managers destroy great chunks of it on whimsical bets like this, which had so little relation to any other aspect of the group's business?

Those were valid points of criticism, but what was not widely known at the time was just how closely involved in the Russian business Taylor himself had been. When, earlier in the year, Bob Diamond with his customary messianic enthusiasm had put up a proposal to the group credit committee that Barclays Capital should take a huge position in high-yielding Russian bonds, Taylor chaired the meeting – as he liked to do, because it appealed to his intellect to grapple with difficult risk propositions and his opinions were rarely challenged in the committee by his subordinates. On this occasion, there were seven people present, of whom only two (not including Taylor or Diamond) could have been counted, in old-fashioned Barclays terms, as real bankers – meaning

---

[1] Barclays closed its Moscow representative office early in 1999, and later announced that it was closing the accounts of all its Russian-based corporate customers. 'The systems have broken down in Russia and therefore we can't do business there,' said a spokeswoman.

people steeped throughout their careers in the art and science of credit assessment. The minutes record that at least one of those two objected vehemently to the whole scheme. Taylor himself proposed a reduction in the limit Diamond had asked for, but was in favour of the concept in principle.

'Can't we twist your arm?' he said to the objector. 'We really need a unanimous decision on this.' There was talk of trying to hedge the political risk – possibly by taking insurance cover at Lloyd's, or possibly by some arrangement with a Russian bank which would itself represent a layer of unquantifiable risk. It is not clear whether any effective hedge could have been, or was, put in place; but Diamond got his approval and went ahead with the trade.

Barclays shares lost 78 pence to £13.37 on the announcement of the Russian losses, but there was still more bad news to come. Attention was now turning to the hedge fund sector. George Soros himself was said to have lost $2 billion in Russian markets, and several other funds had been hit by the general turmoil, including the much-admired Long-Term Capital Management of Greenwich, Connecticut, which was down in value by no less than 44 per cent in a month.

Hedge funds were the most fashionable investment vehicle of the 1990s, and LTCM was the chicest of them all, the apotheosis of the cult of the rocket-scientist securities trader. The $4 billion fund was founded in 1994 by one of Wall Street's most famous players, John Meriwether,[2] and boasted among its managers a pair of Nobel prize-winning economists, Robert Merton and Myron Scholes, fêted for their work on the theoretical basis of derivatives trading. LTCM investors enjoyed returns of over 40 per cent in 1995 and 1996, slipping to 17 per cent in 1997, but were told very little about what was done with their money. The fashionable talk was of a 'black box' of secret investment techniques.

The techniques were not really so mysterious, however. In the crucial period of 1998 the fund had been borrowing many times its own capital in order to invest in 'credit spreads' which are bets on the relative improvement or deterioration of the credit rating of different

---

[2] Meriwether featured in the most celebrated Wall Street anecdote of the 1980s, told in Michael Lewis's wonderfully funny account of life at Salomon Bros, *Liar's Poker*. Meriwether and his boss, John Gutfreund, liked to bet on serial numbers on dollar bills. 'One hand, one million dollars, no tears,' Gutfreund challenged one day. 'No, John,' Meriwether replied. 'I'd rather play for real money. Ten million dollars. No tears.' 'You're crazy,' said Gutfreund, backing away. 'LTCM investors might agree,' said one London newspaper when news of the fund's crash broke.

financial instruments. This involved, for example, holding 'long' positions in German government bonds and 'short' positions (through derivatives contracts) in Italian government paper, in the expectation that the two would converge in credit rating terms with the approach of European monetary union.

But when Russia began to default on its obligations in August, credit spreads in all markets widened dramatically as investors stampeded to buy only the safest instruments – chiefly US Treasuries but also British gilt-edged stock. LTCM's prize-winning formulae suddenly ceased to work. With huge trading losses, the fund was in breach of its banking agreements and at risk of failing to make payments due on derivatives contracts. On 22 September, Bear Stearns, the Wall Street firm which handled LTCM's settlements, pulled the plug by calling in a $500 million payment which LTCM could not make.

What followed was probably the scariest moment on Wall Street in modern times. LTCM was found to have borrowings of the order of $120 billion. The US Federal Reserve spoke of a risk of 'systematic upset and contagion' in the markets, meaning that not only Wall Street but the whole global banking system was perceived to be in danger. Normally averse, on free-market principles, to bailing out busted financial firms, the Fed swiftly called a meeting of America's fourteen most powerful banks, which were collectively owed $80 billion by LTCM, and asked them to put together a rescue. $3.75 billion of capital was raised, in exchange for 90 per cent ownership of LTCM.

One of the non-US lenders of that $120 billion was Barclays, which – in response to requests from both the Federal Reserve and the Bank of England, and having been given only half an hour to make a decision – contributed $300 million to the bail-out syndicate but declined to reveal the extent of its lending exposure. 'Barclays Capital has a number of well-established financing and trading arrangements with LTCM,' said the official announcement. 'Barclays believes that this recapitalization provides sufficient liquidity for LTCM to realize the inherent value of its portfolio over time without disorderly liquidation. Barclays does not expect a negative impact on its own profit and loss account as a result of this situation.'

Taylor himself – 'always articulate enough to make even his failures sound like triumphs', as the *Guardian* commented that week – took a positive view. The fact that LTCM had been saved and had not caused a systemic collapse was a signal that the summer's market crisis was at last coming under control. Barclays had not risked any of its shareholders' money on an outright gamble in LTCM's 'black box', as other banks – including UBS, Dresdner of Germany and even the Bank of China – appeared to have done. On the contrary, Barclays' lending to LTCM had been theoretically secured against government securities. Furthermore, several other British banks, including Abbey National (which surely had no business to be dabbling in such a dangerous world) and NatWest, were also reported to be exposed. In Taylor's view Barclays had done nothing to be embarrassed about. Its participation in the bail-out was merely an act of good citizenship in the banking community – a confirmation, even, that Barclays still had a seat at the highest table. The $300 million was, he believed, a sound investment.[3]

But that was not how the City saw it at the time. It was merely another cause for grumbling about Barclays' failed investment banking strategy and its proneness to accidents. How many more tottering hedge funds was it exposed to? What startling exposures would Barclays Capital suddenly reveal if Brazil and the rest of Latin America followed Asia and Russia into deep crisis? 'Barclays Capital is simply dragging down the share price and obscuring a perfectly good retail business. It has to go,' one institutional investor told the *Sunday Times*, after the share price had fallen to an intra-day low of £8.27, down 15 per cent in a week and more than 57 per cent from its peak of £19.49 six months earlier.

'One does not want to throw the baby out with the bath water,' Taylor responded, rather woodenly by his usual high standards of off-the-cuff oratory. 'I take the message from the stock market very seriously. But some investors are in a state of sheer panic. I think everybody has to calm down a little. That is a complex issue and not the sort of thing you do because you have had a few bad days in the markets. There is an enormous amount of promise here . . .'

But in his heart, Taylor knew it was a promise of more trouble to come. He was already beginning to ponder how long he might stay in the job. Having said when he joined Barclays that he intended to stay for ten years, he had announced in August (four and a half years on) that he was 'now into the second half of my time here'. He sometimes surprised institutional investors in private meetings by saying that Barclays might need a different kind of leadership for the next phase of the business cycle, and he might not be the right person. Colleagues sensed that he was uneasy, that the Russian débâcle had particularly stung him, and that his restless intellect was searching for a new

---

[3] A year later, the LTCM bail-out loan was being repaid in an orderly fashion, with the promise of satisfactory dividends to come on the equity portion.

direction. At an 'awayday' brainstorming session of senior executives, in preparation for the bank's October board meeting and with the global market crisis looming large in everyone's thinking, he unburdened himself of the idea of a complete demerger of the corporate and retail banking businesses.

It was broad-brush stuff, reflecting both Taylor's obsession with extracting best value for shareholders and his tendency to allow big ideas to override detailed practicalities. The discussion group raised a series of obvious objections. Which side would keep the Barclays name, and how much would the other side suffer from the loss of it? How would the capital be divided? Would there be enough of it to support two separate businesses? Andrew Buxton – whose strategic thinking began and ended with the idea of Barclays as the great global institution it had once been – was absolutely opposed to the demerger concept. But it had taken root in Taylor's mind. He was determined to raise it at the board meeting. The board's response to him was to be the catalyst for the end of his Barclays career.

Which brings us back to Andrew Large, who had been contributing all summer to Taylor's uneasiness. Large was one of the City's best-known merchant bankers, and had spent five years from 1992 as the 'head prefect of the Square Mile', in the words of one profile-writer: chairman of the Securities and Investment Board, the umbrella regulatory authority for all aspects of the financial services industry. Large was, like Andrew Buxton, a Wykehamist – though three years junior to Buxton at school and, with his earnest, bookish manner, a rather more typical Winchester product.[4] After an economics degree from Cambridge and a period of travelling the world he had begun his career with British Petroleum in 1964. Later he studied at Insead, the celebrated French business school, before joining Orion Bank, one of the successful City consortium ventures in the syndicated loan and eurobond markets of the 1970s. From there he moved to Swiss Bank, leading its London operation and eventually becoming the first non-Swiss director on its main board.

I first met Large in Malaysia in 1985, where I was seconded by Barclays to work on the privatization of Malaysian Airline. He came to call on behalf of Swiss Bank, sniffing for a role in any future international placing of the airline's shares. I remember his owlish stare and careful

---

[4] It was Christopher Fildes of the *Daily Telegraph* who dubbed the languid, non-intellectual Buxton 'a Wykehamist disguised as an Etonian', and Martin Taylor, for obvious and opposite reasons, 'an Etonian disguised as a Wykehamist'.

note-taking, and his determined sales pitch, based on a tenuous claim to empathy with local conditions – as the son of an army doctor, he had spent part of his childhood in pre-independence Malaya.

Until he joined Barclays as a deputy chairman in May 1998, Large never had a reputation for causing friction. ('One to one, he's really a very nice chap,' one Barclays director told me.) Indeed, in his decade of working for and with the heads of Swiss Bank Corporation, he had been notably diplomatic; and he had later become a valued non-executive director of several major companies, including English China Clays and Nuclear Electric. Small, quiet and bespectacled, he was also physically tough – a keen skier and walker – and a workaholic, inclining towards the manic. One of the few criticisms quoted about him before he joined Barclays was that 'he does not know when to stop'.

At the Securities and Investment Board, his most famous battle was with Mick Newmarch, the burly chief executive of the Prudential and one of the most powerful figures in the City, who had voiced opposition to the terms of reference of the new Personal Investment Authority established under SIB's wing. But Large won the argument by a knock-out, and Newmarch resigned.

Not knowing when to stop was very much the issue with Large at Barclays. His appointment as deputy chairman, announced in February to take effect on 1 May 1998, must have seemed like a splendid idea at the time. He had excellent corporate contacts all round the world and special knowledge of the European banking scene. He had worked in a 'universal bank' which successfully combined retail, wholesale, trading and investment businesses. He was well respected by the Bank of England and the Government for his regulatory work. He would bring formidable professional skills to Barclays' internal audit committee. The problem was that he had been hired as a four-days-a-week executive without a defined job, and at only fifty-six he was not ready or willing to settle into an avuncular advisory role, to be consulted here and there and wheeled out for lunch with important customers. So he set out to create a job for himself.

The ultimate job that he wanted was, his critics supposed, the chairmanship of Barclays itself, when Andrew Buxton reached his scheduled retirement date in April 2000. That may well have been a possibility in Buxton's mind when he appointed Large. The route which might have taken Large to the top, according to this theory, was via the chairmanship of Barclays Capital. The former Treasury civil servant Sir Peter Middleton had, after all, stepped down from that chairmanship, along with his other executive duties, on the day of

Large's arrival. So the appointment would have looked like a seamless succession.

Large's difficulties are believed by some Barclays people to stem from the fact that he really had misunderstood himself to have been offered the chairmanship of Barclays Capital (or indeed of BZW, which still existed at the time) by Andrew Buxton when they first discussed his appointment during the previous autumn. Large has never commented on any of these speculations, beyond telling friends that he 'may have assumed a bit too much' and ought to have been more careful before he signed up. By the time Large took up his post, Taylor had made it clear that he did not want another deputy chairman in Middleton's position, outflanking him as the champion of the group's investment banking interest. And Bob Diamond, as chief executive of Barclays Capital, had made it clear that he did not want another executive layer in the Barclays hierarchy above him. 'Bob's one of those people who always believes he could do his boss's job better than his boss,' said one ex-BZW director. 'And his boss's boss's job for that matter.'

So the Barclays Capital chair was not offered to Large. And its non-availability was confirmed three weeks later by the announcement that Hans-Joerg Rudloff was to become (rather confusingly) 'chairman of the executive committee' of Barclays Capital, without a corresponding title within Barclays Bank itself.

A consummate trader, Rudloff was one of the founding grandees of the eurobond fraternity and a former chairman of Credit Suisse First Boston. Some detractors regarded him (though he was still only fifty-eight) as 'yesterday's man', since he had stepped out of the mainstream to launch an investment business in Eastern Europe and to recover from heart surgery. But he far outshone Large in terms of market celebrity – among many other accolades, he had once been accorded a seventeen-page verbatim interview in *Euromoney,* the *Hello!* magazine of the international capital markets. At Credit Suisse First Boston in the early 1990s, Bob Diamond had been a member of Rudloff's executive committee. The two admired each other, and Rudloff was an easy and valuable fit for Barclays Capital, both as a figurehead with a famous name and as a genuinely wise old owl of the markets. He did not want to become involved in management again, but simply to reactivate his legendary circle of contacts around the world in order to bring in deals. He never did chair the Barclays Capital executive committee, which was actually chaired by Bob Diamond. But his arrival confirmed the fact that Large's putative path to the top of Barclays was comprehensively blocked.

That was not enough to stop him, however. As Taylor came under pressure during the summer Large's attempts to create a more active role for himself in various parts of the bank became more and more of an irritant. Senior executives from Buxton downwards found themselves addressing a stream of notes and queries from the under-employed deputy chairman. Again Taylor felt himself to be under attack, and he reacted badly. But 'it was the board meeting in New York that really did it,' a close friend of Taylor told me – and not, in this case, the sort of 'friend' who is really a spokesman for the person concerned. 'Something happened in that meeting that really got to him. He was never the same after that.'

The meeting took place in New York on Thursday, 1 October 1998. The venue was the St Regis Hotel, a fine old hotel on East 55th Street in Manhattan, decorated in what New Yorkers like to think of as Louis XV style. The meeting was planned as part of a series of events to underline the bank's international profile on the eve of the IMF/World Bank meeting in Washington. There was to be a Barclays Capital client seminar at 75 Wall Street that afternoon, addressed by Eddie George, Governor of the Bank of England, who had diverted via Concorde en route to Washington. And there was to be a grand cocktail party in the Frick Museum in the evening.

But it was hardly a time for a display of cool cosmopolitanism. There were extreme worries throughout the banking community. The threat of LTCM's meltdown had raised the spectre of widespread bank-ruptcies and emergency nationalizations. Most banks' shares had fallen sharply, and Barclays' had suffered more than those of any other British bank.

Martin Taylor was, by his own admission, tired and stressed, though he took exception afterwards to suggestions that he was more or less a nervous wreck. Some of those suggestions appeared to emanate from the highest levels at Barclays, and became the subject of lawyers' correspondence. Perhaps even more stinging to Taylor, they were also given an airing by his old paper, the *Financial Times*, in a piece by Jane Martinson on 28 November headed 'A lonely maverick': 'mercurial' and 'sensitive' were among the descriptions quoted. 'He was obviously under pressure ... and maybe his temperament is not the type to keep grinding away when things are difficult,' said one anonymous source. 'He lives in a world of his own intellect,' said another. 'He is a loner.'

But whatever his state of mind on 1 October, even his most loyal supporters might have advised him that it was the wrong moment to surprise his board with a set of barely sketched plans which would have fundamentally changed the nature of Barclays.

That is exactly what he tried to do, however. But he did not take them by surprise. When the non-executive directors arrived at the St Regis on the evening before the meeting, Buxton called them together. Normally imperturbable, the chairman seemed on this occasion genuinely agitated. He wanted to warn them that Taylor was going to propose a demerger, but that – to judge from reactions at the awayday – most of the senior executives were opposed to the idea. To draw this out, he intended to ask each director in turn to express a view on the proposal.

The board duly convened the following morning, and went about its business. In the early part of the meeting the most senior executives below board level – including Bob Diamond of Barclays Capital and Patti Dunn of Barclays Global Investors[5] - were present to talk about their divisions' activities. Then the board went into closed session in the normal way. In the slot reserved for his monthly commentary, Taylor, as anticipated, offered in outline the radical blueprint which represented the culmination of all his thinking since he had first voiced his doubts about the future of BZW to the board in January 1997.

The solution for Barclays Capital, he said, was a European consolidation. It should be merged immediately with Barclays corporate banking business, and within two years it should be spun off from the retail bank, ideally into a merger with a European competitor. Even though he believed that the rescue of LTCM had staunched the threat of market catastrophe and that Barclays Capital really was a better business than BZW had been, the lesson he wanted the board to draw was that the presence of Barclays Capital was simply too big a drain on the group's capital and too dangerous to the health of the rest of the business.

The retail bank, meanwhile, needed to achieve domestic consolidation through a merger with a former building society – possibly Halifax – or another retail bank – possibly NatWest. But no acceptable merger deal could be achieved while fears about Barclays Capital were so damaging to the group's share price. Barclays could not pursue both these strategic options at once. 'We have to choose,' he told the board. This was the only way forward; some directors understood him to be

---

[5] The group's fund management arm, formed from the 1996 merger of BZW Asset Management and Wells Fargo Nikko Investment Advisors and headquartered in San Francisco.

saying that this was the only basis on which he saw himself staying in post.

In the days after Taylor's resignation, eight weeks later, two journalists, Neil Bennett of the *Sunday Telegraph* and Kirstie Hamilton of the *Sunday Times*, produced the first well-informed accounts of this meeting. According to Hamilton, Taylor 'stunned the directors ... He had no papers to back up his proposal and had not briefed his colleagues. He drew virtually no support for the plan and some directors, including Buxton, were aghast.' Bennett said that Taylor had wanted to force through the consolidation of Barclays Capital and the bank's corporate business within the year, taking the rationalization and redundancy costs (estimated by analysts at £100m) out of 1998 profits.

Taylor let it be known afterwards that he had not actually asked the board for a hard decision to split the group there and then. He had merely sought authority to examine the proposition further, and that was why he had not presented a more detailed paper. But it sounded like a weak excuse, and the fact that he had failed to line up any significant support beforehand was merely indicative of how untenable his position had become. After his torrid experience with the sale of BZW, when every manoeuvre that should have been kept secret was leaked to the press day after day, he believed he could not trust some of his fellow directors not to pass his new proposals straight to the Sunday newspapers. And he had few supporters left anyway, as was rapidly apparent when Buxton did as he had said he would and went round the table for comments, executive directors first, then non-executives.

Besides Buxton himself, there were four executive directors. Of those, Andrew Large was clearly opposed to a demerger but other participants in the meeting do not recall his contribution as being especially antagonistic towards Taylor. He was, after all, speaking from the experience of Swiss Bank, which ran comparable businesses side by side. Oliver Stocken, the finance director, was not close to Taylor and had rarely been included in his innermost counsels; he too was opposed. That left John Varley, head of retail banking, and Chris Lendrum, head of corporate banking, the two junior executive directors elected to the board less than four months previously. Both of them, like Large, had a personal stake in the outcome of the debate, since it was bound to affect their future careers. Of these two, according to one source, only Varley spoke 'mildly in favour' of Taylor's proposal; according to another source, Varley was, like Taylor, very angry at the outcome of the meeting.

Most of the non-executives turned out to be of the same view as has been ascribed to Buxton himself, that Taylor was overreacting under pressure, that it was important for Barclays to remain a big, broadly based player in the forthcoming consolidation of European banking, and that Barclays Capital still added glamour and prestige to the group – and perhaps, by implication, to the board itself. None of them was obviously sympathetic to Taylor, and it is worth pausing to ask why.

Taylor had not always been without allies in the Barclays boardroom, but he had never had many. Former ICI chairman Sir Denys Henderson, who led the board committee which recommended Taylor for the Barclays job, had retired in April 1997. The former Chancellor of the Exchequer, Lord (Nigel) Lawson of Blaby, with whom Taylor was on good terms, left in April 1998. The Dutchman Jan Peelen, a former Unilever director and a Taylor sympathizer, had gone in August 1998. All three had first been appointed by previous chairmen, rather than by Buxton. Bill Gordon, who had risen on merit all the way through Barclays from junior clerk to executive director in charge of banking and was well respected by Taylor, had retired on the day before the New York meeting.

As to the more recent non-executive appointments, Taylor had never taken much interest in cultivating them: 'I asked him one day what Arculus [David Arculus, the chairman of Severn Trent plc, who joined the Barclays board in February 1997] brought to the party,' said one colleague. 'Don't ask me,' Taylor had replied, with barely a flicker of interest. 'I leave that sort of thing to Andrew.'

So what was left was very much Buxton's board. Not one of the seven non-executives (including at this point Sir Peter Middleton) was an influential Taylor ally. At least one – Sir Nigel Rudd, chairman of Williams Holdings and Pilkington – was generally reckoned by the press to be hostile to Taylor's position, having taken an opposing view in the earlier battle over the dismantling of BZW and barely concealed his anger at the way in which the BZW sale had been conducted. Peter Jarvis, chairman of Debenhams and former chief executive of Whitbreads, was thought to be in tune with Rudd, and so was the longest-serving director, Sir Nigel Mobbs of Slough Estates.

So the tide was running strongly against Taylor. The discussion was not a shouting match, as some newspapers subsequently portrayed it. Nor was it, as *Sunday Business* claimed, an 'all-night' session: it was all over by lunch-time. But it certainly triggered a strong emotional reaction in Taylor. His head was in his hands as one director after another told him, in effect, to stop panicking and go away and do his homework properly. For 'Two-brains' Taylor, adviser to cabinet ministers, it was a humiliation. Several people present thought that Taylor might resign there and then, before the end of the meeting. At least one interpreted what he said as meaning that he had actually done so. Buxton brought the discussion to a conclusion by calling – to Taylor's undisguised dismay – for a further strategic review of Barclays Capital which would take at least three months to complete. The meeting broke up in a mood of high tension. Directors went off in huddles to assess the damage, and to compose themselves for the rest of the day's programme. Having held back from the brink, Taylor left the question of his departure open. Gossip in the bank during October said he would be gone by the end of the year.

When they returned to London, Taylor and Buxton finally discussed the situation. Taylor outlined the conditions on which he was prepared to stay. None of the parties concerned has revealed what those conditions might have been, but it is a fair bet that one of them was the removal of Andrew Large from his executive position. Certainly it was believed by some senior executives, well before Taylor resigned, that a decision had already been reached to make Large non-executive and that on that basis Taylor had agreed to stay until 2000. It is known that Buxton spoke to Large, and reports later suggested that the stumbling block was a failure to agree on how much Large should be paid for accepting the change of status. Whatever happened, Buxton failed to deal with the problem of Large until it was too late to hold on to Taylor.[6]

For a brief interlude, however, the crisis seemed to have been defused. As a precautionary measure, Spencer Stuart, Barclays' favoured head-hunters, were quietly commissioned to begin a 'paper search' (that is, to produce a list of candidates, but not to contact them) for Taylor's eventual successor. As October turned to November, world market turmoil subsided and Barclays' share price began rising again. Internal morale seemed to be improving. The press had turned its attention to troubles afflicting two other bell-wether British businesses, British Airways – where chief executive Bob Ayling was being forced to cut back his expansion plans in the face of the sudden economic downturn – and Marks & Spencer.

The great retail chain was, like Barclays, a high street institution whose affairs are of much wider public interest than those of ordinary

---

[6] It was finally announced on 3 December that Large would become non-executive at the end of the year, though he would remain a deputy chairman.

businesses, and the crisis which had suddenly overtaken it carried echoes of the situation at Barclays. M & S had announced a profit fall and was clearly losing it pre-eminent market position. A vicious succession battle had broken out in its normally placid Baker Street headquarters – with the role of boardroom *éminence grise* being played by Sir Martin Jacomb, just as he had played it at Barclays a few years earlier (see Chapter 9). M & S chairman and chief executive Sir Richard Greenbury was under pressure from institutional shareholders to split his dual role and to identify his eventual successor as chairman. He had been forced to fly back from holiday in India to reassert his authority after his deputy chairman, Keith Oates – an ambitious 'outsider' of a mere fifteen years standing in M & S - had begun lobbying internally for the chief-executive half of Greenbury's job.[7]

Amidst such distractions, the pressure on Taylor abated, and he found time to make a week-long trip to the Far East. But his position remained uncomfortable: he still had to talk to institutional shareholders, and found some of them urging him to follow a strategy very much like the one the board had shot down. Meanwhile, the promises made to him about his freedom of action were not, in his view, being kept. Large was still there, and making it clear that he intended to play a full part in the proposed strategic review of Barclays Capital which was so irksome to Taylor. And there were now rumours in Lombard Street of a plan to force Taylor himself out early in 1999 and to invite Andrew Buxton (who was scheduled to retire in April 2000) to stay on as chairman until 2002.

Early in the week of 16 November, there was another discussion between Buxton and Taylor, which seemed to leave Taylor, once again, deeply upset. Buxton was also perturbed; he was about to leave on one of his regular trips to the Middle East, and considered cancelling it. But an elaborate schedule of meetings (one of them with President Mubarak of Egypt) had been arranged for him and after consultations with other directors, he decided it was safe to leave Taylor's concerns aside until he returned. He set off on Friday night for Jeddah.

By Sunday, 22 November, however, Taylor had snapped. Following his usual habit, he spent the weekend walking and thinking and making his mind up. It may well have been another leak to the media that brought him to boiling point.

---

[7] Oates was, in fact, forced out of M & S at the end of November, Greenbury having secured the appointment as chief executive of his preferred successor, Peter Salsbury, a lifelong M & S man; Oates was promptly identified as a candidate to succeed Martin Taylor at Barclays.

'Barclays ponders demerger options,' wrote Neil Bennett in the *Sunday Telegraph*.

> Barclays is considering the demerger of its retail and corporate banking businesses in a dramatic move to reflect the fundamental changes that are taking place within the financial services industry. The group is drawing up strategic plans for its future and is said to have concluded that the two parts of the bank are becoming increasingly divergent and could be broken up within the next two years.
>
> In preparation for a full demerger, the bank is expected to draw Barclays Capital, its capital markets arm, into closer co-operation with its corporate banking business. Then the two operations would be combined under a single management. A demerger would be the final stage. 'The process would certainly be evolutionary, not revolutionary,' said one observer ... If the recent talks between Barclays and Halifax result in a merger, for example, the corporate bank could be spun off with sufficient capital to service its blue-chip list of multi-national clients.

This was the first substantial leak of the plan discussed at the New York meeting, and during the days that followed someone at Barclays accused Taylor himself of being the leaker – a suggestion which Neil Bennett specifically refuted on the following Sunday. Though neither of them ever commented publicly about it, Taylor is believed to have blamed Large for the story. Whether or not this exposure of the demerger scheme was damaging to Taylor's position in the internal debate, it certainly reawakened his fury about Barclays' culture of leaks. He had decided that enough was enough, and that it was time to resign.

As is so often the case in corporate dramas, the senior secretaries seem to have been the first to know. Contrary to all normal protocol, the chairman of Barclays was well back in the queue. On the Monday, Taylor told his immediate colleagues he had decided to go ('I can't stand it any longer,' he told one startled executive. 'I'm not going to hang around and go when they want me to go. I've decided to precipitate the crisis.'). But he took no formal action to resign. On the Tuesday morning, Sir Peter Middleton, elsewhere in London at a board meeting of United Utilities, received a call from his secretary at Barclays suggesting discreetly that he might like to drop in at the bank.

There he found an atmosphere of frozen confusion. Lendrum and Varley were already under the impression that Taylor had resigned, but Taylor had not yet made contact with Buxton. The deputy chairman, to whom Taylor might otherwise have tendered his resignation, was Andrew Large, who was in Australia and to whom Taylor had no intention of speaking anyway. Stocken was out of the office at a board meeting of MEPC, the property company, and could not be reached until the evening. Middleton took it upon himself to track down Buxton and Large (the chairman was, in fact, in flight between Middle Eastern capitals) and to set up a board meeting for the first possible time they could return to London, which was Thursday evening. Having heard the news by telephone from Middleton that night, the astonished Buxton finally received it by fax from Taylor himself.

Middleton, supremely Whitehall-trained in crisis management, was now in his element. Next he asked two senior non-executive directors, Sir Nigel Mobbs and Peter Jarvis, to come to the bank on Wednesday morning. Mobbs, who is a deputy lieutenant of Buckinghamshire, was expected on public duty, and Jarvis was expected at a Rank Organization board meeting, but both dropped everything and answered the summons. Middleton had made sure that Taylor's formal departure would not become effective until the Thursday meeting, so that no premature announcement would have to be made to the Stock Exchange. Mobbs talked to Taylor privately over lunch to see whether he might be persuaded to change his mind. But Taylor was immovable, and in any case the speed with which the news was spreading through head office would have made the decision extraordinarily difficult to reverse. For the rest of the day, Mobbs and Jarvis took soundings among the bank's senior executives as to what should happen next.

Support for Taylor, they discovered, had been ebbing away since the October board confrontation. As for the idea that Andrew Large might replace him as chief executive, there was no support at all. Oliver Stocken, who had been about to retire, was prepared to stay on temporarily as finance director but was not a candidate to become acting chief executive. Neither John Varley nor Chris Lendrum could be convincingly promoted into the job immediately, though both were much-touted candidates for it in the months that followed. That left Sir Peter Middleton, who had passed his sixty-fourth birthday in April and retired from executive duties in May, but who was still at the height of his powers and by common consent the most formidable operator in the bank. Nor was he lacking in ambition, though he had been enjoying his semi-retirement. He had already taken complete command of the situation, and is said by one colleague to have found the task of provoking Andrew Buxton into a robust response to the crisis 'like pulling on the proverbial piece of string'.

Buxton did at least get back to Lombard Street in time for the Thursday evening meeting, as did Large – whose attempt to express some conventional words of regret to Taylor was met with an explosion of rage which echoed across the fifth-floor lobby. The board duly met in the early evening of Thursday – without Taylor, who was by then ensconsed with his lawyers – and confirmed the decision to put Middleton centre stage. After a long night of discussions with advisers and PR people as to how to present the story in the least damaging way, the world was told on Friday morning (most Barclays staff beyond Lombard Street finding out via Radio 4's *Today* programme) that Taylor had for all practical purposes already gone and that Middleton was now acting chief executive and chairman-designate. Buxton would now step down a year earlier than planned, in April 1999, to make way for Middleton – who had first made his name in the 1970s as a Whitehall press officer, and now gave a virtuoso display of press-handling to remind his colleagues of his former professional skills in that area.

There was 'nothing peculiar at all' going on in the bank, he declared baldly, in the face of all available evidence. 'I suppose you could say this could have been handled better, but I do not think what we have done is bad.' As for Taylor, Middleton's tone was sympathetic: 'If Martin's heart has gone out of the business, it was much better for him to go rather than have him limp on.' As for his own elevation, he was supremely disingenuous. 'So that we didn't find ourselves looking for a chairman and a chief executive at the same time, the board asked me if I would become the next chairman. I said yes. Then they asked a rather more difficult question: whether I would be acting chief executive.' Insiders suggest that this may actually have been the other way round: the board asked him to step in as acting chief executive, and his price was that Buxton should step aside early and allow him to be chairman.

Even Middleton's skills, however, could not hide the cracks in the great edifice that was once one of the world's most respected banks. Barclays' global investment banking strategy had been reduced to rubble. All talk of mergers and acquisitions to strengthen its traditional retail business had come to nothing. Its market capitalization, at the lowest point, had sunk to the level of newcomers such as Halifax and Abbey National and to half that of Lloyds TSB. A bank which for almost a hundred years had produced a seamless succession of competent senior executives had been forced to draft in a retired civil servant as emergency chairman and to turn to head-hunters to fill the vacant offices of chief executive and finance director. 'This makes Marks & Spencer look like an orderly succession,' said one fund manager. 'I don't know about chickens, but they're certainly headless.'

Barclays had not collapsed and died. Nor had it lost its name, as the Midland Bank – once the biggest bank in the world – had done, having been subsumed into its parent HSBC. But it had fallen a very long way and made a fool of itself on the way down. Was that fall the fault of a handful of individuals, or of the market forces and collective folly of two turbulent decades? Or was it the fruit of the seeds of Barclays' ancient history? Let us examine the evidence.

2

ORIGINS

1896–1966: The rise of joint-stock banking – The great
amalgamation – The Local Head Office system – The triumph
of Frederick Goodenough – The wisdom of Cuthbert
Fitzherbert – The rise of Deryk Vander Weyer

My father entered Barclays Bank as a junior clerk at Filey in North
Yorkshire on 13 January 1941, a week before his sixteenth birthday. He
was probably the youngest employee of Barclays' York district on that
day; history has failed to record the name of the oldest, but there must
surely have been a chief clerk on the verge of retirement who was
willing and able to pass on to him some of the folk memories of the
origins of Barclays.

There might, for example, have been someone still working in the
district in 1941 who had started his career in the Scarborough Old
Bank, Woodall Hebden & Co., founded in 1788 and part of the
great Barclays amalgamation of 1896. Or – chronologically a little
easier to find – one or two veterans of the York Union Banking
Company, known as 'the Farmers' Bank' before it became part
of Barclays in 1902. They in turn might well have encountered, in
their distant youth, elderly people who remembered George Hudson,
York's celebrated 'Railway King', who had been a director of the York
Union from its foundation in 1833 and its chairman during the
1840s.

To have begun as recently as 1833 made the York Union a relative
youngster. To be really old in Barclays terms would mean pre-dating
the Lombard Street partnership of Barclay, Bevan, Tritton & Co., which
could trace its beginnings to around 1690. It is not, however, the
intention of this book to tell the whole three-hundred year story of

Barclays, which has already been written down more than once.[1] This will merely tell the story of the ups and downs of the last thirty-five years, but even that short period cannot be explained without a brief diversion into history to illuminate the distinctive social structure and psychology of Barclays. For that purpose, we really have to begin in the second half of the nineteenth century.

Once upon a time, goldsmiths in Lombard Street and other kinds of tradesmen throughout the country developed the practice of providing safe custody for the cash and valuables of their wealthy patrons and issuing negotiable bank notes in exchange for them. That was the origin of what we now call 'high street banking'. Many of the early bankers were Quakers,[2] partly because Quakers tended to combine the qualities of prudence, firmness of moral judgement and elaborate courtesy which made good bankers, but partly also because they were excluded by discrimination from pursuing other professions which might have suited them, such as the law.

But individual tradesmen-bankers and small private partnerships were not equipped to cope with the needs of the rapidly expanding Victorian industrial economy. Bigger companies (such as George Hudson's York and North Midland Railway Company) needed bigger banks, and banks needed continuity of capital which was too often disrupted in private partnerships by questions of inheritance from one generation to the next. These pressures created a new vogue for joint-stock (that is, shareholder-owned) banking, though in the early days of that movement – beginning in the provinces in 1826 and moving to the capital in 1833 – there were many failures and scandals, and fierce debates as to which form of ownership provided the most reliable foundation.

---

[1] The three essential volumes are *History of Barclays Bank Limited*, by P. W. Matthews & A. W. Tuke (1926), *Barclays Bank Limited 1926–1969*, by A. W. Tuke and R. J. H. Gillman (1972) and *The DCO Story*, by Sir Julian Crossley and John Blandford (1975). In 1989, the then Barclays chairman Sir John Quinton decided to commission a 'tercentenary history' to be written by Leslie Hannah, Professor of Business History at the London School of Economics, and Margaret Ackrill of Oxford, for publication in 1992. This was to cover the whole three hundred years, but with particular emphasis on the last thirty. Interviews were conducted with many leading Barclays figures, including my father, and the book was duly completed. But – perhaps because 1992 turned out to be such an unhappy year for the bank, perhaps because it was too frank in its account of modern times – it was not published. I was not given access to it, but I am told it is a weighty tome, and particularly good on the early history of Quaker banking. Happily for its authors, I understand that it may appear (its later chapters having been rewritten) in 2000.

[2] Members of the austere religious sect founded by George Fox in 1649. Quakers were dedicated to social work and silent worship; they opposed slavery, war and religious ritual.

A leap forward for joint-stock banking came with the Companies Act of 1862, which introduced the concept of limited liability for shareholders; before that date, their risks were unlimited. The trend by then was also towards the absorption of weaker private partnerships by stronger joint-stock banks – the Birmingham & Midland Bank, soon to become the Midland Bank and the undisputed market leader, being the prime mover. The advantages of strength through amalgamation were made all the more apparent by the Barings crisis of 1890, when the aristocratic merchant banking house nearly ruined itself on an Argentine speculation – providing a very early warning, as it were, of what it would do to itself 105 years later – and would have brought down a number of other City firms if it had not been bailed out by the Bank of England.

Barclay, Bevan, Tritton & Co. – founded in Lombard Street in the City of London by a Quaker goldsmith, John Freame, whose daughter and granddaughter married into the Barclay family[3] – was, we may guess, a reluctant participant in this tide of change, yet was extremely well placed to take advantage of it through a vast network of personal and business relationships. In 1888 the firm had amalgamated with Ransom, Bouverie & Co. of Number 1, Pall Mall East, whose distinguished list of customers had once included Gioacchino Rossini and J. M. W. Turner, and whose partners happened to include a member of the Bevan family. In 1894 Barclay, Bevan, Tritton, Ransom & Bouverie also absorbed Hall, Bevan, West & Bevans of Brighton and other towns in Sussex. The organization by now extended to eight branches beyond Lombard Street, but the idea of turning their confederation of cosy banking parlours into a mighty but impersonal joint-stock corporation was not congenial to the Barclay partners. What concerned them more was the risk of losing business as other banks joined forces around them.

London banks operated a lucrative sideline as agents for country banks, clearing payments for them and providing liquidity in the form of bullion when needed. As amalgamations proceeded apace, so the

---

[3] The Barclays are descended from Robert Barclay of Ury in Scotland, born in 1648 and known as 'the Apologist' in honour of his book *The Apology for the True Christian Divinity, as the same is held forth and preached by the people called in scorn Quakers* (1676). Rather curiously, the Apologist's son David Barclay married John Freame's granddaughter Priscilla as his second wife, Priscilla's aunt Sarah Freame having already married David's son James Barclay. Every partner of Barclay, Bevan, Tritton & Co. from first to last, and a significant proportion of all the local directors who followed them in Lombard Street, could trace lineal or collateral descent from this connection. Genealogy plays a fascinating but rather distracting part in the whole Barclays story; I shall confine it as far as possible to footnotes.

need for London agencies reduced. The multiple merger which created the modern Barclays in 1896 was done, as one of its partners privately admitted at the time, 'in order to protect our valuable agency business. We found that the gradual absorption of banks by their larger neighbours was affecting us in this way, and our new departure is therefore to some extent an act of self-defence.'

The Barclays, Bevans and Trittons were connected by marriage, cousinage and Quaker inheritance – as well as by their role as agents – to many other banking families around the country. But negotiations took several years, and came close to being abandoned, before the Lombard Street partners were able to bring their plan to fruition. Initial agreement was reached with Jonathan Backhouse & Co. of Darlington[4] and Gurneys, Birkbeck, Barclay & Buxton of Norwich – the latter bringing with it seven other Gurney partnerships dotted around East Anglia. To this was added, in the final scheme, Goslings & Sharpe in London,[5] Woodall Hebden & Co. in Scarborough, and eight other banks in the Home Counties and East Anglia – including, most importantly from the dynastic point of view, two banks in which the Tuke family were prominent: Sharples, Tuke, Lucas & Seebohm in Hitchin, Hertfordshire and Gibson, Tuke & Gibson of Saffron Walden.

The new bank had authorized capital of £6 million, of which £2 million was paid up, and deposits of £26 million. It was called Barclay & Company (it did not become Barclays Bank Limited until 1917) and it is said that the fair-minded Quaker founders chose the name Barclay simply because it came first alphabetically among the surnames of the 1896 board of directors. Had there not been two Barclays at the table (one from Lombard Street and one from Norwich) the bank might therefore have been named after one Francis Bassett from Leighton Buzzard. The first chairman was Francis (sometimes called Frank)

---

[4] The history of Backhouse & Co. provides a splendid illustration of the service which London agents provided for country bankers. In 1819 a dispute arose between the Quaker banker Jonathan Backhouse (who married a Gurney) and a local grandee, the Earl of Darlington. The Earl instructed his tenants to pay their rent in Backhouse's notes, intending to accumulate a greater quantity of them than Backhouse could possibly pay in gold on demand. But Backhouse found out, and rushed to London by post-chaise to obtain a large supply – some £32,000 worth – of bullion from his agents. He then hastened back to Darlington, but at Croft on Tees one of the front wheels came off his chaise. Rather than wait for a repair, he piled the gold at the back of the chaise, so 'balancing the cash', and continued the journey on three wheels. When Lord Darlington presented his pile of notes, they were all promptly cashed.

[5] Goslings & Sharpe, the Fleet Street banking house originally known for its sign of 'Ye Three Squirrels', was the oldest company in the 1896 amalgamation, dating from 1649–50.

Augustus Bevan, a partner in Lombard Street since 1861 and the son
of Robert Cooper Lee Bevan, who had been the recognized leader of
the City's private bankers in the previous generation.[6]

Barclay & Co. was now a joint-stock bank, but only in form. As a
footnote written by A. W. Tuke seventy-five years later confirmed,
'Barclays has of course itself been a joint-stock bank since 1896, but I
use the term here to denote those of our competitors who have been
joint-stock in soul as well as body since they were formed.' The official
announcement in June 1896 explained the distinction: the directors of
Barclays were 'selected from among the existing partners, and local
management will remain in the same hands as heretofore, the private
character of the banks being thus preserved'.

The news caused quite a stir in the City: 'The spirit of the age
cannot be resisted,' declared the *Bankers' Magazine*. 'Amalgamation is
the order of the day.' But reactions were tempered by a certain prejudice
among the more sophisticated financiers and merchants of the City,
who regarded joint-stock banking as an activity of no great intelligence
or merit, and its practitioners, as often as not, as provincial dullards
lately come up to town. This was a prejudice which survived well into
the next century: no clearing banker (as they were also called) was
invited to join the innermost élite of the Court (or board of directors)
of the Bank of England until 1932, when Edward Holland-Martin[7] of
Martins Bank, known for some reason as 'Ruby', became an executive
director of the Bank. More significantly, City snobbery about clearing
bankers survived well into the 1980s, when it emerged as a powerful
undercurrent in the tussles between Barclays and BZW: but more of
that (much more of it, in fact) a little later.

There was another aspect of the amalgamation which reverberated
into the modern age. That was the decision to preserve the 'private
character' of Barclays by turning each of the former private bank

---

[6] Supposed to be descended from Jestyn-ap-Gwrgant, the last Prince of Glamorgan, Silvanus
Bevan moved from Swansea to London in 1715 and began business in Lombard Street as an
apothecary. His son Timothy then married Elizabeth, daughter of David Barclay and
granddaughter of the Apologist. A son of that marriage, Silvanus Bevan the third, joined the
bank in 1767.

[7] Perhaps not a very good choice: he was briefly given the job of speaking to the press on
the Bank of England's behalf. 'Though a most affable character, he turned out to know
more about horsemanship than public relations,' recalled one journalist of the day. Though
Martins later became part of Barclays, the first Barclays man as such to join the Court was
Ronald Thornton, a vice-chairman, in 1966 – he was obliged to step down from the Barclays
board in order to do so. He was followed by Deryk Vander Weyer in 1986, and by Andrew
Buxton in 1995. Sir Martin Jacomb, chairman of BZW and deputy chairman of Barclays,
also joined the Court in 1986, but was never classified as a clearing banker.

headquarters into a local head office, wherever it happened to be. This system was in direct contrast to the highly centralized management structure being adopted by the Midland and others, but Barclays was very proud of it.

'All ordinary business could be transacted by the former partners – now local directors – without subjecting a customer to any annoyance which might be involved in the submission of his proposition to an official at the head office in London, to whom he was unlikely to be more than a mere name,' wrote Tuke and Matthews in 1926 – though in practice head office had to have a say in larger lendings. It was Tuke's uncle Henry, a local director at Chelmsford until 1946 and one of the last practising Quakers in Barclays, who inscribed a rejected loan application: 'Turned down by head office though I cannot think why, since it had my recommendation.'

> The system [Tuke and Matthews continued] is designed to preserve the great advantage which the partners in a private firm enjoyed over the local manager of a rival joint-stock bank in the intimate knowledge which they possessed concerning the personal character and business capabilities of their customers, founded as that knowledge was in all probability on the experience of several generations. At all events the fact that it has not been thought necessary, after testing it for nearly thirty years, to vary the system in any important particular, seems to point to the experiment having been in the main successful.

One of the advantages of the local head office system was that it made all the more painless the absorption of other banks into the Barclays network over the years after 1896. There were many of them, but those which have special resonance in this story include Parsons, Thomson & Co. of Oxford in 1900, J. & J. W. Pease[8] of Darlington in 1902 and Bolitho, Williams, Foster, Coode, Grylls & Co. Ltd in Cornwall in 1905. In each case, all the family partners or their inheritors were able to become local directors, whatever their professional standing as bankers: thus at Newport Pagnell, Francis Littleboy – formerly of Bassett, Son & Harris, one of the smaller 1896 signatory firms – was designated 'local director and ledger clerk'.

---

[8] The Peases were one of the most powerful nineteenth-century Quaker mercantile families in the north-east of England, with banking interests in Whitby and Hull as well as Darlington. They were involved in the financing of the first railways in the region, and the development of its iron and steel industry. Their Darlington bank was, however, a small affair which did business chiefly with members of the family. It was in some difficulties when Barclays absorbed it.

In these early years, Barclays' strengths were very much in rural England rather than in industrial, metropolitan or foreign business. It ranked fourth or fifth in terms of total deposits; in the City itself, it was not among the leaders in providing banking facilities for stock exchange members; and in terms of total numbers of branches it was far behind the aggressively expanding Midland – then under the formidable leadership of Sir Edward Holden, its chairman from 1908 to 1919 and certainly the greatest British commercial banker of the age.

The inadequacy of the Barclays network in industrial Birmingham, Lancashire and South Wales, and in outer parts of London, was not made up until twenty years after the first amalgamation – with the acquisition of three joint-stock institutions, United Counties Bank in 1916, the London Provincial & South Western Bank in 1918 and the Union Bank of Manchester in 1919. Barclays now counted as one of the 'Big Five' English banks (along with Lloyds, Midland, Westminster and National Provincial) but the Treasury and the Bank of England began to take the view that the process of consolidation had advanced far enough.[9] After 1920, the only new domestic acquisitions were small or failing ones; the last of them was Gunner & Company of Bishop's Waltham, Hampshire, which was absorbed in 1953. Major F. H. Gunner, DSO (who retired a year later) was thereby the last person to be made a local director of Barclays by the original mechanism of turning his private bank into a local head office.

The consolidation of Barclays as one of the Big Five, and the foundation of its overseas empire, was essentially the work of the one man who towers above everyone else in this story: Frederick Crauford Goodenough. Rather surprisingly, he was not from one of the founding families. By contrast, as the historian David Kynaston puts it (in *The City of London*, Volume II), he was 'the crucial outsider who came to exercise an enormous influence over what could have been a *mélange* of squabbling families'.

Goodenough was a lawyer of formidable energy, ambition and management ability who had been assistant secretary of the Hudson's Bay Company and had then worked at the Union Bank of London under its Governor, Sir Felix Schuster, who counts as the second titan of turn-of-the century joint-stock banking – the first being Holden of the Midland. Schuster ran the Union Bank for almost thirty years with

---

[9] In order to respect the letter, if not the spirit, of the Treasury Minute of 1920 forbidding further amalgamations, the Union Bank of Manchester continued to operate as a separate bank until 1940.

an iron hand, and it is a fair guess that Goodenough modelled his own later career on that of his ex-boss.

He joined Barclays as secretary at the time of the 1896 amalgamation. In that capacity, and as general manager from 1903, he worked with Frank Bevan to pull the merger together and make it work: though the group's deposits quadrupled during the period from 1896 to 1917, when Goodenough succeeded Bevan as chairman, growth during that period was somewhat held back by the old private bankers' preference for the status quo. Once he was in complete command, Goodenough was able to drive Barclays forward at a more determined pace.

He was in office until his death, aged sixty-nine, in September 1934, by which time deposits had almost quadrupled again – to £380 million. He was an autocrat who terrified his underlings – with the assistance of his equally formidable secretary, Miss F. R. Cummins, MBE, the first woman to become a member of the bank's permanent staff. His board meetings rarely lasted more than twenty minutes. According to Tuke, 'he never encouraged members of the board to lift up their voices during its proceedings,' except when he had primed someone to support one of his propositions; nor was he above 'nobbling chosen directors and leaving others in ignorance'.

He was barely on speaking terms with his own deputy chairman, Sir Herbert Hambling, the former chairman of the London Provincial & South Western Bank: Hambling kept his own court in his old head office in Fenchurch Street, where Goodenough suspected him of plotting revolution. Similarly, Goodenough sustained a long-running stand-off with Montagu Norman, the Governor of the Bank of England from 1920 to 1944 and a hugely dominant figure in City life. Norman was said to have attended Goodenough's funeral at Broughton Poggs in Gloucestershire only to satisfy himself that his adversary was well and truly dead.

In his portraits and photographs, Goodenough is a grim figure. He did not tolerate weakness, and had no sympathy for physical frailties. Tuke tells the story of his own father, W. F. Tuke, a benign long-serving general manager (and after Goodenough's death, a stop-gap chairman) in conversation with Goodenough after the two of them had interviewed a senior staff member who had given a rather poor impression of himself.

'That man's no good,' said Goodenough.

'He was so frightened of you he could not speak,' replied Tuke the elder.

'Frightened of me,' Goodenough barked. 'No one has ever been frightened of me in my life.'

'How blind can one be to one's shortcomings?' concluded Tuke the author.

But whatever Goodenough's shortcomings as a human being, he was a great builder. After the Treasury Minute of 1920 effectively forbade the Big Five from enlarging themselves further at home, he set out instead to plant the Barclays flag in every corner of the British Empire and beyond – and it was this project which was to be his lasting memorial.

Facing down the opposition of Montagu Norman – who refused to allow the new overseas operation an account with the Bank of England – he created Barclays Bank (Dominion, Colonial & Overseas) Limited. Known within Barclays simply as 'DCO', this was formed by the merger in 1925 of the Colonial Bank – which operated in the West Indies and West Africa – with the Anglo-Egyptian Bank and the National Bank of South Africa. The merger was backed by Barclays capital, though Barclays owned only 70 per cent and eventually only 56.5 per cent of the shares of DCO – until 1971, when the minority was bought in and DCO finally began to be integrated into the group. If Goodenough had really had his way, he would have bought the Chartered Bank, which covered India and the Far East, and the Australia & New Zealand Banking Corporation as well, but that was beyond what Barclays' capital could support and far beyond what the Bank of England would countenance.

Having entered the Barclays pantheon, it seemed perfectly natural that Frederick Goodenough's family should become part of the bank's dynastic system – though it is hard to think of any other major public company in which it might have happened, and there are some, such as Shell and ICI, which have always discouraged the idea of sons following their fathers. Goodenough's son Will, having served in the Coldstream Guards during the latter part of the First World War, became a local director in Oxford at the age of twenty-four, married a Gibbs from another great banking family, and became vice-chairman of Barclays, aged thirty-five, on the death of his father – who had hoped to live long enough to see his son follow him straight into the chair.

In A. W. Tuke's opinion, Will Goodenough was as able as his father but *suavior in modo*; that is, a lot more pleasant to work for. He became chairman of Barclays in 1947, having already earned a baronetcy and served four years as chairman of DCO – where his successor was his sister Barbara's husband, Julian (later Sir Julian) Crossley. Goodenough

Junior followed into the Barclays chair one of its less distinguished occupants, Edwin 'Tom' Fisher,[10] and there were high hopes for a bright new era – hopes which were disappointed when, borne down by stress, Will Goodenough collapsed. He had quite literally grown old before his time. He was forced to retire in March 1951, aged only fifty-two, and died a few weeks later.

By then Will's son Roger had entered the bank, destined to become senior local director in Oxford. This creation of a new Barclays family alongside the old ones had a curious effect on the psychology of the organization: over the years, I believe it became a mark of power for anyone in the senior management ranks, whether 'family' or not, to have a son, son-in-law, nephew or godson (though I know of no daughters, and only one daughter-in-law) in the bank. I believe that was part of the reason why my father was keen for me to join Barclays in 1981, when I declared my intention to leave my first job with Schroders – the other part of the reason being a benign parental wish just to make sure I had a proper job. 'We like fathers and sons here,' his colleague Henry Lambert told me when I went for the first interview. When I told the personnel manager of Schroders I was moving to Barclays, he said 'Of course, I know it's your family business.' Thus do questions of kinship loom large, and sometimes confusingly, throughout this story.

It is a moot question, however, as to how much of the modern Barclays has ever been owned by any of its families, old or new. Respecting the privacy of the founders' firms, no details were ever published of the original individual shareholdings of Barclay & Company, though it was known that the Lombard Street and Norwich partners were the biggest fish in the pool. By the time the United Counties and London Provincial & South Western deals had been completed, the capital of Barclays had been divided or restructured eight times, and the paid-up capital had risen to £8,820,356. Within that total, a holder of a single £20 share from 1896, on which £8 was paid up, was by 1920 the theoretical possessor of one fully paid £4 'A' share and six fully paid £1 'B' shares, the 'B' shares having some advantage in terms of dividends. He might also have taken up his rights in a series of new issues over the period.

These technicalities make it impossible to calculate the percentage

---

[10] Like the Goodenoughs, Fisher did not come from the founding families: having trained in the law, he joined the bank as assistant secretary in 1908, was a captain in the Life Guards during the First World War, and became a general manager in 1925. He dropped dead at Buckingham Palace during a meeting (on some charitable matter) with the then Queen.

of the bank's shares still held by the founders, but it is clear that by 1920 they had been significantly diluted. It was part of Barclays folklore, however, at least until the late 1960s, that the families controlled at least 50 per cent of the shares. When the share register was eventually analysed, they turned out to own less than 1 per cent.

But the key to the psychology and style of Barclays was – uniquely for any major shareholder-owned British company – that the founders simply carried on down the decades of the new century behaving like partners and owners of their local businesses, retaining a social prestige and civic eminence which did not accrue to the functionaries of competitor banks. The Midland Bank remained true to its own origins, dominated at board level by provincial industrialists. The Westminster Bank in 1938 had ten directors (out of twenty-seven) who were Etonians, and seven who were married to daughters of lords; but its professional staff were just that, classless from the general manager downwards.

Barclays was different: as we shall see shortly from a visit to the Oxford local head office, the senior Barclays local director in any territory was an important figure in the public (and sporting) life of his county. He was also at liberty to apply his own preferences and interpretations to the conduct of business in his territory: 'In the Luton District, Head Office instructions should be regarded as a basis for discussion' was the not-entirely-facetious formula used in the days when A. W. Tuke's son Anthony was a local director there. If, as was very frequently the case, the senior local director was also a main board director of Barclays Bank, he was actually senior to several strata of head office management – the assistant general managers, regional general managers[11] and general managers – through whom he the-oretically reported to his own peer group on the board. It was one of the legacies of this bizarre structure that in the 1980s and 90s, Barclays people in control of their own fiefdoms at home and abroad could never quite be relied upon to carry through the strategy handed down to them from the top if they thought they had a better strategy of their own.

But it was certainly a clubbable organization to which to belong. Some of the families – the Tukes and Seebohms, for example – came up to town and became important players in the development of

---

[11] Originally, senior local directors reported on a day-to-day basis, at least in theory, to the general managers, who acted as a group with no individual definition of role. An intermediate layer of regional general managers was introduced in 1969, after the merger with Martins Bank (see Chapter 3).

Barclays as a whole. Others – including the Gurneys and Birkbecks in Norfolk[12] – tended to stay at home in their own fiefdoms, preserving the style and dignity of an earlier age. But all were secure in their positions, despite a growing contrast in the pre-Second World War banking industry between what A. W. Tuke called 'the amateur and the professional'.

'From time immemorial,' he wrote, 'our local directors, and the partners of the private banks before them, had many advantages in competing locally with the branches of the joint-stock banks, but they were with few exceptions untrained and inexperienced in the wider fields of business life. To be the son, son-in-law or nephew of a partner was sufficient qualification. The upbringing of the senior officials, and indeed of the branch managers, of the joint-stock banks was totally different: highly trained, well equipped theoretically, and strongly competitive; in fact thoroughly professional in their outlook and performance. As long as this contrast persisted, the advantages and disadvantages of the two systems happened to cancel each other out.'

As new banks were added on, so the number of local head offices grew. Soon there were thirty-three of them, each preserving a character nurtured by the longevity in office of local directors who were appointed after the briefest of apprenticeships in their twenties and sometimes simply refused to retire. At York, for example, James Melrose remained in post until he was over 100, attending the office every day well into his ninety-eighth year. In 1942, there were still two local directors *in situ* – a Bevan in Brighton and a Gurney in King's Lynn – who had been there since the 1896 amalgamation. Managers in the Windsor district who reached retirement age in the early 1990s might well have begun their training as clerks under Cecil Woodbridge, who was a local director from 1900 to 1951.

The ambience of Barclays in the 1930s and 40s is best caught not in the formal histories (though A. W. Tuke, who was chairman of the bank from 1951 to 1962, was an admirable writer and a conscientious historian) but in *The Eagle Looks Back* (1951), a slim 'silver jubilee' anthology of contributions to the *Spread Eagle*, the bank's staff maga-

---

[12] Descended from a Norman knight, Hugh de Gournay, the Gurneys had been merchants, and bankers in an informal way, in Norfolk since around 1650. Their first bank proper was established in Norwich in 1775. When its bicentenary was celebrated in 1975, the invitations and menus reproduced elaborate heraldic artwork from the 1875 centenary which turned out to be the work of my own great-grandfather, William Robert Weyer, a Norwich artist and stained-glass window maker.

zine.[13] It begins with a Foreword by the ubiquitous Tuke. 'The Bank takes pride in the work of its staff in prose, verse and picture,' he says, commending a book which 'reflects so much credit on them . . . and on the Bank itself.' But perhaps its most notable item was written by a distinguished customer, rather than a member of staff. It is a piece from 1931 called 'How I Joined Barclays Bank' by no less a figure than Sir James Barrie, the author of *Peter Pan*. Rather elaborately concocted, it reminds us that well into the modern era only the wealthier middle and upper classes had personal bank accounts at all.

For Barrie, the decision to open an account with Barclays required 'recklessness tempered with stratagem' as well as 'an ingratiating manner'. 'My appearance is against me,' he wrote, 'for I take Banks to be like Clubs, where the committee blackball all candidates except those who are unknown to them.' Finally, with clenched teeth, he plucked up courage to enter the Barclays branch in Kinnaird House, Pall Mall East – where he was perhaps fortunate not to have bumped into Frederick Goodenough, whose London flat was above the Pall Mall offices. Even though Rossini and Turner once banked there, the fearsome Goodenough would certainly have taken against anyone exhibiting extravagant artistic or literary tendencies within his portals.

'Have you ever been in a Bank?' Barrie continues. 'Bankers are of medium height, slightly but firmly built, forty or forty-one years of age, and stand in an easy attitude, with nothing about them to suggest their vocation save that they keep their hands in their trouser-pockets. They have pleasant voices, but you do not catch what they say, and all that is expected of you is to bow when they have completed a sentence.'

At last, after undergoing some uncomfortable scrutiny from the Bankers and signing the requisite documents, the author is presented with his cheque-book, evidently a potent symbol of financial elevation. 'Cheque-books are in blue covers,' he adds helpfully, 'and are of a shape which makes them wobble in the hand like a trout.'

Other articles, by members of staff, help to build up a kind of watercolour sketchbook of life in Barclays. There is 'How to deal with Companies . . . If one must', by C. I. Burge ('The average Englishman,

---

[13] The magazine itself, a genteel publication filled with essays, artwork and photographs illuminating Barclays folk's travels and pastimes, was killed off in a cost-cutting drive in the 1970s by my father in his most unsentimental mood. Ironically, it had been a family joke in earlier years that he was a devoted reader of the *Spread Eagle* for its Deaths and Retirements columns, with an eye to plotting his future promotion path. Its replacement, a tabloid-style staff newspaper largely devoted to management propaganda, was a lesser product both in style and substance. The passing of the old magazine is one of those things that Barclays pensioners sometimes remember to regret.

of course, has always found great difficulty in comprehending English Company Law and Practice; it is only the foreigner who really understands the subject.') Then there is 'In Defence of Illegible Signatures' by C. A. R. Brown. There are reminders that almost every male staff member of that era had served in one or other of the two world wars: an account of life in a Japanese prisoner-of-war camp by C. L. Hard, and a poem called 'The Passing of the Brave: An Echo of 1914–18' by 'H. G. T.' These bring to mind the gentle *Dad's Army* comedy of the bank manager Mr Mainwaring, captain of the Home Guard at Walmington-on-Sea, with his chief clerk, Mr Wilson, and his junior, Pike. The attitudes and disciplines of military service were a factor in all British corporate life – and thus essential to an understanding of how Barclays ticked – until the Second World War generation began to retire in the 1970s and early '80s.[14]

Finally, *The Eagle Looks Back* offers a pleasing reminiscence of the idiosyncratic make-up of the Barclays network, by way of a description of Baty's Bank in Newcastle, absorbed in 1911 to become Barclays' Cattle Market branch. This was a famous meeting place on market days for Northumberland livestock men who found good sport by sending their Border terriers down a trapdoor in the bank's floor, known as the Ratting Hole. On non-market days, staff were often engaged in manufacturing shotgun cartridges for the manager, Mr Baty, who was an ardent sportsman. 'During the reign of Mr Baty and his son Isaac who followed him ...' writes A. L. Brady, 'no serious attempt was made to obtain ordinary banking business and it was not until the 1930s that real efforts were made in this direction.'

This, then, was the bank that my father joined on that wartime winter's day when he took the bus from his parents' home in Bridlington, past his grandfather's farm at Flamborough Head, up the rugged coast to Filey, the seaside resort and fishing port that was to have brief post-war fame as the home of the great Butlin's holiday camp. He was, we may suppose, an archetypal Barclays clerical recruit of the era. At Bridlington Grammar School he had won prizes until he was eleven, but had then been eclipsed by brighter 'scholarship boys', and was a middle-of-the-road performer by the time he passed his School Certificate exams at fifteen.

No one in his family had ever been to university, and it does not seem

---

[14] The board of Barclays at the beginning of 1969 included no fewer than five holders of the Military Cross, one of them Marshal of the Royal Air Force Viscount Portal of Hungerford. The seven general managers included one MC and one holder of the Military Medal.

to have been suggested at that stage as a possibility for him. His father, a genial, unambitious man who liked golf and beer, was manager of the Hull branch of the Norwich Union insurance company, which had strong connections with Barclays. His mother (who died before I was born) was a more forceful person with higher hopes for her son. Both would have agreed that Barclays was a safe and respectable career choice. The highest aspiration that they or he might have had as he left for his first day's work was that he might one day be manager of a local branch.

But war broadened his horizons, as it did for so many thousands of other servicemen. In 1942 he was called up in the Green Howards, a Yorkshire infantry regiment, and swiftly selected for officer training. He served in India and Burma, and commanded a signals school at Poona. Attached to the Maratti Light Infantry, he was, at twenty-one, one of the youngest majors in the Indian Army. At the end of the war he was in Calcutta, leading patrols to clear corpses from the streets after the independence riots. He applied for a permanent commission in the Indian Army, but the days of expatriate officers in Indian regiments were over. So he took his demobilization papers and returned to Barclays Bank.

When he reported back for duty at St Nicholas Street, Scarborough branch on 8 September 1947, he was a changed man. He had had a taste of command and gained an inkling of his own potential. Like many wartime officers of humbler social origins who had rubbed up against the pre-war officer class, he had become rather left-wing, absorbing the Fabian ideas of Harold Laski and approving of the government of Clement Attlee; I think he remained a socialist at heart until the late 1960s, even though he once joined the local Conservative Association in an attempt to win more business for his branch.

He had also become something of an autodidact. He read voraciously and had ambitions to take a London University economics degree by correspondence. But back in Barclays in 1947, he was a junior clerk again, with no more status than Pike in *Dad's Army*. When he was transferred that winter to Helmsley – now my own home and in those days a very quiet little agricultural market town, dominated by the vast surrounding estate of the Earl of Feversham – the first thing that happened to this bright, ambitious 23-year-old ex-major was that the senior cashier, one Walter Harrison, sent him out to buy a packet of cigarettes.

But it would be wrong to suggest that the bank as a whole had, like Mr Harrison, failed to react to the post-war mood of social change. Its reaction did not encompass a shift towards open meritocracy – which was still a working lifetime away – but it did take the form of a new awareness of the need for professionalism. The task of introducing this was entrusted to Cuthbert Fitzherbert, who was appointed as the bank's first general manager in charge of staff matters in 1945, and was a vice-chairman from 1948 to 1964.

Fitzherbert's curriculum vitae, incidentally, offers a fine model of the Barclays local director class – with one unusual feature to it, in that he was a Catholic, educated at the Oratory School rather than Winchester or Eton. He was descended from an old Derbyshire squirearchical family, a graduate of New College, Oxford and was wounded as an officer of the Coldstream Guards in the First World War. His father, William Fitz-herbert-Brockholes, was a director of the Union Bank of Manchester. Cuthbert joined Barclays in 1922, becoming a local director in Dar-lington four years later and moving in due course to Preston and Bir-mingham. In the second war, though past forty, he returned to service with the Coldstream as a training officer at Pirbright – a period which he himself regarded as the most fulfilling of his life. As one of his grand-daughters told me, 'he was a man driven by duty'.

His great contribution to Barclays, immediately after the war, was to introduce management training and rudimentary career planning, and to establish a staff training school in Wimbledon to which even local directors returning from military service were sent for refresher courses. He was also charged with recruiting a new generation of future leaders to supplement the thinned-out ranks of the founding families. This he did, but entirely according to his own lights: legend has it that his preference was for Guards officers, New College men, and most ideally of all, guards officers who had (like himself) been Masters of the New College Beagles.

These recruits (including his own son-in-law, John Parham, who became a local director at Windsor) were in terms of social classification exactly like family members, except perhaps in some cases a bit brighter: referred to collectively by the rest of the bank as 'blue-bloods', they joined the family members on what was officially known as the Special List, guarded by Fitzherbert and his successors, of those who might eventually rise to be senior local directors and members of the board. Instead of being appointed local directors almost immediately as in the old days, however, they were now put through a relatively rigorous apprenticeship of courses and attachments to branches at home and overseas. They were considered to be on probation until they were finally confirmed as local directors, and even then (as happened to Edwin Fisher's son) they were sometimes weeded out. 'Even the passing of the examinations of the Institute of Bankers was encouraged, if not exacted,' noted A. W. Tuke. 'In one way and another the gifted amateur was converted into a highly trained and intelligent professional.'

But what was not about to happen was any significant integration of the two streams of Barclays life. Special List men (there were no women) were never branch managers, but could expect to be local directors by their early thirties, with dozens of branch managers reporting to them. The best of the non-Special List people, on the other hand, could not expect to be branch managers until their mid-thirties; if they were really outstanding, they might become local directors or assistant general managers in their mid-forties.

This form of corporate apartheid is illustrated by the early careers of those who rose to the top of the bank in the same era as my father – who was thirty-six when he became branch manager at Chester in 1961, and only then beginning to be marked out as a rising star. By contrast Timothy Bevan, great-grandson of Francis Augustus, joined Barclays – after Eton, the Welsh Guards and reading for the bar – on April Fools' Day 1950, and became a local director, aged thirty, in Nottingham in 1957. In the same year, 32-year-old Henry Lambert (son of a Barclays local director, head boy of Winchester, exhibitioner of New College and lieutenant-commander RN) became a local director in Lombard Street. Both joined the board of the bank in 1966, eight years ahead of my father.

John Quinton, who joined the bank in 1953 (and became its first non-family chairman of the modern era in 1987), provides a rarer example – of an exceptionally bright graduate entrant who was not part of the Special List system. He was the son of a Barclays branch manager in Norwich, and had worked for the bank in his vacations from Cambridge. When he applied in Norwich for a permanent job after graduation, he recalls, he was interviewed by a junior local director, Richard Gurney – who decided before he could make a final decision to call in his aged father, Quintin, a local director since 1920. Quintin Gurney, in turn, was not satisfied until he had called in his wife to confirm the decision. At last the job was offered, and John Quinton – who as a young man, and even as a middle-aged man, had eagerness and efficiency written all over him – made what was considered to be spectacular progress, becoming assistant manager at Piccadilly Branch in 1961, aged thirty-two. Years later, when he was senior enough to see his own personnel file, he found the words 'Mr Fitzherbert is interested in this man' inscribed upon it. Yet even this was not enough to allow him to jump tracks and catch up with the men of his age-group on the Special List.

It was a system built on the ancient belief that true leadership qualities are born rather than acquired. Even those whose advancement was frustrated by it could see that it had some advantages: providing continuity, shared values and a depth of local knowledge and community involvement, and encouraging an élite officer corps to think strategically from a relatively early stage of their careers. It had the effect of turning Barclays into a grand social institution when its greatest rival, the Midland, was concentrating on merely being a commercial bank. But, in the cosily uncompetitive marketplace of the era, it did not do Barclays any harm. On the contrary, A. W. Tuke's analysis demonstrates that by 1957, as Midland began to lose vigour and Barclays' post-war emphasis on professionalism showed through, Barclays was starting to open a lead.[15]

In the rather placid period from 1947 to 1966, therefore, Barclays was not troubled by any pressure to abandon its traditions; on the contrary, it remained thoroughly pleased with them. The bank's recruitment preferences were widely known, so that even as late as the mid-1970s it was possible for me to encounter, at Oxford, an undergraduate from Winchester who described Barclays as 'a good Wykehamist institution',[16] and a young Guards officer who said, 'Barclays? Frightfully good place, they pick all their top chaps from the Brigade, you know.'

Meanwhile the local directors, though reinvigorated by Cuthbert Fitzherbert's training programmes, carried on in their time-honoured way. Some had labradors slumbering under their office desks. Down in Cornwall, Major Simon Bolitho, MC kept in touch with his district by taking the train eastwards from Penzance and instructing branch managers to join the train at one stop, report to him in his compartment, and alight at the next station. In Birmingham in the 1960s, a local director was told that the home of one of his branch managers had been burned to the ground in the night, though the family were all safe. 'Glad to hear it,' he responded, 'but what about the servants?'

As for branch operations, the pen-and-ink clerical practices of the nineteenth century were not wholly replaced by mechanical book-keeping until April 1960, when the last handwritten entry on a customer's statement was made. Bank clerks of that era – still active today, perhaps, as treasurers of Conservative branches and old folks' luncheon clubs – acquired a facility for totalling columns of figures by mental

---

[15] Since banks did not declare their true profits until 1969, leadership could only be measured in terms of total volumes of deposits.

[16] Even very recently, a Wykehamist remarked to me how surprising it was, given the Barclays connection, that a former Lloyds Bank chairman, Sir Jeremy Morse, had been appointed Warden of the school.

arithmetic which is lost to younger generations. The first computer
was installed, at Cavendish Square branch in London, in 1961.

In every respect, this was a period in which, as my father put it in
his 1980 presidential address to the Institute of Bankers, 'the broad
banking stream moved steadily forward, its surface relatively unruffled
by storms'. Any impulse that the clearing banks might have had towards
competitive expansion was held back by almost continuous government-imposed credit restraint, the policy then relied upon to coun-
teract 'overheating' in the economy, and by a gentlemanly reticence to
break ranks. Inflation was modest, property prices rose gently and
interest rates fluctuated in a narrow band of 4 to 7 per cent. Deposit
rates were kept in line among the banks by a semi-official cartel. No
interest was paid on current accounts, and no tariff of charges was
published: annual account charges were imposed, without discussion,
as managers thought fit. Lending money was not a difficult business:
the prevailing margins over base rate provided a comfortable cushion
of profit, and any customer respectable enough to have been offered a
loan in the first place was unlikely to go suddenly bust. Branches
opened only from 10 a.m. to 3 p.m. It was 'an age of relative economic
stability, albeit slow decline,' my father wrote, 'the age of Butskell
politics[17] and the consensus of the centre'.

Despite the sluggishness of the economic environment, my father
himself had made quite a splash as manager of Chester branch, tripling
its business in three years and moving it into rather grand premises in
what had once been the King's School, forming part of the cathedral
precincts. He understood, up to that point, that he was being groomed
to become manager of the large Water Street branch in Liverpool
where he had been assistant manager in the mid-1950s. But it was by
now obvious that he had the potential to go higher. In 1964 he became
a local director's assistant in Liverpool, and in the following year he
finally broke through Barclays' glass ceiling to become a local director.
He often described himself as a 'late developer', measuring the fulfilment of his true abilities from some time after he turned forty in
January 1965. Barclays might also have been classified as a late developer,
having proceeded at a steady but unspectacular pace through the
decades since Frederick Goodenough was at the height of his power
and ambition. But, like its faithful employee from Bridlington, the
bank itself was about to embark on a meteoric phase of advancement.

[17] The perceived similarity during the 1950s of the conservatism of R. A. Butler and the
socialism of Labour leader Hugh Gaitskell.

3

ZENITH

1966–1979: The birth of Barclaycard – The partnership of Derek
Wilde and John Thomson – The discovery of marketing – The
acquisition of Martins Bank – The buying-in of Barclays DCO –
The global vision of Anthony Tuke – The Fringe Bank crisis –
Relations with the Labour government – The creation of Barclays
Merchant Bank – Barclays at its zenith

If sexual intercourse began in 1963, as the poet Philip Larkin said, then
consumer debt as we know it today began in 1966 with the launch of
Barclaycard. This was, perhaps, Barclays' one great contribution to
social change in Britain. It was also the bank's boldest and most
successful product launch ever, unmatched by any of the gimmicks and
deals it has offered its personal customers over the succeeding three
and a half decades.

Credit cards were, of course, an American invention. The concept
began with account cards issued by merchants and retailers, and was
developed by a few local US banks in the 1950s. In 1959, the Bank of
America – headquartered in San Francisco and rapidly emerging as a
world leader – decided to develop the concept more aggressively. 'It
got so bad we might as well have been dumping these things out of
airplanes,' said one executive: cards were mailed out, unsolicited, by
the thousands. As the recipients went on spending sprees, losses soared
in the early years. But the utility of the plastic card grabbed the
American public's imagination in a big way, and soon the British banks
were studying the prospects for their own market.[1]

---

[1] With almost 30 million card-holders by 1970, BankAmericard dominated the US credit
card market; as a defensive move, Bank of America spun it off into a separate company, now
Visa International.

Barclays had been represented in San Francisco since 1949, and enjoyed a relationship of mutual admiration with Bank of America. In December 1965 Barclays' San Francisco office was upgraded to become a subsidiary bank in its own right.[2] During visits to mark the occasion, Barclays' general manager Derek Wilde struck an agreement to gain Bank of America's help in the creation of Britain's first credit card. Barclaycard was launched six months later.

Wilde was one of the wisest and most forward-thinking executives ever to make his way through the meritocratic wing of the Barclays hierarchy. Born in Sheffield in 1912, he entered Barclays as a clerk in 1929 and rose through the trustee department, where he was talent-spotted by A. W. Tuke to become a general manager in 1960. Tall, kindly, shrewd and calm in judgement, he was a hero to many younger Barclays men, including my father. He was also extraordinarily good at presenting new ideas in a way which was acceptable to the back-woodsmen on the Barclays board. As senior general manager from 1966, he worked in a highly effective partnership with the chairman. John Thomson, an Olympian figure from the family side whose broad vision took Barclays forward during this period by several leaps.

Thomson (knighted in 1972) was chairman from 1962 to 1973, and probably the last holder of the office to be universally liked by his colleagues and admired and respected by the outside world. A tall, boney Wykehamist with a deceptively gentle manner and a passion for the Turf, he came to the top by way of being head of the Oxford district, where his family bank, Parsons, Thomson & Co. had been absorbed into Barclays in 1900, eight years before he was born, and where he had been a local director since 1935. He was also at various times lord lieutenant of Oxfordshire, honorary colonel of the county's territorial regiment, Deputy High Steward of Oxford University and a steward of the Jockey Club.

Thomson had been preferred for the chairmanship over Frederic (later Lord) Seebohm, who was one year his junior and probably a good deal cleverer. Indeed, some contemporaries thought Seebohm (who came from a distinguished line of Quaker social reformers and

---

[2] For the incorporation of Barclays Bank of California, the Rouge Dragon Pursuivant, Dr Conrad Swan, later Garter King of Arms, was commissioned to design a coat of arms incorporating the Barclays eagle with appropriate references to the host state. The crest was duly blazoned as follows: 'Before a snow covered rocky mount thereon a grizzly bear statant proper two mullets azure'. Attempts to devise a Latin motto referring to eagles and bears (the Wykehamist A. W. Tuke suggested *Ursa favente crescat aquila*) were ruled out, however, lest it should be misinterpreted as a provocative Cold War reference to American eagles and Russian bears.

was involved in a range of public and charitable activities outside the bank) the cleverest man the families had ever produced.[3] But there was some ancient enmity between the Seebohms and the Barclays and Bevans in Lombard Street, who preferred the cut of Thomson's jib: that of a pre-war gentleman banker and thoroughbred breeder who devoted one day a week to public duties in Oxfordshire and whose Christmas greeting to staff in the *Spread Eagle* was accompanied by a photograph not in boardroom pose but in a comfortable armchair and a tweed suit with spaniels.

When he retired, Thomson told the *Daily Telegraph* City columnist Kenneth Fleet: 'I have had a frightfully good time.' Shortly afterwards I called on him at Woodperry, his eighteenth-century mansion south of Oxford, to help my father deliver a retirement present from the general managers, a record-player which we proved rather inept at assembling. I retain a pleasing mental picture of him striding with his long, countryman's gait towards us across his Palladian forecourt, dogs at his heels.

Yet the style was misleading. Thomson relished new ideas and encouraged bright people. He was much tougher than he looked. He had big ambitions for the bank and he was prepared to take risks, of which Barclaycard was only the beginning.

The first million Barclaycards were issued unsolicited, mainly to Barclays customers. Reactions were mixed, and sermons were preached on the immorality of encouraging debt, especially for frivolous spending. Until then, most people had access to 'consumer' borrowing only through hire-purchase agreements or catalogue shopping schemes run by door-to-door collectors. Charlie Morland, later a local director and merchant banker but then a management trainee in a branch in Hull, remembered a Yorkshire farmer coming into the bank so enraged by the card (or perhaps at the temptations it had offered to his wife) that he tried, unsuccessfully, to tear it in half in front of the counter. Noel White, who was an assistant branch manager at Scarborough, telephoned my father to tell him what a splendid innovation he thought the card was: 'There's three good things about it,' he said. 'It scrapes ice off your windscreen. It picks Yale locks. And it's getting my customers into debt.'

Those debts were more of a headache than a benefit in the early years, however, even though the bank was charging a hefty interest rate

---

[3] His great-grandfather, Benjamin Seebohm, was a German immigrant who settled in Bradford in 1814 and became a Quaker. Benjamin's son Frederic became a partner in Sharples, Tuke, Lucas & Seebohm of Hitchin, and was also a brother-in-law of Joseph Barclay Gurney of Lombard Street.

of 1.5 per cent per month on unpaid accounts. As the bad debt toll mounted, Derek Wilde's first exploratory trip to California was sometimes referred to in the bank as 'the most expensive business trip in history'. But cards continued to be issued to all creditworthy applicants, regardless of whether they banked with Barclays, and by 1969 there were 1,250,000 Barclaycard holders, able to use their plastic in 600,000 merchant outlets around the world. Now an essential feature of everyday life, the credit card was, in 1966, truly a consumer revolution. Remarkably, the other British clearers took more than six years to respond to the challenge, even though Barclays was busy tempting their customers away throughout that period: it was not until October 1972 that Midland, Lloyds, National Westminster, Williams & Glyn's and Royal Bank of Scotland jointly launched the rival Access card.[4]

There were other seminal developments in this period which attracted less attention than Barclaycard. In June 1967, Barclays made history by installing, outside its Enfield branch, the world's first automatic cash dispensing machine. In the same year, a tiny subsidiary business was created within the head office – at first operating for regulatory reasons as an offshoot of Barclays Bank (France) Limited, then under the name of Barclays Bank (London & International) Limited – to borrow and lend in the fast-growing eurodollar market, and to lend sterling to British companies for periods of three to seven years, activities which were not permitted to the clearing bank in its own name. The unit's balance sheet grew very rapidly but it was, as it were, the seed of great trouble to come. It became, in due course, Barclays Merchant Bank, which became part of BZW, and was thereby a grandparent of today's Barclays Capital.

Meanwhile, Derek Wilde had picked up another idea from Bank of America. That was the science of marketing, then completely unknown to British banks. The Barclaycard launch had given an inkling of the possibilities of other markets and services to be explored, but the very word 'marketing' was barely in circulation on this side of the Atlantic: it meant identifying customer needs, designing products to meet them and campaigns to sell the products, setting profitable goals for the progress of those products and measuring that progress. It was all new, and the person Wilde chose to run with it was my father, who was dispatched first to San Francisco in January 1968 to study Bank of

---

[4] The name Access was proposed by the advertising agency J. Walter Thompson, which was hired to market the card. It narrowly avoided being called 'Omnicard', 'Supercharge' and 'Three-in-One'.

America's techniques, and then to the Oxford Centre for Management Studies (now Templeton College) to write a thesis on their application to Barclays.

The notes of his Californian trip make particularly vivid reading. There was, for example, the matter of the physical design of bank branches. In Britain (recalling Sir James Barrie's nerve-racking experience at Pall Mall) lay-out tended to emphasize the dignity of the institution and its superiority over the customer: the manager's office was an inner sanctum to be approached with some trepidation; the counter was a solid mahogany barrier between customer and cashier, and in the 1960s (partly due to pressure from the staff union) it had been surmounted by a steel-framed glass screen to protect against shotgun raiders.

In California, by contrast, 'the major difference from us is the extreme philosophy of "openness",' my father recorded. 'Although the branch manager has a "conference room" for more bashful customers, he and his loan officers sit out on the "platform" in the Banking Hall and interview there. Though Bank of America's 939 branches had 214 hold-ups in 1967, the counters are low and narrow and there are no anti-bandit screens. Such a device would be anathema ...' As to the way staff were trained to handle customers, 'great emphasis is placed on tellers saying "Hullo" with a smile, as well as recognizing customers by name and saying "Thanks" as they leave.'

Bank of America's 'expansionist spirit' and 'quite uninhibited' devotion to business development was, he observed, a function of the buoyant growth of the Californian economy, the absence of government-imposed credit restraints and 'a deep-seated difference in the national temperament'. Arming himself against the predictable responses of the backwoodsmen at home, he concluded that 'we should not automatically react against American marketing methods, though they do not automatically transplant'. On the contrary, a British version of such methods might well be attractive to a 'younger, less traditional' generation of customers.

His Oxford thesis explored these ideas in great detail, and in due course he was invited to present his findings to the board. When he finished, he claimed to have overheard one old soldier on the board mutter to his neighbour, 'What on earth's this young feller talking about?' Nevertheless, the concept of marketing was embraced, and in October 1968 my father was transferred from Liverpool to Lombard Street as an assistant general manager – at a salary of £6,385 per year – to set up the first marketing department of any British bank.

Barclays was 'determined to remain in the forefront in the quality of the service it provides for customers, and in the use of modern management techniques to ensure the growth and profitability of our business', said the internal circular from the general managers announcing the new department. Among the techniques to be applied – even to local head offices – was 'Management by Objectives', the first serious attempt to measure segmental business growth and profit. At the same time, the difficulty in Barclays' decentralized power structure of imposing anything radical from the top is delicately hinted at in other parts of the circular: 'It may be possible for the Department to help in the development of a planning mechanism ...' but rest assured, the carefully chosen words seem to imply, the new outfit will 'co-operate fully with existing Departments to whom, for the present, all correspondence on marketing should continue to be addressed'.

While my father gathered a team around him to tackle this challenge – which was to be the making of his name in the City – another development was taking place which took Barclays towards the leadership of British banking. The Treasury Minute of 1920, banning further domestic bank amalgamations, had been breached significantly only once, in 1962, when National Provincial had received the consent of the Bank of England to acquire the District Bank, an operation of some 580 branches concentrated in the north of England. in 1967, however, a Prices and Incomes Board report on bank charges[5] indicated a softening in official attitudes: 'The Bank of England and the Treasury have made it plain to us that they would not obstruct some further bank mergers.'

The first bank to react to this signal was Martins, even older than Barclays in its origins[6] and the last independent clearer headquartered in the north; its base was in Liverpool, and its network of 737 branches was strong throughout the north-west where Barclays was relatively weak. Martins was simply too small to compete in the modern world: it had an impressive corporate customer list, but repeatedly came up against lending ceilings imposed on it in relation to its capital by government and Bank of England restraints. It also lacked the critical

[5] The report recommended that the banks should compete on deposit rates, rather than fixing them by cartel, and should move towards full disclosure of their profits and reserves – recommendations which, according to one authoritative account, 'did not command ready or widespread acceptance and were not at that time carried further'. True profits were revealed for the first time at the end of 1969: Barclays came out top of the table, and Midland bottom.

[6] Martins claimed descent from the Elizabethan merchant and financier Sir Thomas Gresham (1519–1579) who propounded the principle: 'Bad money drives out good.'

mass to develop an international business, or to invest effectively in computerization. In short, it needed a merger partner. A first tentative discussion with Barclays in 1964 had caused a row in the Martins board and had not gone forward. The City had for some time expected that Martins might link up with one of the Scottish banks.

But in late 1967 Martins' directors let it be known that they were prepared to entertain approaches from the London clearers. The Governor of the Bank of England, Leslie O'Brien (later Lord O'Brien of Lothbury) ruled that this should take place by tender through the Bank, rather than by competing take-over bids in the public domain. In January 1968, while these arrangements were under discussion, the two smallest of the Big Five, National Provincial and Westminster, outflanked the competition by announcing that they were not in contention for Martins but were about to merge with each other – thereby overtaking Barclays, Midland and Lloyds both in balance sheet size and numbers of branches.

The first response to this, on 7 February, was that Royal Bank of Scotland (which owned Glyn, Mills in London and William Deacon's Bank in Manchester) announced a merger with the National Commercial Bank of Scotland, in which Lloyds had an interest. The following day, Barclays and Lloyds announced that they too intended to merge (Lloyds, which was then about two-thirds of the size of Barclays, having first rebuffed a tentative approach from the now fading Midland) and that – both separately and, if permitted, in combination – they would then bid for Martins.

This was all too much for the Bank of England and the Treasury, which confirmed their approval of the National Provincial–Westminster marriage but referred the Barclays–Lloyds–Martins juggernaut (which would have had balance sheet footings of £5.8 billion to National Westminster's £3.5bn, and a market share in England and Wales of around 48 per cent) to the Monopolies and Mergers Commission. Any further merger proposals were banned by the Bank of England until the Commission had time to report.

After long consideration, the Commission rejected the Barclays–Lloyds proposal. There was concern that such a concentration of resources would restrict even further the availability of loan money to the more entrepreneurial and innovative parts of industry, which had never been well served by the banks. And there was a fear, expressed in evidence to the Commission by the Bank of England, that one mega-merger must inevitably lead to another, in which the Midland would be next to be swallowed.

But the Commissioners' six-to-four vote against did not count as a decisive margin and the question still had to be referred back to the Board of Trade (under the presidency of Anthony Crosland), which decided that Barclays and Lloyds could not get together – to the deep disappointment of John Thomson, who had been at the centre of all the negotiations, but perhaps not surprisingly, given the potential market share of the merged group. On the other hand, the Board was content that whichever was the highest bidder in the Bank of England's tender process – and it happened to be Barclays – should be free to buy Martins.

Barclays' offer for Martins became effective on 1 November 1968, and was technically completed by the passage of a private Act of Parliament a year later. Three Martins directors – Sir Cuthbert Clegg, Sir John Nicholson and John Keswick – joined the Barclays board. One Martins executive, Len Walton, became a general manager. The merger proceeded painlessly, to the relief of many Martins managers who had preferred the prospect of a deal with Lloyds – which was at a low ebb, and going through something of a leadership crisis – having feared that they would be crushed by the more assertive Barclays people. Thomson, in his fair-minded way, decreed that (since Barclays was the larger partner by a factor of roughly six times) management jobs should be allocated to Martins men across the bank as evenly as possible in a one-in-seven ratio.

Martins already operated on a decentralized basis which was compatible with the Barclays local head office structure, and was even accustomed to the vestigial presence of a founding family, though the Holland-Martins had long since ceased to have a dominant influence: the only one to become a Barclays local director, in a non-executive capacity at Bristol, was Admiral Sir Deric Holland-Martin, GCB DSO DSC, brother of 'Ruby' and former Second Sea Lord.

Sir Brian Pearse, who was finance director of Barclays before he was head-hunted by the Bank of England to be chief executive of Midland Bank in 1991, joined Martins from school in Liverpool in 1950, and was a general managers' clerk at the time of the merger. Shortly afterwards he was appointed branch manager in Sheffield, and he remembers the surprise of discovering the Barclays two-tier social structure. Asked by one of his new colleagues what his future ambitions might be, Pearse admitted that he thought he would like to be a local director.

'Forget it, Brian, that's for the blue-bloods,' came the reply, though in fairness Pearse did rapidly advance to local director, in Birmingham in 1972. In the tribal way of Barclays, old Martins men would continue to identify themselves as such many years after the name of Martins (and its grasshopper symbol) had been expunged. But the integration of the two clearing banks was a relatively simple step compared to the next phase of Barclays' advance towards its zenith, which was the integration with its own sister company, Barclays DCO.

It was not until well into the 1980s that Barclays was briefly one bank – before dividing again, in spirit, with the birth of BZW – but it is often forgotten that until October 1971 it was not even one public company but two, Barclays Bank Limited and its 56.5 per cent-owned affiliate DCO. The two were always closely linked at board level – Freddie Seebohm was chairman of DCO from 1966 and deputy chairman of Limited from 1968, for example – but in every other respect they were entirely separate, and by no means always on brotherly terms. Until efforts were launched in 1971 to start rationalizing the structure, Barclays' foreign interests was extraordinarily ramshackle.

The problem, first of all, was that Barclays Bank Limited was not purely a domestic bank. It had owned since 1922 a substantial branch banking business in France and had operated in Rome since 1925. In England – in order to service its customers' foreign currency and trade finance needs and to offer sterling facilities to foreign banks – it operated 'Foreign Branches' in Fenchurch Street and the West End of London, in Bradford, Manchester, Liverpool and other cities – in some cases, side-by-side with DCO branches. After 1959, when a board decision was made to expand Limited's international activities, new representative offices were opened (in chronological order) in Zurich, Brussels, Beirut, Tokyo, Frankfurt and Milan. Interests in Canada and Switzerland were owned jointly with DCO.

And DCO, meanwhile, was not primarily an international bank but an overseas domestic one. Its three constituent parts, the former Colonial Bank, Anglo-Egyptian Bank and National Bank of South Africa, continued until the late 1950s to operate very much as they always had done – even to the extent of using different internal forms and maintaining separate advances departments for the processing of loan proposals. DCO men were not by nature sophisticated internationalists, but in their own favourite phrase, 'bush bankers'. According to Julian Wathen, who became general manager in charge of DCO staff in 1966 and later a vice-chairman, they were 'damned good at chucking a safe on the back of a truck somewhere in Africa at three in the morning and opening for business that day 500 miles away across a desert. But not terribly good bankers.'

Wathen – a man of great zest, who likes to talk freely – was in some ways being unfair to himself and his colleagues. All over Africa and the Caribbean, and in Israel, Cyprus and Malta, DCO men ran well-respected branch banking businesses which were market leaders in their territories. Some of the ex-Colonial Bank operations dated back to the 1830s; DCO's local directors were as important in the social hierarchy of Ibadan and Bridgetown as their domestic counterparts were in Norwich and Cambridge. But they were administrators, rather than financiers, good at commanding local staff and operating current account facilities, but not good at lending. In Ghana, where Wathen arrived as a local director in 1961, DCO held £17 million of deposits but lent only £3 million of it back to local customers, the balance being largely deposited with head office in London. Such lending as did take place was seasonal and short-term, as funds moved around the DCO network to finance Sudanese and Egyptian cotton, then South African maize, then West Indian sugar.

But this simple model – capable, in Frederick Goodenough's original masterplan, of replicating itself in every corner of the Empire and beyond – was struggling in the 1960s to adjust to a changing world. As colonies and dominions became independent nations, there were new regulatory barriers and political hostilities to contend with. In Egypt, Libya, Sudan and Tanzania, DCO's businesses were compulsorily nationalized. In other parts of Africa they were obliged to become locally incorporated, in some cases with a percentage of government ownership. In South Africa, by now an international pariah, it was thought politically expedient to remove the name of DCO from the old National Bank of South Africa, which re-emerged as Barclays National Bank (see Chapter 8).

Meanwhile, there were ambitions to expand in New York and California, to follow the growing fashion for investment in consortium banking in various parts of the world, and to be a player (as Barclays Bank Limited was also trying to be) in the eurocurrency loan and deposit markets – competing against a flood of foreign banks opening up in London. With the tribulations of sterling throughout the late 1960s, there was increasing awareness of a need for a bigger capital base to compete with aggressive dollar-based banks such as Citibank and Bank of America. All these factors created pressure for rationalization and co-operation between the two wings of Barclays, which Derek Wilde and Freddie Seebohm set out to address.

The result, in September 1971, was that Barclays Bank Limited bought in the 43.5 per cent of DCO which it did not already own, offering its own shares and loan stock in return, and DCO changed its name to Barclays Bank International Limited. The domestic Foreign Branches and overseas representative offices of Barclays Bank Limited became part of International. But this was a tidying-up rather than anything approaching complete integration: the two wings were to retain separate management structures until 1984. They also retained separate characters, which made them deeply uncomfortable with each other.

'What is remarkable is that two such different banks should have shared a head office at all,' said one old DCO man. 'We barely spoke to each other. Limited people thought DCO people were pirates. DCO people loved to quote a remark attributed to Julian Wathen: "We always thought the word Limited in our parent's name had more than one connotation." '

DCO men were used to the easy-going, clubbable, sometimes rather louche life of the white man in Africa, to being sent up-country to take care of themselves. Many had joined DCO because they enjoyed their time abroad during National Service; very few were graduates or had any intellectual leanings at all. Being relatively few in number they enjoyed a powerful *esprit de corps* and – though DCO was no less hierarchical than any other British company of the period - they considered themselves less rule-bound and stuffy, and more merit-ocratic, than their stay-at-home counterparts. They were particularly suspicious of their new colleagues from the Foreign Branches, which had the reputation of being a dumping ground for second-raters in the domestic bank – 'Buck your ideas up or you'll be transferred to Chief Foreign Branch' being, supposedly, a common exhortation to idle clerks. Senior Limited executives, for their part, resented the loss of the little bit of glamour, and the possibilities for travel, that attached to their foreign business.

And like the Martins men, DCO's senior managers in London now had to contend with the 'blue-bloods' – of whom, within their own ranks, Julian Wathen was a rare example, being descended, through his mother, from Sir Thomas Fowell Buxton, Bt and his wife, Hannah Gurney, and being the brother of a local director at Norwich. But no one ever doubted that Wathen deserved his advancement, if only as a reward for huge enthusiasm and energy. What came as a shock to DCO men was to meet so many blue-bloods of high station but lesser ability.

'It was very, very surprising and deeply unattractive,' said one senior DCO manager who was transferred into the domestic bank to do planning work. 'Having been in an organization which was unusually open, where one felt that everybody was a worker, you came to one with this "Special List" system. Of course it produced some highly competent and able people, but it also produced some other people who may have been extremely nice and may have carried the banner for Barclays locally perfectly well, but in many cases were not what you would call professional bankers.'

One of the results of this system at the time of the 1971 restructuring, was the parachuting in of Anthony Favill Tuke, son of A. W. Tuke,[7] to succeed Freddie Seebohm as chairman of what was now Barclays International. There were several veteran DCO candidates available, but Tuke had already been chosen, by mysterious inner processes at board level, to succeed Thomson as group chairman in due course. His appointment to the International chair represented a logical welding of the apex of the new structure. He had spent a period in South Africa as a young trainee, but had then spent virtually the whole of his Barclays career up to 1968 (when he became vice-chairman of DCO) as a local director in Luton and Birmingham. But he was an internationalist by inclination and a robust, practical banker who rapidly won over his new colleagues.

Tuke and Wathen now formed a powerful partnership. 'Anthony and I had a vision', recalled Wathen, 'that we should turn the bank into a proper international bank. We wanted to compete with Citibank and see them off. We didn't see why we should be buggered about by the Americans. We were already Britain's biggest overseas bank but because of nationalization and localization we had a lot of expatriate staff becoming available: in Ghana when I went out there we had sixty-five expats, when I left there were thirty-five and ten years later there were only going to be three. This new vision was a wonderful way of finding jobs for our people ... But it had one weakness, which was that we didn't have the right people.'

The vision had its first public airing at a meeting in the Great Hall of 54 Lombard Street called to reassure London DCO staff about their

---

[7] A. W. Tuke was in turn the son of W. F. Tuke, who – though already past seventy – served briefly as chairman of Barclays Bank Limited after the death of Frederick Goodenough. W. F. Tuke's father was William Murray Tuke, a partner in Gibson, Tuke & Gibson of Saffron Walden and a local director there after the 1896 amalgamation. William's brother James Hack Tuke was a partner in Sharples, Tuke, Lucas & Seebohm of Hitchin. A third brother, Daniel, was a well-known Victorian 'alienist', or expert on mental diseases. The Tukes were originally tea and cocoa merchants in York, but the cocoa business was too closely connected with slavery for their liking: so the Tukes handed it over to their managing clerk, Joseph Rowntree.

future prospects. It was apparent that there would be some redundancies arising from the amalgamation of Foreign Branches and DCO branches in London, Manchester and Liverpool. But other fears were immediately put to rest when Wathen began to talk about the round the world trip he had just completed. There would soon be a subsidiary bank in Milan, for example, and full branches in Brussels and Amsterdam. As for more exotic locations, John Blandford recorded in *The DCO Story*:

> So many fields for future expansion had Wathen discovered on his journey to the Far East that the staff opportunities were almost unlimited ... Singapore was fast becoming a Far Eastern centre for international finance; Hong Kong would be a good place for a branch; in Tokyo we already had a representative but a branch might be profitable in the long term. Australia was a closed country as far as domestic banking was concerned but there were opportunities there for merchant banking which was now coming into the scope of our thinking. Fiji and Tonga were also visited by Wathen ... Local restrictions presented fairly formidable obstacles in those places but not in the New Hebrides where it was planned to open a branch – surely the farthest removed from Head Office in the entire history of the bank.

It was this performance, perhaps, which created the legend of the inexhaustible Wathen opening a Barclays office wherever he spotted land from the window of an aeroplane. The new strategy would attract, with hindsight, the criticism that once Barclays International had ceased to be a public company answerable to shareholders in its own right, it lost a proper sense of investment discipline and went on a global spending spree – taking it into territories and businesses it was not equipped, in manpower or brainpower, to conquer. Several disasters were to follow – in Italy, Hong Kong and the United States, among other places – and some successes – notably in Spain (some colourful legacies of the great expansion will be visited in Chapter 7). But for the time being, as the Barclays empire extended itself from 35 countries in 1971 to more than 80 a decade later, and Anthony Tuke counted 148 airports visited in only six of those years, Barclays was saluted wherever it went as one of the world's great financial institutions. Tuke, incidentally, wanted to call the whole group (as opposed to the non-domestic subsidiary) 'Barclays International' to underline that status – but the grandees of Barclays Bank Limited sniffed a take-over by DCO, and would have none of it.

Meanwhile, also dating from the autumn of 1971, changes were afoot on the domestic front which were to lead to one of the deepest crises of the modern City of London – but from which Barclays was to emerge strengthened in experience and reputation.

In the period following the November 1967 devaluation of sterling, government lending restrictions on the clearing banks had proved increasingly irksome, whilst the growing 'wholesale banking' sector – merchant banks, foreign banks in London and an increasing range of smaller or 'secondary' financial institutions, all able to obtain funding through interbank deposit markets – was eating into the clearers' dominance of corporate lending. In 1969 a joint Treasury–Bank of England committee was set up to examine how the strains on the banking sector might be relieved, within the context of a more effective monetary policy framework overall. The arrival of a Conservative government in June 1970 invited the possibility of a more 'free-market' approach, and in January 1971 the Bank presented a radical set of proposals, known as 'Competition and Credit Control'. At the core of this was the abolition the clearing banks' interest rate cartel, so that each bank would fix its own rates according to its reading of market conditions. The convention whereby clearers kept 28 per cent of their assets in cash and various forms of liquid instruments was also to be replaced, by a 12.5 per cent 'Reserve Asset' requirement. Lending ceilings were to be removed, leaving interest rates as the Treasury's only instrument of monetary control.

This scheme was endorsed by the Tory Chancellor of the Exchequer, Anthony Barber, and came into effect in September 1971, at a time when the economy was sluggish and Bank Rate stood at only 5 per cent. What had not been foreseen in those conditions was that, combined with other expansionist Conservative policies, the relaxation of lending capacity would swiftly lead to an uncontrollable boom, in which money would pour not into productive industry but into the property sector and stock market speculation, by way of massive growth in secondary banking. Suddenly, it was the era of Slater Walker and Keyser Ullman – whose managing director Stanley Van Gelder recalled that 'what you bought for a million pounds one day you sold for two the next, and that person sold for three the day after.' 'We were having bank money thrust at us from all directions,' recalled another property developer, Ronald Lyon, whose business went under in 1974 with around £50 million of debts.

Margaret Reid, in her definitive account *The Secondary Banking Crisis, 1973–1975*, described the situation thus:

Long-established restrictive attitudes within the High Street clearing banks were abandoned in the tussle for new lending business. Sedate bank managers ... became like salesmen, actively marketing that commodity then in plentiful supply, money. New personal loan schemes, packages for small firms and longer term loans for industry abounded, while managers became more open-handed with overdrafts to individuals, who borrowed heavily to play the stock market boom which was well under way. *The Economist* urged readers who fancied their touch with equities ... to 'go to your bank manager and demand a loan with which to flutter in the City'. Above all, loans to cash-hungry and active property companies expanded dramatically.

In the two and a half years before this boom turned to catastrophic bust, total sterling bank advances to UK resident borrowers rose by 148 per cent. Within that total, lending by secondary banks more than trebled and borrowings in the property and financial sector more than quadrupled. The fringe banks funded themselves almost entirely in the wholesale deposit market – making, on a grand scale, the classic banking error of borrowing short and lending long. One of the most active of these businesses was Cedar Holdings, where deposits rose from £3 million to £67 million in the space of three years.

In August 1973, my father was promoted to senior general manager of Barclays, the pinnacle of the bank's professional hierarchy.[8] The first big test he had to face, and perhaps the biggest he ever faced in more than forty-seven years with Barclays, was the crash of Cedar Holdings.

By late 1973, boom was turning to incipient panic as interest rates rose to 13 per cent in an attempt to restrain rapidly rising inflation. Britain's coal miners were threatening strike action, and oil prices were about to be quadrupled by OPEC. Property and share prices were on the verge of a precipitous fall. In November, a crisis in another fringe bank, London & County Securities, though swiftly resolved by the Bank of England, signalled the beginning of a run of trouble in the sector. In mid-December, it became apparent that Cedar – which specialized in second mortgages for individual borrowers, as well as holding property interests of its own – was unable to meet its obligations

---

[8] But at that point still ranking below board level and therefore junior in status to those local directors who had seats on the board. He was in fact made a director of Barclays Bank Limited nine months later, in May 1974, as one of the first board appointments by Anthony Tuke, whose letter appointing him came with a reminder that 'assuming you are still a general manager, you would be expected to leave the Board when you give up your executive duties.' Family appointees, by contrast, usually stayed on the board for some years after retiring.

in the money market. The Governor of the Bank of England, Gordon Richardson – also new to his job, having succeeded Leslie O'Brien in July – took the view that a default of this size could cause what he later called 'a contagion of fear' throughout the whole banking system.

So on Wednesday, 19 December 1973, Richardson and his deputy, Sir Jasper Hollom, summoned to the Bank the directors of Cedar (led by the Morrison family, descendants of Baltic Jewish immigrants who had settled in Glasgow) and the representatives of Cedar's four largest institutional shareholders, which were the Phoenix Assurance, the pension funds of the nationalized coal and electricity supply industries, and the Unilever pension fund; also summoned was Cedar's lead bank, Barclays, and a variety of professional advisers. They convened early in the morning, expecting to finish before lunch: the Governor told them that he would like them to stay until a rescue had been achieved. The meeting developed, as Charles Gordon described it in *The Cedar Story*,

> into an unprecedented eighteen-hour cliff-hanging series of discussions, wrangles and arguments between the four institutions themselves, between them and Barclays, between all of them and the Cedar directors and also between the Cedar directors themselves. It was only after the great liquidator [Kenneth Cork], adviser to Barclays, had his say, that the rescue was assured. The agreement was eventually signed just before 3 a.m. on Thursday morning, by which time there were over thirty cold and hungry participants, some of them resentful, some deeply angry, some baffled, some just plain petrified, but all of them weary out of their minds. Nor were they mollified to read in *The Economist* after Christmas, that this was 'How The City Was Saved'.

Barclays was represented in this epic encounter by Timothy Bevan, vice-chairman and heir apparent to Tuke, along with my father and another general manager, Doug Horner. As the night progressed, the Barclays team dug its heels in, agreeing to lend £22 million of the £72 million needed to save Cedar, but insisting that the four institutions take the major slice of the risks involved. In Charles Gordon's account, it was Bevan who was most intransigent: 'He gave the impression, indeed he proffered it, that he did not care about the outcome.'

This great-grandson of Francis Augustus Bevan and product of Eton and the Welsh Guards was 'of youthful if not schoolboy appearance . . . high intelligence and low boiling point, astutely concealing a first-class mind from his colleagues . . . But what Bevan could not conceal was his volatile temperament, and he had many critics who did not find the Bevan quick fuse particularly electrifying. He did not seem to care as much about making friends as he did about influencing people.' My father, on the other hand, was 'more ameliorative ... not a member of the founding families but could easily have been considered one ... He was mature and sensible and had a cast of judgement which made him one of the best, if not the best, general managers produced by Barclays in recent history.'

My father's own recollection was that, in the heat of that night's battle and several subsequent ones, he himself was rather less emollient than Gordon's account suggests. He had the impression that Governor Richardson never quite forgave him for showing insufficient respect, and he had a sharp altercation with one of the institutional participants, Viscount de L'Isle and Dudley, the chairman of Phoenix Assurance, who had won the VC with the Grenadier Guards shortly after the Anzio landing in 1944. He also happened to have been, since 1945, a non-executive local director of Barclays in Pall Mall, where his Bevan grandfather had been a partner.[9] After his brush with my father, de L'Isle lodged a formal complaint with Bevan. 'Look here, Deryk, you've been frightfully rude to Cousin Billy,' Bevan said to my father in a prefectorial tone, making him even crosser.

But whatever the animosities created, the City had indeed been saved from a major disaster. Within the same week the Bank of England had marshalled the clearers into the 'Lifeboat' mechanism, which saved from catastrophe a number of other secondary banks. Barclays and the other clearers accepted Richardson's stipulation that they had to man the Lifeboat with no upper limit on their commitment of bail-out loans; when the line was drawn under it in August 1974, they had collectively put up £1.2 billion. The banking crisis was thus absorbed by the City, acting quietly, firmly and, after the early ructions, in harmony, with little or no prompting from the Treasury or Downing Street. As Margaret Reid wrote:

> It is one of the most remarkable events in banking history that the big banks unhesitatingly put up the vast sums required for the Lifeboat, often to protect concerns which had lately been competing wildly with them for business, for the greater good of safeguarding the whole financial system. According to what was sometimes said at the time, it could only have happened in Britain.

---

[9] De L'Isle's mother was the daughter of Roland Yorke Bevan, a younger brother of Francis Augustus. Roland cemented the connection between Barclay, Bevan, Tritton & Co. and Ransom Bouverie of Pall Mall by marrying the daughter of Lord Kinnaird, Ransom Bouverie's grandest partner.

Barclays had played a part in the lending boom, and had its own bad debt problems in the property sector, particularly in the West End of London, besides its exposure to fringe banks. But the problems were localized and swiftly brought under control. The resolution of them brought to the fore a new generation of toughened managers, capable of handling complex loan recovery projects – among them Brian Pearse and the young Andrew Buxton.

The losses associated with the Lifeboat operation were in the end not large – Barclays share was around £10 million – and the bank's central role in the rescue confirmed its status as a market leader. This was particularly so in relation to National Westminster, which suffered a crisis of confidence in November 1974 when rumours spread that it had made heavy losses connected with loans to the Italian financier Michele Sindona and was over-stretched by its commitment to the construction of the NatWest Tower in Bishopsgate. NatWest was unable to raise a rights issue, an *Evening Standard* article implied, and was being heavily supported by the Bank of England. The rumours were denied in an unprecedented public statement by the NatWest chairman, Sir John Prideaux – a man of such supreme bankerly gravitas that my father once remarked he should have been running the country – and were swiftly dispelled.[10] From that point onwards, however, whatever the relative positions in terms of balance sheet totals, Barclays was indisputably the leader and aggressor in the clearing bank field.

Indeed, if you ask old-time Barclays people to name a time when all last seemed to be well with the bank, they will mostly point to the latter part of the 1970s. On the domestic front, the volatility of 1972 to 1975 gave way to a period of relative stability, albeit against the background of low economic growth, strained public finances and constant industrial unrest which characterized James Callaghan's Labour administration.

The Labour ministers of that era were more comfortable for the clearing banks to deal with than their Thatcherite successors turned out to be. There was a distant threat of nationalization, but it was manifested more in party conference motions from the left wing than in concrete policy proposals. In any case, the way in which the banks operated in the domestic market was not so distant in spirit from that of the nationalised industries.[11] Working relationships were established

---

[10] Lloyds also had a damaging crisis in 1974, losing £33 million through fraudulent dealings in its Lugano branch in Switzerland.

[11] In *The National Wealth*, Dominic Hobson observed that despite everything that happened to banks in the 1980s, this spirit was still abroad as recently as 1992, when one person in two

with Denis Healey, the Chancellor of the Exchequer, and Joel Barnett, his chief secretary. Harold Lever, the Labour MP for Manchester Central, millionaire card-player and Chancellor of the Duchy of Lancaster, was skilled at reassuring the City that the rantings of Tony Benn and Michael Foot were not to be taken too seriously. My father felt at ease among these Labour politicians – who were, like him, clever, iconoclastic, provincial grammar school boys by background. He particularly enjoyed bantering with Healey, who called him 'young Deryk' and made jocular remarks about recruiting him to run the state-owned banking giant of the future.

Meanwhile, in the late 1970s Barclays was beginning to deploy its marketing skills to lead a movement bringing banking to 'the unbanked', the 45 per cent of the British adult population – a very much lower proportion than in the United States and most of Europe – which did not yet have a bank account, receiving its weekly wage in cash. Though trade unions, for reasons of their own, were generally opposed to this development, the *Daily Mirror* played an unexpected part in the campaign to persuade working people to open accounts, after one of its own staff was shot dead in a raid on a wages van. A new swathe of small current account customers created pressure on branch resources, demand for quicker progress on electronic banking and cash machines, and a need for a more scientific approach to credit assessment and pricing of services. It also raised the distant spectre of obsolescence for the traditional bank manager. But still the clearing banks operated in a comfortably protected market, in which the building societies were barely recognized as a competitive threat.

If the war in the high street was yet to come, the war within Barclays over the handling of large corporate customers had begun with a skirmish, but one which was easily won by the old guard. Charles Ball (now Sir Charles Ball, Bt) had been recruited in 1976 from Kleinwort Benson to be chairman of Barclays (London & International) Limited, renamed Barclays Merchant Bank (BMB), the domestic bank's first vehicle for medium-term sterling and eurocurrency lending. He had been charged with building BMB into something which would add prestige to the group (the Midland, for example, already owned Samuel Montagu & Co., one of the élite members of the Accepting Houses Committee) but he was a mercurial merchant banker who quickly became uncomfortable with the bureaucratic caution of Barclays.

surveyed thought that the clearing banks were owned by the state. 'It matched their daily experience. Like nationalized industries, banks treated consumers with contempt.'

Within a year, Ball proposed that all medium-term corporate lending should be channelled through BMB, but neither the local directors nor the strong men of Barclays International would have it. Deeply frustrated, Ball resigned and BMB's lending brief was henceforth defined in very restricted terms.

My father, who had been sympathetic to Ball, succeeded him as chairman of BMB, which now found a niche for itself between the power-blocs of the group in the fields of specialized (often tax-based and strictly sterling only) domestic lending, equity-related corporate advice for customers too small or too racy to be clients of the grander merchant banks, and 'development capital', which meant direct equity investment by the bank in growing companies. This beefing up of BMB was led by a new managing director, Lord (Tom) Camoys, whom my father recruited in 1978 from Amex Bank, the London merchant banking subsidiary of American Express.

The 7th Baron Camoys had begun his career with N. M. Rothschild where, as a very young man, he was chosen to be general manager of a joint venture in the euromarkets with National Provincial. That became Rothschild Intercontinental Bank, and was sold in 1977 to American Express with Camoys as its chairman. In the meantime he had inherited from a cantankerous, hard-drinking and several times bankrupt father his ancient barony (first created in 1264) and had bought from his father's trustees the even more ancient family home of Stonor, near Henley. My father observed at the time how pleased the grandees of the Barclays board had been to find him recruiting an Eton-and-Balliol peer of the realm; but even so, at the last stage, Tim Bevan insisted on telephoning Theodore Barclay – one of the powerful 'uncles' of the founding families, but by then long retired to his Suffolk estate – to test out the name of Camoys with him.

The 38-year-old Camoys came with a reference from Leopold de Rothschild, a director of the Bank of England as well as the family firm, who had said 'Don't be fooled by his boyish looks, he's tough,' and indeed he was. A chain smoker, he was combative, self-confident, lordly when the occasion required[12] and very ambitious, sensing the possibility of reinventing the whole of Barclays as a new J. P. Morgan, with himself at its head. He brought with him a group of corporate financiers of his own age – Oliver Stocken and Christopher Haviland from Rothschilds, and his Balliol friend Jonathan Scott from Charter-house Japhet – who began to give BMB the veneer of a real mer-

---

[12] Indeed, he is now Lord Chamberlain, the administrative head of the Royal Household.

chant bank rather than a dumping-ground for Barclays men who were too difficult or clever for the mainstream bank. ('I don't know about these merchant banker types,' my father said after interviewing the fastidious Scott, in his spare time an art expert who hunted with the Beaufort. 'This one's a world authority on Piranesi, for God's sake.')

Camoys tried to persuade Barclays to adopt a more specialized sector-based approach to industrial lending. This accorded with other American models, such as Citibank, which covered large companies through sector-based teams within a worldwide corporate division, and with advice to Barclays from McKinseys a few years earlier. But the local directors – already beginning to sniff the breeze of rationalization wafting in their direction – were not about to cede their largest customers to an upstart unit in London. Nor would Barclays International part with its dollar-based lending to the oil and gas industry, in the North Sea and elsewhere. An experiment with powerless 'group co-ordinators' had achieved very little.

Freddie Seebohm, in his last year as a non-executive director of Barclays, was asked to write a report on these questions, and opted for a compromise which caused least offence: everything stayed more or less where it was except for shipping, aerospace and commodities customers, for whom BMB was allowed to set up specialist lending teams. Group co-ordinators became 'corporate finance directors', overseeing global relationships with selected large companies. Finally, at the end of 1981, they were formed into a Large Corporate Division which drew power away from the bank's other fiefdoms, and in due course became (alongside the bank's Treasury) the biggest battalion in the war with BZW.

In the opposite direction, my father had by now embarked on a campaign to rein in, and in some cases abolish, the local head offices. This was not easily done and was not completed for a decade, often having to wait for the retirement of the senior local director concerned. In the mid-1970s there had been thirty-five LHOs; it was accepted by the end of the decade that the smallest ones were not economically viable, whatever their historic significance. The first three to be closed were Swansea, Truro and York – there were mutterings that my father had taken undue satisfaction in axing the latter – followed later by Brighton and Darlington. By 1989 there were still twenty-three, though they were now renamed 'regional offices'.[13]

---

[13] By the beginning of 1999, there were ten regional offices remaining, but even these were under threat of a further sweeping rationalization. Perhaps surprisingly, three of the ten were still run by family and Special List men – David Barclay (son of Theodore) in London, David

These tides of change produced new tensions in addition to those you might expect to find in any large corporate empire. In Barclays there were tensions between DCO men and Limited men, between local directors and head office, between down-to-earth branch managers and smart-alec merchant bankers, between meritocrats and hereditaries. But in these years, all the tensions were overcome by a much bigger factor: pride in being Barclays.

Internationally, Barclays was greeted in every port of call with the awe and respect that might greet a visiting Royal Navy aircraft carrier. The expansiveness of Tuke and Wathen had reached its apotheosis in the United States, where the group had gone from two offices (New York and San Francisco) in the 1960s to 600, in 36 states, by 1981, with branches in all the major cities and a vast network of outlets of a finance subsidiary called BarclaysAmericanCorporation. *Business Week* magazine carried a cover picture of Tuke, standing in front of the great brass doors of 54 Lombard Street. Walter Wriston, president of Citibank and the most aggressive international banker of the era, acknowledged Barclays as a serious competitor.

In the City of London, there was universal admiration for an organization which produced dynastic chiefs of the calibre of Thomson and Tuke and professionals of the quality of Derek Wilde and my father – as well as strength in depth below that. When Governor Richardson asked in 1977 for Wilde (by then a vice-chairman) to be released from Barclays to become chairman of the Lifeboat-rescued Keyser Ullman, he observed to Tuke that Barclays had the deepest reserves of competent management of any British bank. Barclays people themselves, as several have told me in the course of researching this book, believed quite simply that 'we worked for the best bank in the world'.

My father had been promoted again, at the beginning of 1977, to be vice-chairman responsible for finance, marketing and corporate business development. In that year he also accompanied Tuke to Mexico City for the International Monetary Conference, an annual meeting of top executives of a hundred or more of the world's largest commercial banks. Tuke was chairman of the conference and my father was its 'programme director'. It was a highlight of both their careers and probably the all-time peak of international recognition of Barclays by its peers. From then until the end of Tuke's chairmanship, in April 1981, the bank was at its zenith.

Marris, a Buxton descendant, in the Midlands, and the Hon. Andrew Cairns in Luton. This was an indication not so much of the survival of the old system but of the fact that it sometimes produced very capable managers.

4

TABLE MANNERS

An interlude on Barclays' eating habits, architecture and uncles

Before we contemplate Barclays' decline from its zenith, it would be sensible to pause to eat. Barclays' social structure was defined by its eating rituals as much as by its promotion ladder. During my father's most driven phase, as a young general manager at the end of the 1960s, he once came home with news that he had been reprimanded in the Chairman's Mess, as the senior dining room was called, by an elderly board member – history does not relate which, but it was almost certainly either Theodore Barclay or Emlyn Bevan, the two 'uncles' who dominated the bank from their local directors' parlour on the ground floor of 54 Lombard Street – for scooping Stilton from the middle, rather than slicing it horizontally.

He was also witness to a long-running debate about fish knives, eruptions of which from time to time overrode all discussion of serious business at the lunch table. For the detail and origin of this dispute I am grateful again to Charles Gordon, who provided an elegant account of it in *The Cedar Story*. Fish knives, he wrote, were a Victorian invention designed to deal with a new delicacy of the era, namely whitebait. But 'the staid, anti-new-fangled upper class Quakers from East Anglia' favoured the older fashion of eating fish with two forks, 'So two fish forks it was, at home and at the bank' until well into the 1960s. By then a younger member of the clan, Richard Fenton Barclay – in fact a first cousin of Theodore, though twenty years his junior[1] – was serving duty both as a Lombard Street local director and as manager of the luncheon arrangements: fed up with forks, he plucked up

---

[1] Both being eighth-generation descendants of the Apologist.

courage during the uncles' annual August absence to break the tradition.

So, getting on for a century behind the times, the controversial new
eating irons were introduced. When the two old boys returned from
holiday and saw how the table was set on the first Friday, they exploded.
Young Richard was summoned to the presence at short notice and told
that he had the choice of two postings, Australia or Barbados. He chose
the latter, and probably had a very nice time there. But if, as Charles
Gordon supposed, Richard Barclay had once been 'on his way to the
very top', his career prospects were now ruined. Gordon once
recounted the tale to the property magnate Charles Clore, who
observed, 'They got it wrong. They should have made him chairman.'

But the uncles prevailed, and their unspoken, unbreakable rules of
East Anglian country house etiquette continued to hold sway in the
dining room. The bachelor Bevan had, after all, been a local director
in Lombard Street since 1929, and Theodore Barclay (son of a canon
and husband of a bishop's daughter) had been with him since 1934.
From their parlour, arranged and furnished like a partners' room of
old, they controlled much else in the bank besides its table manners –
while they bickered endlessly about the level of the central heating, sat
in their stockinged feet in mid-morning waiting for the messenger to
clean their shoes, and received queues of stockbrokers and discount
house men seeking to borrow short-term money: business was done
in person, never over the telephone.

It was the uncles who were believed by lesser staff in the 1960s to
have control – as senior representatives of all the original proprietor
families – over more than 50 per cent of the bank's shares. This
estimation must have included shares held by friendly institutions
such as the Sun Alliance insurance company, of which Theodore was
chairman, as well as by multifarious family members. But when it was
eventually explored in detail at the time of the buying in of the DCO
minority, it turned out to be wildly wrong. The families spoke directly
for less than 1 per cent.

Nevertheless, the uncles' grip was unshakeable and they played a
major part in decisions as to who reached the top of the bank, many
such matters being decided during shooting lunches at Theodore's
Higham estate near Bury St Edmunds long before they came to the
board in Lombard Street.[2] In 1962, for example, they had strongly

---

[2] Theodore Barclay liked to assess Special List recruits by inviting them to shoot. This could
be an intimidating experience. One young man arrived at Higham on Friday evening, was
shown to a bedroom where he changed into his dinner jacket, and hurried downstairs

favoured the candidacy for the chair of the congenial Oxfordshire landowner John Thomson over the colder, more intellectual Freddie Seebohm, who was suspected by them of looking down his nose at duller-minded colleagues.

The uncles were also prime parties to the deal, fixed and written down (not in board minutes, since no board can formally bind its successors years ahead, but in a private memorandum) before Thomson's retirement in 1973, which settled the chairmanship for the following fourteen years, saying first that Anthony Tuke would follow Thomson for seven years. Chiefly at the instigation of Emlyn Bevan, it went on to decree that Tuke would be followed for seven years by Tim Bevan. In practice they were to serve eight years and six years respectively, but the succession was cemented in principle in 1968 when Tim, aged only forty-one, succeeded Emlyn as a vice-chairman[3]. The younger Bevan's status as heir–in–line was widely known throughout Barclays from that date onwards.

We shall examine the consequences of that decision shortly, but for the moment let us return politely to the table. Whatever the level of seniority, it was always wise to mind your manners in Barclays – to remember, for example, that the distinctive, decorated plates laid, with special cutlery, at the end of a meal, were strictly for fruit. If the Chairman's Mess ran like the members' table of a St James's club, the assistant general managers' mess, one stratum down – a hallowed sanctum for men promoted from the lower ranks and anxious, as it were, to imitate their betters – observed formalities which were even more rigid, including the saying of grace. Woe betide anyone who invited as a lunch guest a Barclays visitor from abroad who did not rank as the equivalent of assistant general manager in his 'group grade'.

I ate only once in the Chairman's dining room in the old Lombard Street head office building, and when I did so I inadvertently committed a terrible *faux pas*. The occasion was a dinner hosted by the chairman of BZW, Sir Martin Jacomb, to welcome Graham Pimlott and Callum McCarthy, who had been recruited in late 1989 from Kleinwort Benson to run BZW's corporate finance division.

---

thinking he might be late. In fact no one else had come down yet so he selected the most comfortable armchair and sat down to read a copy of the *Field*. After a few moments, Theodore entered the room, ramrod straight, and stared at him. The young man leapt up. 'Good evening, sir, I'm frightfully sorry, is this your chair?' 'They're all my chairs,' came the gruff reply.

[3] These two Bevans were quite remote cousins, being descended from different sons of Silvanus Bevan the Third.

I had just returned from Hong Kong, where I had been managing director of BZW for Asia excluding Japan. I was about to take up the over-titled and ill-defined job of 'Head of International Corporate Finance' – in fact a purely administrative function, as assistant to Pimlott, which had been invented by Oliver Stocken, who had been acting head of corporate finance, both to solve the problem of what to do with me on my return and to suggest to the arriving Pimlott that there was some useful structure to support him. Though the title sounded important, it did not imply that anyone anywhere in the world actually reported to me. Initially some people thought they did, however.

'You're my new boss,' a young French corporate financier greeted me brightly in the corridor of Ebbgate House, BZW's headquarters, on my first working day in the new job.

'Am I really?' I replied, startled. 'Who are you? Who do you think I am?'

The dinner was my first encounter with Pimlott, the man who was to put an end to my career in the bank two years later. 'So you're the one who's coming back to run it all,' he said amiably enough as he shook my hand. I cannot claim to have experienced a chill of foreboding, but I was about to be reminded that Barclays' table manners were a lot more rigid in the modern era than its career structures.

Not realizing that my Nemesis had arrived, I was more interested to see the portraits of former chairmen and Norfolk School landscapes in the dining-room. Appropriate to its East Anglian connection, Barclays has, or had, a collection of the works of John Sell Cotman, John Crome and their followers; my father (one of the few senior Barclays people in recent times to have any interest in art) made some additions to the collection on the bank's behalf. Among the portraits, there was said to be one which had been finished posthumously by means of a discreet visit to the undertaker's parlour, the subject (possibly poor old Tom Fisher) having passed on between sittings.

So I took a glass of champagne and slipped away from the pre-dinner drinks party in the ante-room. An immaculate, tail-coated messenger – a former corporal or sergeant in the Brigade of Guards, at a guess – followed me and, standing very close to my ear, hissed, 'Leave your glass outside, sir.' Puzzled, I indicated that I was happy to hang on to the glass, which was still full, while I looked at the pictures. He remained stiffly at attention nearby, glowering furiously at me, until the rest of the party eventually joined us, Jacomb to the fore. Later I found out that the senior person present was always ushered ceremoniously into the dining-room first, and that pre-prandial glasses were always expected to be left outside.

My introduction to such rituals had come much earlier. As an Oxford undergraduate in 1974, I was invited to lunch at Barclays local head office, the Old Bank in the High. Though again I failed to realize the significance of the occasion for my own destiny, it provided a perfect cameo of the arcane construction of Barclays, and a connection with several of its most notable figures.

The Old Bank is a handsome, stone-built, eighteenth-century commercial building. It began life as the office of Parsons, Thomson & Parsons, a private banking partnership founded in 1771 by William Fletcher and Herbert Parsons, two men's mercers or dealers in cloth – Fletcher being well-known as a specialist in clerical clothing, knee-britches, silk waistcoats and stockings.

In due course Fletcher's line expired and a share in the bank passed to Guy Thomson, a Parsons relation by marriage. In the early nineteenth century both he and Herbert Parsons lived, literally, above the shop. But they prospered considerably, and soon moved up in the world. Both families acquired Oxfordshire estates, the Thomsons moving to Woodperry, south of the city. Guy's son, John became secretary of the South Oxfordshire hunt and a name to conjure with among the county's sportsmen; the Parsons did their hunting with the Old Berkshire.

When the firm was amalgamated into Barclays in 1900, there were three Parsons partners and two Thomsons; the senior Parsons joined Barclays' London board, but the business in Oxford carried on much as before. Twenty years later, when Barclays acquired another local bank – Gillett & Co. of Oxford and Banbury, which specialized in farm lending – the two organizations continued for some years as separate entities, with local head offices barely a hundred yards apart in Cornmarket and the High.[4]

After the Second World War, the Oxford local head office was the personal fiefdom of the chairman-to-be John Thomson, a great-grandson of the first Guy. Throughout his chairmanship and for some years afterwards, Thomson remained an advisory, or non-executive, local director at Oxford. The lunch I attended there was hosted by his

---

[4] The Gillett partners were also keen on their hunting. The most celebrated of them, Archer Tawney, found himself at Oxford one morning with the keys to the Banbury safe in his pocket. This being around 1850, before the Great Western Railway connected the two places, Tawney took horse and galloped the full twenty-two and a half miles, reaching Banbury just as the bank was due to open its doors.

successor but one as senior local director, Roger Goodenough, who was the great Frederick Goodenough's grandson and was also, indirectly, my personal benefactor: the bulk of my school fees – at Glenalmond in Perthshire – had been paid by a Goodenough Bursary, an award under an endowment scheme established by the Goodenough family for the education of Barclays' staff children.

The Goodenoughs were not original Barclays grandees, but by the third generation they certainly behaved as though they were. It was one of the strengths of the old Barclays system that only the more promising sons and cousins of the favoured families were encouraged to join the bank, and even they were on probation before they were appointed local directors. Sir William Goodenough's eldest son, Richard, who inherited the baronetcy, thus managed to avoid a career in Barclays altogether. But his second son, Roger, joined the bank in 1950 after Eton and Cambridge, and became a local director in Birmingham in 1958. With the multiple inheritance of his grandfather, his father, and his DCO uncle, Sir Julian Crossley, weighing heavy on his shoulders, he took charge of the Oxford district in 1969. The university connection was an important one for the bank, and Goodenough evidently felt a duty from time to time to offer the bank's hospitality to undergraduates with appropriate connections. Hence my invitation to lunch, on a warm day in my first summer term.

Thin-lipped, balding, schoolmasterish, Roger Goodenough seemed (as his father must have done) older than his years – he was no more than forty-six at the time. My father warned me I might find him 'uptight'. That he certainly was: the typical undergraduate's unauthorized overdraft, he told me sternly in response to my pale attempt at a joke on the subject, was 'indistinguishable from theft'.

Also present was a younger local director from the Special List, Charlie Morland, who later became a colleague in BZW and a friend. He was the son and grandson of distinguished diplomats but was assumed by people in the bank who made a hobby of such matters to be related both to a line of Morlands who had once been partners in Ransom Bouverie & Co. of Pall Mall and to the founders of the Oxford brewery, Morland & Co., of which Sir John Thomson was also chairman. He was also a nephew of John Keswick, the taipan of Jardine Matheson of Hong Kong, who had joined the Barclays board from Martins. In the interwoven way of Barclays, Morland was also connected to the Buxtons: while his father, Sir Oscar Morland, had been a code-breaker at Bletchley during the war, his mother had shared a house with Elizabeth Buxton, widow of Captain Joseph Fowell Buxton

(Grenadier Guards, killed in action in Tunisia in 1943). Elizabeth was the mother of Andrew Buxton, and the wife-to-be of another Barclays director, Sandy Grant.

The less rarefied and interwoven stream of Barclays life was represented by a man called Chalkley, who was the district manager, Barclays' equivalent of warrant officer rank: he exuded strong disapproval of all students, overdrawn or otherwise. Lunch was a leisurely affair, the table laid with historic silver, including, I think, a pair of those elegant silver pheasants often found in squirearchical diningrooms. Though this was a time of economic crisis, frequent industrial strife at the nearby Cowley car factory, rising inflation and impending property crash, I do not recall much discussion of the great issues of the day. Goodenough, whose family farmed near Lechlade in Gloucestershire, held forth about the state of the crops. On other occasions, I was told, he liked to talk about drains.

He and one of my fellow guests, an undergraduate from my college with far more social polish than I had, then discussed in all seriousness whether it was better to have a hand-bell on the dining table to summon the servant, or a more discreet foot-operated electrical one beneath. This exchange embedded itself in my memory to such an extent that for many years now I have kept an ornate Korean bell in my diningroom, in case I ever find I have acquired a butler.

After cheese and fruit, we were offered not only port – the decanter circulating, correctly, to the left – but Madeira and fruitcake, a nineteenth-century habit which I have only ever encountered at one other table. Needless to say, it was at another Barclays lunch, a decade later and in the incongruous setting of the International division's 1960smodern Fenchurch Street tower. It would be accurate to describe the guests on that later occasion, visiting American bankers, as stupefied by the elaborate fare on offer.

More regular luncheon guests of Barclays throughout the era we have revisited so far might have achieved the same state of stupor, but they might not have been so surprised. While my father was chairman of Barclays Merchant Bank in the late 1970s, he observed that the cost of in-house lunches at its offices in Dashwood House, Old Broad Street, was extraordinarily high even by Barclays standards – approaching £50 per head. An enquiry followed, in which some of the catering staff were discovered to be cooking the books as well as the lunches: resignations followed. At the same time, an attempt was made to curb the excesses of the meals themselves, resulting in a ban on chocolate mints with coffee which endured for several years, and for which my father was often mentioned by disgruntled lunchers as being to blame.

Happily, one of those acquitted in the enquiry was the chief steward of the dining-rooms, a cheerful South Londoner called Derek Hankin. He had an artificial hand and was known to my father as 'the one-armed bandit', but he was much loved by everyone else. It was suggested in some quarters, unfairly, that his acquittal may have had something to do with the fact that he knew the drinking habits and other misdemeanours of the directors of the firm, especially those who occasionally made use of bedrooms provided for overnight accommodation – BMB men being generally more raffish than run-of-the-mill Barclays managers. In later days at BMB in Gracechurch Street, when I worked in an office adjacent to the dining-rooms, Derek seemed always to be engaged in some mischief or other, placing bets, collecting pools coupons, running all-afternoon drinking sessions and offering bargains to his friends. When I had a farewell party in my flat in Chelsea in 1984 before leaving for the Far East, I enquired about the possibility of buying some wine. Moments later, he rang me confidentially at my desk, though I was only feet from where he was sitting.

'The claret's two pound a bottle, Martin,' he whispered. 'And the whisky and gin's a fiver. He's overloaded his van, know what I mean?'

Having received a none-too-convincing assurance that this did not mean either of us was defrauding the bank, I placed a modest order. Derek came to the party with a car-load of booze and waitresses. He and my father greeted each other warmly, though the latter threatened to institute another court of enquiry into the whole affair.

We digress, perhaps, but only in the interest of building up a collage of pre-1990s Barclays life through its eating and drinking habits. The Oxford lunch lasted well past three o'clock, and afterwards I slept for an hour in the PPE Reading Room of the Bodleian Library. The Oxford local head office lasted – despite several proposals, mostly from my father, to close it down to cut costs – until 1987, when Roger Goodenough retired from executive duties. He had been elevated to the main board of the bank by Anthony Tuke in 1979, and in former times he might have expected to keep his seat until he was at least sixty-five. But John Quinton prevailed on him as part of an exercise to reduce the board to a workable size, to step down in 1989, aged sixty-two. He continued briefly to hold the title of advisory director for the Thames Valley region, which by then had its head-quarters in unhistoric Reading.

Derek the one-armed bandit had also long retired by the time I returned from the Far East, and his breed of part-of-the-family City messengers and butlers, many of them ex-servicemen, partially disabled or otherwise disadvantaged, had been rendered extinct by the arrival of cost-reducing contracted-out catering and security services. In their place were pasty young men in ill-fitting Group 4 uniforms, and brisk manageresses from Forte or Granada.

The head office building at 54 Lombard Street which contained the scene of my disgrace in the Chairman's dining-room was demolished very shortly afterwards. It dated in concept from around 1932, when Barclays completed the long-drawn out process of buying all the commercial properties adjacent to the old office of Barclay, Bevan, Tritton & Company, which dated from 1864. But it was held up by the acquisition of the redundant church of All Hallows, Lombard Street in the middle of the site,[5] which took until 1938, and then by the war and the priorities of post-war reconstruction.

In the end, building work did not begin until 1956 and did not finish until the early 1970s, but what emerged was very much a pre-war building, imperious but much less flamboyant than, for example, Edwin Lutyens's headquarters for the Midland Bank at Poultry, the 'palace of finance' commissioned by the Midland chairman (and former Chancellor of the Exchequer), Reginald McKenna, in 1929. There was a certain plainness to the exterior of the Barclays building which the Quaker founders would have approved of, and a certain country house style to its sixth floor where the chairman and his immediate colleagues lived which would have made the Quakers' Edwardian descendants feel at home. *Country Life* and the *Field* were to be found on the reception table, and space was abundant in the public area and senior offices; indeed, the floor area of the Great Hall and all the lobbies and corridors somewhat exceeded the square footage of office space. My father's room had an antique fireplace and wing chairs, and a vast curved desk which had been specially acquired for a rather exotic bachelor vice-chairman of the 1960s, Sir Thomas Bland[6] – who insisted on having refrigerated carnations provided for his daily buttonhole, even when travelling abroad, and kept his gloves on a long string threaded through the sleeves of his overcoat.

But the old building, like the old management structure, was con-

---

[5] The tower of All Hallows, and some of its Grinling Gibbons carvings, were reused for a new church of All Hallows in Twickenham.

[6] Whose mother was a Barclay, and whose Bland great-great-grandfather was an early partner in the Gurney bank in Norwich.

sidered an embarrassment in the modern age: inflexible, unwired, extravagant and all wrong in its priorities. When it was rebuilt in the early 1990s the vast boardroom with its ornate furnishings was replaced by a high-tech chamber with a spectacularly expensive computer-controlled lighting system. All the catering facilities were relocated for efficiency reasons in the basement. In keeping with the exterior of the new building – an exercise in bland modernism, decorated with gold metalwork symbols of vaguely Islamic design, which would not have looked out of place in Dubai – the general impression was of the banqueting floor of a plush international hotel, perhaps a Meridien or a Regent. ('The great advantage of this design', the project manager is supposed to have told a board committee when competing architects' schemes were presented to them, 'is that there's no chance it'll ever become a listed building.')

But one panelled room from the old building – indeed, a survival from the 1864 building, where it had been first the boardroom and later the partners' luncheon room – was preserved and reconstructed, complete with its furniture, as the Chairman's private dining-room. Whatever the symbolism of this, it seems to corroborate Professor C. Northcote Parkinson's observation about corporate headquarters: 'A perfection of planned layout is achieved only by institutions on the point of collapse.'

5

THE MOOD OF THE EIGHTIES

1980–1986: The impact of Thatcherism – The accession of
Timothy Bevan – The challenge of being Number One –
Problems in New York, Hong Kong and Milan – The departure
of Deryk Vander Weyer – Falling morale – NatWest takes the
lead – How John Quinton was chosen

There were many forces, internal and external, that contributed to the turn of the tide for Barclays over the next decade. One of them was Thatcherism. We have seen that Barclays made great leaps forward under the Labour Government of the 1960s, and consolidated its advance during the Labour years of the 1970s. The arrival of the Conservative government in May 1979 seemed at the time to be a further blessing on the bank's good fortune.

Almost immediately, new freedoms were made available. Among the first reforms of the new regime, under the Chancellorship of Geoffrey Howe, were the abolition of exchange control in October 1979 followed in 1980 by the removal of the 'corset' (or Supplementary Special Deposits) scheme, which had been introduced to restrict the clearing banks' ability to lend above prescribed levels.

Too much freedom, however, was to be part of Barclays' undoing. And relations with the new government proved to be far from friendly. 'Margaret had no love for the banks,' Nigel Lawson wrote in *The View from No. 11*. It was a dislike provoked partly – so it was believed both inside and outside Barclays at the time – by the fact that the clearing banks had declined all invitations to make financial contributions to Conservative election campaign coffers. It may also have had to do with the fact that bankers as a species, and especially the upper-class bankers so prevalent in Barclays, were natural Tory 'wets', the patrician adherents of compromise and opponents of change whom Thatcher would gradually weed out of her cabinet and inner circle.

Two of the most prominent wets, Francis Pym, her first defence minister, and Jim Prior, her first employment minister, were East Anglian landowners who in another life would have made perfect local directors of Barclays in Norwich or Cambridge, for example.[1] They and their ilk belonged to the world of unentrepreneurial 'gentlemanly capitalism' which was accustomed to being attacked from the Left[2] but was now about to be savaged by the radical Right as well.

Deeply dyed in that tradition, the Barclays' board – though no doubt Conservative voters to a man – was anxious to keep the bank away from confrontational politics. This was partly – and sensibly – because the bank wanted the business of Labour and Conservative voters alike, but also because of a sense of being an institution which was part of the fabric of national life and above the vulgar fray of politics, as well as commerce.

Unlike the Midland, which over the years had picked two former cabinet ministers, Reginald McKenna and Viscount Monckton of Brenchley, and one former Viceroy, the 2nd Marquess of Linlithgow,[3] as its chairmen, there was no established tradition of bringing politicians on to the Barclays board. The only time an 'outsider' was considered for the chair was in 1947 when (with a view to matching the Midland in grandeur) Marshal of the RAF Viscount Portal of Hungerford, KG GCB OM DSO MC was briefly a runner; but plain Mr A. W. Tuke was preferred instead. It was Tuke, indeed, who first publicly distanced the bank from the Conservatives, by criticizing the Macmillan government's economic policies in his chairman's reports.[4]

The Conservatives in their turn had often been resentful of the banks. Booming profits reported by the clearing banks for 1973, during a bitter winter of coal strikes and power cuts, were held by some Tories, including Enoch Powell, to be a contributory factor in the Labour general election victories of 1974. There were in fact at that time only two identifiable connections between Barclays and the modern Conservative party. The first was Lord Carrington, whose wisdom,

---

[1] In due course Prior (who also became chairman of GEC) proved this point by becoming a non-executive director of Barclays, from 1984 to 1989.
[2] It is still under attack from the likes of Will Hutton of the *Observer*, who wrote in *The State We're In* about 'the network of City institutions, public schools, regiments, landed estates and boardrooms' which in his view was to blame for all modern Britain's economic weaknesses.
[3] Who 'seldom gets down off his elephant,' Sir William Goodenough once observed.
[4] Thereby earning himself the nickname 'The Iron Tuke' from the journalist Harold Wincott, editor of the *Investors Chronicle*.

charm and shrewdness overcame any reservations Margaret Thatcher may have had about his 'wetness', and kept him constantly in demand for top jobs in the City and elsewhere for almost forty years.

Despite protesting that he knew nothing about banking, Carrington (who had been High Commissioner to Australia in the 1950s) had become chairman in the mid-1960s of the Australia & New Zealand Bank, in which Barclays had a shareholding. This led to an invitation to join the Barclays board in 1967. He rejoined twice at later dates between ministerial appointments, and seems to have acted as a discreet political adviser to the bank throughout this period. Carrington found Barclays a 'splendid and civilized institution', though he approached its boardroom with some diffidence, he wrote, having been warned to expect 'High Mass without the incense'. But that did not mean he had to take it too seriously. For a time, my father sat next to him in the boardroom, and was impressed by Carrington's sharp grasp of issues and common-sense contributions to debate – yet mystified by the peer's Etonian mannerism of making jokes about the most serious problems. I once asked Carrington for his recollection of the same meetings and – perfectly illustrating the point – he said, 'Oh yes, I remember Vander Weyer, he was great fun, we used to laugh a lot.'

The other Tory connection was one to be less proud of as time went on: Edward du Cann MP. This former junior minister in the Macmillan government and chairman of the party under Home and Heath had made a fortune in unit trusts – together with Peter Walker, he launched Unicorn Securities, one of the fastest growing ventures in the early days of the unit trust industry, backed by the London & Edinburgh Insurance Co. In 1965 Martins Bank bought London & Edinburgh, and in 1968 Barclays bought Martins: du Cann thus became chairman of Barclays Unicorn, as it was then called, and was also a non-executive local director for the London area. The diarist and newspaper tycoon Cecil King had dinner with him in May 1971 and noted that du Cann was 'tipped as the future chairman' of Barclays. It seems probable that the only source of this tip was du Cann himself, since the succession from Thomson to Tuke had by then almost certainly been decided, and the candidacy of a non-family outsider – even one so sleek and successful as du Cann then seemed to be – is unlikely to have been viewed as a serious alternative.

Du Cann was, however, chairman of another bank, Keyser Ullman, a City firm of nineteenth-century origins which expanded dramatically in the early 1970s under his leadership, absorbing Central & District

Properties, of which he was also chairman, and lending heavily to property developers such as William Stern (later bankrupted for £104 million) and Christopher Selmes. KU's financing of Selmes's take-over of Grendon Trust brought the bank into difficulties when the property market collapsed. KU was one of the Lifeboat's most prominent borrowers and attracted accusations of incompetence from government inspectors. Du Cann himself had large personal debts, and there were those in the bank who wanted to take a firm hand with him. His political prominence made this difficult, but he and his business connections were treated very cautiously at Barclays for ever afterwards.

So Carrington was the only positive connection, and when Margaret Thatcher went to dinner at Barclays in February 1982, she would have been right to assume that she was not among a group of her most ardent supporters. That was certainly how she approached the encounter. She brushed aside small talk ('The "Wets" found the wayward behaviour of £M3 a suitable subject for mockery at dinner parties,' she wrote in *The Downing Street Years*, and it was perhaps some gambit along those lines that fired her off) and harangued the assembled company in the style to which the nation had by then become accustomed. The Barclays men present found her view of their business – and the need for it to play a more dynamic role in the economy – unfounded in any significant understanding of banking priorities. My father, nevertheless, found the experience 'sexy' – I recall that he admired her figure, but not whether, like Alan Clark in his *Diaries*, he was captivated by her ankles.

She was not captivated by the banks, however. 'It wasn't any hostility to the banks as such,' Nigel Lawson told me. 'But there was no doubt that they were a cartel and were extremely bureaucratic. They had been encouraged to be unentrepreneurial – it suited the Bank of England that way, and reflected the sort of economic policies that used to be pursued, where the banks were told who to lend to and who not, that they must lend to exporters but not to importers and so on. They had become accustomed to a quiet life in which everything was directed by government and therefore they were not a very dynamic part of the economy.'

What was worse, in the sharp recession of 1981, the banks had made handsome profits while the rest of industry and business was suffering. This was largely a function of the 'endowment' profit on non-interest bearing current accounts – the higher the prevailing interest rates, the higher the profit – and the government clearly thought the banks should be forced into some compensatory contribution to the national economic struggle. So Lawson, as Financial Secretary, was delegated to make the point by asking the banks to take over the financing of a portion of the Export Credit Guarantee Department (ECGD) fixed-rate loan scheme – creating a useful apparent reduction in public borrowing.

The proposal was put to Jeremy Morse, the chairman of Lloyds who was also chairman of the Committee of London Clearing Bankers, with a hint from Lawson that the alternative would be some form of special tax on bank profits. Morse, however, insisted that the banks were unwilling to take on the export financing. They were already beginning to count the cost of their own Latin American exposures, which in some cases had arisen through pressure from the previous Labour government to provide financing in support of export contracts for companies such as GEC. If the ECGD portfolio looked anything like their own loan books, it was probably in poor shape. A tax might be the lesser evil.[5]

Accordingly, a once-only 2.5 per cent levy, known as the 'windfall tax', was imposed on the value of non-interest-bearing current accounts in the budget of March 1981, taking £400 million from the banks. The bill for Barclays was more than £80 million. Resentment in banking circles, Lawson wrote, was compounded by the fact that Morse had omitted to explain to his fellow chairmen that the tax threat was a direct alternative to the export financing proposition. Although the windfall tax was never repeated, the episode was a warning of less comfortable times to come.

But still Barclays was on the crest of a wave when, in the following month, Timothy Bevan took over from Sir Anthony Tuke as group chairman. This succession had been decided many years earlier: Bevan had been the sole deputy chairman of the group since Tuke's accession in 1973. There had been a possibility that Tuke might stay on a year or two longer, but that fell away when he was invited to take over the chair of RTZ, the mining group. So the timing of Bevan's succession and the consequential changes that went with it were reconfirmed on 30 April 1980 by the Senior Directors Committee – an inner group which had no status under company law but seemed to have inherited the powers formerly wielded by the uncles – and accepted by the full board on 1 May. Various rearrangements took place in October 1980

---

[5] During the same period there was also pressure from the Government to commit to lending to the Channel Tunnel project. On this most banks including Barclays did give way, though in Barclays it was said to be impossible to find any executive who admitted to having supported the proposal.

to smooth the way for the hand-over, my father becoming a deputy chairman and succeeding Bevan as chairman of Barclays Bank UK Limited.

It is very likely that the senior directors did not even discuss the possibility of overturning the preordainment of Bevan in favour of my father or anyone else – Henry Lambert, chairman of the international side, would have been the only other internal candidate. Despite the pepperiness of temper described by Charles Gordon in *The Cedar Story*, Bevan was well liked around the City, and neither press nor shareholders nor investment analysts (who barely existed in the 1970s) had ever questioned his status as heir apparent. He was a central member of the team which had driven Barclays to the top of the world league. And ever since the end of Frederick Goodenough's reign, Barclays had emphasized teamwork at the top, rather than autocracy: 'I'm against big white chiefs,' Bevan told the *Financial Times*. 'Little trees don't grow under a giant beech tree.'

Perhaps the Senior Directors would have felt, if they had talked about him, that my father wanted too much to be a giant beech tree: he certainly never concealed the fierceness of his personal ambition. They would have had to credit him with the benefits that had accrued to Barclays from a decade of dynamic marketing and planning, and to note that he had been saluted professionally by being elected president of the Institute of Bankers. But such speculation is pointless and anachronistic: everyone in the City at that time knew that a non-family man could not hope to be chairman of Barclays if there was a family man available, so that was that.

But within Barclays, there was a rumbling body of opinion that felt otherwise. 'Your father was the personification of everything that was good and professional in Barclays,' I was told by Chris Ball, who ran the bank in South Africa. 'He was the only guy at the top who really saw Barclays as a business,' said one non-executive director. 'They just didn't have the balls to make him chairman,' said Sir Brian Pearse, 'and the whole bank resented it.' When the decision was confirmed at the May 1980 board meeting, my father went round to Tom Camoys' office in Barclays Merchant Bank and drank most of a bottle of whisky with him.

The *Financial Times*, in a feature article headed 'The challenge of being No. 1' marking Bevan's accession, noted that 'Barclays is still very much a family institution,' and quoted Anthony Tuke's assertion that if the family tradition was to be criticized, 'you have got to be able to say that Barclays has lost out'.[6] 'If that is the test,' wrote Michael Lafferty, the FT's banking correspondent, quite fairly, 'then the families' succession certainly seems to have brought great benefits to the bank.' Not only was it the leader of the British clearing banks, but only the top three US banks – Citicorp, Chase Manhattan and Bank of America – were equal or ahead in terms of global reach and size. In terms of return on assets and return on equity, it was also well ahead of the likes of Deutsche Bank, Société Générale of France and Dai-Ichi Kangyo of Japan.

But the article also noted that Barclays' profit strength was derived overwhelmingly from the protected and uncompetitive nature of the British high street banking market. Barclays' net interest margin (the difference between interest charged on loans and interest paid on deposits) was around 8 per cent, more than double that of Deutsche Bank. 'They had to expand internationally to use up some of the profits,' was the comment of 'a typical German banker' on this discrepancy. There were also hints from various Barclays people of the tensions which were to become more apparent as the Bevan chairmanship advanced. Not enough progress had been made in the development of automated banking for the retail market. Clarity had yet to be achieved on the questions of whether corporate business should be separated from personal, or whether the bank should be managed along product lines rather than by geographical territories. With British industry flattened by recession, growth was only available in the domestic corporate market, in which Barclays was already very strongly represented, by the dangerous tactic of buying market share – either by cutting margins or taking on higher-risk lendings.

'We have got to get our act together better than we have got it now,' Bevan admitted, with ungrammatical bluntness. Despite that admission, Barclays was still the leader of the pack: in Bevan's words, in another interview with the *Financial Times* in 1984, Barclays liked to think of itself as a bit more 'sporting' than its competitors. When interest rates moved, it was invariably Barclays which announced its Base Rate change first – sometimes in advance of signals from the Bank of England and on one occasion in 1983 incurring the wrath of Margaret Thatcher

---

[6] Tuke's public defence of his inherited position was, characteristically, more robust than Bevan's. Asked about it by the *Sunday Telegraph Magazine* in 1983, the latter said, 'I don't think that what one's great-grandfather did is relevant; it has little effect on one's career. Do you know what your great-grandfather did? It is a common misconception that we are a banking family.' This despite the fact that there had been a Bevan *in situ* in the Lombard Street banking parlour without a break since 1767.

for doing so while she herself was out of range on a visit to the Falkland Islands.[7] In 1983, Barclays was the first clearing bank to reintroduce Saturday morning branch opening, claiming to have won 5,000 new accounts in the first few weeks as a result. This latter move was pioneered by John Quinton as senior general manager, to whom the Prime Minister is supposed to have said on one occasion, 'Call yourselves competitive? You're not even open on Saturdays.' 'We will be next Saturday,' he was able to reply.

There were indications of change in the high street pecking order, however. Building societies, having shaken off their own pre-1980s lethargy and preference for cartels, were now competing hard for personal deposit accounts, taking their market share from 46 per cent to 57 per cent between 1980 and 1982. The clearing banks, in turn, had entered the home mortgage business, one of the few genuine growth markets available to them and one which they saw as both low-risk and easy to handle within their existing operating systems. The government was beginning to ponder legislation (finally enacted in 1985 and 1986) to allow free competition between the two groups, in which building societies would issue cheque-book accounts and credit cards, while banks would have to deduct tax at source on deposit interest as the societies did.

There was pressure to offer current accounts free of charges, to devise attractive deposit-account-cum-cheque-book deals – of which Barclays' 'Prime' account was an early market leader. Finally, in a concession which was anathema to traditional clearing bankers, interest was offered, albeit at very low rates, on current accounts – here, for the first time, it was Lloyds, not Barclays, which made the first move.[8]

Overseas, the picture was even more mixed. Barclays had some problem loans to Poland and Romania but was not saddled with the levels of Third World (particularly Latin American) sovereign debt which were about to frighten Lloyds out of the international banking

---

[7] Barclays' relations with the prime minister reached their nadir in 1984, when the Strand branch released to the *Sunday Times* some confidential details of the account of Monteagle Marketing Ltd, a company in which Thatcher's husband Denis and son Mark were involved. Though the *Sunday Times* was criticised for the methods used to obtain the information, Bevan felt obliged to present himself personally in Downing Street to apologize to Denis. It was perhaps fortunate that he had already collected, in the previous New Year Honours list, the knighthood which in those days seemed to come automatically to clearing bank chairmen.

[8] Coincidentally, Barclays' first internal report on the pros and cons of paying interest on current accounts was written in 1981 by Peter Ellwood, who many years later became chief executive of Lloyds TSB.

arena. Nor had there been any disastrous large-scale acquisition to compare with Midland's 1980 purchase of Crocker National Bank in California. But several outposts of Barclays' great 1970s expansion had gone to the bad. In the United States (by now accounting for 15 per cent of Barclays group assets) lending to second-line oil and gas ventures, much of it through the Houston branch, led to bad debt provisions of $122 million in 1982. 'Barclays sent out instructions from London to hire basketfuls of loan officers and to lend, lend, lend,' one rival told *Euromoney* magazine. 'What happened is that they tended to pick up all the business the local banks didn't want.' There were loan problems in New York and California, and a string of underperforming branches in New York State bought from Bankers Trust.

In Hong Kong, it was an even more colourful story. Barclays was a very late arrival in a market dominated by the Hong Kong & Shanghai Bank and Standard Chartered as well as a plethora of local Chinese institutions. But visiting Barclays grandees found that unacceptable: Colin Stevens, who moved there as manager in 1980, remembered Roger Goodenough expostulating at the idea of being given Standard Chartered banknotes at the airport bureau de change: 'Why don't we have our own notes?' he demanded.

When Tim Bevan was in the colony during a world tour before he took up the chairmanship, he visited the Governor, Sir Murray (later Lord) MacLehose, and absorbed an upbeat presentation of Hong Kong's economic future. 'We must have more branches,' he declared after the meeting, and Barclays duly expanded, in double-quick time, from one to fourteen outlets. Local Chinese managers were hired who spoke good English but were for some reason not making careers in the better-established Hong Kong banks. A substantial majority of them, and many of the customers they brought with them, turned out to be fraudsters, at least one being apprehended at the airport with a suitcase full of cash.

Meanwhile Trident, a tripartite merchant banking joint venture (one of Julian Wathen's many bold initiatives in the mid-1970s) with Merrill Lynch of the US and Nomura of Japan, had also gone wrong. The co-operation had not worked well, and Barclays had bought out the other shareholders. Renamed Barclays Asia, the unit proceeded to lend heavily into Hong Kong's booming commercial property sector, including the hottest operator of all, Carrian, which was brought down by scandal and plummeting property values in 1983. Barclays' losses in Hong Kong amounted to £66 million, and one Barclays expatriate loan officer implicated in the Carrian scandal spent the next few years in Stanley Jail.

There were similar troubles brewing in Italy, where the manager in charge, Ken Bromley, one of the brightest of the ex-Martins men, had expanded the business rapidly on all fronts. By 1985 Barclays was the worst performing foreign bank in the country, with losses of $23 million. An involvement with a machine-tool leasing company which became the subject of a fraud investigation cost $25 million.

On the other hand, there were successes to be highlighted – a dazzling expansion in Spain, for example, after the take-over of the ailing 38-branch Banco de Valladolid. And the group's profits continued to be remarkably strong, reaching £485 million before tax for 1983, £605 million for 1984 and £840 million for 1985. Until the beginning of 1986, Barclays had topped the clearing bank profits league continuously since true profits were first revealed in 1969.

Tim Bevan meanwhile, managed Barclays 'by interference', as one colleague put it: he involved himself in detailed decisions below the usual level of matters dealt with by the chair – especially personnel decisions which affected members of the families. He also swore a lot, blew his top a lot, and made lots of Etonian jokes. 'He was frightened of his own shadow,' said a senior figure, 'and bloody difficult to work for.' 'He was a very attractive character in some ways, capable of great warmth and sympathy and with a searching mind,' was a more even-handed comment, 'but he lacked self-confidence.'

He sometimes made bold decisions – more branches in Hong Kong, a new showpiece US headquarters building at 75 Wall Street.[9] But more often he leaned on the side of caution. As US and other foreign firms began to bid up City salaries from 1984 onwards, he took a quixotic stand against the trend, making a point of accepting very modest rises in his own salary – which was £133,000 in 1984. 'He thought it created a good impression, but it created a concertina effect for the salary of managers below him,' said one insider to Euromoney, adding, perhaps unfairly. 'And many of us didn't have his private income.' Until the opportunity of Big Bang and BZW came along, he did not communicate any great vision of where the bank was going.

---

[9] Though Bevan cannot be entirely blamed for the outcome, the Wall Street building developed into one of the bank's most expensive follies. It was finished to an extremely luxurious specification - the executive washroom had gilded taps with digital temperature read-outs – but was too small to house all parts of the Barclays group as originally intended. Several BZW departments found excuses not to move in. As it was approaching completion, its basement floors mysteriously filled up with water.

The one thing he did communicate, more by action than by words, was that as executive chairman he and no one else was the bank's chief executive.

And he was never challenged by his board. It met in great solemnity around a vast oval table, hollow in the centre and built to seat more than thirty directors plus the chairman, who was placed on a raised dais at the apex – while the company secretary sat at a kind of schoolboy's desk in a corner behind him. With every seat taken, as they were during the Bevan era, the board was too big by far to be an effective discussion forum. It was extremely formal – no one was addressed by his Christian name – and disproportionately filled with Barclays' traditional backwoods local directors and retired executives, who enjoyed their periodic trips up to town but had little to contribute to the proceedings. The board met at noon and finished in time for lunch at one, and was not given the papers beforehand, even when it had the annual results to deliberate upon – until non-executives objected that it was impossible to assimilate the information in ten minutes before the meeting began. One observer called it 'unbelievably Dickensian, and distinctly divided into aristocrats and peasants. Nobody ever challenged the aristocrats.'

My father became increasingly frustrated by Bevan's management style, and disillusioned by the relative powerlessness of his own position. Soon after the management changes of 1981 were announced, there had been discreet enquiries from the Bank of England as to whether he might become available for other jobs. In the summer of 1983, he was approached to become deputy chairman of British Telecom, which was in the early stage of preparation for privatization. The first contact came through Jeffrey (now Lord) Sterling,[10] the chairman of P & O, who was an *éminence grise* of the Thatcher government as industrial adviser to successive secretaries of state for Trade and Industry – the incumbent cabinet minister being, very briefly, Cecil Parkinson before his political demise at the hands of his mistress, Sarah Keays, in October of that year.

The job offered to my father was a challenging one, to oversee the financial side of BT and act as its senior point of contact with the City through the privatization process. He decided to take it, and the formalities for his release from Barclays were swiftly completed. When

---

[10] Sterling made his name in the City, and as a valued Barclays customer, through his skilful management of Town & City Properties, a victim of the 1974 crash which he merged with his own group, Sterling Guarantee, nursed back to financial health and eventually took into P & O.

he departed on 30 September, there was a rather strained farewell party in the Library, a handsome room on the seventh floor in Lombard Street. Bevan made a short tribute speech which did not seem to satisfy some of my father's close colleagues: one of them, Geoff Miller (who had worked for him almost continuously since they were in Liverpool together in the mid-1950s) threatened to make a speech of his own.

'Deryk Vander Weyer's departure was a blow to all those outside the family groups,' one insider, perhaps a guest at that party, later told *Euromoney*. 'It seems that the worst thing you can be at Barclays is extremely good.' My father was more philosophical, and his farewell speech was gracious. Nor was he bitter in private: in all but the last two of his forty-two years there, Barclays had given him wonderful opportunities, and he was to remain on the board for another five years. In any case, he remarked as we left Lombard Street, 'As one door closes, another opens.' The family, our family that is, retreated to the Ritz for an opulent dinner.

If this were our history rather than Barclays', that would have made a chapter ending. But the bank simply carried on, with Henry Lambert replacing my father as chairman of the UK side and Frank Dolling – a strange, charismatic, weather-beaten man who had once walked 700 miles across Poland as an escaping prisoner of war, and had made almost the whole of his Barclays career in Africa – replacing Lambert as international chairman. (At that time, and for another ten years, it never occurred to the Barclays' board that the bank might be unable to fill all senior vacancies, at however short notice, with internal appointees whose qualifications for the jobs concerned were unquestioned; after that, it was rarely able to appoint an internal candidate to any senior post.)

Several great changes were afoot in the three years after my father's departure. BZW, which was to be the one truly bold strategic development of Bevan's chairmanship, had already been dreamed up in the summer of 1983 – by Tom Camoys while reading the *Financial Times* in a bar in Ibiza. And Barclays' South African operation, one of the foundation stones of DCO, was to be abandoned in 1986. Thirdly, the 'One Bank' project, masterminded by Peter Leslie and Frank Dolling, was at last achieving the complete integration of the domestic and international banks, though not without a great deal of guerrilla resistance on both sides.[11]

---

[11] This integration took three years, and required an Act of Parliament to complete. When it was announced in 1982, Barclays International still had 7000 staff in the UK, in 30 branches.

The fourth great change was harder to observe, but perhaps the most profound in the context of the whole of this story. Like an aircraft-carrier imperceptibly slowing and changing course, Barclays was giving away its lead in the domestic market, in the short term to the more aggressive NatWest, and for the longer term to the better-managed Lloyds.

And connected with that shift, morale was continuing to drop. In 1985, Malcolm Williamson, the bank's regional general manager for London, left to run the Post Office's Girobank subsidiary. Williamson (who was two months older than Andrew Buxton) resigned – so his colleagues suggested – partly in frustration at Tim Bevan's continuing tendency to protect the families' interests, and partly because he had been told that his own career had already peaked. He went on to become chief executive first of Standard Chartered and then of Visa International, the credit card giant. A Lancastrian noted for his sharp dress sense and his love of running marathons, Williamson was often quoted as an example of how Barclays' class structure interfered with promising careers: as the boss for London, he had to cope with the anomaly that part of his region, the Lombard Street district, was run by Alan Tritton, one of the bank's senior family grandees. Williamson was followed through the door by Leslie Priestley, also a regional general manager, who went on to run the Trustee Savings Bank.

Finally, in the first half of 1986, NatWest took the lead in profitability. The pre-tax six-month profit figures were £482 million to NatWest, but only £434 million to Barclays, some 10 per cent below analysts' expectations. NatWest, Midland and Lloyds, all lending aggressively into the growing consumer and property boom, had averaged 31 per cent increases in profit over their results for the first half of 1985, while Barclays had scored only an 8 per cent improvement. Underlying the figures was the fact that Barclays had increased its sterling lending by only 2 per cent over the past year, with no growth at all in the six months in question. It was a direct reflection down the line of Bevan's extreme cautiousness. 'If you try to stick with the quality end of the market you will see your market share go down,' he declared, whilst admitting that 'we could have marginally overdone it'.

With hindsight it can be said that a continuation of Bevan's cautiousness might have preserved Barclays from the worst of its lending problems over the next five years, but that was not how it was seen at the time. The shock of these results, released on 7 August 1986, reverberated throughout the bank. After the 'deconsolidation' of the South African arm (in which the holding had been reduced to 40 per cent) Barclays was now, quite simply, a smaller bank than NatWest, said a 'Dear Colleague' circular from Peter Leslie, adding 'It will take all our efforts to ensure that we restore Barclays to its traditional lead position, and we are taking appropriate action to achieve this objective.' That battle for supremacy would in the end do immense damage to both protagonists.

A more confidential internal analysis written in the same month provided clues to what had really gone wrong. Barclays' 'B & D' (bad and doubtful debts) compared unfavourably with the other clearers partly because of poor quality business picked up during the 'dash for growth' in the 1970s. The standard of professionalism of Barclays managers had also fallen below that of NatWest, which had introduced a powerful new training programme in the late 1970s while Barclays – still proud of the training system first developed by Cuthbert Fitzherbert – had merely maintained what had gone before. Both these points suggested that, even at the zenith of Anthony Tuke's and my father's era in the late 1970s, when everyone thought the bank was in marvellous shape, the sins of complacency and over-confidence had crept in.

Since that time, market share had fallen because of a conscious reversal, over three or four years, of the previous drive for growth, combined with a reluctance to chase ever-decreasing margins and commissions in the large corporate sector. In the home mortgage market, Barclays had lost ground because branch managers, having at one stage been tightly restricted but then told by circular that the bank was keen to get back into the business in a big way, had apparently failed to read the circular.

It was at this turning-point in the mood of the bank that attention turned once again to questions of succession. Bevan's sixtieth birthday was on 24 May 1987, and that was the date on which he had always intended to retire. The question of who should succeed him was, however, far from straightforward. To go outside the existing board of directors and appoint a grand public figure (as NatWest had done with the former Conservative cabinet minister Lord Boardman in 1983) was, as we have seen, simply not Barclays style. The conventional solution was to look to the families, but the choice was unpromising.

Derk Pelly, aged fifty-seven, was a descendant,[12] through his grand-

---

[12] In retirement, Pelly (a talented amateur artist) produced a family tree connecting the descendants of John Freame, Robert Barclay, Silvanus Bevan, John Henton Tritton and John Gurney. He was able to identify 31 relations who had worked in Barclays during his own career from 1952 to 1988.

mother, of Thomas Fowell Buxton, and had succeeded Dolling as Deputy Chairman on the international side. But his role there seemed largely ceremonial, and he was not a serious runner. Neither was Roger Goodenough, who was almost sixty. To most observers inside and outside the bank, there was only one viable family candidate: Andrew Robert Fowell Buxton, whose heir-apparent status had been signalled in 1985 by his appointment as a vice-chairman, and who was universally expected to become chairman in due course.[13] But at forty-eight he was clearly still young for the job.

Youth in itself was not necessarily the problem: Sir Jeremy Morse, the youngest clearing bank chairman ever, had been forty-seven when he took over the chair of Lloyds in 1977. But Buxton was not a recognized statesman of the international banking scene like Morse, who had been an executive director of the Bank of England and chairman of the IMF 'Committee of Twenty'. Buxton's track-record was largely limited to corporate lending in Pall Mall and Lombard Street, plus the negotiation of the BZW acquisitions. Tall, handsome, commanding in presence and in his ability to chair a meeting, he certainly looked the part. He had the reputation of being a courageous banker – willing to lend boldly, but also willing to fight to get his money back. But he was not experienced in large-scale administration; Winchester, Pembroke College, Oxford and a short commission in the Grenadier Guards had not equipped him with strong intellectual credentials; and no one had ever accused him of being a great strategic thinker.

More importantly, he was outranked in age, experience and public profile by Barclays' two leading non-family executives. These were John Quinton, one of the three deputy chairmen (the others being Pelly and Sir Martin Jacomb, the newly arrived chairman of BZW), and Peter Leslie, the chief general manager. In the meritocratic world

---

[13] Andrew Buxton has, like Tim Bevan, tended to downplay his family's connection with Barclays, claiming quite correctly that the Buxtons of Coggeshall, Essex, were better known as brewers (in the firm of Truman, Hanbury & Buxton) than as bankers. Andrew's great-great-great-grandfather Sir Thomas Fowell Buxton, first baronet, was an MP and anti-slavery campaigner who married Hannah Gurney. Their son Thomas, the second baronet, bought into the Gurney banking partnership in Norwich on behalf of his son Geoffrey, who became a partner there in 1874. Geoffrey (brother of Andrew's great-grandfather) was a director of Barclays Bank from 1896 until his death in 1929. Four other Buxtons descended from the first baronet, including Andrew, have been directors, as have at least three descendants with other surnames. But Andrew's own introduction to the bank came through his stepfather, Alexander (Sandy) Grant, who was a director of the bank from 1945 to 1971 and chairman of its Liverpool and Manchester local boards. Andrew Buxton entered Barclays in 1963 and married, in 1965, Jane Grant, who is Sandy's daughter by his first marriage.

of Thatcherite Britain, with investment analysts and financial journalists becoming increasingly focused on personalities at the top of big companies, it was no longer acceptable to opt for a blatantly dynastic preferment, especially in a company in which the dynasty owned so few of the shares.

And after all, as far as the chair was concerned, the dynastic system in Barclays had been less rigidly applied in earlier years – before the rise to behind-the-scenes power of the Lombard Street uncles. Of the nine chairmen between 1896 and 1987, six (three Tukes, two Bevans, and John Thomson) came from the proprietor families; two, Frederick Goodenough and Edwin Fisher, came from general management, and one, Will Goodenough, was an able son of his father.

But such genealogical minutiae were not widely known, so the assumption throughout the bank and outside it was that a family candidate would always have the advantage. And indeed, before the decision to go for a non-family chairman was finally made, there was another family member to be considered – one of whom almost no one outside the inner circle at the top of the bank had even thought. This was Alan Tritton, senior local director in Lombard Street, director of the bank since 1974 and a descendant of John Henton Tritton, who joined the Lombard Street partnership in 1783 and married Mary Barclay.[14]

The first Tritton of the dynasty was remembered for his skilful helmsmanship of the bank during the panic of 1825, when many private banks failed. His descendant Alan was also a very sound banker, and a modest, kindly man with an unusually wide range of interests: before joining the bank in 1954 he had served with the Seaforth

---

[14] Robert Barclay the Second, a junior partner under John Henry Tritton, wrote a tribute to him after his death in May 1833 which offers a model of the ideal Barclays banker of former days: 'He was the most deliberate and exact man I ever knew, and when you have supposed a subject exhausted he would still draw out of the deep stores of his wisdom many new bearings of the case, and set it in a new point of view. In his meridian years he followed up the detail of every part of our concern with minute particularity which kept all the clerks up to the mark, silently overlooking their work and making all his observations in a low tone of voice, so that the same quiet habit of transacting the business prevailed throughout the House. Extreme caution, inflexible integrity and firmness were his characteristics as a man of business, and to these he added punctuality and self-command. He was scrupulously exact in not revealing the secrets of others, and especially careful of being dragged into ill-precedents by the influence of names ... Thus has passed away a great good man – great because he lived in the entire subjection of his natural temperament and passion – good because the fulfilment of his duties to God and men were the business of his life. He has not left his parallel for inflexible integrity, calmness of mind, sound judgement and experience or kindness of heart or suavity of manner.'

Highlanders in Malaya ('Got shot in the Pahang,' he liked to say) and taken part in the Falkland Islands Dependencies Survey – the first time I met him, at a City lunch during the Falklands War, he was proudly sporting a tie available only to explorers of South Georgia. He was also the bank's resident expert on India, and a vice-president of the Royal Geographical Society. And at some point before the mood of the eighties intervened, rumour has it that he was given to understand – by Theodore Barclay perhaps, Emlyn Bevan having placed himself outside the magic circle by dying in 1972 – that he could hope to follow Bevan into the chair.

But the trouble with Tritton was his mannerisms, which made him seem somewhat less statesman-like than he actually was. He was famous in the bank for poking his ears in search of wax with either the earpiece of his spectacles or a wire paper-clip bent out of shape for the purpose – the latter a particularly agonizing performance for his staff to watch. He had the loping gait of an Antarctic explorer, and carried a scruffy airline bag in preference to a conventional briefcase. For all his travels he had, as I saw for myself in Japan, little sense of how to deal with foreign rules of etiquette. The relatively simple protocol of exchanging business cards with Japanese bankers (in which the key thing is to make it very obvious whether you intend to shake hands or present your card first – preferably the latter – but never to attempt both manoeuvres at once) completely flummoxed him.

Tritton was in reality an unlikely candidate for the chairmanship, and several senior Barclays people have told me that they were never aware that he was one. Rumours persist, however, that he was and that Tim Bevan had the awkward task of telling Tritton he was no longer in the running, some time before the formal board decision.

So the choice fell back to Quinton, Leslie and Buxton. There was no shortage of support for Buxton – even from one or two of the executives below him, who thought he would make a better chairman than hands-on managing director – but it was Bevan himself who said that it was time to go for a non-family choice. Sensible succession planning suggested in any case that Buxton would be all the better for a period of intensive grooming before slipping into the job in five years' time.

As between Leslie and Quinton, the clinching factors had to do with morale and presentation. Two years earlier, Quinton had followed Lambert into the siding previously occupied by my father, as chairman of Barclays Bank UK. At the same time, Leslie had become the first chief general manager of the whole group (thus completing the 'One

Bank' amalgamation process) and seemed to have been winning the race. The old-fashioned title of chief general manager was as close as Tim Bevan was prepared to go towards appointing a chief executive, and Leslie, a formidable bureaucrat,[15] usually had Bevan's support in disagreements with Quinton. Quinton was ambitious, popular and clearly a threat to Bevan's own position, as my father had been, so better sidelined.

When it came to taking over the chair, however, Leslie was thought too severe in manner to lift the gloom caused by the profits slip, the loss of people like Williamson and the growing turf war between BZW and the bank. He was also a team player – 'an institutional type of person', as he put it himself – who did not especially crave the limelight. Quinton, with his open, sunny personality, was the man for the job, and he probably wanted it more.

At the time, this was widely hailed as a good and progressive decision. But how the choice was actually made was a mystery to the outside world, the appointment of Quinton simply emerging as a decision of the group board on 2 October 1986. In fact it was presented to the board, like so many other decisions in that era, as a *fait accompli*. Bevan had written to the non-executives on 12 September to remind them of his forthcoming retirement date, adding:

> Directors will also know that speculation has started inside the Bank, and in the Press, regarding my successor, and the matter has, of course, been under consideration by the Senior Directors Committee. I have also been able to have informal discussions with many of the remaining members of the Board and it is apparent that there is overwhelming support for John Quinton (date of birth 21.12.1929) to become chairman for a five year term.

The Senior Directors Committee was chaired on this occasion by Anthony Tuke. Its members, if literal seniority was the criterion, would have included Sir 'Jock' Pease[16] and Henry Lambert (directors since 1965 and 1966 respectively) as well as Bevan *ex officio*. Johnnie

---

[15] My father, who had a high regard for Leslie, once described him affectionately as 'like an East German politburo member'. In fact, Leslie's first ambition had been to become a diplomat, and he would have made a superb Whitehall mandarin. He had a near-photographic memory for documents and figures, and made a point of taking every decision within twenty-four hours of being asked. Uniquely in Barclays, he typed the minutes of his daily management meetings himself, so that they could be circulated for action within the hour.

[16] Sir Richard Thorn Pease, third baronet, was a protégé of Sir John Thomson and a director of Barclays from 1964 to 1989. As vice-chairman during the 1970s, he was the official guardian of the Special List. His great-great-grandmother was a Gurney.

Henderson, the ex-senior partner of Cazenove, took part, and Quinton believes that he argued strongly for Buxton. Denys Henderson was there at his own insistence, having taken offence at the idea of a Senior Directors' Committee which excluded the chairman of ICI, and was impressed by how fairly the discussion was conducted, without the bias towards the family interest that might have been expected.

Bevan's letter to directors contains two other interesting details: it confirms that the Quinton proposal is one 'with which, incidentally, the Governor is content'. And it lists the executive directors who – presumably because their own positions might be affected by the decision – had not been consulted: besides the three candidates, these were Pelly, Robert Sale (the personnel director), Humphrey Norrington (a Special List man who eventually became a vice-chairman),[17] Peter Ardron (senior general manager on the international side) and Tom Camoys. Illustrating the eccentricity of the Barclays power structure, the list omits three executive directors who also happened to be senior local directors – Tritton, Goodenough and Tony Rudge in Birmingham – who for this purpose seem to have been treated as non-executives, and had presumably been consulted ahead of their own immediate superiors, the regional general managers, who were of course too junior even to be mentioned in Bevan's letter.

My father was one of 'remaining members' to whom Bevan had spoken informally, and had expressed himself in favour of Quinton. But still he was surprised that the inner group had come to what he considered to be the right decision. Quinton himself found people trying to trace a hitherto unrevealed link between him and the families. Was his wife related to them? Since he originated from Norwich, was there some connection between his surname and the fact that members of the Gurney family sometimes have the Christian name Quintin? Of course there wasn't, but that was how Barclays people thought. Some of them just took the opportunity to patronize him: 'We must all be very proud of John Quinton,' one Buxton relation said to me, dredging up what may well have been an authentic detail of the new chairman's first holiday job in the bank as a Cambridge undergraduate. 'You know he started as a driver.'

In Tokyo, meanwhile, the Barclays branch manager Michael Tomalin declared that 'Quinton must be just keeping the seat warm for Andrew'.

---

[17] Norrington, another Wykehamist, is the brother of Roger Norrington, the conductor, and the son of the late Sir Arthur Norrington, Master of Trinity College, Oxford, who invented the Norrington table of relative performance of Oxford colleges in degree results.

It was apparent from everything that Quinton subsequently did that he saw himself as anything but a caretaker.[18] But that was certainly how he was regarded by the old guard, and the resentments later expressed towards him reflected, in part, the fact that he refused to read his lines in that scenario.

Of course, they related also to Quinton's own actions and judgements, which will be examined in Chapter 9. But for the time being, Quinton's appointment was cheering news for the bank. At the group's 1986 annual planning conference – a gathering of senior executives from all round the world, held each year in early autumn at a hotel near Heathrow – there was a palpable uplift in the atmosphere when Quinton persuaded Bevan to let him take over the conference chair.

---

[18] One of the factors which contributed to the 'caretaker' theory about Quinton was a note in the annual accounts saying that his service agreement with the bank would expire in December 1989, on his sixtieth birthday. Some people thought this must be the limit of his term in the chair.

6

SOUTH AFRICA

1925–1999: DCO's roots in South Africa – The rise of the anti-
Barclays protest movement – Barclays as the anti-apartheid bank –
The decision to withdraw – The difficulty of returning

Ask any group of people today who were left-leaning students at British universities in the 1970s and early 1980s for an instant word association with Barclays and they will almost certainly answer, in chorus, 'South Africa'. The bank's involvement there was a long-running public relations nightmare, as well as a profound moral dilemma. And the last significant act of Tim Bevan's chairmanship was his decision to put an end to the argument, severing one of the central strands of Barclays' international history.

Barclays' business in South Africa was one of the three foundation stones of DCO in 1925. Its most important root was De Nationale Bank der Zuid-Afrikaansche Republiek Beperkt, originally registered in Pretoria in April 1891 with a concession to form both a bank and a mint. The bank duly established the State Mint in Pretoria, with the exclusive right to mint coin and issue banknotes within the Republic, and leased it to the South African government for £500 per year.

After the South African War of 1899–1902, the bank's name changed to the National Bank of South Africa Limited. Expansion proceeded at a great pace, with the absorption in 1910 of the National Bank of the Orange River Colony, of the Bank of Africa in 1912 and the Natal Bank in 1914. Barclays became a shareholder in the National Bank in 1919, and the National Bank in turn owned stakes in both the Colonial Bank, to which Barclays was increasingly close, and Cox & Co. (France), which was about to become the nucleus of Barclays' French operations. A Barclays director, Arthur Gillett of the Oxford Quaker banking family – who happened to be a lifelong friend of Jan Smuts, the South

African premier – was a member of the National Bank's London board.

In the early 1920s, however, the National Bank's rapid expansion – more than 100 new offices were opened in a single year – began to place strains on its capital. For the year to March 1923, heavy losses were incurred and the whole of the bank's reserve fund had to be appropriated to meet them. Deposits were draining away.

Barclays, meanwhile, had been toying with the idea of encouraging the Colonial Bank to expand into South Africa, but the ever-ambitious Frederick Goodenough could now see the possibility of an enlarged scheme in which a rescue of the National Bank might be effected under the Barclays umbrella. A cable was sent to the National Bank's chairman, James Leisk, with whom Goodenough was already on cordial terms, and the reply was encouraging. With the backing of his board, Leisk quietly took ship to England in December 1924 (boarding at Durban, rather than taking the weekly mail boat from Cape Town usually favoured by prominent businessmen of the day) and entered secret negotiations with Goodenough – who, as ever, simply acted on his own autocratic authority and told his board afterwards.

Eventually, the DCO scheme was completed. The Colonial Bank would take over both the Anglo-Egyptian Bank and the National Bank, with the backing of £1 million of new capital from Barclays. When this had been approved by all parties – only one National Bank share-holder, a Mr George Hay, spoke out against the scheme – the South African bank changed its name to Barclays DCO. But one of the conditions laid down by the National Bank board was that it should not lose its identity entirely – so the phrase 'with which is amalgamated the National Bank of South Africa' appeared on all its stationery, cheques and name plates until the name changed again, in 1971, to Barclays National Bank. The Barclays philosophy of decentralization, as applied to domestic local head offices, was to be applied equally to South Africa: Leisk had Goodenough's assurance that the board and management would be retained intact and that there would be no disturbance in the day-to-day administration.

Thus it was that Barclays acquired a network of more than 300 branches (growing eventually to 900) in South Africa, and eight more in South West Africa, which became Namibia. Though the size and history of the South African operation made it more self-contained than other parts of DCO, it was still very much a part of the Barclays family: in the post-1945 era, all its managers did part of their training in London. As a business, it had more in common with the domestic British branch banking network than it did with the 'bush banking' operations of the rest of Africa. The South African bank served as a useful model and comparitor for developments at home, and in later years was considered to be at least as well advanced in the management sciences of planning, marketing and product development.

It was also the source of a steady flow of dividends, representing about a third of DCO's profits, with no remittance problems and very few calls for capital in return. But from 1960 – the year of Harold Macmillan's 'Wind of Change' speech to the South African parliament in 1960 disassociating the British government from the ruling National Party's policies of apartheid, of the Sharpeville massacre, in which sixty-eight African demonstrators were shot dead, and of the sub-sequent banning of the African National Congress and withdrawal of South Africa from the Commonwealth – Barclays' presence in South Africa was a potential problem.

That problem remained quiescent, however, until the dawn in 1968 of the era of student unrest – the time of the Grosvenor Square protests against America's war in Vietnam and of the Sorbonne riots in France. In April 1968, the 'Haslemere Declaration' by a group of forty British activists – meeting somewhat incongruously in the prosperous Surrey commuter town – drew attention to Barclays' profile in Africa in the context both of a call for opposition to *apartheid* and for increased financial aid for developing nations.

Over the following years, hostility towards Barclays became one of the most fashionable of radical causes. Protesters cottoned on to the idea of buying single shares in order to gain the right to attend annual general meetings, though they were initially defeated by Barclays' arcane structure: in January 1969 they were excluded from the DCO shareholders' meeting because they had bought Barclays Bank Limited shares by mistake. In 1970, the financing of the Cabora Bassa dam and hydro-electric project in Mozambique became the issue of the moment, Portuguese colonial Mozambique being almost as offensive to liberals as South Africa itself, and South African contractors being in the lead in the dam's construction. A group calling itself the Dam Busters launched a series of aggressive protests against Barclays – which was not in fact a member of the £100-million consortium financing the project, but was banker to one of the South African sub-contractors.

At DCO's last AGM, in January 1971, Seebohm faced polite ques-tioning from a clergyman and a representative of the Edinburgh Uni-versity World Poverty Action Group. He pointed out that the dam had the potential to raise the living standards of one and a half million Africans in the Zambesi valley, that Barclays had 700,000 non-white

South African customers and pursued employment policies which challenged the restrictions of apartheid in various ways. But reasoned responses were of no avail, and the anti-Barclays campaign gathered momentum. Colleges, student unions and even scout troops took their accounts away. The words 'Barclays is a piggy bank' were scrawled across the face of a branch in Nottingham, and another at the University of Essex was put to the torch.

Oxfam, the leading charity in famine relief work in Africa, removed its business, and so did the London Borough of Camden, which had been a customer of King's Cross branch. Senior Barclays executives were sent out, on a kind of punishment rota, to debate the issue with student bodies around the country, ducking the projectile eggs and paint. All of this was taking place in a period when – as an initiative of my father's marketing department – university students were being targeted for the first time as valuable long-term customers, and were being tempted with offers of free banking (if they stayed in credit) and free plastic clipboards in Barclays' distinctive shade of blue. It was an uphill struggle.

In my first term at Oxford, filial loyalty drove me to a rather weak defence of Barclays' South African involvement in a debate on whether the Worcester College Junior Common Room bank account should be moved elsewhere. My opponent was a Welsh lawyer called Rawlings, a powerful operator in college affairs, whose case consisted largely of shouting, ''Oo's yer dad, then? Tell 'em 'oo yer dad is!' while I was speaking. He carried the vote by a substantial majority. One of the few people to vote with me, oddly enough, was the extreme-left-wing playwright Doug Lucie – author of some savagely anti-capitalist plays of the 1980s – who was one of my best friends at the time, and who believed that emotional solidarity should always take precedence over cold, even Marxist, reasoning.

The level of anti-Barclays protest waxed and waned over the years according to the general level of agitation from one student generation to the next, as well as in response to developments in South Africa itself. The Anti-Apartheid Movement (based appropriately in Mandela Street, Islington) published in 1975 a twelve-page pamphlet of charges against Barclays, written by one Martin Bailey. From time to time there were demonstrations outside and inside the Lombard Street head office, on one occasion in the early 1980s involving smoke bombs – and a particularly robust citizen's arrest by one of the bank's ex-soldier tail-coated messengers, who was said to have glazed over for a moment under the illusion that he was back in Korea or Aden, and to have been restrained by his colleagues from carrying out some form of summary justice.

Throughout this period, Barclays debated whether to go or stay. In the early 1970s, when the South African economy was booming but there were threats from the South African government to force all foreign banks down to maximum holdings of only 10 per cent in local operations, it would have been easy to sell the business for a handsome price and take the cash out at an exchange rate of two rand to the pound (the commercial exchange rate when Barclays finally sold in 1986 was 3.2, but capital could only be remitted out of the country at a punitively unfavourable 'financial' rate of around 5.85).

In 1977, a debate took place at the Barclays International board in which Lord Carrington argued that the situation in South Africa was bound to get worse and that the bank would be wise to consider an eventual path to withdrawal. Harry Oppenheimer – the liberal-leaning chairman of South Africa's biggest company, Anglo-American – argued for staying on, making the point both that it was possible for Barclays to be a reforming influence through its employment policies and that if the bank had no investment in the African continent at all, South Africa would still be the only country worth contemplating.

The outcome of this debate seems to have been a compromise. Over a period of time, Barclays' percentage holding in Barclays National would be reduced. Within South Africa a policy was to be pursued, where possible, of resisting apartheid in day-to-day operations: Barclays branches did not keep separate counters for whites and non-whites, and employed non-whites outside the geographical areas to which they were normally restricted. When a new training centre was built, a regulation requiring separate toilet facilities for non-whites was observed only until the government's building inspector had been to call; then the extra set was bricked up.

At the same time, attempts were made to establish relations with black leaders. Anthony Tuke made repeated efforts, through lawyers, to meet Steve Biko, and asked the government to let him visit Nelson Mandela – the request was not granted. The Zulu Inkatha party leader, Chief Butholezi, who had been an opponent of violent uprising in South Africa when the ANC was still preaching Marxist revolution, was much easier to reach, and advised that disinvestment by Barclays would not help the black population in any way. The overwhelming majority of blacks with bank accounts preferred to use Barclays or Standard Chartered rather than Afrikaner banks, and the South African government would not have been upset at all to see Barclays withdraw.

The conventional view was that only if a substantial block of all the 300 foreign investors in South Africa decided to withdraw at the same time would it make any real impact. The consensus within Barclays was that it was morally right to stay, even if it would have been economically right to go at the beginning of the 1970s.

Until 1982, Barclays' senior executives in South Africa maintained this stance without raising their heads too far above the political parapet. That changed with the appointment as managing director of Barclays National Bank of the 42-year-old Cambridge-educated Chris Ball, who had joined Barclays from Barings a decade earlier. Acting on his own initiative, rather than according to any strategy agreed with head office, Ball rapidly emerged as one of the South African business community's most outspoken voices against apartheid.

He cultivated contacts in London with Thabo Mbeki and other ANC exiles, and drew the personal hostility of President P.W. Botha. His telephones were tapped, and it emerged during Archbishop Tutu's Truth and Reconciliation Commission hearings, after the ANC came to power, that Ball's name had been on a secret police list of potential candidates to be murdered.

In September 1985, Ball was instrumental in arranging for a group of leading South African businessmen – led by Gavin Relly, Harry Oppenheimer's successor at Anglo-American – to fly to Zambia to meet the ANC leader in exile, Oliver Tambo, at Zambian president Kenneth Kaunda's private game-hunting lodge. (Contrary to some press reports at the time, Ball was not at the historic meeting itself, because his presence was required at the annual Barclays planning conference in London.) Though the ANC's official position favoured total disinvestment by foreign companies in South Africa to be followed by widespread nationalization, the exiled party was also a customer of Barclays in Zambia, and it was clear that there was scope for further discussion.

Back in Lombard Street, however, the issue of South Africa was coming to a head in a different way. 1985 was also a year of widespread rioting within South Africa and of fierce arguments between Margaret Thatcher and other Commonwealth leaders over the imposition of trade sanctions. Some foreign banks, led by Chase Manhattan, were refusing to roll over their loans to South Africa, which in turn declared a four-month freeze of the repayment of principal of its foreign debt. Catching the mood – and perhaps prompted by Chris Ball – Bevan suddenly struck a much more challenging note than in any of his previous statements on South Africa, which had tended towards the apologetic. In November 1985 he denounced apartheid as 'repugnant, wrong, un-Christian and unworkable', at the same time revealing the extent of Barclays' contacts with the ANC. This was followed, four months later, by a declaration that Barclays would lend no more money to South Africa (it had £800 million outstanding) and would take no part in formal debt rescheduling negotiations until 'there are changes which confirm an end to the bankrupt policy of institutionalized racial discrimination'. He also called for the early release of Nelson Mandela.

Even the chanting of that particular mantra was not enough to assuage Barclays' radical critics. Since the 1977 board debate, Barclays' ownership of Barclays National Bank had been reduced first to 60 per cent, then to 50 per cent, and in 1985 – through a rights issue in which Barclays did not take up its rights – it had been diluted to 40.4 per cent, so that it no longer had to be consolidated in the group's balance sheet. But still the Anti-Apartheid Movement had Barclays in its sights, and the strengthening of US sentiment against the South African regime made Barclays unacceptable as an 'authorized depository' for the funds of several American states. The battle for student bank accounts had been comprehensively lost: Barclays' market share in the sector had fallen from over 25 per cent to 17 per cent. In the first half of 1986, Barclays had fallen 19 percentage points behind the now-dreaded NatWest in the student sector. And the share price was beginning to suffer as well.

At the same time there were voices within the bank saying that, with or without the political flak it attracted, South Africa was not relevant to Barclays' future, which would be found in the high-growth markets of Europe, North America and the Far East. This analysis was promoted by Peter Leslie and supported by those such as Martin Jacomb who saw the nascent, capital-hungry BZW as the vehicle which would propel the group towards that future. Meanwhile, South Africa had contributed only 2.7 per cent of group profits in 1985, compared to a recent peak of 16 per cent in 1983. Its economy was sinking into difficulties, the rand was weak and advice from the British Foreign Office was that the National Party was capable of hanging on to power, by whatever brutal means, for many years to come.

For all of these reasons, most of the Barclays' board – Anthony Tuke and Johnnie Henderson being two notable exceptions – were prepared to agree with Bevan that it was time to cut South Africa adrift. The decision was taken at the May 1986 board meeting (which took place in New York, to celebrate the completion of the new 75 Wall Street headquarters building) and the deal was announced in November:

Barclays' stake would be sold for £80.3 million (representing a book loss of £42 million) to Anglo-American, De Beers and Southern Life. Bevan admitted that the price was much less than might have been raised if the sale had happened two or three years earlier. But clearly it was better at this stage to be able to make a significant investment in the US, for instance, rather than in South Africa 'which is uncertain and disapproved of by the rest of the world'.

Was it the right decision? It cannot be argued with hindsight that capital released from South Africa was invested productively in the US, or anywhere else. Chris Ball and others believe that if Barclays had hung on in South Africa for another six months, the political pressure to withdraw would have abated. Margaret Thatcher was said to have been furious with Barclays (again) after the sale. Other companies such as Shell – vulnerable to consumer opinion at home through its petrol stations just as Barclays was through its branches – stayed on right through South Africa's troubled period, maintaining both a clear anti-apartheid stance within the country and a robust defence of Shell's position to the rest of the world. When Barclays reopened an office in Johannesburg in 1995, President Mandela himself told the delegation from Lombard Street, 'You should never have sold.'

Barclays was in fact the first major international bank to return to South Africa – ahead of Citibank, for example, though one or two lesser names, such as Société Générale of France, had stayed put all along. The new Barclays representative was Philip Howell – a former army officer and another descendant of Thomas Fowell Buxton – who found a warm welcome from the new political and business establishment.

But an enormous amount had been sacrificed in nine years of absence. In a market where Barclays once held a market share bigger than its market share at home in Britain, it now had a single office of fewer than seventy people. First National Bank, as its former subsidiary was now called, had meanwhile grown to a market capitalization equivalent to £5.8 billion, so that the 40 per cent stake sold for £80 million in 1986 would now have cost well over £2 billion to buy back. And though First National is still run by an ex-Barclays man, Viv Bartlett, with fond feelings for the old firm, the emotional hangover of the sale and the very different evolution of the two banks over the last decade has made remarriage exceedingly unlikely.

And South Africa is now a particularly difficult banking market for Barclays to break into any other way. Four large local banks, including First National, hold 80 per cent of the country's banking assets. Every international bank in the world is competing to do business with top companies such as Anglo-American, but those who want to develop a broader business are under political pressure to offer banking services in poor black districts where they generally fear to tread. Barclays hoped to establish a niche investment banking business under the Barclays Capital banner, but the strategy was vague and – like every other aspect of Barclays' international development – a low priority while there were so many urgent problems to be dealt with at home.

Perhaps most significantly for Barclays' future in Africa as a whole, the South African banks were beginning to become a competitive threat in the still profitable but much-ignored black African territories of Botswana, Ghana, Kenya, Uganda, Zambia and Zimbabwe. Though rarely highlighted in any public presentation of Barclays, those businesses remained among the most profitable in its portfolio.

They had needed no new capital from London for decades, and indeed in some cases had actually remitted capital back through special dividend payments. By the mid-1990s, Africa had the most efficient computer systems in the Barclays group, providing centralized real-time data-processing via satellite links to England. The conditions of daily life in Africa create constant difficulties on the ground, but these are precisely the kind of problems which long-serving Barclays International and DCO men were trained to cope with, unlike the challenges of the international capital markets. Senior international managers returned to Africa – after arduous stints in New York or Hong Kong, or on the many battlefronts between Barclays and BZW – with a sense of relief and home-coming. Old colonial standards still quietly applied; until 1992, for example, there was an internal rule against providing hot running water in the servants quarters of Barclays expatriate staff houses in Kenya. It was still considered radical to suggest that a black African manager – the most likely candidate being Isaac Takawira, a former official of the Zimbabwean treasury – should be considered for the job of running Barclays' operations throughout Africa.

If one territory was passing through a bout of political or financial instability (as in Zimbabwe in 1999, when Robert Mugabe began seizing white farmers' land without compensation), other African territories would usually be doing well enough to compensate in the combined results; and even in the troubled territories, Barclays as the best name in the local market would benefit from any 'flight to quality'. Lending margins were counted in whole percentage points, not in basis points (hundredths of a per cent) as they are in London and

Johannesburg. Market shares of 35 to 40 per cent were normal, and profits of £100 million a year continued to roll in.

There is a school of thought which says that the inevitable path for South Africa is one of economic decline and of descent into the corrupt and undemocratic practices which hold sway across most of the continent. In which case, there will be no need for regret if Barclays' business dwindles away. But there is another school of thought which says that, under South Africa's economic and political leadership, there is hope for the emergence of a more prosperous, better-governed African bloc in the early decades of the twenty-first century. In that case, Barclays' decision to pull out of South Africa in 1986 will have been one of its greatest mistakes.

7

BIARRITZ TO TOKYO

1973–1986: An interlude in France – A series of job interviews –
Joining Barclays Merchant Bank – Cold calling in America –
Diplomacy in Malaysia – Guerrilla war in Tokyo

The sale of Barclays National Bank in South Africa marked a historic change in the shape of the group; there was a tidy symbolism in the fact that it was announced within a few days of the official birth – in London on 27 October 1986, the day known as Big Bang – of Barclays de Zoete Wedd, or BZW, the investment bank through which Barclays aimed to be recognized as a new kind of global market leader. But before we examine how that project came into being and why it ended in failure, there is time for a diversion around the Barclays empire: to illuminate some of its byways and to explain how I came to be, at 9 a.m. London time on that special date, waiting in a Tokyo basement for someone to shout 'Bang!' down a long-distance telephone line.

My Barclays career, such as it was, dated from June 1981 to January 1992. But I had a foretaste of life in the great organization in 1973, between leaving school and going up to Oxford, when I worked for several months in the Biarritz branch of Barclays Bank SA in France. It was a charming interlude, and a glimpse of Barclays at its most proud and eccentric.

Barclays in France began life in 1915 as an offshoot of Cox & Co., the Army Agents, which had followed the British Expeditionary Force across the Channel the previous year. Standing behind Cox & Co. in its French banking venture was the London & South Western Bank, which merged first with the London & Provincial Bank in January 1918 and then with Barclays in October 1918. The Colonial Bank, which was to become part of DCO in 1925, was also a shareholder in Cox & Co. (France).

By the end of the First World War, Cox & Co. branches had been opened in Paris, Boulogne, Rouen, Marseilles, Le Havre and Lyons, and a local banking business acquired in historic premises in Bordeaux. As peace returned, branches sprouted for the benefit of British tourists and residents along the Côte d'Azur, at Nice, Menton, Cannes and Monte Carlo. There was even an office in Oran, in the then-prosperous French colony of Algeria.

Cox & Co. (France) became Barclays Bank (Overseas) Limited in 1922 and Barclays Bank (France) Limited in 1926. But it never became part of DCO, remaining a proud trophy and direct subsidiary of Barclays Bank Limited. The decentralized management system which applied so congenially to domestic local head offices was extended with even more latitude across the Channel: it was accepted that the French did not like to be told what to do by the British, and that interference from head office in London should be kept to a minimum – a state of affairs which was to persist well into the 1980s.

On the other hand, the directors in London were by no means averse to periodic visits to Paris and the Riviera. The chairman of the French bank was by tradition a family grandee from London - for many years it was Emlyn Bevan, and during my brief encounter in 1973 it was Sir Roderick Barclay GCVO KCMG, a former British ambassador to Belgium who was a first cousin of Theodore.[1]

There was also a resident British director in Paris. After the Second World War this was Lionel Gurney Buxton MVO MC, and as late as 1991 it was Joseph Gurney Barclay, Sir Roderick's son and a sometime manager of London's Curzon Street branch. The holder of this pleasant post was by tradition largely ignored by the French managers around him. After all, few British bankers speak French with sufficient confidence to do so in board meetings, and though most senior French bankers speak English quite well, few are willing to do so on their own home ground.

Back in the 1920s, more branches were added for the convenience of British tourists: at Le Touquet in the summer season only, at Aix-les-Bains, where prime minister Baldwin liked to spend his extended holidays, and in 1927 at Biarritz, the grand resort of the Côte Basque which had been specially favoured by the nineteenth-century Empress Eugénie, Spanish-born wife of Napoleon III, whose villa became the

[1] Sir Roderick's father was a missionary. His maternal grandfather, Henry Birkbeck, was a local director of Barclays at Norwich; his paternal grandmother was a Buxton, daughter of the second Thomas Fowell Buxton, whose mother was a Gurney. Thus he carried the bloodlines of four of the founding East Anglian families.

exceedingly grand Hôtel du Palais. Edward VII had been another habitué of Biarritz, obliging Herbert Asquith to travel out to see him there in 1908 in order to kiss hands on his appointment as prime minister.

The Barclays branch stood, appropriately enough, on the avenue Edouard VII, next door to an English tea-room. It overlooked the casino and the Grand Plage. By the time I got there, Biarritz was a rather forgotten, geriatric resort, and had barely begun to develop its modern tourist reputation as Europe's prime rendezvous for surfers. Our manager, Monsieur Lavignasse, lived in a handsome apartment above the bank. He had followed his father in the job, and his son was subsequently manager of Barclays at Toulouse. This was a Clochemerlian backwater of Barclays, its only moment of greater importance having passed briefly in 1940 when the general management from Paris retreated to Biarritz as the Germans advanced on the capital. But within Biarritz, Barclays carried itself with some self-importance. To its French customers, a cheque book issued by 'La Barclays' had something of the snob value of employing an English butler.

Accommodation for my stay was arranged as the paying guest of one such customer, a local doctor, Guy Larue de Charlus, whose grandfather had been mayor of the town. The house was a turreted nineteenth-century villa, where I lived on the attic floor unseduced by a dumpy little Portuguese housemaid in the room next door. It was apparent that the Larue de Charlus family thought it exceedingly smart to have a Barclays *stagiaire* staying, my predecessor in the house having been one Oliver Tritton of the founding family – of whom I never heard again. Madame Larue de Charlus had South American connections and occasionally gave Proustian dinner parties for what passed for the local 'diplomatic corps' – the consuls and vice-consuls of Brazil and Portugal. It was all a fine education for one who had just left a brutish Scottish public school. I learned the etiquette of eating asparagus and of picking at duck legs with the fingers, and how to spot the difference in taste between claret in magnums and single bottles.

At work, I dealt with the problems of Barclays customers from England who had lost their holiday money on the casino tables or had valuables stolen from their cars. I also acted as courier, or courier's minder, for very large quantities of Spanish pesetas exported illegally from Spain (often in shopping bags on local buses) by rich Spaniards who feared a socialist coup after Franco's death[2] and wanted to put

---

[2] He was over eighty and in fact had two years to live.

their money elsewhere. Barclays was particularly favoured for this purpose over the state-owned French banks, which the Spaniards did not trust. Once the loot was paid in at our counter, a clerk and I would be dispatched with it to the Banque de France branch in nearby Bayonne. Most of it was exchanged for gold ingots, which were then placed in our vault; a legendary quantity of bullion was eventually amassed there. It would have made for a spectacular robbery caper movie in the style of Claude Chabrol's *Bonne Année*.

From time to time, in the approved Barclays manner, we received important visitors. Sir Roderick Barclay passed briskly through. Then came Monsieur Pringle, the resident director in Paris, whose manner I recall describing in a letter home as 'quavering', rather as I imagined the manner of an ageing *haute couturier*. He spoke French with a very affected English accent, and was well imitated after his departure by our mischievous cashier.

It was apparent, even from this four-month glimpse, that the strength of the Barclays name in France was chiefly with wealthy private customers. By the early 1980s, when all the significant French-owned banks had been nationalized, Barclays was the largest non-state-owned commercial bank in the country. It was regarded, with the neighbouring operation in Spain, as a jewel in Barclays' crown. But by then the idea of Barclays as the bank for *grandes dames* and tax-dodging Spanish Dons who liked to drink Earl Grey in English tea-rooms had been abandoned in favour of the idea of Barclays as the new J. P. Morgan, the multi-national corporate bank. But it never worked, as we shall see, and several disastrous moves later Barclays in France was discovered to be losing hundreds of millions of pounds. Diminished and battered, it then decided to concentrate once again on the up-market retail sector which was its true destiny in the first place.

As for me, I went up to Oxford with the ambition of becoming a journalist. But after two years of idle undergraduate life, I had rather forgotten about being a writer. So I went along with my father's suggestion of a summer job in the City. He fixed me up with a stint at J. Henry Schroder Wagg & Co., one of the leading merchant banks, where I spent a happy six weeks as a clerk handling bills of exchange issued by companies, accepted by Schroders (which was an Accepting House) and sold into the discount market.

Schroders was brisker and more businesslike than Barclays in Biarritz, but it also left a warm impression. The chairman, the elegant 15th Earl of Airlie, took the trouble to call me to his office on my last day and invite me to 'come back and see us' next time I was in the City. I remember his sunlit office, with its fine antique furniture, a painting of himself as a child sitting on his grandfather's Grand National winner, a leather-bound edition of Joseph Conrad and a view of the dome of St Paul's. When I applied for a permanent job with the firm in the graduate recruitment season of the following winter, an offer arrived straight away. After some unpromising interviews with other banks, I happily accepted Schroders' offer.

One of the other banks which interviewed me was Barclays International. I had sent an application, no doubt, at my father's suggestion though he was not insistent about it: even if he already hoped I might one day join him in Barclays, he certainly thought it a better idea for me to start my career in a good merchant bank. I was interviewed in an office in Gracechurch Street by a personnel manager by the name of Kettle who gave off signals, which I later discovered to be common throughout Barclays, of suspicion towards all graduates: anyone who had idled away three years at university was likely to be undisciplined, ignorant of the real world and too brainy for his own good.

At the time, I thought the interview completely ridiculous: Kettle picked on the fact that I had been involved as treasurer in college theatricals. He became convinced that, far from being suited to banking, I ought really to be going into the world of entertainment, an option which had literally never entered my mind. Oddly enough, I now spend a good part of my time running a local arts centre and music festival and dabbling in amateur acting, so perhaps he was unusually perceptive. What was certain is that he did not want to recruit me, and rather curiously I received no further communication from Barclays, not even a letter of decline.

So I joined Schroders, which – though it was and is a first-class name in the City – had more in common with a gentlemen's club than with investment banking as it is today. Its banking division, where I was placed, lent only to the bluest of blue-chip companies, and was staffed by blue-chip Oxbridge public school types and smooth Chelsea-dwelling Europeans. I was paid only £2,814 a year in salary, but we only worked from 9.30 in the morning until twenty to six in the evening, and rarely spent less than half an hour on *The Times* crossword after lunch. It was extremely sociable, and some of the smarter people in the department moved in such exalted circles that, on one celebrated occasion, Princess Margaret rang up and asked to speak in succession to three young men at adjacent desks. Though cleverness and wit were admired, naked displays of keenness and ambition were generally frowned upon. In my first three years there, I only once – visiting a near-bankrupt engineering factory in Kilmarnock, which one of our American clients was buying – felt I had glimpsed the gritty world of industrial finance. I never glimpsed at all the high-pressure, big-bonus, cut-throat world in which we would all find ourselves a decade hence.

After three years I was bored out of my mind and beginning to think about changing career to journalism. But then everything changed: I was posted to Brussels to work in a Schroder joint venture with Mitsubishi Trust of Japan. This began with two weeks' training in Mitsubishi Trust's Tokyo headquarters, an experience which awakened in me a enduring fascination for the East. The job itself – managing a portfolio of syndicated eurodollar loan participations – proved much more fun than anything I had done in London. I liked living in a foreign city, working in a small team of mixed nationalities and being accountable for my own little section of the business. The loans we made were typically to state-owned banks and development agencies in Latin America. When repayment fell due, long after I had moved on, most of them never came back. But it seemed like a good idea at the time, as did so many of the market fashions touched upon in this book.

When my time was up in Brussels after eighteen months, I knew I did not want to go back to Schroders in London. So I answered an advertisement in *The Economist* for a loan officer's job in a Paris consortium bank called Société Financière Européenne – in which Barclays had a small shareholding. I went for an interview, but heard nothing and returned to rejoin the crossword team in London. Then I told my father about the Paris interview, and suddenly I was caught up in the Barclays system. He asked Tim Bevan, who sat on the board of the Paris bank, to enquire whether they were going to offer me a job: they were not, but perhaps Barclays International would be the place for me. I was summoned to see the chairman of Barclays International, Henry Lambert, who uttered the (to me) famous words, 'We like fathers and sons here.' He also said, encouragingly, 'If you want to work in Paris, I'm sure you can work for us there,' and more ominously, 'Of course you'll have to fill in all the forms and come back to talk to our personnel chap.'

The personnel chap, Bob Harvey, turned out to be a colleague of my father's from early days in Yorkshire; they had been foreign clerks together in Hull, processing letters of credit for imports of Polish bilberries. But it was apparent that he was a good deal less devoted to the concept of fathers and sons than his chairman. Nor was he impressed by what I had been doing in Brussels, managing thirty or forty loan accounts amounting to $70 million. In Barclays, he said, $70 million would be just one rather modest loan – a boast which must eventually have turned into a regret when 70 per cent of all Barclays' Third World debts had to be written off.

And had I passed the Institute of Bankers' exams, Harvey demanded. No, I hadn't; Schroders did not require them. That clinched it. For the second time in five years, it was obvious that Barclays International were not keen to employ me. So I was passed on to Barclays Merchant Bank.

There I was interviewed first by Tom Camoys, hunched thick-set over a huge, untidy desk in a densely smoke-filled room. It was late afternoon. He poured us both a neat shot of Grant's Standfast whisky. His manner was brisk, though not as brusque as I saw him on subsequent occasions. On the subject of inheritance (I foolishly implied that I thought he might have to offer me a job because my father had given him his) he quickly put me straight: he judged people solely on how they performed, he said; he regarded his own lordly handle as a complete irrelevance.

But still I was not sure whether they were just taking me in to please my father. The next interviewer was the head of the banking department, Gervase Buxton (a first cousin of Andrew), who asked me whether I was really, seriously ambitious.

'Well, since you're more or less obliged to give me a job, I'd better be totally honest . . .' I began.

'I bloody well am not obliged to give you a job,' he replied crossly. But he gave me one anyway.

BMB was as different in atmosphere from Schroders as it could possibly have been. Though the families and the Special List were represented by the likes of Gervase Buxton and Charlie Morland, the place was predominantly staffed by ordinary Barclays managers picked out of the branch network because they were unusually clever or awkward. Compared to the *boulevardiers* of Schroders, they were tough, unpolished and intensely competitive. And they knew about real banking: how to take fixed and floating charges on company assets, how to take a grip on the customer's cash flow if he looked as if he was in trouble. They taught evening classes for the Institute of Bankers and they kept talking about Clayton's Case, of which I knew nothing.[3]

---

[3] I do now, if only out of curiosity: Devaynes v. Noble (1816), known as Clayton's Case, established that 'in the case of a current account, payments in are, in the absence of any express indication to the contrary by the customer, presumed to have been appropriated to the debit items in order of date'. The reference is from Chorley & Smart *Leading Cases in the Law of Banking* (Fourth Edition, 1977), of which my copy is inscribed, optimistically, 'Martin: a little light reading for Xmas, Father'.

They worked through routine procedures and strictly hierarchical relationships, not in the casual officers' mess style of Schroders. My first
boss, Neil Harland, was an exceptionally able and aggressive manager
from Hartlepool, who gave me a hard stare and began, 'Listen, son, I
don't care who your antecedents are . . .'

But we soon got on terms and I began to enjoy myself. My induction
was completed by a month-long course at Ashdown Park, a former
monastery in Sussex which was the bank's management training centre.
There I was grouped with twenty assistant managers from branches
around the country, all older than me, all graded slightly lower than
me on the Barclays' career ladder, and all deeply suspicious of me, both
because of my surname and because I came from the merchant bank,
which they regarded as a dangerous unknown quantity. Only two out
of twenty were graduates, none were very bright, but several had sharp
commercial minds and they were all loyal Barclays men (no women)
steeped in the folklore of banking life. They expected nothing more
from their careers than a gentle progression to branch manager. They
saw the bank in rigidly hierarchical terms, talking possessively about
the staff below them ('My MA' meaning in this context 'the manager's
assistant one rank below me', rather than 'my master's degree') and
almost reverentially about the local directors above them.

Once the ice was broken we got on well – the last-night party was
one of the drunkest nights of my life – and we even met for a reunion
dinner in London. But after that I never saw any of them again. They
did not know it but they were an endangered species; I wonder how
many still have jobs in the bank. Ashdown Park was sold in the early
1990s, as a cost-cutting measure.

When BMB became part of BZW in 1986 it was regarded with
contempt by the incoming partners from de Zoete & Bevan and Wedd
Durlacher; it had never raised its game to compete with the grander
merchant banks, because top companies preferred to take advice from
an independent source rather than from a clearing bank subsidiary,
and because the government preferred to give its major privatization
mandates to trusted houses like Warburgs and Kleinworts. Fenced in
on all sides by the Barclays group structure, BMB's only natural client
base was among fast-moving second-rank entrepreneurs such as Gerald
Ronson of Heron Corporation and Michael Ashcroft of ADT (later a
controversial Tory Party treasurer). But within the limitations imposed
on it, BMB was good at what it did.

In the month that I joined, for example, it completed the £54
million privatization of National Freight Corporation, Britain's largest

road haulage business, by means of a highly geared management and employee buy-out. This bold, complex deal made millionaires, over the following years, of a large group of ordinary lorry drivers. It also yielded a remarkably valuable nest egg for BMB, which took a £600,000 shareholding in NFC for its own account and in due course passed it on to BZW. The under-performance of the more fashionable parts of BZW was repeatedly disguised by profits on the NFC stake.[4]

There were other smart investments through the 'development capital' subsidiary, and clever, tax-efficient loan schemes which were sold through BMB to the Barclays' network. Having been recognized as someone with a lively brain but little technical knowledge and no aptitude for routine administration, I was encouraged to work on new ideas. One was a fantastically complicated mechanism to help breweries lend money to pubs; another was the first formula ever used in Barclays to measure the risks involved in interest-rate swaps, now a multi-billion daily trading business but then a sinister, untested concept.[5]

BMB was fun. It had the advantages of a small company of fewer than 200 people. Though everyone was acutely conscious of their rung on the job–grade ladder, it was democratic, with much friendlier relations between directors, juniors, secretaries and messengers than had been the case at Schroders. It was enlivened by an annual intake of graduate recruits who were mostly pretty, self-confident Oxbridge girls with names like Pippa, Antonia and Lucinda – regarded as untrainable temptresses from another planet by the more traditional Barclays managers, but nevertheless a fragrant addition to the organization. With Derek the one-armed bandit as master of ceremonies, BMB had superbly sweaty Christmas disco parties – my father, as chairman, had fallen off his chair while making a speech at one of them.

In 1983 I migrated within BMB to what liked to think of itself as an élite unit of high-flying deal-makers. It was called Corporate Services Division (CSD), and its name gave most of the game away. For the first time, BMB was to be allowed to hunt for transatlantic corporate finance business, but the unit was forbidden to call itself 'International'

---

[4] In the three years from 1989 to 1991, BZW raised over £57 million from the sale of the £600,000 NFC investment, representing almost half of all BZW profits for the period. But for NFC, BZW would have had to declare a loss for 1990, when in fact it showed a £5 million profit.

[5] Not even my ornate formula could have identified the real risks of interest rate swaps as transacted with British local authorities. A controversial High Court judgement – finally upheld by the House of Lords in January 1991 – deemed such transactions to be unlawful for the local authorities and therefore unenforceable by the banks. Though Sir Martin Jacomb raged against 'this astonishing judgement', it cost BZW £36 million.

or to use the word 'Finance': BMB's own domestic corporate finance department (which, like the corporate finance divisions of more established merchant banks, offered advice on mergers, acquisitions, share issues and flotations) was called 'Corporate Advisory Division', to avoid the appearance of competing with Barclays Bank's Corporate Division (which, of course, offered finance). The label 'Corporate Services' would suggest to most businessmen a supplier of, say, roller towels and computer stationery, but it was all we were allowed. We would have made a better return for Barclays shareholders if we had tried to live up to the name, and set ourselves up as contract office cleaners.

CSD was the brainchild of a young Etonian called Charles Ryder – the brother of Richard Ryder, who was an aide to Margaret Thatcher in Downing Street, and later Tory Chief Whip. Ryder was manically, almost apoplectically, keen to do deals, and made his name during a brief secondment to New York, where he came within an ace of pulling off an international take-over deal – between a US chemical group and a Norwegian fertilizer maker – under the noses of the giant Wall Street investment banks. This won him the support of Camoys, who encouraged him to scour the United States for more of the same. Barclays offices across the US were generally pleased to see Ryder, because he at least gave them a new reason to call on potential customers. But the Barclays hierarchy in New York and London treated the initiative, like all other attempts to broaden the scope of BMB, with deep suspicion.

Ryder's partner in this enterprise was Tessa Bamford, a tall and forceful blonde ('Tessa's the head girl,' another female graduate trainee once observed) who made a great impression on Barclays managers wherever she went. The two of them roared backwards and forwards across the Atlantic, making brave efforts to find opportunities for business, especially with high-growth high technology companies on the West Coast. The concept was exciting – they enthused, for example, about the potential of a little-known company in Seattle called Microsoft – but the odds against turning it into a substantial flow of business for Barclays were insurmountable.

The team's secondary function was to look for ways of breaking into privatization work for the British government. BMB had little standing in conventional big ticket share sales. So we tried to look for unusual angles and new ideas, with the help of Dr Lynda Rouse, a former political adviser to Nigel Lawson as energy minister, and Jeffrey Thomson, an economist seconded, and eventually detached, from the Department of Energy. It was a matter of some competitive prestige at that time to recruit high-flying civil servants into the merchant banks: Schroders had the brilliant Gerry Grimstone, Kleinworts had Callum McCarthy (who moved firms to run BZW in Tokyo and New York before becoming the regulator of the gas and electricity industries). Thomson, an owlish figure with a habit of splattering himself and his desk with Tippex correcting fluid, made a more modest impression, though he later made a name for himself as an 'equity strategist'.

This crew enjoyed a liberal travel budget, but generated very little revenue during the nine months I was attached to it. It was clear to me that I had no talent as a 'calling officer', particularly when we had so little to sell. The concepts of privatization, on the other hand, were intellectually interesting and the potential in that field, at home and overseas, seemed genuinely wide open.

The nadir of my spell with Ryder's team was a ten-day trip to the United States in April 1984. It provided a glimpse of the hollowness of Barclays' strategy in that huge market. I went first to New Orleans, where I met up with a BMB director based in New York, Alex Duma (an Albanian, as it happened, though you would never have guessed from his Wodehousian English manner). Why we went to New Orleans remains a mystery, except that we were lunched by an adviser to the Louisiana governor, Edwin Edwards, who tried to interest us in lending a large sum of money for a gas pipeline project. If the deal was being offered to us, a couple of innocent bozos from England in town for less than a day, you could be pretty sure that every other bank in town had already turned it down. It was a fundamental illustration of Barclays' problem in the US. Within two years, the New Orleans office had been closed.

But on we went to Houston, scene of previous Barclays disasters in oil and gas lending: 'de luxe hotel, nice skyscrapers, no business prospects whatever' would have been a fair summary of my trip notes. I continued on my own to Dallas and Tulsa, in the dusty plains of Oklahoma. In Dallas the local Barclays manager, a brash Texan called Charlie Mc-Kinney, took me to call on several local corporate chiefs with whom I died the death of the actor who has not simply forgotten his lines but has never been given any lines to learn, and has no talent for improvisation.

The treasurer of American Airlines stared at me as though I were a cockroach on his office carpet. At a dinner in Dallas's exclusive Palm Restaurant with another big-hitter, I failed to utter a single word beyond 'Hello', 'I'll have the steak', 'Mmm' and 'Goodnight'. When I flew to Tulsa to call on the First-Third Bank, the pilot of the South

West Airlines plane went into an extended holding manoeuvre, and eventually said on the intercom, 'You-all might think we're lost up here, but we're not. We're jus' goin' aroun' in circles for a while.' That seemed a fair, even an optimistic, summary both of my career and of Barclays' American strategy.

Though Tulsa was one of the remotest extremes of my banking career (the others include Sapporo, Kathmandu and St Petersburg) the First-Third Bank, a modest regional operation, was, in fact, one of the few destinations on that trip where Barclays genuinely had something to offer. 'Correspondent banking relations' with local banks all round the world was something Barclays did well and took great care over. It had traditionally been the function of Barclays Bank Limited's London Foreign Branches, and for that reason was treated disdainfully as a sideshow by ex-DCO international managers. But it was actually one of the best selling points Barclays ever had abroad.

Many hundreds of obscure foreign banks kept their sterling accounts with Barclays, and appreciated the way they were looked after when they came to London. A team of correspondent banking managers travelled the world to maintain the relationships, making bankers' small talk and handing out golf balls and credit-card wallets embossed with spread eagles. The larger US regional banks which had been the recipients of this service over the years had now become potential eurobond issuers, so at least I had something to talk about. I even had a pre-prepared proposal to deliver. Nothing ever came of it, but it was the only moment of the trip when I briefly ceased to feel embarrassed.

On the way back to Dallas I ate something called a chilli dog at Tulsa Airport and considered despondently my prospects for promotion or wealth or escape from a career to which I seemed so completely unsuited. I spent the weekend in Dallas, in a drab hotel room which looked down into the internal atrium of a mall complex with an ice-hockey rink and giant plastic foliage.[6] I spent much of Sunday trying repeatedly to telephone one of the BMB graduate girls with whom I thought, wrongly as it turned out, I was conducting a relationship. Eventually the phone rang back, but it was not her.

It was a BMB director asking me whether I would mind, as soon as I got back to London, getting on another plane to go to Kuala Lumpur with Christopher Haviland to bid for the mandate to privatize the Malay-

---

[6] I found myself back in the same hotel, now called the Meridien, a dozen years later, making a speech about the British economy to the Dallas British–American Chamber of Commerce: I had become a lot less tongue-tied in the intervening years.

sian telephone system. Kuala Lumpur was, it seemed to me, roughly where I might have emerged if I had dug a hole in the basement of the Dallas hotel and kept on digging. It seemed a good omen: escape was at hand.

But not before I had endured another dozen hopeless meetings in Birmingham, Richmond, Charlotte, Atlanta and Memphis. The latter has a particularly fine turn-of-the-century hotel, the Peabody, where the Albanian Duma threw a spectacular tantrum at reception over some minor inadequacy of his room arrangement. The Peabody was famous for a gaggle of ducks which lived on its roof and once a day marched in line from the elevator to the ornamental fountain in the middle of the lobby. Similarly, our gaggle of Barclays calling officers, sometimes as many as five of us at the same meeting because so many parts of the group insisted that other parts could not call on potential customers without them, marched in and out of the offices of bemused American businessmen. In between meetings we discussed, endlessly and obsessively, the Byzantine internal politics of Barclays. If the truth be told, it was all a fantastic waste of shareholders' money.

The following Tuesday, Christopher Haviland and I took off for Malaysia. The British Airways plane broke down for twelve hours at Muscat. Passengers who took the option of disembarking spent a sweltering day in a comfortless concrete lounge, but we stayed put in first class (to which BMB directors, and anyone accompanying them, were entitled). We eventually landed in Kuala Lumpur in the early hours of Thursday morning. The neon-lit shophouses on the route to the Hilton hotel were my first glimpse of southeast Asia: the characteristic smell of the Malaysian capital – a hot, damp mixture of diesel fumes, cooking oil and durian fruit – is still with me. We did not win the telecom privatization mandate – it went to Kleinwort Benson's local associate – but a few weeks later, we went out again and picked up the mandate for the flotation of Malaysian Airline System.

Barclays' history in that part of the world dated from shortly after Julian Wathen's stirring 1971 speech in London. A Singapore branch, principally a foreign exchange dealing and 'offshore' banking operation, opened in 1972. A representative office in Kuala Lumpur followed in 1974. The first KL representative was Eric Staines, a genial Scotsman who was a legend in Barclays International for his princely lifestyle and his skill at working the expatriate benefits system. To follow Staines or to be junior to him in any posting was – as I discovered for myself in Japan in 1985 – a material blessing, because he always found the best houses, golf clubs, limousines and accoutrements of office, and he insisted that expatriates working under him should spend their living allowances (set by him and rubber stamped in London) to the limit, in order to demonstrate that it was impossible to live on less.

The KL representative's job initially included coverage of Thailand, where Barclays had some aspirations to do business, and Burma, Vietnam and Cambodia, where there were no aspirations at all. But this geographical spread enabled Staines to persuade London to allow him the fullest trappings of ambassadorship, which included a mansion in the city's most exclusive residential district, Kenny Hill – later called Bukit Tunku, after Tunku Abdul Rahman, the first prime minister of Malaysia, whose house was nearby.

Staines moved on to open an office in Seoul – where, according to stories told down the years around Barclays campfires, he rented the best townhouse available then sent a message to head office to the effect that the smog in the city made the acquisition of a weekend house on a nearby lake absolutely essential. Once that was approved, he sent another message to say that the speedboat necessary to reach the weekend house had also been purchased at a bargain price.

His successor in KL, in 1976, was John Carruthers, also a celebrated figure in the bank, but for more admirable reasons. A former major in the 2nd Gurkha Rifles, Carruthers had once been ADC to the last British governor of Singapore, Sir William Goode – with whom he can be seen, in a historic newsreel clip often shown on Singapore television, descending the steps of City Hall after the swearing in of Lee Kuan Yew as Singapore's first prime minister in 1959. Historians have often wondered what statesmanlike thought – about the end of Empire, perhaps – Goode was sharing with his aide as the crowd surged towards them across the Padang: Carruthers confirms that it was 'What the hell have you done with the Rolls, John?'

Carruthers' grandfather had been general manager of the Anglo-Egyptian Bank, which was one of the founding components of DCO in 1925.[7] His father also worked for both Anglo-Egyptian and Barclays. John always denied that he knew anything about banking, but he was in many ways an ideal representative: discreet, diplomatic, well informed about local politics and tycoonery, liked by the local banking authorities and frugal in the way he ran his office. He and his second wife Rukiah, a flashing-eyed Malay many years his junior, were also impeccable hosts, making KL the most popular stopping point in the

---

[7] Though, perhaps surprisingly in a Barclays context, he was not related to Sir William Carruthers of the London & Provincial Bank, who was a Barclays Bank director from 1920 to 1936 and whose son was a local director at Cardiff.

region for touring Barclays grandees. John was one of the few people I knew in Barclays in modern times who held on to his job until he reached retirement age. Now based in Labuan, an offshore financing centre on a Malaysian island close to Brunei – gone upriver, you might say, like a character in Anthony Burgess's *Malayan Trilogy* – he is still a part-time adviser.

I treasure a recollection of sitting on a verandah with Carruthers and his young brother-in-law, Hashim Shukor, late at night, drinking brandy and smoking dense, teak-brown Burmese cheroots. Above a cacophony of insect noise from the undergrowth, Rukiah harangued us at length about some complex matter involving herself, John and the women who worked in the Barclays office – one of whom, Zarina, the Malay-Indian manageress of the traveller's cheques section, was reckoned by my father to be the world's most beautiful Barclays employee. Whatever the subject of the complaint, it lasted fully ten minutes with barely a pause for breath. When it was over, Carruthers drew deeply on his cheroot.

'Thank you, my dear, for that spirited interjection,' he said slowly, in his authentic colonial drawl.

A patient, phlegmatic approach was needed at all times in Malaysia. I was attached not to the Barclays office but to Malaysian International Merchant Bankers, a joint venture between Barclays (which had bought its stake from the Crown Agents) and a local state-owned investment institution. An American bank, Continental Illinois, was also a share-holder, but was going bust in Chicago at the time, so took no active part. For ten months I sweated in poorly air-conditioned rooms over the airline prospectus, treading a delicate line between local sensibilities. There were constant, unstated tensions in the office between Malay managers, acutely conscious of status, and Chinese who had better technical skills but scant hope of winning top jobs. The organization was dominated by a culture of poisonous whispering. Outside the office, there were constant rumours about the corruption of politicians and big businessmen, but no one dared speak against the government of Dr Mahathir Mohamed, even among friends. The oppressive tropical climate (and, in the season of Ramadan, the Islamic rule of daytime fasting) seemed to make people unusually volatile and ill-tempered.

Attitudes to the British were deeply contradictory. On coming to power in 1981, Dr Mahathir had launched his 'Buy British Last' campaign, in response to Margaret Thatcher's decision to stop sub-sidising overseas students at British universities. Any hint of British superiority provoked stinging reactions. Yet the Malaysians wanted our know-how, and many senior Malaysians and Singaporeans remained at heart, deeply Anglophile: they had been educated at English universities; the richer ones kept flats in Bayswater and sons at English public schools. The chairman of MIMB, an extraordinarily brilliant retired surgeon and university administrator, was a classic example: he was capable of fierce anti-British outbursts, yet he treated me like an adopted son.

How was Barclays regarded in that part of the world? It was a great name in banking, and its top people were received with courtesy by senior officials of the region's central banks and finance ministries. But if you asked local businessmen what they thought Barclays did in the region, they would probably have said foreign exchange in Singapore, and traveller's cheques everywhere else. One of the tasks of the KL representative office was the pursuit of Malaysians who had failed to pay their Barclaycard accounts in England.

The 1970s strategy of opening offices to fly the flag in every capital and taking minority participations in local banking ventures like MIMB almost always created more headaches than successes. Barclays was seen to be there, but often it merely scratched the surface of the local business scene. In its minority investments there were often problems of lack of control and seldom advantages in terms of direct corporate relationships created. Barclays never localized itself in Asia to the same extent as Standard Chartered, Hong Kong Bank, Citicorp or Indosuez, the cleverest of the French banks. The best way to make that happen would have been to buy or merge with Standard Chartered, a deal which arose as a possibility first in the late 1970s, again in 1988, and yet again in 1998, but never happened.

Towards the end of my Malaysian stint, Charlie Morland came to visit. One purpose of his call was to ask me whether I would like to open a representative office for BMB in Tokyo. I accepted without a second thought; there was nothing interesting for me to return to in London, and Japan had held a deep fascination for me since my first visit in 1979. But the job offer came with a warning; if Malaysian office politics had required a crash course in diplomacy, Barclays group politics in Japan would need the skills of a UN negotiator. Not only was there a disputed demarcation line between BMB and Barclays Bank, but (preparations for the launch of BZW having advanced in my absence) there was now to be an adjacent office of our stockbroking partners, de Zoete & Bevan, run by its own representative, a noted eccentric of the Tokyo British community called Simon Grove.

When I arrived in Tokyo in September 1985, neither of these fronts turned out to be as hostile as I had expected, or at least not for a while. The bank there was best described as being in a state of comfortable indolence, without much appetite for an internal fight.

Barclays Bank had first opened a representative office in Japan in 1969, advancing to a full branch three or four years later. Unlike NatWest – which could claim to have taken part in the financing of the post-war reconstruction of the Japanese electricity industry – or Warburgs, Schroders and Kleinworts, there were no long-standing corporate links to be exploited. There were no Japanophiles in Barclays' senior echelons, and indeed there was an ingrained anti-Japanese prejudice among Barclays International managers of the Second World War age group which made it difficult to find anyone willing to be posted to Tokyo at all.

The exception was Colin Stevens, a cultivated bachelor who served as manager there from 1973 to 1980. Stevens himself says that 'nobody had a clue' what business could or should be done by Barclays in Japan: but in the tightly controlled Japanese system, foreign bank branches were allowed just enough scope for corporate lending to allow them to cover their operating costs. There was foreign exchange dealing, and the facilitation of trade finance for Japanese trading companies exporting to black Africa, and correspondent banking relations; there were current accounts for British expatriates. There was a handsome office on a prestigious ground floor corner site in the Mitsubishi building in Marunouchi, the city's most presitigious business district.

And most importantly, once again, there was the Barclays name, that hugely powerful calling card. When my parents visited Tokyo in 1975 with Anthony Tuke and his wife, Japanese companies sent so many bouquets of flowers to the Tukes' suite at the Okura Hotel that they had to be moved to a bigger one.

In Kyoto, the Barclays delegation was entertained by Nomura Securities to a fantastically elaborate banquet in a private villa, served by authentic geishas – photographs of which clearly show the agony experienced by middle-aged westerners when made to sit for three hours cross-legged on tatami mats eating raw fish with chopsticks.

Stevens did his best to capitalize on the value of the Barclays name to develop local relationships, and made many personal friends among the Japanese. But when he moved on to Hong Kong in 1980 he was replaced by the legendary Eric Staines, who played lots of golf with the British Airways station manager and acquired a weekend cabin on Lake Yamanaka. To the extent that there was any attempt at business development under the Staines regime, it was done through managers

detached from Japanese banks (Mr Yoshida from Mitsui, Mr Murai
from Dai-Ichi Kangyo, Mr Kurokawa from Sumitomo) each retaining
useful connections, and somewhat confusing loyalties, with his own
original grouping.

It would be fair to say that there were two ritual greetings for Barclays
executives meeting on foreign territory. The first was to exchange
neckties, each district or country having its own design combining the
spread eagle with some local insignia.[8] The second involved the host
manager warning the visitor, politely or bluntly, not to tread on his
patch. Staines did indeed present me with a Barclays Japan tie
(emblazoned with *tori*, or temple gateways) but since he was not
personally very interested in doing business with Japanese companies,
he barely bothered with the second part of the ceremony. The truth
was that neither he nor I could think of any useful business that I might
find to do with Japanese companies. BMB had no track record in the
eurobond market or in international mergers and acquisitions. We
might be able to sell some bonds (Barclays' own issues of perpetual
floating rate notes, for example, of which we did sell large quantities)
to Japanese banks. Beyond that, just like a decade earlier, nobody had
a clue.

What was of more pressing concern, if not to Staines himself (whose
chief worry was that I might spend less than his recommended figure
on furnishing my rented flat) then to Alastair Robinson, his fiercely
impatient boss in London, was to do with reporting lines. As we have
seen, in the battle between 'product' and geographical territories,
geography had always won out in Barclays. The top man in any given
territory, whether he be senior local director in Oxford or managing
director in Ghana, was lord of all he surveyed. The idea that I should
be operating in Japan but not reporting to the Tokyo branch manager
(in fact I reported to Christopher Haviland in London) was deeply
offensive to traditional thinking.

As to relations with de Zoete & Bevan, there were no ground rules
at all, other than an instruction from Haviland and Camoys that I was
to do my best to get on with Simon Grove. Grove had been a naval

---

[8] I still own a modest collection of Barclays ties, though it seems unlikely that I shall ever
wear any of them again. Within the bank, these ties had social as well as geographical
significance: the upper stratum of the domestic bank – hidebound by the sartorial rules of
their class – would no more wear a tie with a badge on it than they would wear brown shoes
with a dark suit. Old DCO men, on the other hand, loved the tie ritual. When I lunched
with Julian Wathen at his club in the course of researching this book, he wore, in my honour
as it were, the tie of the long defunct York District, combining white rose and spread eagle.
'No one ever wears bank ties any more,' he lamented.

attaché in the British Embassy (engaged in exotic cloak-and-dagger work, according to rumour) and had then become the local representative of Grieveson Grant, a stock exchange firm for whom he had built a useful business selling gilt-edged stock to Japanese institutions. Grieveson had been bought by Kleinwort Benson, whose representative in Japan was the young but extremely grand 3rd Viscount Trenchard. The two had immediately gone to war with each other, and Grove had been pushed out; his Grieveson partners had then recommended him to de Zoete & Bevan.

The de Zoete partners, meanwhile, had no Japanese presence, but were keen to spend some of Barclays' money to acquire one. Grove was swiftly recruited, though it was difficult afterwards to find any de Zoete partner who admitted to having proposed him. Grove certainly made a striking first impression – a bibulous, bowler-hatted, bewhiskered Pickwickian figure, then in his mid-fifties, he was a scholar of arcane aspects of Japanese culture (especially concerning sex), a fluent Japanese speaker and a fascinating conversationalist. But as the representative of a thrusting new global investment bank, he was an extraordinary choice. Camoys was so taken aback when presented with Grove as de Zoete's chosen candidate that he ordered a psychological profile on him. The psychologist's report declared Grove to be one of the sanest specimens he had ever examined.

For all his oddities (of which he was proud) I liked Grove. He had rented a pair of small office suites, one for him and one for me, in the basement of a building conveniently located next door to the Ministry of Finance, where I was to spend much of the following two years negotiating BZW's operating licence. He had also recruited an unusual collection of staff, including a brilliant girl who was a Tokyo University law graduate (the ultimate Japanese academic achievement); a beautiful but sad receptionist whose previous job had been in the wardrobe department of Tokyo Disneyland; a charming chauffeur called Eguchi who had been a trainee fighter pilot at the end of the war; and a Japanese-speaking Irish student rugby player who turned out to be a brilliant gilts salesman.

All this made for a stimulating winter of 1985, but Grove's days were clearly numbered. He had upset one of the senior de Zoete partners by including in his Tokyo stockmarket research bulletin an item about Japanese women wearing no underwear under their kimonos. But worse, the new head of international equity business in London was Nicholas Sibley, former managing director of Jardine Fleming in Hong Kong, a noted wit and bon viveur, a collector of vintage Rolls-Royces

and an A-list celebrity of the Asian financial community. Sibley and
Grove knew each other of old, and were not well matched. By March
1986, Grove was out – though he was soon in work again, happily
running an office for Westdeutsche Landesbank with, as he boasted, 'a
five-year contract and a Deutschemark pension'.

His replacement was Michael Connors, a protégé of Sibley's from
Jardine Fleming, also a high-level Japanese scholar and a leading investment research analyst in the electronics sector. Connors was blunt,
down-to-earth, very sure of his own views, fun to work with and
completely unbankerlike – in another life he might have been a poly-
technic lecturer; if he was twenty years younger he would have been
an e-commerce entrepreneur. Most importantly, he had the full confidence of Sibley, which meant that he had an open cheque-book to
recruit and to build a full-sized securities business just as fast as we
could persuade the Ministry to let us operate one. That was what
we set out to do, some distance behind most of our major British
competitors.

We soon found that we had not only taken on the combined forces
of the international securities industry and the Japanese Ministry of
Finance, but that we were engaged in a guerrilla war with Barclays
Bank as well. Eric Staines had been winkled out by Robinson,[9] and
replaced by Michael Tomalin, who was as aggressive and ambitious as
Staines was laid back, and who (having once worked for Rothschilds,
and having recently run Barclays' merchant banking offshoot in New
Zealand) sincerely believed himself to be an investment banker. When
he arrived in Tokyo to find Connors and me building an investment
bank that did not report to him, all hell broke loose. The tussle that
ensued between the two wings of Barclays – in one of the world's most
important and expensive financial centres, in which neither side of
Barclays had a viable business foothold – was to develop into one of
the great farces of Barclays' history.

When Big Bang arrived on 27 October, we were still in our crowded
basement and not yet licensed to conduct any business. The only thing
we could do to mark the change was replace the rather handsome
spread eagle door-handles (which I still have) with new ones carrying
the BZW logo, said by many people to look like a Czechoslovakian
motorcycle badge. But we did arrange for Nick Sibley to shout 'Bang!'

---

[9] Staines seemed to enjoy some protection from the old Barclays International powers-that-
be, and was detached by the bank to run a Pestalozzi Children's Village charity in the south
of England until his retirement: he died playing golf.

down a loudspeaker phone from the new BZW headquarters, Ebbgate House, as the London market opened for the first time on the new basis of 'dual capacity', with firms like ours making markets and broking stocks at the same time. Sibley − always a relaxed performer − missed his cue, so the moment was rather a damp squib. But it would have been as nothing anyway, compared to the internal explosions and external crashes that were soon to come.

8

THE BIRTH OF BZW

1983–1991: Camoys' brainchild – Buying de Zoetes and Wedds –
The culture clash – Sir Martin Jacomb arrives – What autonomy
meant – Buxton steps in – Onwards and upwards – Sir Peter
Middleton takes over

There is a particularly pleasing image associated with the moment of
conception of BZW, and it is well described in Andrew Lorenz's
official history *BZW: The First Ten Years*, on which I shall draw
extensively for detail in this chapter. The image is of Tom Camoys
reading the Financial Times in his favourite bar in San Antonio, Ibiza,
the peer's regular summer holiday bolt hole. San Antonio is now
famous for attracting British holiday-makers rather younger and coarser
than Camoys, but anyone who knows him well would bet good money
on him outlasting them in a night out on the town. He still visits the
same bar every summer.

What he read on that day in the summer of 1983 was that Cecil
Parkinson, the Secretary of State for Trade and Industry, had reached
an agreement with Nicholas Goodison, the chairman of the London
Stock Exchange, under which exchange members would do away with
the demarcation lines between brokers (who bought and sold stock on
behalf of clients) and jobbers (who made markets by buying from and
selling to brokers) and the barriers to entry which protected both
groups. They would also abolish fixed commissions. In return, the
Government would drop a case which it had launched against the
Exchange in the Restrictive Practices Court. These manoeuvres
reflected two underlying streams of thought: the Government and the
Office of Fair Trading saw the Stock Exchange as a bastion of protected
interests, inimical to free trade, and the Bank of England was increasingly concerned that the City would lose business to New York, Tokyo

or Frankfurt unless its under-capitalized, old-fashioned securities firms were strengthened and reformed. Camoys himself had for a long time felt that the way for BMB to break out of its niche might be through an alliance with a powerful broking firm – some years earlier he had tried to open discussions with Cazenove & Co. on the subject but met a blank response. Now at last the possibilities were opening up.

From the bar, Camoys called Dennis Ford, a director of BMB in London. Ford had previously run Barclays Bank in California, where things had gone badly wrong on the lending front. But he was a brilliant conceptualizer and just the man to start putting the flesh on the bones of Camoys' idea, which was to buy both a broker and a jobber and to build an integrated investment bank on the Wall Street model. Ford set to work on a strategy paper. A few days later Camoys returned to London and went straight to see Tim Bevan.

Despite his reputation for caution, Bevan was receptive to the idea. Like Camoys, he had long been interested in the idea of a Barclays presence in the Stock Exchange. It was, after all, part of his heritage. Bevan's grandfather, father and brother had all been partners of Pember & Boyle, a broker specializing in gilts business which was in due course bought and swallowed by Morgan Grenfell. Francis Augustus Bevan's cousin David had founded his own firm, later called D. A. Bevan Simpson, which had become part of de Zoete & Bevan.[1] A Barclay cousin, Anthony, had been the long-serving senior partner of another well-known firm, Shepperds & Chase. In his time as a Lombard Street local director in the 1960s, Bevan had dealt every day with the funding needs of stockbroking firms. This was natural territory for him. He gave Camoys the go-ahead, making it clear that if a deal was to be done, it should be done in the Barclays style, on a grand and first-class scale.

The first approach was to the grandest name of all, Cazenove, with which Barclays had two very strong connections: the former senior

---

[1] Sir Timothy may have been somewhat less encouraged by the example of his great-uncle Gerard Lee Bevan, son of Francis Augustus, a stockbroker with Ellis & Co. and an associate of the notorious City rogue Clarence Hatry. Gerard was described as 'an elegant, plausible man who traded on his family connections and whose hereditary privileges left him arrogant, vain and irresponsible'. In 1921, he used the City Equitable Fire Insurance Co. as a vehicle for some highly speculative investments; it went bankrupt, and Ellis & Co. was hammered with £2 million of liabilities. Gerard absconded abroad, was arrested in Vienna and eventually convicted at the Old Bailey on sixteen counts, serving several years in jail. 'He deliberately, when past middle age, did everything he could to forfeit his position and to ruin the fortunes of himself, his partners, his friends and his clients, and what for?' wrote a City commentator of the day. 'I ask, "What was his kink?" The only answer which comes to me is: "Vanity – pure vanity".'

partner, Johnnie Henderson[2] had been a non-executive director of
Barclays since 1978 and was chairman of Barclays' trust company
subsidiary; the partner in charge of Cazenove's overseas business,
Stephen Carden, was the brother of Richard Carden, a Special List
man who had been head of Barclays in North America and was later
head of corporate banking. But the Cazenove partners, uniquely among
the leading stock exchange firms, had absolutely no interest in abandoning a *status quo* which gave them a very powerful position in the
corporate and institutional end of the market and as much personal
wealth as (being already wealthy men) they felt they needed.

But most other partnerships had weighed the opportunity otherwise,
and were up for sale. Favourites on most buyers' list included Rowe &
Pitman, which was snapped up by S. G. Warburg, and Hoare Govett,
which went to the American bank Security Pacific. Camoys' team
homed in on de Zoete & Bevan, which ranked at the lower end of the
top bracket of London firms in turnover and research ratings, but
reckoned itself the most profitable in terms of return per employee.
Founded by a Dutch émigré in 1798, the firm had a good corporate
client list, including GEC, British American Tobacco and the mining
group RTZ, and a strong position in the gilts market. In the frenzied
round of flirtations of late 1983, de Zoetes already had two other
suitors, Kleinwort Benson and Bank of America, but when Tim Bevan
put in a first call to Jim Titcomb, the senior of de Zoetes' three
managing partners, he found him amenable to the idea of a deal with
Barclays.

The next task was to secure a jobber to complete the tripartite
structure. The market leader, Akroyd & Smithers, had again gone to
Warburg. The second-ranked player was Wedd Durlacher Mordaunt,
a firm formed from the merger of three late-Victorian jobbing partnerships: Durlacher & Co., which originally specialized in railway
stocks, breweries, distilleries and rubber estates; Wedd Jefferson which
dealt in fixed interest securities; and Bone Oldham (in which the
Mordaunt family were partners) dealing in breweries, food companies,
dairies and hotels.

Wedds, advised by John Craven's corporate finance boutique
Phoenix Securities, was looking for a broker to team up with, and de
Zoetes was looking for a jobber. They were not ideally matched –
Wedds had a well-developed international business, while de Zoete's

---

[2] Henderson was ADC to Field Marshal Montgomery during the Second World War, Lord
Lieutenant of Berkshire and a pillar of the racing establishment.

turnover was 95 per cent domestic – but, as other alliances swiftly formed around them, a process of elimination brought them together and made them obvious targets for Barclays. 'There was only one choice in jobbing if Barclays was going to be serious,' John Varley told Andrew Lorenz. 'Wedds wanted us to go for de Zoetes, and de Zoetes was a damned good business, well run, consistently profitable. The decision seemed to make itself.' To the brokers and jobbers Barclays had the advantage of being British, of having a very strong capital base, and of being prepared – in the traditional Barclays way – to offer a high degree of management autonomy.

But not everyone in Wedds saw it that way. Some of the senior men in the jobbing firm favoured an alliance with the directors of Kleinwort Benson (led, at this stage, by Martin Jacomb, before he was head-hunted to become chairman of BZW) who were more their kind of people than the stuffy Barclays clearing bankers, and they were offering publicly quoted shares in Kleinworts as consideration for the take-over, rather than untradeable Barclays loan stock. De Zoetes were less keen on the Kleinworts alternative, partly because they sensed that a first-class merchant bank like Kleinworts would dominate the merger, whereas they themselves would have the upper hand in relation to the second-division Barclays Merchant Bank.

With these factors in the background, Andrew Buxton conducted the negotiations personally. He secured de Zoete & Bevan for around £42 million, though his colleagues were surprised to discover that he had thrown into the bargain a seat on Barclays' main board. It was initially assumed that this would go to the senior of the three de Zoete managing partners, Jim Titcomb, but in the end it went to the gilts specialist Ken Sinclair; it was a promise that was rather grudgingly kept, and not until 1988. The deal consisted of a modest slice of cash up front and a package of BZW 'Founders Shares' and Barclays loan stock. How these elements were distributed among the de Zoete partnership (which was expanded at a late stage to include a large number of younger members of the firm) remained a closely guarded secret, but the seniors were said to have been relatively generous to the juniors, allowing them a higher proportion of the equity interest as an incentive to stay. There were also individual 'golden handcuff' contracts, tying valuable people in for up to five years. The level of pay-out for the most senior people was around £2 million, as was indicated by Ken Sinclair's holdings, which as a director he had to declare in Barclays' annual report: in 1988 (in addition to the cash portion received when the deal was done) he had £1,150,000 of Barclays loan stock and

604,871 £1 Founders Shares in BZW Holdings. Partners in the second layer made around £1 million each.

Wedds was a more difficult proposition for Buxton, because of its internal disagreements. Buxton did not want to pay more than £50 million, but the asking price was £100 million. It was an extremely difficult business to value – the past, under a highly restrictive and fragmented Stock Exchange regime, was a very poor guide to the future – so it came down to hard bargaining. Ken Sinclair, whose style always tended to be both blunt and urgent, called on Buxton unannounced one morning to tell him that he would just have to pay up to get the Wedds deal. According to legend, however, the Wedds partners had got together by then and agreed (though not unanimously) that Barclays was the better bet. They were prepared to settle somewhere in the middle, in the £70 million region. But when Buxton came to see them – on Valentine's Day 1984 – he put £100 million on the table. The Wedds men practically bit his hand off. On 12 March the deal was announced. Barclays would take stakes of 29.9 per cent in both firms immediately, with the intention of increasing its stakes as fast as the Big Bang timetable allowed. Camoys was now chief executive designate of what was about to be Barclays de Zoete Wedd.[3]

It was at this stage that the relative strengths of the three parties in political infighting – and the fundamental differences of character between bankers, brokers and traders – began to become apparent. From the first 'getting to know you' social events, at which representatives of the three sides wore different coloured buttonhole flowers to identify themselves, the contrasts were potentially troublesome. It was not easy even to find a social format that suited all three: bankers liked opera, brokers liked cricket and golf; jobbers liked nightclubs. A joint outing to the ballet, early in the courtship, was voted a disaster by all sides. 'Until tonight,' one Wedds partner confided to his Barclays neighbour, 'I thought ballet was a make of shoes.'

It was the brokers and bankers who were least likely to get on. Before 1984 I hardly ever met a stockbroker: though broking and investment research rapidly became fashionable career choices of the 1980s, they

---

[3] It took a further nine months to decide on the name and logo, neither de Zoetes nor Wedds being happy to appear at the end, to lose their names altogether or to appear under a Barclays spread eagle. The only artefact ever produced which did carry the eagle in conjunction with the names Barclays, de Zoete and Wedd was an *imari*-ware ashtray commissioned by Simon Grove and me as a gift for guests at the opening party of the Tokyo representative offices in October 1985. Mine is perhaps the only one in the world still on display; the inscription has faded, but it has still outlasted the firm. The ashtray's value as a collectors' item is probably small.

were lines of work which graduates of my mid-1970s generation had seemed to drift into only as an under-achiever's alternative to TEFL, or teaching English as a foreign language.[4] Bankers thought of brokers as unreliable, smooth-talking lightweights; brokers thought of bankers as stuffed-shirt dullards, more interested in the trappings of office than in maximizing the bottom line. It was a head-on culture clash, and on the whole it was the brokers who had the best of the encounter.

The de Zoete leaders were after all, in different ways, formidable people. Jim Titcomb was a devout Christian, a respected corporate financier and a man who did not lack for certainty in his own opinions; he made it clear from an early stage that he had no intention of being told what to do by Camoys (whom he was once heard referring to as 'that fat little man') and retired once the take-over was complete. Rex Cooper, who became BZW's first deputy chief executive, was an elegant figure (known as Sexy Rexy to his younger staff) with a tendency to waffle, but a skill for handling people and an unshakeable belief in the superiority of his profession. Ken Sinclair, though short on charm, was an acknowledged heavyweight of the gilts market and an effective manager, fiercely protective of his own subordinates. Behind them came a phalanx of cocksure partners, good at their business but determined not to be moulded into a corporate BZW ethos and largely blind to the idea of inter-departmental co-operation within a diversified financial conglomerate.

Within de Zoetes itself there seemed to be a number of long-running personal feuds and a good deal of day-to-day petulance, but the brokers could unite at least in their contempt for BMB, whose corporate client list looked so inadequate beside their own. There was contempt also for the size of BMB directors' offices in Gracechurch Street, which were certainly spacious, and for their walnut-veneered desks, which were undeniably enormous – the de Zoetes senior partners shared one small room, which they used only for meetings with visitors. At one stage during the 'disclosure' process, in which each party was entitled to ask the others for any details and explanations it thought necessary,

[4] Tommy Fellowes, a money-broker and the brother of Sir Robert, who was the Queen's private secretary and is now vice-chairman of Barclays Private Bank, told me the following story. On a business trip to Japan, he was taken sightseeing to the shrine of Nikko on Lake Chusenji and was shown a rocky promontory high above the lake. 'This is very sacred place,' his Japanese host explained. 'Very popular suicide spot for students who fail examinations. What do your British students do when they fail examinations?' 'Aha,' Fellowes searched for a suitable answer. 'Well, I suppose most of them become stockbrokers.'

a memo arrived at Barclays from de Zoetes asking whether it was true that BMB was a dumping ground for useless and difficult relations of the founding families and difficult offspring of other Barclays employees. Could a list be provided of such black sheep? The enquiry was passed to John Varley for an answer. His reply had two names on it, his own and mine.

'I suppose you could say de Zoetes had a certain intellectual arrogance,' said John Cousins, who had been brought in to the partnership to develop its international activities. 'We thought we were clever, and I think we *were* clever. We thought of ourselves as the most profitable of the big broking firms, meaner and tighter in the way we ran things. We thought BMB was woefully inferior.'

The Wedds partners were less difficult to assimilate: since bankers and jobbers are both fundamentally concerned with risk, there was the beginning of a meeting of minds. But still the jobbers found the bankers ponderous, bureaucratic, unattuned to markets. 'We're trying to get used to you bankers and all your memos,' Nick Durlacher (who became head of BZW's futures trading activities) said to me the first time I met him. He pronounced the last word 'mee-moes', as though he had never come across it before.

The senior Wedds men were old-style City gents – I last saw one of them, Dickie Durlacher, on the day after the October 1987 crash, pottering from office to office collecting orders for bin-end bargains in vintage port. They were never as assertive as de Zoetes in the preparatory phase of BZW, and they were knocked off-course in July 1985 by the defection to Kleinworts of eight of their key men, led by Charlie Hue Williams and Willie Mellen, who were members of Wedds' management committee, and Barry Bennett, a top trader – a departure which left behind, as the clear rising star of the next Wedds generation and (at £2.7 million) the largest individual recipient of the firm's sale proceeds, Jonathan Davie, who will play a crucial part in the later part of this story (see Chapter 13). At the same time trading conditions were becoming increasingly difficult for market-makers, while de Zoetes appeared to be doing well on rapidly increasing turnover. Some de Zoetes partners raised the possibility of dropping Wedds altogether at this stage, but Camoys and Buxton were determined to stick with the deal. There was however an adjustment in the purchase prices of both firms, with some of Wedds' money being given to the smarter operators of de Zoetes instead. The final price for Wedds was closer to £80 million, and the final pre-Big Bang investment by Barclays in BZW (including the value of BMB and Barclays Investment

Management, and the capital costs of furbishing BZW's first home, Ebbgate House) was around £250 million.

Ebbgate House was as symbolic of the early uncertainties and tensions of BZW as 54 Lombard Street was of the solidity and self-confidence of Barclays Bank a generation earlier. Though its best offices and meeting rooms had a fine view of the river, it was a building of no architectural merit whatever, a late-1970s speculative development which happened to have a central atrium big enough for BZW's equities trading floor. It had inadequate lifts, peculiarly ugly public areas and no interesting artwork, ancient or modern. It rapidly became very overcrowded. The rear part of the building was partly occupied by a grim multi-storey car park, in which thieves amused themselves all day long among a fleet of expensive company cars.

By the time the merger terms and building plans had been finalized in mid-1985, another important decision had been made: the name of BZW's first chairman. Camoys himself had been an early candidate, but the de Zoetes people would not have him. Bevan had initially favoured Kit McMahon, the deputy governor of the Bank of England, but McMahon (who went on to have a torrid time as chairman of Midland Bank instead) turned him down. John Craven of Phoenix Securities, formerly of Warburgs and later of Morgan Grenfell, was considered. But Camoys's own candidate – and an extraordinarily good choice for the job – was Martin Jacomb, then a vice-chairman of Kleinwort Benson.

Once referred to as 'the thinking man's City grandee', the Etonian ex-barrister Jacomb was already a big name in the City. He was a hugely persuasive performer: his early career in Chancery work[5] had taught him to extemporize on complex subjects with ease and elegance. Elaborate sentences delivered in slow, resonant tones combined with piercing blue eyes and a deceptively frail physique to create a mesmeric effect – especially on foreign bankers, who regarded him as something of a guru. Though he was closely associated with the reforms and innovations of the 1980s, his gravitas personified older City values. He disliked confrontation, but his authority, emolliently exercised, was to override many internal BZW conflicts.

Jacomb had been a vice-chairman of Kleinworts, and a leader of its corporate finance team, since 1976. In the early 1980s he moved to

---

[5] As a barrister, Jacomb had specialized in tax cases, but he also defended John Aspinall, the zoo-keeper, against an injunction brought by a neighbour to stop him keeping tigers and bears. On another occasion, he appeared for the widow of Lloyd George's chauffeur, left penniless by her husband's will.

become head of the firm's investment management division where, by his own account, he was not a great success: this counted against him in the race for the chairmanship of Kleinworts, for which he was passed over in 1983. But his name came to the fore in the following year as the leader of the Kleinwort team which advised the government on the privatization of British Telecom. At £3.9 billion, the first BT share sale was by far the largest ever attempted in London: during one meeting with the Chancellor, Nigel Lawson, Jacomb was the only City figure present who thought it could be done. But the issue was a success and Jacomb was credited with many of the original ideas which made it work. He had a rare ability to articulate common ground between ministers, civil servants, bankers, brokers, lawyers and BT executives, all working under pressure in unexplored territory.

Meanwhile, as chairman of a committee of 'wise men' advising the Governor of the Bank of England, and deputy chairman of the Council for the Securities Industry, he helped to draft the rules of the post-Big Bang City, favouring regulation which was efficient without being excessively onerous. (He achieved minor celebrity in due course when he remarked that insider trading was 'a victimless crime'.) He was an obvious candidate to be the first full-time chairman of the Securities & Investment Board, the watchdog body established in 1985, but he declined the invitation, preferring to take up the challenge of BZW.

Perhaps the most significant feature of Jacomb's appointment was that he was also, at his own insistence, to be a deputy chairman of Barclays Bank — the first outsider to come into the bank at that level since Sir Herbert Hambling Bt, whose own bank, the London Provincial & South Western, had been acquired by Barclays in 1918. What was important about this was that Camoys, as BZW chief executive, reported through Jacomb to Bevan, and not to the chief general manager of the group, Peter Leslie, thus establishing for better or worse the idea of BZW as an 'autonomously managed' division of the bank. It was probably the only formula that the collective ego of BZW would have accepted, but it was to be the cause of endless trouble and friction in the years to come.[6]

An early example of BZW's idea of autonomy came in January 1987, when the firm's banking analyst, Terry Smith (who had once worked in Barclays' own planning department and whose salary leap in

---

[6] A classic example of BZW's resistance to integration with Barclays was the investment bank's refusal to accept the 'All-In-One' computer system, the group's first attempt at a worldwide e-mail intranet. This was scorned by BZW as being technically inadequate, but the real reason was a simple fear of Big Brother-like surveillance.

joining BZW was already a cause of bitterness with his ex-colleagues), produced a 'Sell' note on Barclays itself, making biting criticisms of its senior management. 'There is something wrong at Barclays,' it began. Tim Bevan had originally assumed that BZW would not make markets in, or comment on, Barclays shares at all; he certainly had not expected personal abuse from his expensive new subsidiary.

'I imagine you're going to fire him,' he said to Jacomb when they met for a Barclays board meeting that day. On the contrary, Jacomb responded, 'This is the best demonstration of the independence of our analysts which we could possibly find. It's a great opportunity.' Bevan never quite accepted that concept ('If you are a family and one of the junior members criticizes you in public, you feel rather bad about it,' he said later) and neither did many other people in Barclays. The ten-year civil war between Barclays and BZW had commenced in earnest.

And it was far from sweetness and light within BZW itself, even though trading conditions in the first half of 1987 were very favourable, with volumes in equities trading running at three or four times pre-Big Bang levels and BZW gaining a reputation as not only the biggest market-maker in numbers of stocks but also the most efficient in settlements. Camoys was still battling every inch of the way to create a recognizable management structure in which people did what they were told, reported what they were doing in an orderly way, and shared knowledge which ought usefully to be shared without breaching the disciplines of client confidentiality (known as 'Chinese walls'). No one made it easy for him, and his temper became shorter as time went on. 'It was bloody hard and very, very stressful,' he said. In June 1987, still only forty-seven, he suffered a stroke, followed by an enforced period of rest and recuperation.

That would have left Rex Cooper of de Zoetes in charge of BZW, a situation which Barclays (now under John Quinton, Bevan having stepped down in May) was not quite ready to stomach. The solution was to send Andrew Buxton, the bank's vice-chairman and deputy managing director, over from Lombard Street to Ebbgate House as acting (and part-time) chief executive. Since Buxton was the as-yet-untarnished heir apparent to the Barclays chairmanship, the move flattered BZW by emphasizing its importance in the group. At the same time, it gave Buxton the opportunity to observe his new creature at closer quarters. Since he had bought their firms on such favourable terms to them, and since he was a good deal less demanding and more even-tempered than Camoys, he was welcomed by the de Zoetes and Wedds people, and his presence was doubly reassuring in the aftermath

of the October 1987 crash (see Chapter 10). 'We like Andrew,' Rex
Cooper said to me during a visit to Hong Kong, 'He's a very sensible
chap. He takes decisions when we need them. He doesn't shout at us
like Tom.'

As to what Buxton actually did while he was at Ebbgate House,
Andrew Lorenz's account provides some useful pointers:

> He went to considerable lengths to instil the sense of financial discipline
> that he felt was lacking in the firm: he introduced systems to monitor
> expense accounts and overseas travel, and even looked at some expense
> accounts personally. Confronted by serried ranks of BMWs and Merc-
> edes, Buxton made a point of cycling to Ebbgate House ... He would
> regularly walk the trading floor, where at night he would tell people to
> go home and not to work themselves into the ground.

The passage reveals several truths about Buxton: that he is well-
meaning, parsimonious, inclined to focus on small management details
rather than the big picture, and not entirely comfortable in the role of
City grandee (I spotted him once cycling to work along the Embankment in a T-shirt). Lurking within the sentence about expenses there
is perhaps a reference to Buxton's best-known memorandum during
his stay at BZW, which said that he had observed from his window a
large stream of black taxis drawing up every day to take people to lunch
in the West End, and that he expected directors to organize a taxi-
sharing scheme. When visiting Ebbgate House long after he had
ceased to be acting BZW chief executive, Buxton would occasionally
challenge waiting taxi-drivers and tell them to go away.

Buxton's other contribution was to try to persuade Camoys, with
whom he had never been on close terms and whom he may have seen
as a rival for the chairmanship, to retire. But – so it was rumoured –
the bank was not prepared to pay enough to make it worth Camoys'
while to go. He insisted on returning to become deputy chairman of
BZW with a roving ambassadorial brief, and it was a job which suited
him well. He was a less articulate spokesman for the firm and the City
than Martin Jacomb, but he had a quietly authoritative presence which,
together with his habit of constantly chewing nicotine gum to stop
himself smoking, made a big impression on foreign officials and tycoons,
particularly Asians. His title could open almost any door. On his
overseas trips he also stirred, on every appropriate occasion, the battle
between BZW and the bank: 'I really had to bash him,' he muttered
to me, after a short courtesy visit to the office of Michael Tomalin at
Barclays in Tokyo.

Camoys's tenuous hold on power is symbolically illustrated in the bank's 1987 annual report, in which a picture of the (still recuperating) peer is rather obviously pasted in at the back of the senior management team photograph, like a Russian politician who has been mysteriously absent for the May Day parade. The process had by then begun of searching for his permanent replacement as BZW chief executive, with no chance either of the strong men of BZW agreeing on a promotion from within their own group or accepting the parachuting in of anyone else from Barclays. Early in 1988, to general applause from the financial media, the job was awarded to David Band, a Scotsman who had been European head of J. P. Morgan and who seemed to personify everything that Barclays hoped BZW might become. He was to be, in a rather idiosyncratic way, the kingpin of BZW for the next seven years.

Meanwhile, the expansion of BZW continued, both before and after the 1987 crash, at an unstoppable pace. A high-powered team recruited from Kidder Peabody established a US treasuries trading operation in New York, with $100 million of capital. In London, a Capital Markets division had been created under a humourless Californian brought in from Bank of America, Ken Green, who was unkindly described by one of his staff as 'the kind of officer who got shot by his own troops in Vietnam'. Green bought in a gang of eurobond traders from Samuel Montagu and a startlingly aggressive swaps team from Lehman Brothers, one of whom, when I attempted to enquire about his plans to do business in Tokyo, told me (with some prescience, perhaps) that my career in BZW was 'dogshit'.

All of this in due course came (together with the gilts and other bonds businesses) under the control of Ken Sinclair, who stood no nonsense from anyone. When he eventually fired one of the most cantankerous traders, he phoned a colleague first: 'I'm about to get rid of that bastard X and I've got a little list here,' he growled in his Essex tones. 'It starts with a figure of how much I'm prepared to pay him to go. Then it says how much I'm going to knock off that figure every time he says "fuck" during the interview.'

On the corporate finance side, BZW ranked twenty-third in the City league table for 1986, which was about as low as could be. Its resources consisted of the old BMB team, which had a modest record with small-to medium-sized companies but no blue-chip clients at all except Barclays itself, and a clever privatization team which notched up some successes (British Steel, National Bus, Scottish Electricity) but could never beat Warburgs or Kleinworts to the biggest mandates. The transatlantic efforts of Charles Ryder's team ('that Gucci-shoed lot', as one de Zoetes partner dismissively put it) had come to a halt, and most of them had left the firm. Elsewhere in the building was de Zoete & Bevan's corporate team, still operating under its own name and working with other merchant banks to provide the broking skills required for major take-overs and share issues. The refusal of de Zoetes to contemplate any form of integration in corporate finance was at first taken as a manifestation of their general refusal to behave as though they had actually been bought by Barclays. But it gradually became clear that they were right, because they had a successful, distinct business, and their blue-chip broking clients were not in the least interested in switching away from traditional merchant banking advisers to take up the offer of an 'integrated' service from BZW. So de Zoete & Bevan remained, in that respect, de Zoete & Bevan throughout its time under Barclays' ownership, and is still identifiable within CSFB.

Everything BZW tried to do to beef up its merchant banking corporate finance side seemed to go wrong. The highest-profile client at the time was the entrepreneur John Gunn, but his British & Commonwealth conglomerate came to grief after the 1987 crash and its £400 million take-over of the Atlantic Computer leasing group resulted in complex litigation, and losses to Barclays, which dragged on for a decade. Meanwhile, there was an attempt in 1987 to buy the entire corporate finance department of Hill Samuel; that proved impossible, but a team of a dozen executives was poached, bringing with them a handful of medium-sized clients. A new star was recruited in Nick Wells from County Bank, but he had to resign within a year to fight a court case (in which he eventually cleared his name) connected with the notorious Blue Arrow rights issue, on which County had advised.[7]

Next, Martin Jacomb launched a raid on his old firm, Kleinwort Benson. In October 1989, Graham Pimlott, an up-and-coming mergers and acquisitions specialist and a former secretary of the Take-over Panel, was persuaded to jump ship. He in turn persuaded the ex-DTI official (and former head of Norman Tebbit's private office there) Callum McCarthy to come with him. Half a dozen other Kleinwort people were lined up to follow them, until Kleinworts appealed to the Bank of England and injunctions began to fly. Two other Kleinwort directors did move across a year later, but the coup was aborted and in

---

[7] NatWest's merchant banking subsidiary was, up to this point, much more successful in corporate finance work than BZW. But the Blue Arrow scandal virtually destroyed its reputation and did immense damage to NatWest itself, provoking several senior resignations. It was partly due to Martin Jacomb's insistence on very high standards of 'compliance' and ethics that BZW steered clear of such scandals.

the meantime Barclays had turned its attention instead to a possible bid for the whole of Morgan Grenfell. That would have brought in a huge corporate finance business led by some very powerful personalities, and would have left Pimlott in an awkward position before he had even taken up his job at BZW. No wonder he was edgy and defensive from the start.

I shall reveal in Chapter 10 what happened to me when I returned from Hong Kong at the beginning of 1990 to work for Pimlott as the co-ordinator of the division's international activities. These consisted of an entirely unplanned selection of small teams around the world, mostly created as adjuncts to BZW's broking businesses and following strategies all of their own, sometimes in co-operation with the local Barclays Bank and sometimes in outright competition with it. In New York, for example, a laconic ex-Morgan Stanley partner called Dan Morris, hired by David Band, had built up an M & A team over which we seemed to have no influence at all. 'At this early stage in the promulgation of our divisional strategy,' said a rather feeble planning document drafted by me in July 1990, 'it would be fair to say that [what we want to do] is not necessarily accepted by the M & A group in New York or by [Barclays Bank there]. We are not yet in a position to say with confidence that the New York team is focusing on an optimum strategy . . . We are addressing these weaknesses, together with the New York management . . .'

One way in which we addressed the weakness – representing an apotheosis of the BZW spirit of cleverly articulated non-cooperation – was to establish an entirely separate corporate finance department above a shopping mall in Short Hills, New Jersey, to house a team of information technology specialists hired from the nearby headquarters of AT&T. They were supposed to do global M & A work in the IT sector, reporting directly to Callum McCarthy in London. The man in charge was a portly Hungarian called Gross who, on the day I visited him, wore a lumberjack shirt to work, drank beer from cans at his desk and entertained me to a very long lunch in a Mexican restaurant. The venture lasted about eighteen months before it was quietly closed down.

My 1990 planning document projected losses in the early stages but, by very inventive means, a profit of £20 million for the division by 1993. Sure enough, according to Andrew Lorenz, 'corporate finance hit the £20 million mark in the fourth year of the Pimlott regime'. But the truth is that BZW never made it into the big time in corporate finance, in the sense that it never acquired a list of first-class clients providing repeat business, and rarely made a splash in mega-merger advisory work. What it did eventually acquire (for which the credit mostly belongs to Amir Eilon, whom Pimlott hired from Morgan Stanley was an ability to structure very complex financing deals, using BZW's power in securities distribution and the strength of Barclays Bank's balance sheet. Of the original Camoys conception, that much at least was achieved.

On the equities side of the house, led initially by Howard Coates, a senior research analyst from de Zoetes, and Nick Sibley from Flemings, the BZW empire expanded at a breathless pace throughout the late 1980s. Hong Kong, Tokyo and New York were already on the map, and a Barclays stockbroking operation was taken over in Amsterdam. A stake was acquired in a highly professional Australian broking firm, Meares & Philips, establishing the principle, particularly favoured by Sibley, that the way forward was to find like-minded businesses, buy into them, and let them get on with what they were doing without undue interference from London. 'They know the sort of thing,' was a Sibley catch phrase. More businesses were bought or developed according to this principle in Madrid, Singapore, Toronto, Frankfurt and Paris – though the latter, the partnership of Puget-Mahé, turned out in due course not to know the sort of thing at all and to need some severe re-education from London.

By the end of the decade, more than half of equity revenues were coming from the international businesses. But revenue did not mean profit. An attempt by Coates to build a more substantial New York operation by hiring forty analysts and salesmen from the collapsing Drexel Burnham Lambert had turned into a disaster. All over the world, BZW's dedication to producing elaborate, glossy, investment research products (very much driven by Coates's own enthusiasm for research) had added a thick layer of costs, on which it was impossible to measure a return. In Tokyo the great bull market had come to an end and BZW had lost £30 million in 1990; the division as a whole lost £45 million, and the truth was that in the entire period since Big Bang it had contributed no profit at all to BZW. In January 1991 Howard Coates, in Andrew Lorenz's ambiguous phrase, 'left equities to become a deputy chairman of the division'.

There was a move to replace Coates with John Varley, the impeccable corporate financier and management bureaucrat who had succeeded me as managing director in Hong Kong. But the Equities men would not accept a boss who was not one of their own breed. So at Ken Sinclair's instigation the job went to Jonathan Davie, a gilts specialist who was very much what we had learned from the American author Michael Lewis to call a Big Swinging Dick of the trading floor. Varley came back as Davie's number two. They immediately closed the ex-Drexel New York operation, and set about chopping other costs wherever they could.

It was a painful time, but not so painful as to suppress the appetite of BZW staff at all levels for personal enrichment. Throughout the firm, remarkable creativity was achieved in the reasons (other than actual profitability, of course) people found to justify asking for more salary and bonus for themselves and their team mates: market share, research poll ratings, morale, dissatisfaction with management, job offers from elsewhere. This attitude of mind was driven not so much by the division heads and senior executives – who had already been enriched either by the sale of their partnerships or by the contract terms on which they had joined the firm – as by the so-called 'marzipan layer', the up-and-coming late-twenties-to-mid-thirties thrusters. Ten years earlier, a typical member of this group might have defined his ambition in terms of a seat on the board of a first-class firm, a long career there and whatever wealth came with it. Now – wherever he was in the City – he thought chiefly in terms of maximizing the earnings potential of a three-to-five year stay with any given employer. It was a shift which reflected not only the greed provoked in perfectly decent people when large sums of money are waved in front of them (I became noticeably greedy myself at times) but the insecurity of the new City, in which it really was foolish to try to plan beyond a three-to-five year horizon.

So money was uppermost in everyone's minds, and – in a firm which lacked either a glorious history to live up to, or a well developed team spirit – money was by far the most powerful motivation. When Pimlott arrived in Corporate Finance, he observed that we were paid less than our peers at Kleinworts and immediately raised everyone's salary: mine went up from £65,000 a year to £100,000 in the space of eighteen months, and when I wrote a note suggesting that the only sensible way forward, given the paucity of revenues, was to try to devise a way of cutting the salaries again and placing more emphasis on genuinely performance-related bonuses, people looked at me as though I was mad. There was a Catch-22 in all this: BZW did not have the profits to pay bonuses on the scale of the American houses, so it had to pay bigger salaries to attract people to join; but those salaries made the overhead so high that the profits could never be attained.

And BZW still had some 300 individual holders of Founders Shares (including former partners of Meares & Philips and Puget-Mahé, as well as de Zoetes and Wedds) whose devotion to the value of their personal interest in the firm was seen by Barclays as an obstacle to co-operation and restructuring. In late 1990, a deal was struck to buy out all these interests at the extremely generous price of 150p per £1 share, making a total cost of £111 million and theoretically valuing BZW at £771 million, more than 20 per cent above the market value of Warburgs, which was three times more profitable. The deal added about £20 million to the wealth of the former de Zoetes and Wedds partners. It was struck on all the shareholders behalf by Jonathan Davie and Simon de Zoete, a pairing who were to play a major hand in BZW's ultimate fate, with much the same skill as advocates of their colleagues' interests.

Once the Founders Shares had been bought in, there was another (but smaller) bundle of money to be handed out. Some time shortly after Big Bang it had been recognized that while all the ex-de Zoetes and Wedds partners and many senior recruits into the firm had long-term financial incentives to stay, the Barclays contingent in BZW and some others who had turned out to be useful had no such advantages. Yet the ex-Barclays businesses – specialized lending, money market dealing, fund management, development capital and the National Freight stake – were making good money for BZW, while the equities and corporate finance divisions were merely racking up costs. So a 'phantom option' scheme was invented, giving us all a notional stake in the firm's performance over the coming years. In the autumn of 1991, the scheme was unwound, producing a round of (somehow tax-free) bonuses; in my case the figure was a gratuitous £32,000.

The unwinding of the phantom options also produced a virtuoso farewell performance from Martin Jacomb, who was about to step down as BZW chairman – his five-year contract had already expired, and he was preparing to move on to chair Postel (the post office and telecommunications workers' pension fund) and the British Council. At a meeting of phantom option-holders in the Ebbgate House canteen, speaking without notes, he slid gracefully past the question of how the options had been valued, unravelled the tax consequences, promised more incentives to come without giving away anything specific, and congratulated us on the businesses we had built. Jacomb was a pro: he understood what made investment bankers tick – chiefly adrenalin and greed – and he made you believe what he said. He knew how to work a room, whether it was full of Japanese ministers or Essex traders. On another occasion close to the end of his tenure, he came to speak at a corporate finance divisional conference: 'We have it within our grasp,' he said of the firm's prospects. With an eloquent hand gesture he repeated, very slowly, 'We have it within our grasp.' We all believed him again. When I saw him in 1998, not long after the dismantling of BZW, he spoke of 'a sense of the deepest regret' about the fate of the project.

Jacomb's successor was a very different animal, and if anything an even more formidable operator. Sir Peter Middleton missed out on his true ambition, to be cabinet secretary and head of the Home Civil Service, but he was considered quite a catch for BZW when it was announced in April 1991 that he would take over. Aged fifty-eight, had been permanent secretary at the Treasury since 1983, but he was by no means the standard Oxbridge-educated Whitehall mandarin type. He came from Sheffield, where he attended both the grammar school and the university – studying economics and statistics – before national service in the Royal Army Pay Corps. At the Treasury he was private secretary to Ted Heath's Chancellor of the Exchequer, Anthony Barber, and a notably skilful press officer in the days before the label 'spin doctor' had been invented. The Labour Chancellor Denis Healey spoke warmly of Middleton's 'genius for dealing with the media' and of his welcome capacity for 'a little gentle subordination'.

It would be impertinent to try to guess at the political beliefs of so inscrutable a figure as Middleton, but he was probably the only senior civil servant to win high marks from both Healey and Margaret Thatcher. At the only BZW meeting I ever attended with him (the subject was what if anything we should do about the prospect of privatisation work in Kazakhstan) he made an oddly disobliging off-the-cuff remark about Thatcher, but his Whitehall reputation was that he had her ear and could make her listen. He first attracted the Tory prime minister's attention at Chequers, early in her first term of office, when he delivered a masterly seminar on EEC budgets which fired her to go into battle in Brussels for a rebate of 'our money'. He was, as Nigel Lawson wrote, 'the closest approximation to a monetarist the official Treasury could produce'. It was his 'perceptibly unmandarinlike commitment' (Hugo Young's phrase in *One of Us*) to the thrust of Thatcherite economic policies that won him the job of permanent secretary to the Treasury.

For the next six years his political boss was Nigel Lawson. But Lawson's Treasury career ended before Middleton's did, and the former Chancellor had already arrived in 1990 as a part-time executive director of BZW. The edgy relationship between these two powerful men

became a curious sidelight for observers of BZW. Lawson was generally
assumed to have been Martin Jacomb's own choice to succeed himself
as BZW chairman – though the idea seemed to fade quietly away
as Lawson became increasingly preoccupied with the writing of his
memoirs. Middleton was clearly John Quinton's choice to succeed
Jacomb. These choices mirrored the style of the choosers: Jacomb the
smooth, high-level political operator, Quinton the banking bureaucrat,
who had himself once been seconded into the civil service.

There was certainly a competitive edge between Middleton and
Lawson. In *The View from No. 11* the latter wrote a carefully spiked
description of his permanent secretary:

> Although I always enjoyed his quickness, his intelligence and his political
> sensitivity . . . he and I were somewhat wary of each other. In many ways
> I could not have asked for anyone better; but I was never sure that his
> habit of cultivating the Press, which he had acquired during his years as
> the Chancellor's Press Secretary, was always helpful. A good civil servant,
> who has to serve with equal commitment Ministers of all types and of
> both political parties, has to become to some extent all things to all men;
> but in Peter's case this characteristic was particularly highly developed.
> He was 'turned on' most by the interface with the City, where he
> eventually ended up. He was at his best as a troubleshooter, taking a grip
> of a complex specific issue in a way few others could have done.

But perhaps more significantly, Lawson (who did not waste many of
his 1100 pages on such incidental anecdotes) records that he and his
financial secretary, John Moore, once beat Middleton and Terry Burns,
the Treasury's then chief economic adviser (now Sir Terence, and
permanent secretary) at snooker – during a Budget planning weekend
at Chevening. Victory had been achieved despite the dilettante
approach of the ministers. The mandarins, on the other hand, 'took
the whole thing very seriously, and arrived with their own cues'; what's
more, to make sure that no such perverse result ever happened again,
they set aside time before the next year's encounter for intensive
practice at the Reform Club whose name, Lawson added mischievously,
'appears to satisfy their modest appetite for change'.

Lawson may in his turn have thought it a perverse result that he
should have 'ended up' in the City (to adapt his own phrase) as a
director of BZW subordinate to Middleton. Certainly one Barclays
non-executive formed the view that Lawson extracted himself from
his BZW duties, while remaining on the main Barclays board, not just
to make time for memoir writing but also to avoid having to take

orders from his former permanent secretary. In the same cocktail-party conversation, the non-executive concerned vented himself of the view that Middleton was 'ninety-nine per cent for Middleton and one per cent for anything else'.

That seems a harsh judgement of someone who in the end held Barclays together almost single-handedly through the crisis of Martin Taylor's departure. Middleton has had many unequivocal admirers in Westminster, Whitehall and the City – including my father, who had numerous dealings with him and who recognized him (as Healey had done) as a fellow Yorkshireman, an iconoclast, and a man of unusually powerful will and intellect. Even so, an element of what the non-executive said recurs in other people's remarks about Middleton. This, they say, is a man who has rendered outstanding service to Barclays, even perhaps (in returning from retirement) beyond the call of duty, but who is also acutely clever at managing his own position.

9

BOOM AND BUST

1987–1992: Quinton makes his mark – An explosion of property
lending – An unpopular rights issue – The turn of the tide –
The Imry loan – Quinton's heart trouble – Too much
restructuring – Brian Pearse goes to Midland – Relationships
break down – the crowning of Andrew Buxton

As soon as he took over, John Quinton declared that he wanted Barclays
to become the McDonald's of banking, a place where 'you're greeted
with a smile and you're not kept waiting'. It was a bold image for a
new era ('McDonald's?' you could almost hear the boardroom back-
woodsmen mutter. 'What is this place McDonald's?') and it certainly
worked in one way. For the next two years, any customer who wanted
to buy a house or build a shopping centre found borrowing the
necessary money from Barclays as easy as buying a hamburger.

Barclays was, in this respect, striving to catch up with a national
trend, rather than leading it. The total volume of mortgage lending in
Britain rose from £19 billion in the 1985/86 fiscal year to £27 billion
in the next, a sure sign (though not much remarked upon at the time)
of an incipient boom in house prices. Between 1985 and the vertiginous
1989 peak of the property market, average house prices in Britain more
than doubled. Banks and building societies, exercising to the full the
competitive freedoms given to them by the Thatcher government,
were equally irresponsible in fuelling the boom, though it was the
banks which in the end came off worse.

High street lenders in this period seemed, with hindsight, to have
taken leave of their common sense as well as their own rules of
prudence. They offered mortgages in ever larger proportion to house
valuations, sometimes over 100 per cent. They offered higher multiples
of loan applicants' earnings (rising from two and a half times to three

and a half, or four) and some ceased bothering to check whether the earnings figures given by applicants were real. As interest rates began to rise (from the end of May 1988) in response to inflationary signals, banks failed to spot the fact that the more mortgage money went out, the more consumers would have to cut back on household spending in order to maintain their interest payments, bringing damage to small businesses and retailers who also happened to be the banks' borrowers.

Barclays, as we have seen, was slow to jump on this bandwagon, largely thanks to Bevan's innate caution. But under John Quinton, it rapidly caught up. In 1987, total group assets grew by 11 per cent but within that figure, lending to the property and construction sectors in the UK and on home mortgages grew from £5.7 billion to £8.8 billion, an increase of more than 50 per cent. The bank's new zest – and its urge to be loved by its personal customers – was symbolized more than anything else by Quinton's decision to sponsor the Football League championship for three years at a cost of £4.5 million, placing giant Barclays hoardings behind the goalmouths at every important football ground in the land.

In the Tuke era, Barclays had sponsored cricket (Colin Cowdrey was on the Barclays' payroll as a part-time roving ambassador) and the British ski team. Bevan's preference was the supremely élitist sport of ocean racing. Quinton, in contrast, was a long-standing season ticket holder of Tottenham Hotspur. His decision to sponsor the entire Football League was regarded – according to taste – as a populist masterstroke or a plunge downmarket. Either way, it broadcast the Barclays name as it had never been broadcast before.

At the same time, the Connect card, Britain's first debit card, was introduced, and Barclays claimed to offer more cash dispensers, more convenient opening hours and fancier savings products than any of its rivals. This was a return to the trend-setting Barclays of earlier years, the bank with the 'sporting' attitude which Bevan had talked about but failed to sustain.

The high growth path which Quinton wanted was rapidly achieved, but it came with a problem. In common with other international banks – and more prudently than some – Barclays had bitten the bullet during 1987 and made huge provisions against its exposures to Third World countries. The write-off figure was £716 million, wiping out 70 per cent of what would otherwise have been the bank's first £1 billion-plus pre-tax annual profit. At the same time, BZW (which had made a net loss of £11 million for the year, having been hit badly by the October 1987 stock market crash) was beginning to demonstrate a voracious appetite for capital. These depletions at a time of rapid growth in domestic lending had brought the bank up against its capital ratios. For the past three years, the group's ratio of equity to total assets had been gently declining: Barclays needed more capital of its own. A large-scale rights issue – which was bound to be deeply unpopular with shareholders – began to look inevitable.

The issue was first planned to take place in late 1987, but the crash of Black Monday stopped it. Brian Pearse, returning from New York[1] in the spring of that year to take up the post of chief financial officer, found draft rights issue paperwork waiting on his desk. It did not happen, however, until March 1988, by which time, Pearse says, 'the money had already been lent' into the surging boom. The announcement of the deeply-discounted[2] £924 million capital raising (Barclays' second rights issue in three years and the second biggest ever in the London market at that time) was extraordinarily unpopular, both with institutions and with small shareholders. Many of the latter were forced to accept adverse tax effects when they sold old Barclays shares in order to subscribe for new ones. 'This issue is wicked, unkind and unfair,' declared Joseph Gurney, a non-banking member of the Norfolk dynasty. 'If I could find a way of stopping it I would.'

For three weeks – shepherded by Cazenove, the bank's broker – Quinton was obliged to trot round the City calling on pension fund managers and insurance companies to explain his strategy and justify the cash call. In characteristic style he declared an 'open-door lunch policy': investment analysts and their clients were encouraged to drop in to hear the story, which was summed up in a slogan that would later haunt the corridors of Lombard Street: 'Number One by '91'.[3]

'We are not going madly for a dash for growth,' he defended himself, while tacitly admitting that the issue proceeds had already been committed. 'This money is needed to cover the growth we are

---

[1] Pearse, who 'would register anything up to 12 on a Beaufort Scale of bankers and is now coming back to blast through Head Office', according to the *Daily Telegraph* columnist Christopher Fildes at the time, had done his best to knock the US operations into shape and to achieve some co-ordination between the conflicting aspirations of Barclays and BZW. But the group's US strategy remained remarkably confused. Pearse's successor was intended to be a high-profile American banker recruited from Citibank, but at the last moment there were cold feet in London about the scale of the recruit's proposed business plans. He was paid off, and the New York job was given instead to John Kerslake, a safe but stolid pair of hands from Lombard Street who achieved an almost invisible profile for himself on Wall Street.

[2] Rights shares were offered at 250p, a discount of almost 50 per cent to the prevailing market price, on the basis of one new share for every two held on 19 April 1988.

[3] Later transmuted by City wags into 'In the poo by '92' and 'On the floor by '94'.

experiencing anyway and which we need capital to support. We are
not rushing frantically to beat NatWest or to fund a major acquisition.
We have growth in good quality business coming through so strongly
that if we did not have this issue we would eventually have to call a
halt.'

For all Quinton's ebullience and openness, the sales pitch was hard
going. Five of the largest shareholders – Prudential, Mercury Asset
Management, Allied Dunbar, British Telecom's pension fund and the
unit trust group M & G – were reported to be unhappy. S. G. Warburg's
investment analysts issued a 'Sell' recommendation on Barclays shares,
which tumbled from 481p before the issue announcement to 425p.

'It is early days to talk about revolt,' said Pearse, as the bandwagon
gathered momentum in the wrong direction. 'Rights issues are never
popular, nor are banks.' When it came to a shareholders' poll, there
was even a hint that Quinton might resign if the issue was voted down.
Most institutions clearly preferred not to precipitate such a crisis,[4] but
they abstained in droves to make their point. Less than 15 per cent of
eligible votes were cast.

It was the end of Quinton's honeymoon with the financial press.
Many commentators would say it was the beginning of all the troubles
that were to follow for Barclays over the following decade. But once
the dust had settled, it did not seem so bad. A few days later, Andrew
Buxton took over from Peter Leslie as managing director, and struck a
worldly, upbeat note: 'The bank is running very well, judging by our
ability to put on good new business ... [But] we should certainly not
be involved in a race to be the biggest by assets. That's like the Dallas
banks, each trying to build a head office taller than the others' ... We
are going to be one of the strongest banks in the world.'

Buxton himself was presented to the media as a hands-on, trouble-
shooting manager and a sophisticated banker. He had run a super-
tough 'Special Team' set up in 1974 to handle borrowers in deep
trouble after the fringe bank crisis. As a local director in Pall Mall, he
had relished dealing with fast-moving, entrepreneurial customers in
the property sector, and had worked on the principle that 'in our Pall
Mall business you hope that you make rather more than you lose!'[5]

[4] The Co-operative Insurance Society, with 4 million shares, was the only large institution
to declare publicly that it had voted against the rights issue.
[5] It would be unfair to infer from this remark and what follows in this chapter that Buxton
was unusually susceptible to racy customers at Pall Mall or elsewhere. Barclays generally liked
to think itself broad-minded, shrewd and professional in dealing with entrepreneurs of
colourful reputation. During the Guinness trial, for example, Sir John Quinton, supported
by Sir Martin Jacomb, offered a character reference for one of the defendants, the property

When he had been sent in to BZW in 1987 as acting chief executive, after Tom Camoys suffered a stroke, he had enjoyed that too: 'There's nothing like day-to-day involvement to teach you new things.'

As to the relationship between himself in his new role and Quinton as executive chairman, there would be no problem at all. 'The chairman and the managing director meet a lot to agree a joint policy,' he said, but the managing director manages; that was all there was to it.

And the fruits of the rights issue saga, when they were unveiled at the end of the year, looked startlingly good. Pre-tax profit was up by 29 per cent to £1.39 billion, within a whisker of NatWest at £1.41 billion. Barclays had now overtaken its rival once more in terms of total assets and market capitalization. There had been a storming rise in domestic banking profit, offset only by further mishaps in the US and an unexpected £24 million blip in New Zealand. Even BZW was modestly in profit, at £33 million. In the home mortgage sector, still very much in the competitive spotlight, Barclays had piled on another £2.5 billion, increasing its exposure to the housing boom by more than 50 per cent. Though higher interest rates in the second half of the year began to take the edge off the nation's appetite for consumer debt, corporate lending was going on strong, with a year-on-year increase of 38 per cent.

Within the general figures for corporate lending, there was a great deal more exposure to the property market. Total exposure to property, construction and housing had multiplied two and a half times between the 1986 and 1988 year-ends. This was the golden era of 'off balance sheet lending', in which the banks did huge damage to each other by inventing ways of lending which did not have to be shown on the property developers' balance sheets and so concealed from other lenders the true extent of the developers' debts.[6] It was also the period in which the City of London responded to the threat from Docklands by relaxing its planning restrictions to allow taller and denser developments

---

and petrol station tycoon Gerald Ronson, who was a long-standing customer and whose syndicated loan arrangements I once managed. Quinton also took the lead for Barclays in dealings with Robert Maxwell, whose private companies borrowed £200 million from the bank. In *Maxwell: The Final Verdict* Tom Bower records Quinton lunching with Maxwell in November 1990, when the hidden truth, according to Bower, was that the Maxwell empire was already in dire financial trouble: 'Quinton, who deluded himself that he could understand London's more maverick entrepreneurs, was easily persuaded by his host of the health of Maxwell Communications Corporation's finances.'

[6] This was the kind of lending scheme I had been encouraged to devise at Barclays Merchant Bank in 1982–3; it was usually achieved by setting up as the borrower a new company, owned partly by the developer and partly by the bank but not strictly 'controlled' by the developer and therefore not required to be consolidated in the developer's accounts.

Silvanus Bevan the Third, who joined the Lombard Street bank in 1767.

Francis Augustus Bevan, chairman of Barclay & Co. 1896–1916.

The premises of Barclay, Bevan, Tritton & Co. in Lombard Street in 1864.

The board of Barclay & Co. in 1900.

Frederick Crauford
Goodenough, chairman
1917–1934, a terrifying
autocrat.

In Kyoto, 1975. Seated, left to right: Deryk Vander Weyer, Lady Tuke, geisha,
Sir Anthony Tuke, geisha, Marguerite Weyer, Colin Stevens. The hosts were
executives of Nomura Securities.

Deryk Vander Weyer
in 1977.

The board of Barclays Bank Limited in 1980;
Sir Anthony Tuke is in the chair.

Sir Timothy Bevan (centre) introduces Deryk Vander Weyer to Margaret Thatcher at 54 Lombard Street, 1982.

The first staff of BZW Tokyo, 1985. The author is seated third from right, Simon Grove third from left. Mr Eguchi the chauffeur is seated extreme left.

史蹟了仙寺
60年9月28日　6番

The opening party of BZW Tokyo, 1985. Rosetted, left to right: Simon Grove (obscured), Rex Cooper, Lord Camoys, author. The guests are the British ambassador, Sir Sydney Giffard and his wife.

The senior management of Barclays in 1987.
From left to right, seated: Sir Martin Jacomb, Sir John Quinton, Peter
Leslie, standing: Brian Pearse, Owen Rout, Andrew Buxton, Humphrey
Norrington and (pasted in) Lord Camoys.

The author with BZW's Hong Kong equity dealing team in 1988.
Kinson Hui, the dealing director, is on the author's left.

'The team taking BZW to the top' in 1993. From the left: John Spencer,
David Band, Graham Pimlott, Donald Brydon.

Martin Taylor deep in thought.

Martin Taylor and
Andrew Buxton in
happier times.

Sir Peter Middleton,
formidable operator and
skilled press handler.

Bill Harrison: 'short, rough
and Brummie'.

Sir Andrew Large:
workaholic Wykehamist.

Matt Barrett with
his second wife
Anne-Marie Sten.

within the Square Mile: the result was a forest of construction sites, notably along London Wall and in the area of Cannon Street station, which produced in the early 1990s a glut of unlettable office space.

Meanwhile, loans to many other kinds of businesses – hotels, retailers, motor dealers – were also secured on (and judged by) their property assets. Bricks and mortar were what lending bankers thought they knew and understood. Warnings from economists inside and outside the bank about the overheating of asset prices, and the interconnected effects which could follow across the whole economy, barely registered at all with lending officers down the line. And the more streamlined structure of the modern Barclays was in itself a contributory factor to the troubles to come: lending officers now had their proposals sanctioned on a much more centralized basis than in earlier days, when the ingrained knowledge and caution of long-serving local directors might have weeded out some of the worst proposals before they advanced through the system.

In an interview with *European Banker* in December 1992, shortly before he retired from the Barclays chair, John Quinton admitted: 'I did not see the recession coming. I think I would have needed an enormous capacity for foresight to see it coming. Not many people did.' But he had not been totally blind to the dangers building up. He recalled that he had told the Governor of the Bank of England in early 1988 that he thought property lending was 'getting overblown', and that he had sought to put a cap on it in Barclays. But a 'cap' did not mean a ban; far from it. There was a concern, first of all, that if Barclays as the biggest lender to the sector had called a complete halt, the decision might have provoked a minor property crash there and then. What was proposed was merely that Barclays should take on no more than 15 per cent of all new lending in the sector.[7] But even that caused uproar with lending managers (those at Pall Mall local head office in particular) whose in-trays were overflowing with hot propositions from valued customers. The 'cap' was circumvented in every possible way, often by redesignating proposals to make them fall under sector headings other than property.

'In practice there was a good deal more property lending done within that cap.' Quinton admitted to *European Banker*. 'We have been

---

[7] In practice the bank had no accurate measure of its total exposure to the property sector until some years later, when Martin Taylor asked his risk director Alan Brown to find out. The exercise took several months of research, and produced the answer that Barclays was around 50 per cent overweight – that is, property in all its forms represented a larger portion of Barclays' risk portfolio than of the British economy as a whole by a factor of 50 per cent.

caught out by a number of lendings that were made in the 1988–9 era which, with hindsight, we should not have made. I think we could have been sterner in those days.'

The warning signals had been flashing for a year by the time base rates hit 14 per cent in May 1989. But still property exposure continued to mount. And Barclays was a lender to all the most exciting names: Olympia & York (the Canary Wharf developer), Mountleigh, Rose-haugh, Speyhawk. But the loan which was to cause most trouble was to a company called Imry, and it is worth dwelling on in a little more detail.

In the spring of 1989, a private company called Marketchief, formed for the purpose, took over Imry Merchant Developers plc, which had to its credit such prestigious developments as Royal Mint Court, the office complex opposite the Tower of London of which Barclays itself was to become a major tenant. Imry's managing director was Martin Myers, a famously persuasive operator known as 'the red squirrel' (and later, apparently, 'Ginger Spice') for the colour of his hair. Imry developments then in hand included the Shires shopping complex in Leicester, and the West Quay development in Southampton. Marketchief was owned through a Jersey investment company controlled by a low-profile German entrepreneur, Wolfgang Stolzenberg, who also had large property interests in Canada. Myers was a partner in the deal, which was designed to make money for the principal players by taking out Imry's public shareholders in an advantageous way – that is, by using borrowed money to do so. Barclays funded the Marketchief bid with a £215 million loan.[8]

Once the take-over was completed, Marketchief changed its name to Imry Merchant Developers Limited, so that the name Marketchief disappeared. Loans to property companies are usually secured by mort-gages over the properties they own, or by arrangements which prevent other creditors getting to the property assets first. But in this case, the bank's inspectors later discovered, the security was not put in place until long after the loan had been drawn.

Whatever the technicalities, it was a very large loan to the property sector, a year after such lending was supposed to have been capped on John Quinton's instructions. And when commercial property values had crashed two years later, Barclays apparently had no choice but to refinance Imry, increasing its loan exposure to a breathtaking total of

---

[8] Though not at the first time of asking: the proposal had been turned down by Strand branch before it was picked up and pushed by Pall Mall local head office.

£422 million. By the end of 1992, the £196 million outstanding from
the original Marketchief loan, and a further £44 million of other debt,
had been written off. Another £100 million of debt was converted
into redeemable preference shares, giving Barclays power in Imry's
boardroom, and a team of BZW specialists was sent in to carry out
a 'financial reconstruction'. Stolzenburg (whose Canadian company,
Castor, had collapsed with £800 million of debts) had by then been
forced out.

It was one of the largest individual corporate debt write-offs in
British banking history. It was also 'quite possibly the worst loan of this
recession that we're aware of', according to Chris Ellerton, banking
analyst at S. G. Warburg.[9] 'It's extraordinary that a bank of Barclays'
stature would allow itself to get exposed to this extent on its own.
There has been a question mark over the judgement of Barclays during
the last two to three years and this underlines that question mark.'

Naturally, Barclays-watchers were interested to know whose judgement had been at fault. Many of them assumed that a giant property
loan emanating from Pall Mall must have come ultimately to the
attention of Andrew Buxton, since he had been a specialist in that field
in earlier days. But Buxton let it be known that he had not been closely
involved. A spokeswoman for Barclays told the press that 'usual loan
procedures were followed in this case. This was authorized by a loans
committee at the highest level.' Pressed on the question of whether
the Imry losses would damage the standing of Andrew Buxton (the
extent of the write-off was revealed in November 1992, just before
Buxton took over the chair) she repeated, 'No, the loans were authorized through usual procedures.'

What were those 'usual' procedures? A loan of such a size needed
three signatures, one of which had to be that of an executive director –
of whom there were four at the time. Traditionally in Barclays, loan
proposal paperwork would circulate to signatories individually, each
one adding his own marginal comments. This was regarded as more
rigorous than calling the signatories together as a committee, since it
obliged each person to express an independent view rather than allowing them to hide behind a collective decision. On occasions, however,
signatories did meet around a table to discuss a specific proposal, and
that was the case with Imry. Barclays never revealed who the three

---

[9] Ellerton was one of several banking analysts in the City who were unusually well informed
about Barclays, having started their own careers there. His grandfather, Sir Cecil Ellerton,
was deputy chairman of Barclays Bank in the 1950s, and was responsible for building up its
position as a leader of the London foreign exchange market.

signatories were, though one of them was understood to be Mark Deverell, who had recently returned from running the bank in Australia to take up the head office post of director of risk management. The *Sunday Telegraph* of 20 December 1992 carried a rather elegant cartoon of Buxton, busy wiping the words 'Imry Loan' off a large slate.

Once it had been sanctioned by three signatures, the loan would have passed to an advances review committee and finally it would have been reported to the board of the bank, in a schedule of large lendings presented by the finance director. Having completed all these stages, every loan decision was regarded as a collective one. And this one was regarded, at the time of its approval, as straightforwardly attractive: an inspector's report later said that it had been regarded in Pall Mall as a 'stone-bonker', which is Barclays slang for a piece of lending, at an attractive margin, that an experienced banker could do with his eyes shut.

But that did not help Mark Deverell or the Pall Mall local director in charge of corporate business, a former National Service drill instructor called Philip Plumridge. Their careers with Barclays came to an end in early 1993, shortly after Buxton's accession to the chair. In Deverell's case, the bank did not hesitate to let the press know that it held him to blame. Many people thought they had been made scapegoats. As the finance director, Peter Wood, remarked to the *Financial Times* shortly before they departed, 'If we fired everyone who made a bad loan, we'd be a pretty small bank.'

But this is to jump ahead of the story. By the time Quinton wrote his chairman's annual report in February 1990, the economic picture was one of slowing growth but still some distance short of recession. British businesses were scaling back their investment plans quite sharply, though loan demand remained strong, which 'is normal at this stage of the business cycle as cash flow weakens' – an ominous phrase in retrospect. Profits had roared ahead again by 20 per cent to £1.7 billion, but had been knocked back by a second slice of 'country risk' provisions, of £983 million, meaning that Barclays had now had to provide for the actual or probable write-off of some 70 per cent of all its loans to Lesser Developed Countries.

Quinton ended his report with a paragraph reminding investors of the successful outcome of the 1988 rights issue, which had proved 'wholly justified' and had 'given us fresh impetus'. Barclays was now 'in a very healthy position to prosper in what promises to be a challenging decade'. But Quinton himself was not in a healthy position. In the following month, the sixty-year-old chairman underwent heart bypass surgery at the Wellington Humana Hospital in St John's Wood.

As heart surgery goes, it was straightforward. An announcement was swiftly issued on Quinton's behalf that he hoped to be back at work in 'a few weeks' – as indeed he was, looking cheerful and fit, having lost some weight. Bouts of tiredness are to be expected after such an operation, but Quinton seem determined to overcome the after-effects by will-power, and to return to a normal work schedule as soon as possible.

That was not to be however, because a complication had developed in the form of Hepatitis C, a debilitating blood infection for which there was no immediate cure. After a while Quinton himself realized there was something seriously wrong. With hindsight he reckoned that he was operating only at 60 per cent of his full powers. Others have speculated that the medical trauma may have in some way affected his judgement – as can happen with heart surgery patients, who often display post-operative changes of temperament.

When I had dealings with him over the arrangements for my father's memorial service in September 1990 he seemed in good spirits, if not quite as ebullient as the Quinton who had breezed through Hong Kong and Taiwan a year or so earlier. But fifteen months later, when I went to see him in his office in Royal Mint Court[10] on the day before I left BZW, he seemed distinctly diminished. I too was in a low state, having just been fired. My purpose in going to see him was not to ask for my job back – you can never do that – but to try to make sure before I departed that he knew just how badly BZW was being managed. When I got there, however, it suddenly seemed a point-less exercise. I asked after his health. He asked whether I was being treated decently for severance pay. Regret hung in the air. It seemed inappropriate to say so – so I didn't – but what struck me most was the stately, even presidential, scale of his office, with its tall Georgian windows and its high-backed, brown leather desk chair. It was a sad little meeting.

But by then, of course, things had been going horribly wrong – more so for him, as it turned out, than for me – for quite some time. During 1990 the recession had begun to bite, and the down-side risks of a near-doubling of Barclays' UK balance sheet in five years became apparent. There were provisions for bad and doubtful debts of almost

---

[10] During the rebuilding of the Lombard Street head office, the senior management of Barclays temporarily relocated to the splendid neo-classical Royal Mint building designed by James Johnson and Sir Robert Smirke, where coins were minted from 1810 to 1975.

£800 million on the domestic loan book, and more than £100 million on Barclaycard, which had been heavily hit by fraud as well as unpaid debts. Standard and Poors, the credit rating agency, had cut its rating for Barclays bonds from AAA to AA+, knocking Barclays out of the category of undoubted world banking leaders. Instead of being able to boast about growth of quality business, Quinton was now on the defensive. 'We don't force money on anyone,' he told the *Financial Times*. 'Obviously there was an over-expansion of lending, but how far we can be blamed is arguable.'

As for the bank's struggling customers, 'We always try to be as helpful as possible ... The last thing we want to see is a customer go bankrupt.' But that was not the way the customers saw it out in the field. Branch managers who had metamorphosed into slick loan salesmen in 1987 (with, for a time, their smiling photographs on their business cards) had turned back into ruthless debt collectors. Nineteen ninety was the year in which small businessmen and mortgage borrowers seriously began to hate the banks again.

And demoralization was spreading in the ranks. Early in 1991 there was talk of a plan to cut up to 20 per cent of Barclays' 87,000 UK employees – 5000 jobs were abolished by 'natural wastage' during the year. For executives dealing with large corporate customers at home and abroad, there was constant friction with BZW, and jealousy over the high pay packages of the investment bank hot-shots. Managers throughout the group found their jobs being 'regraded' and their departments and reporting lines continually restructured.

Most controversially, Quinton and Jacomb unveiled in 1990 a plan designed by the consultants McKinsey & Co. (who have redesigned Barclays half a dozen times in the past thirty years, but rarely to good effect) to bring BZW and Barclays closer together by creating a Markets and Investment Banking Division (MIB) which would include BZW and the bank's Treasury (or money market dealing) operations and would report to Jacomb. This pleased nobody. It was clearly an attempt to reduce the autonomy of BZW, and it meant merging BZW's Treasury operations into the bank's. But the managers of the two Treasury operations hated each other with a special passion, and whoever came out on top, the restructuring was a recipe for vicious antagonism.

Then, when Sir Peter Middleton arrived from Whitehall to succeed Jacomb in November 1991, it all changed again. Middleton did not like the new structure, so he set about reversing it. Instead of BZW becoming part of MIB, MIB became part of BZW. These were arcane manoeuvres for the outside world to observe ('Small earthquake in Barclays: not many dead,' said the *Daily Telegraph*) but internally the battle was all-consuming. Middleton, with his formidable clarity of mind, won the boardroom argument. But as far as Quinton was concerned 'It was probably the most difficult decision of all for any of us to sign for.' One of its effects was that foreign exchange dealers from Barclays instantly moved on to higher BZW pay scales, garnering large bonus payments as they did so and leaving their ex-colleagues in the bank in a well of bitterness.

Meanwhile, far from downplaying the grimness of the domestic and global economic situation, Quinton had taken to putting it in the plainest terms. In a conference speech in 1991 he said: 'There is a real threat that the recession in the United States, the United Kingdom and elsewhere will deepen and awaken comparison with the Great Depression of the thirties.' The pressures facing international banks could result in 'a shake-out on an unprecedented scale' over the following five years. By the summer of 1991 – when the Chancellor of the Exchequer, Norman Lamont, was claiming to have spotted the first green shoots of recovery – Quinton was warning loudly that he saw no such thing. He was also having to defend the bank on all sides (ranging from an appearance before a House of Commons select committee to a call from his car to the *Call Nick Ross* phone-in show on Radio 4) against accusations that the banks had exploited small business customers by raising interest margins as conditions got more difficult. Analysis of all the clearing banks' published accounts confirmed that margins were widening, and the publication of various 'codes of conduct', committing the bank to 'open and fair relationships with our customers' did little to help.

In the first half of the year, Barclays made another £800 million of provisions, and revealed that loans to small businesses were turning bad at the rate of £1 million a day. The half-year profit of £378 million, down 37 per cent, had also been hit by big losses in the United States, mostly on property lending.

But Quinton was not so dispirited as to want to retire early. His original five-year term would have taken him to the annual general meeting in April 1992, but before his illness the board had agreed to his proposition that he should stay for two years beyond that. After the heart operation, however, the board had begun to worry, not so much about the state of the business under Quinton's command – real panic about the extent of the trouble in the property loan book did not take hold until 1992 – but about the relationships between the senior executive team. A first low point was reached on 31 January 1991, when the Bank of England – concerned at that point about the weakness of the Midland Bank, whilst regarding Barclays as amply blessed with first-class managers – asked Quinton whether he would release his finance director, Brian Pearse, to become chief executive of Midland.

Though Midland's problems were well known, the Bank of England's solution to them was unexpected. The bank, which had been a world leader long before Barclays, had come disastrously unstuck: its ownership of Crocker National Bank in California from 1980 to 1986 had cost it $1 billion in losses, and it had dropped another £100 million betting the wrong way on interest rates. It had heavy exposures to Third World debt. Its chairman, ex-Bank of England deputy governor Sir Kit McMahon, seemed to have lost the confidence of his former colleagues. Lord Hanson and Robert Maxwell had acquired stakes in Midland in anticipation of a take-over, and even the Saatchi brothers, from the world of advertising, had revealed themselves as potential bidders.

In Barclays it was believed that Midland's problems would be solved through a take-over by Lloyds, out of which Barclays might collect some unwanted bits of Midland debris. But the Bank of England thought otherwise, and it is (or was) part of the way the City works that requests from the Bank for executives to be released to take on urgent tasks elsewhere are hard to refuse. Quinton, who regarded Governor Eddie George as 'probably my best friend in the City', was prepared to acquiesce without argument. For his own part, Pearse recognized that he was probably in his final job at Barclays (he would be sixty in August 1993) and that with Buxton ahead of him there was effectively no chance of becoming managing director or chief executive. So he was ready to accept the challenge of Midland. But Buxton did not want to lose Pearse, and a furious shouting-match ensued between Buxton and Quinton.

Some of the non-executives also thought the decision was a bad one, and it was this perhaps more than any other single incident that led to the suggestion of Quinton's judgement becoming wobbly after his operation. 'It was a crazy decision,' said one director. 'Of course it's what the Governor wanted and that carries enormous weight. But Pearse was just about the only professional banker left in the place. In that case, the answer should have been "Bugger the Governor, what about Barclays' shareholders?" '

Some Barclays people thought Pearse was fortunate to have been offered a job at Midland for which he might never have been considered at Barclays. But as with Peter Ellwood of Lloyds TSB, history emphatically proved this judgement wrong. Pearse himself said later that Midland's problems, particularly in relation to Third World debt, were probably not as bad as they looked, and that the place 'just needed confidence again'. Blunt, cheerful, boundingly energetic, a traditional high street banker to his fingertips, Pearse was the ideal man for the job.

And the way he went about it offered several useful lessons to his old employer. One of his most notable actions was to take some 200 managers out of Midland's regional centres and put them back into branches. He also called a halt to a policy of retiring most managers at the age of fifty, even inviting some of them to come out of retirement and go back to work. The Bank of England completed Midland's management reconstruction by giving Pearse a sympathetic chairman in Sir Peter Walters, ex-head of BP, and a wise deputy chairman in Sir Peter Leslie (now, having retired from Barclays, also chairman of the Commonwealth Development Corporation). Early in 1992, Hong Kong & Shanghai Banking Corporation came on the scene as the new owners of Midland, bringing an overlay of strong management, strong branding skills and superior computer systems.

HSBC treated Pearse respectfully for a while, allowing him to continue the job without interference, but eventually the autocratic HSBC chairman, Willie Purves, decided to bring Midland closer into the fold, and Pearse's role came to an end. But by the time he moved on in 1994 (to become chairman of Lucas Industries, the car component maker) he had been knighted, and had also been made considerably richer by his Midland share option deal. His old Barclays' colleagues watched wistfully, and the press occasionally wondered whether it might not be possible for them to persuade him to come back.

Meanwhile, the period of drift that followed Pearse's departure at the end of March 1991 was even worse for morale and progress. Peter Wood, the bank's treasurer, was the obvious successor to Pearse in terms of financial skills. But he was a controversial figure because of his undisguised hostility to BZW, and he was not named as finance director until June. Personal relations between Quinton and Buxton were going from bad to worse. Tensions between the bank and BZW were running high. One non-executive observed that the board of the bank was even more powerless than usual during this phase, because any recommendation put to it was assumed to have been arrived at as a delicate compromise between executives who personally hated each other: the board was treading on eggshells, in fear of creating even more strife by asking for changes.

As the deterioration continued, Martin Jacomb reported to Denys Henderson, the leading light of the non-executive directors, that the normal relationship between an executive chairman and his managing director seemed to have ceased to function. With Henderson in the lead, the Chairman's Advisory Committee of the board (the renamed Senior Directors' Committee) then put it to Quinton that it might be better for him to become less executive, and to allow the managing director to manage. They asked for greater definition of roles between Quinton and Buxton. But it soon became obvious that this was not working either.

Rumour spread around the City that, as one director put it, 'there was a shambles in Barclays'. Henderson and Sir Derek Birkin found themselves being called in by two of the most powerful institutional investors in the City, Mick Newmarch and Hugh Jenkins of the Prudential, to try to explain what was going on. Towards the end of 1991 the plot took a new twist, when Quinton suddenly took on the additional job of chairman of football's newly formed Premier League, a post which, according to one sports correspondent, demanded 'the patience of Mother Teresa and the pugnacious political instincts of Boris Yeltsin'. It also required a significant portion of his depleted energies, and some Barclays directors made it clear that they thought he should not have taken it on.[11]

Quinton's position was beginning to look vulnerable, and the 1991 year-end results made the tensions worse. Profits were down again, by 30 per cent to £533 million, and the dividend (which had risen steadily in recent years) remained flat. Provisions on domestic lending had risen to £1.3 billion. America was still in trouble. Two much-trumpeted acquisitions in late 1990, of Merck Finck & Co. in Germany and L'Européenne de Banque in Paris, had brought added costs rather than profits. Around the world, only Spain and the two unreconstructed relics of DCO, black Africa and the Caribbean, were really performing well. BZW was doing better – with profits of £61 million – but that meant more demands for giant bonuses, and more hostility between senior people in the two wings of the group.

The state of the competition was also very much a factor in Barclays' morale. NatWest – whose £1.4 billion 1988 profit still stood as an all-

---

[11] Quinton himself later claimed that he had spent only 'about two hours a week' on the Premier League, compared to 'sixty or seventy hours' on his Barclays work.

time record for any British bank — had also come to grief by this stage, brought low by heavy losses in the United States, in its investment banking ventures and on lendings to Robert Maxwell. It had also suffered a huge blow to its reputation in the Blue Arrow rights issue scandal, which led to several changes in top management. Midland, as we have seen, was on its knees. But the bad news for Barclays was that Lloyds had now emerged as the front-runner and stock market favourite of the clearing bank sector.

A decade ago, Lloyds had been enfeebled by its encounter with Latin American debt. In the mid-1980s, when banking glamour was measured by size of commitment to the new world of investment banking, Lloyds — which had withdrawn from any commitment to that world at all — was the dullest dog in the pack. A failed bid for Standard Chartered in 1986 had completed the picture of a bank condemned to a modest niche in an ever more competitive domestic market.

But Lloyds had quietly conceived a strategy which was to give it, by the latter part of the 1990s, not only acknowledged market leadership but a stockmarket valuation which was at times more than twice that of Barclays. Under the leadership of two remarkable men — Sir Jeremy Morse, its brilliant, other-worldly, chess-playing Wykehamist chairman, and Brian Pitman, its plain-speaking, branch-banker-man-and-boy chief executive — Lloyds set out to make itself the most efficient bank in Britain. While Barclays was still buying extravagant foreign businesses, Lloyds was selling them to reinvest the proceeds at home. While Barclays was piling on fine-margin large corporate lending, Lloyds was edging out of it. Costs were ruthlessly chopped out of its branch network — £150 million pounds' worth in 1991 — and saleable products (such as life insurance, through the acquisition of Abbey Life) pushed in. Lloyds also had big bad debt provisions for 1991, but not nearly as big as Barclays'. And its profits and dividends were up. While Barclays and NatWest had been making all the noise and doing so much damage to themselves in their five-year tussle for supremacy, they had failed to notice the cool intelligence of the Lloyds team creeping up to pass them.

Meanwhile, Barclays' non-executive directors were doing what they were paid for, and grappling with the bank's leadership crisis. At the beginning of the new year, Buxton had set a new cat among the pigeons by telling Quinton that he wanted to retire — though still only fifty-two. The thought of eight more years in the bank, even if the last six of them were almost certain to be spent as chairman, had lost its charm. The prospect of a portfolio of non-executive directorships (he was already on the board of SmithKline Beecham) was more appealing. Quinton suggested that they repeat the conversation in front of Sir Martin Jacomb – on whom he relied heavily during his debilitated phase – which they duly did. It is easy to suspect the Buxton resignation threat (which became common knowledge in the senior layers of the group, gossip of it even reaching me at my desk in Ebbgate House shortly before my departure) as a ploy to shift Quinton, but it may well have been totally genuine. Whatever else had been said about him, Buxton has never had a reputation either for deviousness or for being a workaholic.

The climax came in April, when Quinton arrived back from a fortnight's holiday in Mauritius. Denys Henderson and Nigel Mobbs came to see him. In view of your health, they said, it would be better if you retired and Andrew became chairman. Quinton (who would achieve forty years' service with the bank in mid-1992, so becoming entitled to his full pension) did not fight against the idea. The board was split as to whether he should go immediately, or whether he should be allowed to stay on more dignified terms until the end of the year. By choosing the latter course, however, the board succeeded in making matters worse: instead of achieving a clear shift of power to the new chief executive and chairman-designate, a situation was created in which the two protagonists simply continued to tussle to the bitter end. Quinton rejected flatly a suggestion from Buxton that he should vacate his office. Barclays being Barclays, many senior managers made matters difficult by continuing to show traditional deference to the chairman, rather than transferring their allegiance to Buxton.

The intention may have been to leave Quinton his dignity intact, but the announcement was not well handled. 'These changes have been planned for several months,' Quinton felt it necessary to say. 'There has been no coup.' 'It would be wrong to say there was a coup,' a bank spokesman tried to underline, 'but there was some modest encouragement from the non-executives for Quinton to go early.' It was noted that Quinton would be the first Barclays chairman ever to leave the chair alive and not remain on the board for several years afterwards as a non-executive director. However it was presented it was an ignominious way for Quinton to end his tenure. For a man universally regarded, in the bank and the business world generally, as capable, likeable and energetic, it was a sad reversal. Perhaps the biggest factor in that reversal was simply bad timing – in being ill when he needed to be at the height of his power, just as the bank hit the worst recession in living memory.

The most interesting question is whether any other candidate besides

Buxton was considered for the chairmanship; or whether, as in 1980, the senior directors backed the heir apparent without a second thought. In a *Spectator* article in November 1992, mischievously headlined 'How to Inherit a Bank: Martin Vander Weyer on nepotism at Barclays', I constructed a conspiracy theory about Buxton's appointment as the last gasp of a family cabal led by Sir Timothy Bevan. My reconstruction of the process was based on information (from an impeccable source, though the bank declined at the time to confirm it) that it was Bevan who chaired the Chairman's Advisory Committee meeting which took the final decision. Having now understood the process in more depth, I see that my first version was too crude.

Whether or not Bevan actually chaired the vital meeting, his influence was by then much diminished – and indeed he left the board, earlier than originally planned, at the 1993 annual general meeting. There was no overt pressure in the committee to pick Buxton because he was a representative of the families – even though some directors outside the committee believed that family status *ought* to be a consideration after what one of them described as the 'disastrous experiment' of going outside the families with Quinton. Buxton was simply the obvious, safe choice, a seasoned banker, a man groomed for the job over many years and a man who knew the organization from top to bottom. At the time it looked like a very easy decision.

Consideration of whether or not Buxton had done a good enough job as managing director to deserve promotion seems to have been left aside. Besides his dominant role in the bank's corporate lending activity, he had also been responsible as managing director for cost control: he is said to have ordered plastic flowers to be displayed instead of real ones in order to cut the bank's florists' bill, but that hardly matched what Lloyds had been achieving. On the other hand, he had always been a very good performer at board meetings. I had once seen myself, at a crowded round-table discussion on lending policy in Lombard Street at which I was a note-taker, how easily he could command a room.

The possibility must have been considered, however briefly, of making Buxton chief executive and having someone else as chairman. But the problem with that was that Buxton had better credentials to be a chairman – a certain charisma and self-confidence – than to be a chief executive, which requires a voracious grasp of administrative detail. If he had to have one of the two jobs, it was clearly better that he should be chairman.

So there seems to have been no thought of breaking with Barclays tradition entirely and going outside the bank to look for a chairman. As for the other inside candidates, Martin Jacomb (six weeks older than Quinton and by now a non-executive deputy chairman, but planning to go on in the City until he was seventy) 'would have loved the job', according to one close colleague, but would have been resented by senior executives on the banking side because he was seen as *parti pris* in the interminable battle between the bank and BZW. Nigel Lawson was a possibility (and was said to have been disappointed, before he came to Barclays, not to have been offered the chair of NatWest) but the rest of the board was wary of his intellectual high-handedness and his habit of making long speeches in justification of his own policies during the previous decade.

Sir Peter Middleton (who had joined the board in November 1991) was still something of an unknown quantity when the decision was being taken, though history has shown that he might well have been the better choice. It was widely said in the City that he and Buxton failed to hit it off from an early stage, and that if the pecking order had been the other way round, Buxton would have found Middleton a very uncomfortable boss. As it was, Middleton had little hesitation in expressing his opinion of the Quinton-Buxton regime. In November 1992, shortly before Buxton actually took the reins, Middleton gave an interview to *Banking World* magazine, the journal of the Chartered Institute of Bankers, in which he said:

> I do think the bank was lacking a clear sense of strategic direction . . .
> When I came in, Barclays was in the throes of a reorganization. One thing I learned in the Treasury was that reorganizations should, generally, be avoided. My basic belief is that if you have a problem, solve the problem. Don't change the organization. [As for the contrast between the Treasury and the bank:] If anyone in the Treasury gets into difficulty, the others rally round to help. In a bank if anyone gets into difficulties, others rally around only to push them deeper into it. [And on the quality of decision-making in Barclays:] The quality of decision-making in the bank I find somewhat difficult to understand . . . I think those in invest- ment banking have a much clearer appreciation of the risk they are running than do those in domestic banking. The risk in domestic banking looks easy. It is extraordinarily difficult to assess.[12]

This public dressing-down, not only telling Barclays' domestic bankers

---

[12] Middleton later applied his statistician's training to the development of a new system of risk measurement throughout Barclays, much more rigorous than anything that had gone before.

how to do their jobs but praising their enemies in BZW into the bargain, did not go down at all well in the bank. The board meeting which followed the appearance of the article, one of Quinton's last in the chair, was particularly ill-tempered. But Middleton showed his Treasury mettle, declining to apologize on the grounds that he had merely spoken the truth. 'D'you know that fellow Middleton?' one non-executive director asked me loudly at a cocktail party in Brooks's club some time later. 'He's an absolute shit.'

Even after Middleton's article (or perhaps because of it) the *Daily Telegraph*, for one, was still promoting the cause of Middleton for chairman in November 1992. In practice Buxton was by then already in command and merely waiting for Quinton to leave the building, but he was facing a barrage of City hostility which cannot have been anticipated when the announcement of his accession was made in April. Bad debt provisions at the half-year stage had been more than a billion pounds (with Imry, Olympia & York, Heron and Mountleigh all mentioned as troublesome cases) and pre-tax profit was down to a mere £51 million. Some analysts were suggesting that the level of provisions was still not high enough, and that there must be even worse news to come. The dividend was clearly under threat – Buxton and Middleton were forced to deny a split between them, in which Middleton was said to have been arguing strongly for a dividend cut – that made the board all the more sensitive to the views of the bank's institutional shareholders. The issue on which the institutions were agitated was Buxton himself, and whether he was fit to be both chairman and chief executive.

These roles had never been split in Barclays, in good times or bad, until Quinton was sidelined as chairman after the April 1992 reshuffle. But it was very much the fashionable wisdom that they should be split in all large public companies. That nostrum had been written down in the Cadbury Committee's guidelines on corporate governance and supported by the Governor of the Bank of England in a speech in the very week of Barclays' April announcement. Some members of the board have said that Buxton was told from the earliest stage of his appointment that he would have to divide the two roles and find himself a chief executive – and other sources believe that the job was half-offered to Alastair Robinson, the executive director in charge of banking. But if true, these manoeuvres were not reflected in anything Buxton or Quinton said in public. In November the chairman-in-waiting was said to be 'determined to try combining the top jobs', though if it did not work out successfully he might 'consider splitting them for business reasons'. Quinton, in his *European Banker* interview, explained that 'Each division head is effectively a chief executive and so the chairman is much better placed to combine chairmanship with the role of chief executive. This is the structure which Andrew Buxton has introduced. He does not see it as set in stone, but it may very well prove appropriate.'

But a chorus of disapproval was building up, some of it combined with persistent questioning about the Imry case. 'I would like to see some humility from Barclays and some admission of past mistakes,' one investor told a Sunday newspaper. 'I want to see the role of chairman and chief executive split, not kept within the family network. I want to see a strong, independent figure brought in.' 'Either Barclays will change its mind on this or the issue will explode,' said another.

My *Spectator* article, illuminating (perhaps for the first time for most readers) the Barclays family system of which Buxton was 'the last prince', was widely read and may have had some impact on the debate. The edition happened to be a best-selling one, because its cover story by Hugh Massingberd was a scoop about the marital separation of the Prince and Princess of Wales. The article itself became, so I have often been told, one of the most photocopied *samizdat* documents in the history of Barclays Bank. It was not kind about Buxton. Besides the question marks over his track record, I wrote, the world outside Barclays had found him 'colourless, strangely disconnected, far from user-friendly. "I don't really have any interests," is one of his few quotable remarks ... Despite Buxton's acknowledged skills, the feeling is that he is neither a great communicator nor a world-class banking statesman ... Outsiders can only guess whether "family" interests have any influence. Bevan could not steam-roll the vote, but he could perhaps have made the point that *not* to make Buxton chairman, an appointment expected for almost 20 years and predestined for 150, would be to signal panic to the world.'

The editor of the *Spectator*, Dominic Lawson, often told me that I was too good-natured to be a really attacking journalist. I certainly felt uncomfortable about writing the Barclays piece for him. But it struck a chord with many Barclays people past and present. And I don't think subsequent events have rendered it invalid.

THE PIG CEREMONY

1986–1992: Playing games with the Japanese Ministry of
Finance – Battling with Barclays in Tokyo – The crash of Black
Monday – The pleasures of Asia – A memorial service – The end
of a short career

In Tokyo in the week of Big Bang I conducted the eighth of a series
of twenty-six meetings with officials of the Ministry of Finance which
constituted the 'negotiation' of BZW's local branch licence. Quote
marks are necessary here because this was not really a negotiation at all,
but a Kafkaesque game in which the ministry officials made up new
rules and guidelines whenever we came close to fulfilling the previous
ones and never pretended to be treating all applicants on equal terms,
holding us back or making us dance until it suited them politically to
allow us across the border into the promised land of Japanese securities
dealing.

It is now regarded as part of the collective delusion of the financial
world of the 1980s that every major bank in the world wanted a
presence in the Japanese markets for shares and bonds. Japan in 1986
was still in the upswing of a long boom, built upon the success of its
export manufacturing companies and the thrift of its citizens. But as
savings accumulated, asset values of all kinds soared into the stratosphere.
My neighbour's cramped suburban house was worth £10 million, and
the grounds of the Emperor's palace were said to be worth more than
the whole of California.

Industrial companies borrowed money through eurobond issues at
very low interest rates and used the proceeds not to build factories but
to speculate in the markets for themselves; the equity warrants issued
with their eurobonds were themselves a prime instrument of speculation. The big securities companies, led by Nomura, drove chosen

share prices upwards at will, simply by instructing their enormous sales forces to tell Japan's 20 million-plus private investors to buy them. Shares in mundane companies sold for a hundred times earnings – or even three hundred times earnings – and clever Western analysts like my colleague Mike Connors, an expert in Japanese electronics stocks, found convincing reasons why that was not insane.

It could all be explained in terms of the superiority of the Japanese economic model, the huge productive power of its high-tech industries and various odd but admirable characteristics of the Japanese psyche. So favourable was the combination of circumstances that Japan's growth-path seemed set to defy gravity, and economic history, for as far ahead as any banker or broker could see. Western institutional investors had a growing fascination with Japanese stocks. Japanese savers, as they broadened their horizons, would soon become huge buyers of all kinds of Western paper.

In order to participate in this vibrant marketplace, firms like BZW would have to plant large sums of capital in Japan and wait for the Japanese system to allow it to blossom. But it would surely do that within five years, or maybe ten, and once the breakthrough was made, the smart foreign players would make so much money that their start-up costs would look completely insignificant. 'Believe me,' Connors used to say when we began to add up the likely costs of an operation of over 100 people, many of them hugely expensive expatriates, in sixteen thousand square feet of brand-new office space bristling with electronic wizardry. 'None of this will matter once we get going. There's no point in having a strict budget: the budget is whatever it costs to get into the game.'

The problem was that BZW was starting behind the game: numerous other British, American, German and French firms were ahead of us in the queue for operating licences. The game we were playing was leapfrog, Connors said. Before we began we had to construct a complex façade of shareholding arrangements to circumvent Japanese securities law, which decreed that a commercial bank such as Barclays could not own more than 50 per cent of any securities business. Through the good offices of Denys Henderson, ICI agreed to be the nominal holder of the other 50 per cent for us, but the Ministry would not let us follow precedents set by other banks (including NatWest) as to how to present this transparently cooked-up arrangement in an acceptable way. We were, we believed, being held back deliberately as a negotiating ploy to persuade the Bank of England to grant London banking licences to Japanese securities firms such as Nomura. But the Bank of England refused to negotiate with any foreign power on a tit–for–tat basis, so for months we were stymied. Two interventions by Michael Howard, the junior trade minister sent out by Margaret Thatcher on what was described as a handbagging mission, only served to make matters worse.

So we trooped backwards and forwards from our basement to the Ministry next door, to a dim 1950-ish room in which officials worked long hours at battered gunmetal-grey desks surrounded by mountains of files, with no computers and few telephones. Sometimes we were made to resubmit material already submitted months before. At several successive encounters, armed with a volume of Halsbury's Laws of England and various other learned papers, I pursued an obscure seman-tic argument about the different duties of directors under British and Japanese company law. The twelfth meeting consisted of a getting-to-know-you dinner – at a cost of £1000 – for a senior Ministry official called Miyamoto in a geisha house in Yokohama, at which I sang an excruciating karaoke version of 'My Way'; Mr Miyamoto turned out to have no influence on our case whatever and we never saw him again. In the twenty-sixth and final meeting, my notes remind me, we were still hung up on the question of whether 'underwriting' and 'handling of new issues' were the same thing, even as we waited for a vice-minister to stamp his official seal on our licence.

These tireless bureaucrats were the inheritors of the *samurai* in Japan's feudal power structure, though they hardly looked it: the official in charge of our file, Mr Fujitsuka, had the lank hair and sweaty pallor of a man who rarely saw natural daylight. He was never less than civil to *gaijin*, but on the one occasion when we tried to circumvent him by complaining to someone more senior through the Bank of England, he was imperiously and savagely rude to my assistant, Mr Hirayama, virtually accusing him of being a traitor. Happily, we outlasted Fujitsuka on the case: the twenty-fifth of my twenty-six meeting notes recorded that he had been 'wafted by divine providence to the Kinki regional tax office'; I hope he is still there.

While all this was going on, Mike Connors and I conducted a parallel but more hostile set of negotiations with our colleagues in Barclays Bank, led by Michael Tomalin. It remains a mystery how any major public company could allow two of its divisions, operating in the world's most expensive business centre, to sustain such a complete failure of co-operation. The stand-off between BZW and Barclays was a *cause célèbre* of Tokyo cocktail party gossip throughout my time there. 'The simple answer is that the two Michaels should have been fired,' one senior ex-BZW executive told me. But far from being fired, each of them was supported to the hilt by bosses in London, who regarded Tokyo as one corner of the bigger chessboard of Barclays group power-politics.

There was a serious argument underlying the dispute, about how to maximize the value of Barclays' relationships with Japanese companies and banks and how to achieve brand recognition in a huge market where we were insignificant players. There was a potential overlap in the area of 'debt capital markets', a territory claimed by both parties but not yet successfully cultivated by either. The structure was eventually resolved after eighteen months of civil war by a day-long peace conference chaired by Martin Jacomb, at which, as the official minute-taker, I was able to exercise a certain influence on the nuances of the final agreement.

But at heart the problem was not one of words and products, but personalities. Michael Tomalin, the Barclays manager, was determined to be recognized as the senior Barclays person in Japan, and irate from first to last that Connors and I did not report to him. We told him what we were doing, but only through clenched teeth. Connors was a bold strategic thinker, but he was not a manager at heart and he showed little respect for Barclays hierarchy. He was at his best talking about his own specialism, investment research, or spouting blue-sky ideas about the amazing future of BZW, couched in the vocabulary of advanced electronics and *Star Wars* films, which drove Tomalin to apoplexy. BZW's apparently unlimited recruitment budget (we became the first foreign bank to launch a Japanese graduate recruitment scheme, for example) added to his fury.

The dispute sank into trivial point-scoring about who was invited to what and who sat next to whom at dinner, of which the following is perhaps an especially trivial example. When Barclays sponsored a Royal Ballet visit to Tokyo, Connors and I were not invited to the party. After pressure from the highest level in London, Connors was allowed in but I was still excluded. Happily, one of the most beautiful ballerinas was a friend of a friend of mine and had been told to look out for me. 'Are you Martin?' she said to Tomalin as he greeted his guests. 'I've been told I must meet Martin.' The story went round the town like wildfire.

It was fortunate, at that stage, that our basement and Tomalin's branch premises were two miles apart. But in due course the question of moving together, or 'co-location', arose. Tomalin saw an opportunity to move us under his wing by taking over the NatWest's office space next to his own; we extracted from our Ministry of Finance official some 'guidance' to the effect that he was unlikely to approve of the two operations being on the same floor of the same building. When instead we took a floor of the new Kasumigaseki building next door to our basement, we suggested that Barclays might take another floor in the same building, and thus move over to us. But the idea was dismissed out of hand. In fact it was a good one, and might have saved another joint move, three years later, into the world's most expensive office building, the NTT tower, known locally as the 'Tower of Bubble', where rents were $3000 a square metre.[1]

Overseeing the building of the BZW Kasumigaseki office was also part of my job. The budget for the project really was, in Connors's phrase, 'what it costs', because the Japanese contractors did not tell us what the bill would be until it was too late to change our minds. The final figure turned out to be £3 million, but London only demurred when we said we were building a set of interconnecting meeting rooms which could be opened out into a conference hall to seat more than a hundred (to accommodate investor presentations) equipped with full video cinema equipment and electrically operated blackout curtains. 'Why do you need electric curtains?' was the single question asked of us by BZW's management committee in London.

It was a fascinating encounter with the Japanese system. We wanted urgently to move into the new offices (we had seventy people in a basement designed for twenty-five) but we were told that we must use the building's official contractor for fitting out, and that we would have to wait to do so at the back of a queue of obscure government departments which were moving in on other floors. I sent Mr Hirayama to fight for a better deal on our behalf: he told me that as a teenage conscript in Manchuria in the 1930s he had been driven into battle at the point of an officer's gun, and accused me of treating him the same way. When he returned from the first meeting of interested parties, pale and shaken, I understood his apprehension. The building's super-visor, he said, had ignored Japanese conventions of oblique, consensus-forming discussion; he had simply harangued the meeting like a fascist dictator, expressing special contempt for foreign intruders. We decided to wait our turn.

But being Japan, the problem was solved in the end. We were given a date when the offices would be ready, and they were, in every minute

[1] Even when that move took place, after my time, the tussle continued to the last moment, focusing on which side of the group should have the more prestigious upper floor: BZW won on a technicality, by claiming that the cost of computer wiring dictated it should be on top.

perfect detail. The fitting out took seven weeks from start to finish. In London it would have taken six months. In Japan's pragmatic society, there always was a solution. The Japanese were practically impossible to do business with, but it was a pleasure not doing business with them. And they had the better of us all in the end: after a decade of massive investment in staff and offices by dozens of foreign securities firms – many of them, including BZW, redoubling their stakes to become members of the Tokyo Stock Exchange – the Japanese market peaked on 29 December 1989 and slid slowly down to a third of its peak value. It has never recovered. Flows of business withered away for foreign firms which had accumulated mountains of fixed costs. A market which had once seemed to be driven by investors' admiration for the technological brilliance and drive of Japanese industry was revealed to have been driven largely by gangsterism, political fixing and outright gambling.

The successors to Connors and Tomalin, respectively Ben Grigsby for BZW and Alan Brown for the bank, made friends with each other and set out to make sense of the business, weeding out costs on the equities side and getting rid of low-margin lending to second-rank Japanese corporate borrowers in the bank. Eventually a viable operation emerged, focused on trading in Japanese government bonds and bearing no resemblance at all to what we had planned when we first set out.

But 1989, at least, was an astonishingly profitable year for BZW's Japanese business, because a London-based team trading Japanese equity warrants[2] turned in a profit for the year of £50 million – their manager becoming, after much heated argument between Ebbgate House and Lombard Street, the first person in the Barclays group ever to pick up a £1 million bonus. The irony was that all the warrant traders needed in Tokyo were half a dozen desks and telephones; the rest of the operation was largely superfluous. But the huge one-off profit enabled Connors to claim that 'We're in the Japanese market for free,' even if we never reached, or even glimpsed in the distance, the golden valley of perpetual profits he had so often described.

But that was all after my time. Having secured the licence and built the office, I was expecting to return to London in the autumn of 1987. But then a crisis blew up in BZW's Hong Kong office which created a much more interesting prospect. Hong Kong had been the only overseas outpost of de Zoete & Bevan, which had a small, low-budget operation dealing in Hong Kong shares on behalf of London institutions. With BZW's budget to play with, it had rapidly become

---

[2] Rights to the issue of new shares at a fixed price within certain future dates.

larger and less frugal and it had acquired a new and glamorous managing director – a former Rothschild colleague of Tom Camoys called Barbara Wong. But she was not a stockbroker by background and was not given a friendly welcome by the de Zoetes side of the firm. Over the summer there had been a back-office crisis, involving stacks of unsettled share bargains and emergency all-night shifts to clear them. Various powerful personalities were sacked, or resigned, or were persuaded not to resign by means of spectacular increases in salary. Finally, Mrs Wong herself departed, somewhat to her own surprise. What remained of the operation was unstable, fractious and demoralized. As the manager nearest the door, as it were, I was suddenly appointed managing director of BZW Hong Kong, and sent down from Tokyo to pick up the pieces.

It was a nerve-racking experience. On my second day in the job, Sir Martin Jacomb arrived on a long-planned grand tour. My predecessor had arranged an in-house lunch for him which I now had to host in her place, and there had not even been time to warn the guests that she had gone – there was some discussion as to whether I might don one of the leather miniskirts she favoured to test whether the guests noticed the difference. The guests turned out to be a Who's Who of the local business scene: Willie Purves, the terrifying boss of the Hong Kong Bank, Piers Jacobs, the financial secretary of the government, David Li, chairman of the Bank of East Asia, and Ronald Li, chairman of the Hong Kong Stock Exchange. The latter pair were cousins but well known not to have been on speaking terms for the past twenty years, which made *placement* peculiarly difficult. The menu Mrs Wong had ordered from a nearby hotel turned out to consist of five elaborate courses, served at very leisurely intervals. It was not a success. Somewhere between the third and fourth courses, the guests started to make excuses about leaving.

'This is the most enormous lunch; only Barclays could afford this sort of thing,' Purves said with beady-eyed sarcasm as he prepared to go. 'You must be making wonderful profits.'

I had barely recovered from that fiasco when something even more cataclysmic hit us. 'Heard the news from home?' said a man from Warburgs in the lift lobby, some time after lunch on Friday 16 October 1987, 'Ninety-mile-an-hour winds across Britain.'

It was the day of the great hurricane. Activity in a febrile London stock market was curtailed because most of the windows of Ebbgate House were blown in by the extraordinary storm which swept the south of England. The London Hong Kong dealing desk, with its much-coveted river view, had been reduced (like Sir Martin Jacomb's office on the floor below) to a wreck of sodden paper and broken glass. Rupert Byng, a stylish Old Harrovian salesman, kept his raincoat on, crawled under a desk with his telephone and suavely tried to carry on dealing. But there were few people to talk to, because most clients were in similar chaos, or had failed to reach the City at all.

So business was abandoned, while metaphorical storm clouds gathered over New York waiting for Wall Street's opening. The Dow Jones industrial index fell a record 108 points that day, and over the weekend US Treasury Secretary James Baker made the obscure but incautious remark which triggered the crash of Black Monday: 'The rise in German interest rates is not a trend which we favour.' By then I was on a plane to London, not in anticipation of a crisis, but for pre-planned meetings about my new job.

By the time I reached Ebbgate House, the whole glamorous world of global securities trading to which we had been inducted in the year since Big Bang seemed to be coming to an abrupt end. The FTSE 100 index had recorded its largest ever one-day fall, while the Dow Jones lost 23 per cent. As I arrived on Tuesday morning, London was plunging by another 250 points. The chairman of the New York exchange had said the market was 'close to meltdown'. Trading monitor screens showed red digits everywhere, denoting falling prices.

'There was something sinister about it all, Armageddon-like, coming after the hurricane, with this red blood all over the screens,' former BZW director John Cousins recalled. 'It was panicky for the first two or three hours, then it was more stoical.'

Older hands, who had seen the 1973 share price collapse and lived through the long bear market which followed it, were sanguine. Those of us with shorter experience were less so. Having ascertained the extent of the fall in Hong Kong, I remember describing myself, with commendable honesty, as 'a rabbit in the headlights'. Summoned to see Tom Camoys and Rex Cooper, I ventured a remark about 'the next support level' at which Hong Kong might rally. Much as I admired Camoys, I suspect he knew no more than I did about extremes of market behaviour. But fixing me with a narrow, Clint Eastwood look he said, 'In these conditions, there are no support levels.'

BZW lost the best part of £70 million over those two days, and only found out afterwards how much stock it actually owned at the moment of disaster. But after the initial shock the mood was one of numbness rather than terror. While lesser competitors were accused of refusing to answer their phones, Martin Jacomb entered City legend by telling BZW traders to carry on offering prices whatever the damage: that was the moment at which BZW was recognized as a serious long-term player in the securities business. A van-load of champagne, due to be distributed to staff to mark the first anniversary of Big Bang, was quietly consigned to the cellar.

'In a perverse sort of way I quite enjoyed it,' one old BZW broker told me when I wrote a tenth-anniversary piece about the crash for the *Daily Telegraph*. The most basic fear across the firm was that the gravy train of giant salaries and bonuses, then just beginning to gather speed, had been derailed. But we were quickly reassured. The management reaction in most firms, including BZW, was to declare that strategy would be unaffected by the setback – and strategy at that stage often boiled down to buying market share at whatever cost. The pay spiral continued with barely a blip.

A secondary concern was the fact that all the paraphernalia of expertise and research, on which firms like BZW placed such expensive emphasis, had been shown to be meaningless in a crash. As the great American economist J. K. Galbraith said: 'Markets are driven higher by greed, and people come up with ingenious explanations for their apparent good fortune.' But there was no perceptible dent in the self-confidence of our analysts and pundits.

After the initial fall, the Hong Kong Stock Exchange had suspended business for a week, amid accusations that some of the big hands of the local market had forced the closure in order to protect their own positions. Ronald Li, my recent lunch guest, was eventually forced to resign. There were ugly scenes, and punches thrown on the exchange floor. When trading resumed, it was at a depressed level of turnover for several months. Then it began to recover, and after a year we had almost forgotten the crash had ever happened.

I never developed any real affinity for stockbroking business, but I like to think that I ran an efficient office and that I had a certain talent for encouraging good people. I relied heavily on the senior Chinese share-dealer, Kinson Hui, whose judgement I trusted completely, and when he told me that we ought to have a proper ceremony to give thanks for the safe deliverance of our business after the crash, I was happy to go along with the idea. This turned out to involve bringing a whole roast pig into the office, plastic sheeting having been laid on the floor to catch the dripping fat. Each member of staff in turn clapped hands to attract the attention of the spirits, bowed to the shining red face of the pig and planted a burning joss stick in front of its snout. Then we devoured the greasy pork with our bare hands. Some of the expatriates refused to take part in this pungent ritual, finding it

altogether too pagan and sinister. But I was glad to bow to the inscrutable beast. Like much else about life and business in Asia, the forces at
work were a mystery to me, but I knew I needed all the help I could
get.

The rest of my time in Hong Kong was without doubt the best part
of my banking career. The Hong Kong business itself ran steadily and
happily, and we added to it small offices in Seoul, Manila, Bangkok
and Taipei. In Singapore I completed the purchase of a stake in a local
broking firm, Pacific Union. I travelled out of Hong Kong fifty times
in two years, crossing and re-crossing Asia, absorbing myself in the
intricacies of local business practice, regulation, social etiquette, cuisine
and nightlife. I collected interesting objects and pictures. Unlike many
expatriate businessmen, I genuinely liked dealing with Asian people,
and on the whole they seemed to like me.

The more difficult diplomatic challenge was, as ever, in internal
relations between Barclays and BZW. In Hong Kong, Barclays boasted
a Merchant Banking Division, engaged in putting together packages of
loan finance for industrial and construction projects around the region.
Its head, an able but prickly Fijian Indian, was determined at all costs
that his team should not be made part of BZW. On another front, as
in Tokyo, discussion of 'co-location' of the Barclays and BZW offices
turned into a series of savage dog-fights, in which I felt it my duty to
uphold the spirit of BZW by rejecting any plan which involved sharing
a reception desk or a staff canteen with the bank. But relations were
by no means as bad as they were in London, New York or Tokyo. The
two senior Barclays managers in the region – Mark Tress (a godson of
Sir Julian Crossley, the Goodenough brother-in-law, and thereby a
distant DCO blue-blood) and Peter Geer, a wise old Africa-hand in
Singapore – were both as reasonable and helpful as they could be. But
we were all locked into a structure that was simply a recipe for internal
conflict. If the energy and aggression that conflict generated around
the world had all been directed outwards, at the clients and the competition, who knows what a brilliant success we might have created.

By late 1989 I had been abroad for more than six and a half years,
and I felt it was time to go home. From the point of view of my
banking career, it would have been much better to have stayed in the
East. It is a well-known problem – even in the best run companies, of
which BZW was not one – that managers from overseas, who have
enjoyed more freedom and status than they probably deserve, are
difficult to assimilate back into the home base. Though I did not know
it, I was about to become a classic example of the problem.

Before that issue came to a head, life was overshadowed by other events. My father's health had began to fail seriously during the latter part of his time at British Telecom, when, among other arduous duties, he had to commute monthly to board meetings in Canada. He was diabetic, and a breathiness apparent for some years – the residue of childhood bronchitis – had developed into an incurable lung disease, pulmonary fibrosis. Increasingly gaunt and short of breath, he retired from BT in 1986. In April 1988, on medical advice, he asked to be released from his other board appointments – the Bank of England, Barclays and the property group Haslemere Estates – in the coming September. Sir John Quinton had written back:

> Of course there will be no problem over the change in the date of your leaving the Board, and I will make the necessary arrangements. As you say, forty-seven and a half years is a fair stint. I would add, speaking personally, that in the long history of Barclays Bank no single person has done more to enable it to grow and prosper than you have. All those here who had the privilege of working with you will entirely share my view.

These were kindly remarks, made in private to a man who clearly did not have long to live. To say that no one had done more for Barclays was in truth an overstatement, because Frederick Goodenough – who had cemented the domestic amalgamation, created DCO and run the bank as an autocrat for almost two decades – clearly fitted that description. Derek Wilde, with the support from above of Sir John Thomson, had made a huge contribution in the 1960s. On the international side in the 1970s, Sir Anthony Tuke, with the assistance of Julian Wathen, had certainly made the bank grow, but whether they made it prosper is another question.

My father's condition continued to deteriorate. He could read and paint, but he could not walk more than a few steps. His lung-power became drastically reduced. He coughed continuously. He died at home in Surrey, aged sixty-five, on 15 June 1990. The best of the obituaries of him was written for the *Independent* by Margaret Ackrill (joint author of the unpublished tercentenary history of Barclays), who recalled his 'quick mind and swift eye' and commented on 'a sad end to a vigorous career ... Weyer was an outstanding force for change in a dependable but cautious profession.'

The immediate reaction to his death from Barclays made a deep impression on me. It really was as though the bank was a big family, or a small regiment. My father was one of their own. From the first, it was understood without discussion that the bank would help, where needed, in every aspect of the tiresome arrangements which follow a death. I suddenly understood, better than before, the personal solidarity that was part of the old system – now almost completely destroyed – of lifelong career-building. Barclays' corporate reaction, expressed through the individual actions and words of dozens of people, was in contrast to that of British Telecom, which did no more than instruct a public relations company to send a large bunch of flowers, wrongly addressed.

A throng of Barclays people, including Tim Bevan, came to the funeral in the village church at Chipstead. Even before that, two managers from the trustee department came to the house to reassure my mother that they would handle everything to do with my father's estate and sort out for her any tax matters or other household paperwork she could not face. Their services would be available to her, they said, free of charge for the rest of her life (though, of course, it did not quite work out that way: in the mid-1990s, even the benefits offered to pensioners' widows came under cost-cutting scrutiny, and the tax service was hived off into a private company which charges for its advice).

From head office, Andrew Buxton rang me at my desk in Ebbgate House. He said that the bank would handle all the arrangements for a memorial service, but that 'our usual church', St Edmund the King in Lombard Street (where the name of his kinsman Maurice Buxton, a local director in the Lombard Street parlour, had for many years appeared on the noticeboard as a common councilman of the ward), was closed for rebuilding work. St Margaret Lothbury, behind the Bank of England, was available as an alternative, however, and Barclays would host a lunch party in the adjacent Overseas Bankers Club afterwards.

It was a fine service. My father's former chauffeur, Terry Reed, was detached by the bank to drive my mother for the day. John Quinton gave an address, the governor of the Bank of England read the lesson, and Cathryn Pope, a young soprano from the English National Opera, sang 'L'Amero' from Mozart's early opera *Il Re Pastore*. At the party afterwards, old Barclays men tucked into a substantial buffet and swapped irreverent anecdotes about my father. He had been a very demanding boss to many of them. Evidently he had a reputation for vanity, particularly in relation to his public-speaking skills, and for occasionally enjoying a drink. Sir John Nicholson, chairman of Martins Bank before the 1968 merger, shed a tear as he talked to me. There were also high emotions expressed about the state of the bank and most especially about BZW: 'They're all nutters over there,' one retired general manager declared.

I have often wondered, though I lasted another eighteen months in BZW, whether that lunch marked the beginning of the end of my own banking career. If I was ambitious to rise in BZW (and I confess I sometimes pictured myself at fifty-something, swanning around the world as an ambassadorial vice-chairman) it was perhaps to fulfil my father's ambition for me – itself the product of Barclays' fathers-and-sons syndrome – rather than any real drive of my own. From that day onwards my motivation dropped and my inclination to dissidence grew: it became only a matter of time before I dropped out of the race, either at my own instigation or at theirs. In the end they beat me to it.

I had to sack, or take part in the sacking of, or watch being sacked, quite a stream of people at BZW before it happened to me. So at least I knew what to expect, and I knew that it could never be done elegantly or without bad feeling.

My first experience had been in Hong Kong, when I sacked the office chauffeur, an ill-tempered Cantonese fellow called Andrew. His terminal offence was to have abandoned our most important client – a formidable lady from the Henderson fund management group in London – on a pavement in Kowloon for forty minutes while he apparently went off to have his lunch. When he at last returned to collect her, he responded to her complaint with a tirade of Cantonese abuse. So I summoned him to my office and launched into what I hoped would be a well-phrased and fair dismissal speech.

'I go right now?' he spat, before I had finished the first sentence.

'Er, yes, if you wouldn't mind . . .' I replied, but he had already left the room, never to be seen again.

Sacking corporate financiers in London was not so easy. I had to help Graham Pimlott, the division head, to dispatch a whole list of them one morning, and despite careful choreography, the episode was a farce. The idea was to summon the victims one by one into a meeting room, break the news, then escort them – allowing them to collect only their coats and briefcases on the way – straight out of Ebbgate House to the personnel department across the road, where they would be read their full severance and pension rights. They would be allowed back a few days later to collect personal effects from their desks. It sounded fine, but it just didn't happen according to plan. The first victim, a dentist who had changed profession to banking, could not have been nicer about it, apologizing for causing me such an unpleasant task, just as he might have apologized for the necessity of drilling my molars. But the second victim simply ran out in distress and disappeared, and a third went into clinical shock, returning to sit rigid and ashen-faced at his desk in the middle of an open-plan office, refusing to be escorted away. By then, everyone knew what we were doing, and thought we were complete bastards.

Pimlott had put in quite a lot more practice by the time he got around to sacking me in January 1992. For the previous six months I had been telling friends that I sensed he had me in his sights, and that it was now only a matter of time. We had got off to a good start in the first half of 1990, when he promoted me to 'Chief Operating Officer' of his division, and raised my salary by almost 50 per cent. But the trouble began in the following winter, when I disagreed with him on a variety of minor management decisions. One problem was that I thought I knew at least as much about management as he did, and a lot more about Barclays and BZW. The other problem was that I knew very little about corporate finance. The division was far from profitable: the greater the pressure to perform, the more difficult Pimlott became to work for, as he once acknowledged to me. We were barely bothering to speak to each other by the spring of 1991. Finally, we agreed, amicably enough, that I should transfer within the division to a small team which specialized in overseas privatization work.

Before I moved at the end of June, however, I took part in a meeting about half-yearly promotions which I afterwards realized had left me a marked man. Taking part in the discussion were Pimlott, Callum McCarthy and Amir Eilon. I proposed for promotion to director Huw Jenkins, who was then taking over from John Varley as managing director in Hong Kong. Jenkins had chosen this job rather than return-ing to our division in London: he had 'jumped ship to do admin', Eilon said, and was of no account. But his job was of director seniority I said, and Jenkins was an able fellow whom we would like to keep in our team for the longer term, even if temporarily detached: the promotion would be a gesture of goodwill.

There is no such thing as a fixed hierarchy of seniority across the firm, they said almost as one. There are merely titles which we give out, they might have added, and there is no such thing in BZW as the longer term, or gestures of goodwill. The atmosphere of the meeting was intensely unpleasant. I was not brave enough to say so, but I imagined this to be how Cambodian leaders conducted themselves in what they liked to call Year Zero. I lost the argument and left the room.

Shortly afterwards I made matters worse by sending Pimlott a note to the effect that, since I was no longer his chief operating officer, would he confirm that I was now one of the division's seven or eight 'managing directors' rather than one of its twenty-plus 'directors', on the grounds that as COO I had ranked as a managing director. He took this badly, replying with a three-page-long dictated note which to this day I find almost too painful to read: it concluded by grudgingly allowing me to call myself managing director as long as I accepted that this 'inevitably lifts the stakes'. My short reply was almost suicidally provocative. It is a wonder he did not fire me there and then.

But he did not, and I spent six months helping to organize new BZW offices in Warsaw, Prague and Budapest and pursuing mandates to advise Polish Lot Airlines on the redevelopment of Warsaw airport and a Czech bank on its role in Czechoslovakia's mass privatization programme. This was a stimulating diversion, though by no means as enjoyable as my years of travelling in Asia. My heart was not in it, but at least it kept me out of Pimlott's way.

By the end of the year, the breeze down the corridor from his office was becoming chillier by the day. I sat waiting for the call through the pre-Christmas period, when several other people in the division were chopped out. At the departmental Christmas party, a gruesome affair in a Kensington nightclub, Pimlott (incongruously sporting a battery-lit bow tie) seemed anxious not to have a conversation with me. But I survived the first week of January and began to wonder whether I had worried unnecessarily.

On Sunday, 8 January 1992 I had a late dinner with some friends in Chester Square, ending with a pungent Vacherin cheese and a large quantity of red wine. Waking with a hangover after a night of fierce indigestion, I arrived at the office later than usual on Monday morning; it might have been ten past nine. Jeremy Seddon, the head of the privatization unit, was dancing nervously behind my desk, searching my diary to see where I might be; in his agitated state, he had found my 1991 diary rather than the new 1992 one, and could not understand why he was looking at the wrong day of the week. A big, bald, clumsy man with an eager-to-please manner which made him good at winning privatization mandates, Seddon was not at his best during this episode. Throughout the days that followed, he sustained a tortured 'How not to handle a colleague who's being sacked' performance of the kind usually found in John Cleese's best-selling management training videos.

'You're late,' he barked, uncharacteristically. 'You're expected at a meeting.'

'What meeting?'

'Come on, you'll find out,' he barked again, panic gripping his throat. I suppose it was obvious what meeting this must be before I even saw who else was there: Pimlott and my friend Howard Paget, the personnel director, who winked at me and made no attempt to conceal the familiar form (with pension details and so on) lying on the table in front of him.

'I expect you can guess what this is about,' Pimlott began, talking fast to discourage interruption. 'There's no place for you here any more, I'm afraid, and we're asking you to go. If you can find a job for yourself anywhere else in Barclays or BZW, that's up to you. Howard will explain the position, but I don't want to get into a discussion with you about it now. If you want to come and talk to me about it in a few days' time, before you go, I'll be happy to see you.' And with that he left us to it.

It was an insult and a deep blow to the self esteem. It was 'like a bereavement', as one of the hundreds of other aggrieved sackees in this story put it. But it was also a moment of profound liberation. My first thought was 'Thank God father isn't alive to hear this,' and my second was 'Now I can be a journalist instead.'

That is, of course, exactly what I did, and my second career proved immeasurably more satisfying than my first; so I do not bear a grudge against Pimlott or anyone else. But still I wonder, and many other people in BZW and Barclays wondered loudly at the time, at the sheer wastefulness of the exercise. I was not a high-flying deal-maker, but I was an experienced manager who had done a series of difficult jobs, from Malaysia onwards, with some success. I was well known to Barclays people around the world. The bank clearly had no obligation to keep me for life – especially it had no obligation to keep me because of my father – but it did have an investment in me that might have been worth nurturing. BZW did not want rid of me because I was useless, but Pimlott wanted rid of me because I was becoming a dissident influence in his division. If he had quietly told me to find another job in the group or leave in three months' time, I would have welcomed the opportunity.

But that was not to be. The formula of 'You're fired, but if you happen to find another job here that's up to you' was not designed to be helpful. Tom Camoys, Oliver Stocken and John Varley were all sympathetic, but had nothing to suggest. My friend Humphrey Percy, in charge of swaps and money market dealing, discussed with his boss, John Spencer, whether they might find a place for me, but Spencer's answer was 'It's not worth the hassle of antagonizing Pimlott.' A few days later, a sudden vacancy arose to run the Singapore office, which I had set up, where I was on excellent terms with the local partners, and where I was registered with the authorities as an authorized dealing director. My name was floated, but the answer from the equities division head, Jonathan Davie, I was told, was 'Oh no, we want a real stockbroker to run it.'

So I spent the last week of my banking career on a British government funded trip to Moscow and St Petersburg, lecturing to Russian officials about the benefits of privatization. I did not return to Ebbgate House. I did, however, send one last memorandum to Pimlott, prompted by a mole in the management secretariat who tipped me the wink that de Zoete & Bevan men always asked for bonuses even after they were fired, and sometimes got them. So I itemized the useful things I had done during the previous year, and asked for a bonus on top of my severance pay, which had been set at the theoretical maximum of a month's salary for each year of service. Sure enough, two months later, they sent me another £20,000. It seemed to me to be final confirmation of the mad way in which BZW was run.

Very shortly after that, in the very week that I officially fell off the BZW payroll, I achieved my true ambition. I appeared in the *Spectator* for the first time on the day of the April 1992 general election, which the Conservatives were widely expected to lose. The editor, Dominic Lawson, thought my unsolicited essay might strike a chord with his readers at what seemed to be the end of an era.

My own title for it was *Phantom of the Gravy Train*, and it said everything I wanted to say about my first career. So I reprint it here in full:

Merchant banking was the ultimate Eighties career. It found its time in the middle of that decade in a great blaze of swaggering hubris, just as membership of the Soviet Communist Party peaked as a lifestyle choice a few years earlier. How appropriate, for me, that it should come to an abrupt end just ahead of a general election which, whatever the outcome, completes the postscript to the Thatcher era.

For times change. An occupation which had once been the most luxurious of international gravy trains had transmuted itself into something more like British Rail's new InterCity 225: high-tech but unstable, full of disgruntled and ill-matched people for whom, even though their numbers were shrinking, there were somehow never quite enough seats. It was certainly time to get off. One January morning I arrived to find the decision had been taken for me.

The feeling is one of rage mixed with relief, and nostalgia for the

heyday of a few years ago. And what a heyday it was, for this was a job
which offered practically everything: glamorous travel, an ecstasy of
name-dropping, a gold Mercedes with a chauffeur, a key to the executive
toilet and the opportunity to blunder like Flashman into every boudoir
and battlefield of the financial world.

One of the merchant banker defendants in the Guinness trial, Lord
Spens, was described as a noted stamp collector. Many merchant bankers
have that particular mentality, but, rather than postage stamps, we tended
to treasure the sort of stamps you get in your passport, and the names of
the most obscure and exotic airports en route: Gdansk, Penang, Misawa
and Memphis spring to mind. We collected book-matches from every
restaurant and nightclub, casually displaying them in large glass bowls all
over south west London. An almost random handful gives me The Good
Time Club of Roppongi, Iberia Airways, the Palace Hotel in Prague,
the Tahiti Beachcomber, Annabel's, the Ginza karaoke in Albemarle
Street, Delmonico's off Wall Street, the Lai Lai Sheraton in Taipei and
the Auberge des Trois Bonheurs in the rue Saint-Honoré.

And on the way through, I recall, I shook the silken hand of Asil
Nadir and was shaken by the granite fist of Gerald Ronson. I had my
elbow grasped by the soon-to-be-disgraced Ronald Li of the Hong
Kong Stock Exchange muttering 'We can do deals together,' and I
actually hired the Recruit Company of Japanese scandal fame to recruit
someone. I exchanged pleasantries with President Iliescu of Romania
and I bumped into Richard Nixon in a lift. I wrote a speech (of which
barely a word survived in delivery) for a certain well-known former
Chancellor of the Exchequer. A member of the present Cabinet, in
Tokyo on a handbagging mission, dropped in for coffee. I went backstage
to meet a starlet of the Royal Ballet, played pool with a cowboy in
the Fort Worth stockyards, carried a briefcase through the bazaar in
Kathmandu, got sprayed with holy water by Thailand's highest priest
and held a meeting stark naked in the Riverside Sauna in Seoul.

I could fill pages with these lists, but there was a day in May 1989
which, looking back, seems to have been the zenith (perhaps it was two
days, but memory condenses them). Did I really try to gain access to the
hotel bedroom of Taiwan's Finance Minister, Mrs Shirley Kuo, in the
company of a knighted fellow of All Souls? Did I attend a meeting in
Beijing's Great Hall of the People addressed by President Yang Shangkun,
witness the first of the great student demonstrations in Tian'anmen
Square, and take afternoon tea with a minister of the Papua New
Guinea government who was high as a kite? Did I then go on, posing
uncomfortably as the All Souls knight's wife, to crash Merrill Lynch's

invitation-only cocktail party in a closed pavilion of the Forbidden City? Yes I did, and at the time it seemed as normal a way to spend the day as the dentist at his chair or the potter at his wheel.

But what did I actually do, you may well ask. What is a merchant banker anyway, apart from a man who avoids rhyming slang? Well, at the beginning of the eighties, for instance, I could have told you how to price syndicated loans to Brazil and Mexico; the pricing didn't really matter in the long run because, as everybody knows, practically none of those loans ever came back. Late 1982 found me writing papers on the legality of British local authority interest rate swaps. Woops; eight years later a judge found that some London boroughs had used this particular piece of arithmetic to gamble themselves into perdition. He told us to our grief and amazement that we couldn't make them pay us back, because it had been illegal (for them, not us) all the time. Somewhere in the mid-eighties we discovered cross-border mergers and acquisitions, which meant spending years trying to persuade giant Japanese corporations to buy every famous European brand name from Aquascutum to Zeiss. The end of the decade found us in liberated Eastern Europe, taking tea with ministers and selling them Mrs Thatcher's great gift to merchant bankers, better than any tax cut, the concept of privatization.

In parallel with all this there was Big Bang, the revolution of the London securities market which put us in bed with the brokers and traders, the Big Swinging Dicks of Michael Lewis's *Liar's Poker*, who apparently thought we were pussies. Of course we looked down on them. They were coarse, shallow and greedy (greedier even than we were) and they didn't know how to take tea with the Minister. But they had fun, and sometimes we got to join in. A big international share placing may be the most exciting half hour you will ever spend in business: the adrenalin of a huge risk taken for a very short time; the stadium clamour of a roomful of salesmen who've all seen the film *Wall Street*; the cash-register ring of a colossal profit materializing before your very eyes.

Of course, as always, it can go horribly wrong, now or later. I spent an exhilarating night on a London trading floor selling many millions of dollars' worth of paper called Perpetual Floating Rate Notes to investors in Japan. Now, thanks to obscure changes in international regulations on bank capital, they will show a substantial loss on them for ever. There was another long and memorable night in October 1987 when we watched the Hong Kong stockmarket drop like a Korean airliner over Kamchatka. It was a night which included, in the Far Eastern lunch-hour, a pre-dawn break for beer, darts and fried breakfast (but sadly no book-matches) in the Fox & Anchor in Smithfield. The meat porters probably thought we were pussies too, but we thought we were tremendous.

How was it, you may well also ask, for our employers? More pertinently, how was it for their shareholders, footing the bill for this ten-year ego-trip? It wasn't all bad: collectively we got into and out of all kinds of booms as well as busts, we broke new ground, we were ahead of the game, in some instances we even invented the game. We were proud of what we built but it never looked anything like the three-year plan said it should, and stable growth was not a feature; this was the roller-coaster gravy train. When we were not making enough money for them we thought of ourselves as the go-faster stripes on the livery, adding the lustre their rolling-stock lacked, and we asked for bigger bonuses. When we *were* making enough money for them, which was not often but sometimes, we asked for bigger bonuses still, lest we go and do all this for some other company.

At its best it was so much fun that we should have been paying them, but they didn't know that. Often they did give us bigger bonuses. Sometimes they gave us phantom ones as well, as an incentive to stay, artificial share options which couldn't be cashed in for several years. And what a grim world the survivors found themselves in by the time the day arrived to encash the phantom options, like coming out of your bunker after the bomb to find the banknotes of some obliterated state wafting in the nuclear wind.

Gone is the iconic figure of the eighties, whisked for the last time from the Hong Kong Mandarin to Kai Tak airport in the back of a white Rolls Royce. If he's still got a job at all, he's stuck at Frankfurt on his way back from Warsaw with a Eurotraveller Economy ticket, a ham roll and a bout of flu. He may recover: markets and bank proprietors have short memories, the gravy train may roll again in all its glory. But not for a while. For now perhaps, the iconic figure of the Nineties, the one who's ahead of the game, is the former merchant banker cultivating his garden and relishing his memories: been there, done that, met the Minister, got the book-matches.

THE ANNUAL SHOW

1993–1998: The dividend cut – Buxton splits his job – The
appointment of Martin Taylor – A mixed impression – The share
buy-backs – A turning-point for Taylor – Difficulties in pleasing
the customer – Barclays as seen from an agricultural show

By the time Barclays announced its 1992 annual results, there was no
hope of Buxton hanging on to his dual role as chairman and chief
executive. The dividend had been cut from 21.2 pence per share to
15.2 pence, which was less than its 1988 level, and the institutional
shareholders were furious.

The year-end figures were catastrophic. For the first time in its 97-
year-history, Barclays had made a net loss. The deficit before tax was
£242 million – an embarrassingly close echo of the £240 million
provision on the Imry loan. The loss was not the result of one bad
loan, however, but thousands of them. Total bad debt provisions for
the year amounted to £2,554,000,000. The loss was concentrated in
the UK domestic bank, which dropped £414 million, but it was offset
by a £241 million profit in BZW, attributed largely to 'money market,
foreign exchange, swaps and options and fixed income activities' –
meaning that BZW was now benefiting very substantially from its
take-over of the bank's Treasury operation. With £53 million of 'costs
associated with staff reductions' also reported in the domestic bank, it
is not surprising that morale there was low, and resentment towards
BZW ever higher.

Overseas, there were losses in the United States, and a spectacular
£98 million loss in France, much of it, as usual, on property lending.
The 1990 acquisition of L'Européenne de Banque in Paris had turned,
pound for pound, into one of the worst Barclays' decisions of all time.
This former Rothschild banking house had been bought for its

corporate lending connections and its handsome 1960s headquarters building in the rue Lafitte, which Barclays thought was undervalued; it was not, and nor was it even a very practical building for Barclays to occupy. The acquisition almost doubled the bank's balance sheet in France, and multiplied its problems there many times over. The other exciting European acquisition of 1990, the German private banking group Merck Finck was also emerging as a disaster; all its best investments had remained in the hands of the Finck family, while its loan portfolio turned out to be a big bundle of trouble.

At this all-time nadir in Barclays' fortunes, Buxton finally agreed to split his responsibilities. Rumours began to circulate that head-hunters had been appointed – and that senior insiders were unhappy about it – in early March, but the intention was not made explicit until three weeks later. Even after that, Buxton noted in his annual statement that 'this is not a change that should be rushed'. Indeed it was not: the process took a full six months to complete. A team of boardroom knights – Sir Denys Henderson, Sir Martin Jacomb, Sir Peter Middleton, Sir Nigel Mobbs and RTZ chairman Sir Derek Birkin – was delegated to produce a shortlist of candidates. They were under pressure from the institutions (led by the Prudential, which held 4.5 per cent of Barclays shares) and from the Bank of England to make a swift appointment.

That pressure was not particularly biased towards an outside appointment. Within the bank, however, a critical loss of self-confidence now militated against the possibility of an internal promotion. For the first time in the clearing bank's history, no lifelong career-builder seemed to measure up to the vacant senior job – not even the tough, decisive 54-year-old vice-chairman, Alastair Robinson, an Etonian Essex landowner who was not a family member or a Special List man by origin, but very much in the mould and probably a better manager than Buxton. The finance director, Peter Wood – deeply disaffected ever since Peter Middleton's victory in the BZW–MIB restructuring battle – was a non-runner, and barely waited for the race to start; he left at the end of April to become finance director of Standard Chartered, working for his old Barclays colleague Malcolm Williamson.

Meanwhile, the message which seeped out from the knightly subcommittee was that the new chief executive needed to be 'an agent of change' – meaning an outsider with no Barclays baggage – and might even have to come from America. But the American candidates presented did not impress, and looked very expensive. Only one, an Americanized Briton trained in the finance subsidiary of an industrial conglomerate, made it on to the shortlist. Of the British names floated in the press, Derek Wanless, who had become chief executive of NatWest a year earlier, was certainly the best qualified, but it seemed unlikely either that he would want to move or that the Bank of England would be happy for him to do so. The outstanding candidate, the most unusual, and probably the youngest, was 41-year-old Martin Taylor.

When I first met Taylor, one lunch-time outside the Bow Wine Vaults off Cheapside a dozen years earlier, he was already – as the editor of the *Financial Times*'s Lex column – one of the celebrities of his City generation. The girl who introduced him to me resorted to the special tone that socially acute people use to indicate that they are introducing someone you must surely already have heard of, as indeed I had. When I met him again, on a corporate junk in Hong Kong in 1988 – he was now a director of the Courtaulds textile group – the effect was much the same. His courtly, donnish manners were immediately attractive; he spoke in clever paragraphs and responded alertly to whatever you said to him; he was a natural centre of attention. He was clearly a man who was destined to go a long way.

But it had not always been obvious that he would go a long way in business rather in academia. His passions were cerebral ('ideas and language,' as he put it) from the start. Born in Burnley, the son of an accountant who died when he was eight and stepson of a wealthy wholesaler, he was educated at Eton as the top King's Scholar of the 1965 intake. 'He came top in every exam,' one contemporary recalled, 'but he was one of those slightly strange boys, totally focused on studying, barely aware of people around him. I'd never have imagined him becoming a success in business.'

Going up to Oxford to read English, he decided during his first year that he wanted to read Chinese instead, the issue coming to a head during his Mods examinations in the summer term. Why Chinese? 'Because I wanted to learn a hard language and read ancient Chinese in the original ... It would never have occurred to me to read economics.' He took a second, incidentally, not the first that is sometimes attributed to him by journalists copying each other's cuttings.

After Oxford he joined the Reuters news agency, working in London, Germany and France. He developed an interest in finance and in 1978 he moved to the *Financial Times*, where he rapidly became the leader of the Lex team, revered by younger journalists around him. 'He was a single, shining star, obviously and remarkably brilliant,' recalled Carla Rappoport, now with *The Economist*. 'An extraordinarily good analyst with an encyclopaedic memory for detail. But also very nice. He was one of the rare journalists who could maintain good relations with companies but still write critically about them if he felt he had to. With the rest of us he was always generous with his time, and he had a way of making ordinary questions seem like good questions.' (Someone once observed that Taylor often looked disappointed at Barclays' results meetings, because none of today's City journalists ever asked questions that tested him.)

Taylor somehow sat above the cut and thrust of daily journalism. Despite his Reuters training, he was no newshound: for all his precocious eminence on the paper, he never wrote a front-page lead story. He always went home to Blackheath in time to see his daughters before they went to bed. But he was not a dilettante: there was no surprise when he said he was moving to Courtaulds (one of the companies about which he had written so perceptively) because he had the air of a man who wanted to make things happen rather than merely write about them. 'I became fascinated by the workings of big companies,' he told one interviewer. 'They were in trouble and I was curious.'

Rappoport worried that Taylor was, at bottom, 'way too nice' to make his way in the hard commercial world. But he talked to several potential employers, and what drew him finally to the textile and fibre conglomerate Courtaulds was the opportunity of working for its chairman, Christopher Hogg − a disciplined, thoughtful businessman who became his role model and mentor. One of the lessons Taylor credited to Hogg was 'getting the right balance between patience and impatience': a lesson which he perhaps eventually forgot at Barclays.

But at Courtaulds, all went well. Taylor moved from personal assistant to Hogg to head of the textiles division. In 1990, when the group completed a radical demerger exercise, he became chief executive of Courtaulds Textiles, maker *inter alia* of the Wonderbra, Wolsey socks and Jockey underpants. This was a public company in its own right, with turnover of almost £1 billion but serious problems of over-capacity. He sold off non-core and under-performing businesses, reduced the workforce by 9,000, reduced the group's borrowings and produced an improved profit performance despite the recession. His high status among his former colleagues in journalism ensured him a consistently good press. His recruitment as chief executive of Barclays, announced on 19 August 1993 to take effect on 1 January 1994, was greeted with a round of applause from the media and an almost audible sigh of relief from the bank's institutional shareholders.

'He's known to us and we are positive,' said one succinctly. Andrew Buxton nodded to investors' concerns about his own capabilities by saying 'I think I will be a better chairman with Martin as chief executive.' Taylor deflected comment about his lack of banking experience by pointing out that, coming from textiles, 'I'm quite used to over supplied markets.' 'He may not be a banker,' observed John Jay in the *Sunday Telegraph*, 'but then just look at the mess bankers have made of banking in the last two decades.' It looked like the boldest and smartest City appointment for many months, and Barclays share price rose 4 per cent on the news.

For Taylor himself, Barclays was a less comfortable proposition than Courtaulds, partly because he no longer had the sympathetic mentoring of Christopher Hogg. He knew nobody at Barclays well, and many people had warned him not to take the job because of the bank's internal strife. The traditional bankers in Barclays clearly saw him as a puppy who needed house-training. On the other hand, he had three advantages which made him acceptable to them: he was not from a competitor bank, he was not an American, and he was not one of the insiders who would have been resented even more than an outsider – David Band, for example, or Sir Peter Middleton.

His brief gave him the freedom 'to shoot all the sacred cows', as he put it, but it was not an easy job to come to grips with. As Middleton had said in his controversial interview, the bank's decision-making processes were 'difficult to understand'. Internal information flows were inadequate for a manager of Taylor's analytical turn of mind, 'like going to one of those countries where there are no good maps,' he remarked to one colleague. In the early weeks, he sometimes learned about events in Barclays through the pages of the London *Evening Standard*. And as he learned more, he found the risks in the business to be rather greater than was apparent to the outside world. Though an economic recovery was by then well under way, the bank was still bleeding heavily in certain areas and was extremely vulnerable to any shock – a snap election, for example – which might send the UK property market plunging again.

The 1993 annual results, the first to be announced in Taylor's reign, nevertheless showed a significant improvement, with a return to £664 million of pre-tax profit. Bad debt provisions still added up to £1.9 billion – a large portion arising in the United States, where the group was at last extracting itself from all its retail banking and property lending adventures. France, Germany and Italy lost another £135 million between them. But the domestic bank had produced £632 million of profit, and BZW Division (now including not only Treasury but what remained of the group's ongoing businesses in North America and Asia) produced a spectacular £501 million. The overall trend was clearly in the right direction, but Taylor had serious work to do. He set his own target, by declaring that the profits ought to be three times larger than they were.

He settled to the task, and reports emerging from Lombard Street in the early months of 1994 said that he was a breath of fresh air; that he was accessible and interesting to work for, if sometimes petulant; that he was willing to take decisions. Andrew Buxton, after an arduous eighteen months between the sidelining of Quinton and the arrival of Taylor, seemed content to take a back seat and to spend rather less time in Lombard Street. He spent more time talking to important corporate customers[1], and travelling abroad. Having never shown much liking for touring Barclays' overseas empire in earlier years – he did not like the constant round of formal lunches and dinners, especially if they involved highly spiced foreign food – Buxton now developed an unexpected affection for the Middle East, an area in which Barclays had no substantial businesses and which is among the least favourite destinations of many seasoned business travellers. He made regular visits to the region throughout his chairmanship.[2]

While the press hung on Taylor's every pronouncement, in fact, Buxton was barely heard of again until the collapse of Barings in February 1995, when he emerged in a self-appointed role as the organizer of a rescue syndicate of British banks. During emergency discussions at the Bank of England over the crisis weekend, Buxton extracted commitments of £600 million from the assembled bankers – though the plan swiftly proved unworkable because of unquantifiable risks in Barings' open futures positions, which the Bank of England itself refused to underwrite. To those banks which were reluctant to commit (notably, Standard Chartered, one of whose representatives at the meeting was Buxton's former underling Peter Wood) Buxton said magisterially: 'This is UK Limited and we've all got to contribute. I'm going to put you down anyway.' It is often said that the Bank of England was not previously a fan of Buxton's, but he made such a

---

[1] In 1994 the chief executive of one of Britain's leading retail groups, at a private dinner party, made the following (entirely unsolicited) remark to me, illustrating the most fundamental obstacle to the success of Barclays' corporate and investment banking strategy: 'The people at Barclays keep offering to bring Andrew Buxton to see me, but I can't think of anything I want to talk to him about. All I need from Barclays is cash-handling and a payroll service and an overdraft. If I want anything fancier than that I talk to Morgan Stanley.'
[2] And continued to do so – on a generously remunerated part-time contract with Barclays – after he stepped down in 1999.

favourable impression in this episode that he was promptly invited to join the Bank's Court, or board of directors.

In September 1994 I went to see Taylor at Royal Mint Court to interview him for *Management Today* magazine. I also interviewed, in the same period, Sir William Purves of HSBC, Sir Brian Pearse of Midland and Sir Brian Pitman of Lloyds. The contrast was instructive. The latter three were all of a type: physically robust, conventionally dressed, plain spoken in the accents of their birth and the vocabulary of forty years in branch banking. Taylor on the other hand, though not frail, did not have an impressive physical presence. The lightness of manner I recalled from previous encounters had retreated into a pre-occupied, edgy seriousness. He had acquired a facial habit of lapsing into sudden, distant, cross expressions as tangential thoughts flashed across his mind. He was pale, and wearing an unbankerish modern suit, a green shirt with a soft, button-down collar, and an abstract tie. I did not make a note of his shoes (as Barclays personnel managers always did in job interviews) but I would bet that they were not the regulation black toecap lace-up Oxfords.

None of this mattered a hoot – he was not an actor hired to play the part, after all – but it reinforced the impression of a fish out of water which gradually becomes part of this story. He talked more brilliantly than his three competitors put together but without any of their reassuring weight of experience. Pitman, the most successful British banker of the decade, was probably the least articulate of the four when it came to talking about grand strategy and economics – but then, as one anonymous fund manager commented at the time of Taylor's resignation four years later, 'It takes more than intellectual insight to run a bank. You need a complete thug like Brian Pitman.'

One of the insights that Taylor discussed with me was 'constructive shrinkage', the proposition – unthinkable to 1980s bankers – that it would be better to return capital to the shareholders than to pile on high-risk lending to fill vacant balance sheet space. Lloyds, indeed, had already set the pace in the latter respect, shrinking its balance sheet by 30 per cent.

'If you are trying to grow a business when the market is trying to shrink, you just end up destroying capital,' Taylor said. Developing a new analysis of lending risks begun by Peter Middleton, he was in the process of purging the bank's loan book and introducing a scientific system of provisioning which recognized the risk inherent in any loan as soon as it was put on the bank's books, not when the borrower suddenly went bust years later. Looked at in this way, corporate lending was becoming less and less attractive.

'Cyclicality has been so overwhelming that we tend not to notice the structural downtrend,' he said, offering a good sample of his unscripted skill with words, 'but the fact is that our best customers are borrowing less and less, which means that the universe of lending opportunities is moving towards the riskier end of the spectrum.' When the risk factor was compared with the lending margin, many loans turned out to be earning nothing whatsoever for the bank. 'So if we take them off the books, we make our shareholders richer. That's a wholly beneficial thing to have done.'

Not everything Taylor said in his early days at Barclays was universally well received. Like Middleton, he did not conceal his disdain for the lack of rigour in Barclays' previous decision-making processes. Remarks about increasing the use of computers in credit assessment were interpreted by staff and unions as a threat to managerial jobs in the branch network, though he later tried to undo the damage by referring to the computer programme concerned, Lending Adviser, as no more than a 'decision-making support tool' in a system which gave managers 'maximum freedom within clear constraints'.[3] At BZW, he caused hackles to rise by saying in a press conference that the investment bank had two years to prove itself, though he did not indicate what would happen if it did not.

But his frankness was more welcome when he talked about the challenge of repairing customer relationships after the recession: 'We have not been good as an industry at the more positive features of customer service,' he told me. 'Some very rough justice was meted out to customers during the recession – particularly to small businessmen – and the idea has lodged in the popular mind that banks are inconsiderate, brutal, greedy and incompetent.' 'It is not the historical destiny of banks to be popular,' he admitted on another occasion.

At the end of his first full year in the job, Taylor's magic seemed to be working. Profits had indeed almost trebled, as he said they should, to £1.86 billion. Total assets had shrunk slightly, with the disposal of some fifteen unwanted businesses, and staff numbers were down by 5,000. Arguments about the management structure for corporate business had been laid to rest by the creation of an all-encompassing

---

[3] Barclays internal research over the years since computerized credit-assessment was introduced has proved that, for loans of £10,000 or less, computers do in fact take more reliable lending decisions than humans.

Corporate and Institutional Banking Services division, under Graham Pimlott, acting as a kind of clearing-house within which any remaining border dispute could be swiftly settled. There was talk, for external consumption, of a marked revival in team spirit.

Taylor modestly gave himself six and a half out of ten and 'Could do better' for this performance. 'So far, the improvement has been largely accounted for by making the bank smaller,' he said. 'But now we have a real chance of making the business strong. There is a real momentum developing.' His personal press coverage was consistently glowing: 'Barclays responds to new boy's charm' was a typical headline.

But behind the headlines, the truth was not quite so wonderful. The profit recovery was, in the most direct way, a reflection of the borrowing customers' financial recovery rather than the bank's. Profits had gone from £661 million to £1.86 billion because provisions for bad debts had fallen from £1.87 billion to £602 million. Performance on cost control was less impressive, and certainly less effective than what Brian Pitman had already achieved at Lloyds. The United States was looking healthier at last, but the unresolved problems in France and Germany produced another nine-figure loss from Europe.

As to team spirit, the atmosphere was certainly better than it had been in the depths of 1992, but that was not saying much. There was no meeting of minds between Taylor and Buxton, or Buxton and Middleton. Taylor does not seem to have formed a high opinion of Alastair Robinson, who was now chairman of 'UK banking services' or of Oliver Stocken, now finance director, or of David Band at BZW. The only members of the senior executive team that he seemed to value were Pimlott, whom he regarded as a strategic thinker worth arguing with; rather surprisingly Bill Gordon, the managing director of UK banking and a forty-year Barclays' veteran; and Carlos Martinez de Campos, the Spanish head of European retail banking.[4]

Below the top layer of management, Taylor created a very mixed

---

[4] Martinez de Campos deserves a lengthy footnote. A handsome, bearded Spanish aristocrat, he joined Barclays as its deputy representative in Madrid in the mid-1970s, and masterminded the takeover of the struggling 38-branch Banco de Valladolid. He then proceeded to build up a network of small, low-cost retail branches, concentrated on deposit-taking rather than lending, which gained a remarkably high profile with the Spanish public. The operation remained profitable year-in, year-out throughout all Barclays' troubles elsewhere in the world, and is probably the only large-scale new Barclays venture abroad in the past thirty years which can be judged a complete success. It was achieved partly by accepting as little interference as possible from head office. The formula was replicated in Portugal, but attempts to repeat it in France and elsewhere were generally thwarted by combined forces of local regulators and local banks.

impression. After the honeymoon period of 1994, he came to be regarded as a loner, who preferred to work only with his own small coterie. In the retail bank, people thought he was not interested in the detail of what they were doing and resented the impression that he was far more excited intellectually by BZW. In BZW, on the other hand, he was regarded as out of tune with the spirit of investment banking, more concerned with 'managing by numbers' than with getting the best out of mercurial, talented individuals in fast-moving markets. Or to put it another way, he never hid his hostility to what he regarded as the mercenary, bonus-obsessed, short-termist attitude of most of the senior people at BZW.

At a personal level he could be very amusing; he was a clever mimic, for example. But he could also become suddenly angry. Those who travelled abroad with him – always a good test of working relationships – found him an austere and uncomfortable companion. And (perhaps bearing out Carla Rappoport's view of him as being 'way too nice' for the nastier aspects of business) he was not good at handling difficult personal encounters; when it came to sacking senior people, he pre-ferred others to do the dirty work. He gained a reputation for being happier talking to journalists (often through his corporate spin doctor, Liz Wade) than to colleagues outside his small chosen circle.

In all these respects, Taylor was storing up trouble for later. But the oddities of his style, like his shirt and tie, did not matter while the business was heading in the right direction. After the honeymoon of 1994, the trend was less clear in 1995. Pre-tax profits surpassed £2 billion for the first time, but at the operating level, before bad debt provisions, profits had actually fallen for the second successive year, while Lloyds, Midland and NatWest had reported an average 16 per cent improvement. Analysts observed that the bank's underlying oper-ating costs were still going up. 'They are trying but not succeeding in getting a grip on this,' said one. Taylor declared that 'all the pieces of the jigsaw' were now in place in his strategic shaping of the group, but the market was not sure whether to believe him, and the share price weakened.

But Taylor had a not-so-secret weapon to keep investors happy, and that was his policy of giving them back their capital. This began in August 1995 with a £180 million purchase of 25 million shares, and continued with 40 million shares bought in for £306 million in Feb-ruary 1996 and another 55 million bought in for £470 million in August 1996. The buy-backs were an explicit acknowledgement – which the market admired – that banks with surplus capital have an invariable habit of wasting it on bad acquisitions and foolish lending. The total proceeds of the three buy-backs, £956 million, represented a belated return of the £920 million rights issue monies from 1988 which had been so painfully frittered away. Some commentators saw it as a kind of apology.

Each buy-back transaction followed immediately after a results announcement, and the third one probably marked the high point of Taylor's tenure of office. Half-year profits were up by 15 per cent to £1.3 billion, the shares jumped to a new record price of £8.72, and Taylor was able to say with evident satisfaction that this had been 'one of those rare periods when all our businesses have done well and one of the main motors of profit growth is the absence of problems'. As will be seen in Chapter 12, one of the problems which Taylor thought he had solved at the time of this announcement was the management of BZW, where the new team of Bill Harrison and Bob Diamond was about to take charge.

There was to be a fourth buy-back, after record full-year profits for 1996 were announced in February 1997, but it did not happen as it was meant to. The bank proposed to buy in 26 million shares at £11.37 per share, but was offered only 9.2 million shares by institutional shareholders. Taylor quickly pointed out that this was no bad thing, since it meant that investors wanted to hold on to their shares – and he was in fact able to buy in more shares later, towards a declared target of £700 million worth for the year.

But still there was a misjudgement of the market in February which seems with hindsight to have marked the beginning of a new phase for Taylor. The profit figures had indeed been good enough for investors to hope for more growth in the share price, but much of the comment had focused on the weakness of BZW and what he ought to do about it. From the beginning of 1997, when Taylor first began to wrestle in earnest with that question, nothing quite went according to plan for him.

As the focus of the story switches back towards BZW we should not lose sight of what was going on in the rest of the bank throughout this period. There had been a great improvement in bottom-line performance since 1993 – pre-tax profits had multiplied three and a half times – mirroring the improvement of the economy and the consequent fall in bad debts. But there were still massive problems of costs, competition and morale. Operating profit before provisions, the most basic measure of the bank's business efficiency, had actually peaked in 1993 at £2.6 billion, before Taylor started work. Over the eight-year period since 1989 (when it was just under £2 billion) this key figure had barely kept pace with inflation. At the end of the Taylor era, Barclays still had the highest ratio of costs to income of any major British bank.

And how did the bank stand with its customers and peers? From a peak of almost 30 per cent in the late 1970s, Barclays' high street market share had fallen by 1998 to around 16 per cent – six percentage points behind Lloyds TSB. Building societies, supermarket banks, telephone banks and other new competitors had by then taken more than a third of the market. As to customer satisfaction, a MORI survey conducted in the first half of 1998 found just under half of Barclays' customers 'very satisfied' with the service the bank provided – ahead of NatWest, but well behind Halifax, Abbey National and Lloyds TSB and nowhere near the bank with the highest satisfaction rating, the telephone-banking pioneer First Direct, which scored 80 per cent.

As Taylor and many of his predecessors have observed, banks are rarely loved by their customers. But they are sometimes admired by their peers (as Barclays certainly was at its zenith at the turn of the 1980s) and by managers of other big businesses. Sadly, however high Taylor's personal rating may have once been, Barclays was also now failing on this test. The bank was ranked the 90th most admired company in Britain in *Management Today*'s 1996 annual survey, falling to 146th in 1997, when Lloyds TSB ranked 19th. In 1998 the survey listed only the top 100 companies, and Barclays received no mention at all.

Statistics tell us a great deal, but they make dull reading. To understand Barclays' standing in the world and its inner psychology we must revert to anecdote and travel to the rural heartland where we began. Every year, on the last Tuesday in July, I pack a picnic and take my golden retriever to the Ryedale Show, which claims to be (and I think is) Yorkshire's finest one-day agricultural show. The 1999 show was the one hundred and thirty-fifth, and there are many aspects of the livestock competitions, the produce tents and the Grand Parade of winners that can have changed little since the first show in the 1860s. It is an occasion of brass bands, straw hats, flat caps and farmyard smells, of pony club girls, gnarled hill farmers and show-dog owners who look like their dogs. It is a celebration of the continuity of English life. It is one of my favourite days of the year. And it is a useful opportunity to observe the changing state of Barclays Bank.

Of course, like every English institution, including Barclays, the Ryedale Show changes year by year in ways that we do not always notice: the make-up of the list of trade stands offers a fair cross-section of the changing rural economy, with cut-price 'countrywear' stalls and Aga oven salesmen offering the fantasy of country life to townees and incomers alongside the agricultural machinery merchants and saddlers catering for the real thing. But every year so far one thing, happily, has always been in the same place – right next to the bandstand overlooking the parade ring, the most privileged 'trade' site in the whole show-ground: the Barclays Bank pavilion. Ritually every year, at noon, my mother and I pay it a visit. We go to see if any old family friends are there, but I also have another purpose: there could be no better way of gauging the morale and self-confidence of the bank from one year to the next.

When I first moved my account to Helmsley – the branch where my father had once been sent out to buy cigarettes for Mr Harrison – it still had a manager of its own, Mr Armstrong, who looked after his customers in the old-fashioned way. The elderly Lady Morland at Ampleforth, for example, (mother of Charlie Morland) relied on him to help her with the paying of domestic bills. He was helpful with my own arrangements. On one occasion, asked if he could help identify the man who had looked after the garden of my house for the previous owner, so that we could try to tempt him out of retirement, Armstrong left his office and popped across the road to the Black Swan Hotel, where he (correctly) thought the barman might be the ex-gardener's brother. On another occasion soon afterwards – one which particularly endeared him to me – I asked him for a temporary overdraft limit to fund some building works, and he rang me a few days later at my desk in Ebbgate House.

'Weyer,' I answered the phone in brusque, time-is-money invest-ment-bankerish style.

'Oh, er, yes, er, Armstrong here ... Barclays Bank, Helmsley ... er...'

'Hello, Mr Armstrong, what can I do for you?'

'Well, er, as a matter of fact, I ... I just thought I ought to check that you really do work there ... Er, thank you very much indeed. Goodbye.'

At the Ryedale Show, Armstrong and his generation were always particularly solicitous to my mother, widow of the most famous banker ever to start his career in Barclays' York district. In those days the crowd in the little pavilion (a kind of enlarged Portakabin, surrounded by little white picket fences) always included my father's much-loved but sometimes cantankerous friend Noel White, who had long retired as manager of Scarborough Northway branch and who liked nothing better than to drink beer in the sunshine at the bank's expense while loudly criticizing its current performance. With him would be his friend Ken Braithwaite, who always said he had been made manager of Thirsk branch because Major Andrew Gibbs, the senior local director at York in the 1970s, kept racing stables there and wanted someone sensible to look after its bank accounts. Gibbs – who was related by marriage to Sir William Goodenough, and whose stepson is the 5th Earl of Liverpool – was described by Noel White, usually inclined to castigate his superiors, as 'an absolutely magnificent man'.

But by the 1990s there were no Barclays magnificos left to grace the Ryedale Show, only an ever-changing roll-call of regional product managers (corporate, personal, agricultural) with the haunted look of men who do not know whether they will be there next year – and many of them were not. When Armstrong retired, his replacement was younger and more nervous and (perhaps fatally for his career) bearded: in the first of several rounds of local restructuring, he managed both Helmsley and the neighbouring Kirkbymoorside branch, and his chief topic of pavilion conversation – incomprehensible to anyone not closely versed in Barclays lore – was the way in which the bank kept changing his grading, job description and contract terms. Pretty soon one more change came along, and he and his wife went off to run a bed and breakfast in the Lake District.

During the phase in which the unknown quantity Martin Taylor was casting his eye over his new empire in search of structural logic and cost-efficiency, the demoralization of Barclays managers in the field was palpable. The security and small-town dignity of status which anyone joining Barclays as a junior in the 1960s and 70s had once been able to expect until the end of their working lives had been completely erased – and a good thing too, many people have said to me, because those factors also created a working atmosphere which was complacent and uncommercial. What had also gone was the quasi-regimental loyalty and pride. It had been replaced by consultant-speak downwards, and nervous whingeing upwards and outwards.

The prime example of consultant-speak of that era was a sheet promulgated from Head Office, through training manuals and circulars, called 'Barclays' Group Values'. 'We take full responsibility for our decisions and actions,' it said.

> We admit to our mistakes, so that the effect on customers or colleagues can be put right quickly ... We make our customers' problems our

own – and we resolve them ... We operate in teams, within and across business lines, wherever this will improve the quality of the work and services we deliver. We treat each other as we wish to be treated ourselves. We share the successes, problems and disappointments of colleagues across the group and we frown on those who denigrate others' effort. If we are disappointed with the contribution of colleagues, we discuss with them how it can be improved. We don't complain behind their back.

'Those "group values" sounded all very fine,' one senior manager in London told me, 'but nobody I know bought into them.' In an organization where every executive lived in fear of the chop – as I had done myself in my last few months at BZW – the lines about sharing problems and not denigrating others sounded especially hollow. A manager in the provinces whose employment with Barclays was terminated after twenty-seven years' service sent to me unsolicited at the *Daily Mail* (for which I have occasionally written articles about the follies of the financial world) a dossier about his case which offered a vivid contrast between reality and aspiration.

Though I appear to have a full set of the relevant correspondence, I may not have heard all sides of the case and it would be wrong to name either the manager concerned – let us call him Bill -or his immediate bosses. Nevertheless, the bones of his story are worth repeating. Bill was judged at the end of 1997 to have 'done well' in the difficult area of debt recovery work and to be 'an intelligent and experienced banker'. His department was due to be disbanded, but 'we owe it to him to find him something suitable', one of his superiors wrote. Eventually a job was offered to him, as a Small Business manager, which he regarded as a downgrading and refused to accept. The only alternative was redundancy and the pursuit of a formal grievance procedure. Bill was, no doubt, one of thousands of managers whose careers were destabilized by all that regrading and restructuring, but he chose to express his disgruntlement specifically in relation to the Group Values – those 'one-sided simplistic platitudes, [as] many staff believe them to be'. All typed in angry capitals, it concluded:

> We treat each other as we wish to be treated. My personal view is that the foregoing history of worthless assurances, falsely raised hopes and decisions based solely on expediency are prime breaches of this group value ... My belief is that the bank's business was built on the concept of 'my word is my bond'. In this case, on several occasions those from whom I had no alternative but to accept career assurances have let me down continuously and very badly. My major mistake was to place my

trust in very senior people . . . who have now disclaimed all responsibility
for the situation in which I find myself.

Perhaps, for all his professional skills, Bill was really too troublesome,
or over the hill, to be found another job which he himself would have
considered acceptable. Or perhaps the pressures on Barclays to bring
its costs-to-income ratio into line with Lloyds TSB meant that useful
but disposable people like Bill were simply at the mercy of larger forces.
He is just one of many aggrieved people all over the organization to
have found themselves suddenly devalued.

'Where is old X these days?' I would frequently ask when talking to
ex-colleagues about this book. 'Taken out and shot,' came the reply in
one conversation with a senior manager at Barclays Capital. 'And Y?'
'Shot.' 'And Z?' 'Shot.' 'But I thought he was a top man these days?'
'He was, but the other day they called him over to head office and read
him a lawyer's letter telling him he was to leave immediately and not
to go back to his office for his personal effects.' One of my acquaintances
in Lombard Street was so convinced he was heading for an acrimonious
departure of this kind that he retained Anthony Julius, the late Princess
of Wales's divorce lawyer, to prepare his 'wrongful dismissal' case;
somewhat to his surprise, the call never came, and he became one of
the few to resign entirely of his own accord.

In Yorkshire, I began to lose track. Possibly Helmsley and Kirkbymoorside came under the nearby Pickering branch for a while, but
eventually all three of those branches came under Malton, the largest
town in the district. Eventually, a young man appeared in Helmsley
wearing a badge proclaiming him Manager, but it was not clear whether
he had any of the powers of former incumbents. Still, it was always a
pleasure to go into the branch to be greeted by name by the long-
serving lady cashiers. But contrary to all modern banking trends, it was
advisable always to go into the bank in person to benefit from this kind
of attention, because the telephone number of Helmsley branch had
by then been abolished. All calls now went through to Malton to be
handled by one of those maddening 'Christine speaking, how may I
help you?' remote switchboard systems which demand that you explain
the reason for your call in some detail before − pause for lengthy
interlude of recorded music − you might be put through to someone
who could actually deal with your query. In the era when Britain's first
24-hour telephone bank, First Direct, was scoring 80 per cent customer
satisfaction ratings, Barclays actually seemed to be going backwards,
turning every customer phone-call into a cameo performance in the

style of the manic hotelier Basil Fawlty in *Fawlty Towers*:

'Could I speak to Mrs Smith in Helmsley, please.'

'Can I ask what your enquiry is about, Mr Weyer, so that I can put you through to the correct person . . . ?'

'No, just put me through to Helmsley, please.'

'Could I ask you for your account number first, Mr Weyer, so that we can . . .'

'FOR GOD'S SAKE put me through to Helmsley, will you, I've left a pork chop on the counter . . .'

Eventually, in frustration at this sort of thing, I signed up for Barclays 'Premier' banking service, which for a modest monthly fee offers a personalized telephone banking service co-ordinated with the local branch. I would have signed up for the Internet banking service as well, but when it was first offered the instructions for registering were so complicated that I never got around to completing them.

All of this may seem trivial compared to the boardroom battles and billion-pound blunders which dominate this story, but it illustrates an important point. In an age of competitive advance in all kinds of service businesses, bank customers' innate resentment of banks could only be assuaged by the most meticulous attention to the way in which the customer is handled. The old way, with Mr Armstrong helping ladies to pay bills and cashiers greeting everyone as neighbours, was good but it was never cost-effective. The challenge for Martin Taylor and his ilk was to find a new way which was not just cheaper to run, but equally good from the customers' point of view.

The telephone-banking model created by First Direct and developed by Virgin Direct, Standard Life and Egg (a venture by Prudential Assurance) was an intelligent solution: the customer never spoke to the same telephonist twice, but every telephonist had all the customer's details instantly on screen and was trained unobtrusively to personalize the conversation so that the customer felt properly looked after. For the modern generation, accustomed to shopping and doing business by telephone at all hours, it was a satisfactory way to interact. There was, incidentally, a proposal floating around in Barclays in the early 1990s for the establishment of a *de novo* telephone bank to outdo First Direct. But it never advanced because – in a classic example of the Barclays managerial mind-set – the heads of retail banking saw it as a threat to their territory. By the end of the 1990s, the game had moved on again: de-personalized but quick, responsive communication through the Internet was rapidly becoming the new norm, and in this area Barclays was actually emerging as one of the pacesetters.

But for most of the Taylor era the bank seemed to be stuck half-way between the old and the new, irritating its customers by constant changes in the interests of cost-saving efficiency. The media sniffed (not just at Barclays) a correlation between job cuts, staff demoralization and the rate of errors in handling customer accounts. Stories of widows offended by rude letters to recently deceased spouses, or of lost accounts, or of giant interest claims caused by computer errors, and of refusals on the part of the banks to apologize for any of these things, became the bread and butter of the weekend newspapers' 'personal finance' supplements. Even the *Daily Telegraph* political columnist Boris Johnson, interviewing Taylor about his part-time role as the Labour government's adviser on welfare benefits reform, 'can't resist pointing out that about the time of all these staff cutbacks, service went pretty haywire. He listens carefully while I tell him about the standing order that took eight letters to establish, the £1,000 that was transferred into the account of someone else called Johnson. "Did you get it back?" he asks quickly. There is no doubt that during the period when the bank was in trouble, customer service took some knocks . . .'

Meanwhile, back at the agricultural show at the end of the Taylor era, the old Barclays pavilion has been symbolically replaced by a bigger and brighter one – decorated rather incongruously with photographic panels of yachts and ocean waves, so perhaps borrowed from a boat show. But every one of the managers I knew by name had gone, and even the chorus of bank pensioners seemed to have disappeared, abandoning their claim to a free pint of beer. No one recognized my mother (not that she minded) or asked who we were.

'We *are* customers,' she said to the hostess in Barclays uniform who gave us a drink, feeling that some explanation needed to be volunteered for our being there.

'I hope you are,' the hostess replied rather sternly. But something more than hope and cheap wine was needed to restore a relationship of mutual esteem between the bank and its customers. That task lingered to confront Martin Taylor's successors. Taylor achieved several important things in Barclays: improving its structure and its ability to analyse risk, disposing of underperforming assets, focusing on its shareholders' expectations. But for all his brilliant clarity of vision, he had neither solved the bank's problems of excessive operating costs, nor rebuilt the morale and faith of its managers in the field, nor truly succeeded in pleasing its customers.

12

THE BAND COCKTAIL

1988–1996: The man from J. P. Morgan and his appetites – The
peak of BZW's performance – The second Big Bang – The
death of David Band – Taylor's doubts begin to show – Bill
Harrison arrives – Bob Diamond arrives first – Tenth birthday
celebrations

Perhaps the most enigmatic figure in the whole, short history of BZW
was David Band, who was its chief executive from 1988 until his sudden
death, aged fifty-three – from a heart attack, at the end of a challenging
ski-run in Val d'Isère – on 28 March 1996.

In many ways, Band personified what Barclays wanted BZW to
become. Throughout his seven-year tenure, BZW seemed on course
to achieve that aspiration. Yet Band, like BZW itself, turned out to be
fatally flawed – programmed to self-destruct. And after he had gone,
BZW lasted only eighteen months until Martin Taylor decided to
dismantle it.

Band was head-hunted for BZW by the exclusive search firm of
Norman, Broadbent, but he was already well known to Tom Camoys
and Oliver Stocken. He was the European head of J. P. Morgan &
Co., and chairman of its London securities business – and it is worth
diverting briefly into a character sketch of Band's previous employer,
because it says a great deal about the role model Camoys had in
mind.

The most blue-blooded of Wall Street banking houses, Morgan was
probably the institution that every other ambitious commercial bank
in the world most wanted to emulate in the 1980s. Dedicated, in the
words of J. Pierpont Morgan Jr, to doing 'first-class business in first-
class ways', it shunned all but the most blue-chip corporate and private

customers, and was known for its excellent access to governments and central banks around the world.

Its officers were well trained, clean-cut, low-profile. Though it may be a trick of memory, I seem to recall every Morgan executive I have ever met wearing a single-breasted navy blue suit, a plain, custom-tailored shirt and a heavy but unflamboyant silk tie, probably polka-dotted, predominantly yellow.

Morgan people tended to make long careers in the bank, which meant that they shared a degree of collegiate trust not found in firms which relied on mercenaries and trading stars bought in from elsewhere. They thought in terms of long-term relationships rather than one-off transactions: 'Not the fast buck' was an in-house slogan. They were able to list (in 1992) 97 of the top 100 US corporations as clients, and many of those relationships went back for several decades.

To Americans, Morgan exudes a certain Britishness, attributed to the founding J. P. Morgan's early experience working with his father in the London banking venture which eventually became Morgan Grenfell. To British admirers, however, Morgan is the ultimate expression of a refined, cosmopolitan style perfected on Wall Street but rarely achieved in the same combination in the City, except perhaps in the parlours of Rothschild and Lazard. One bank analyst interviewed by Professor David Rogers of New York's Stern School of Business, author of *The Future of American Banking*, summed up the Morgan style thus: 'Their internal co-operativeness is stunning. There is that much collegiality. They are also very patrician. They constitute rich people dealing with rich institutions. And they are also as anonymous and faceless as one can get. People there are always selected for their character and manners. Civility is highly valued.'

'Everything there must be in good taste,' another observer told Professor Rogers.

> They have exquisite taste as people, in conduct, in personal appearance, in clothes, in the appearance of the offices, in the artwork ... People at Morgan are well groomed, not like those at IBM or Merrill Lynch, where it is a result of deliberateness, but rather by birth. They pride themselves on not being *nouveaux riches* like some of their competitors ... Until recently, and even now, Morgan people were not interested in money, but in elegance of conduct.

To have climbed the ladder to the highest level at J. P. Morgan, as David Band had done by his early forties, was to be marked out as a class act in international banking. The other strong contender for the

BZW job was a product of Europe's, rather than Wall Street's, business aristocracy: John Loudon, then a director of N. M. Rothschild, son of former Royal Dutch/Shell chairman Jonkheer (the Dutch equivalent of Sir) John Loudon and younger brother of George Loudon, the chief executive of Midland Montagu. Loudon Jr would have been a good catch in social terms, but Band with his Morgan aura was the favoured candidate, with particularly strong backing from Camoys.

Yet more than once I heard it said with a chuckle that J. P. Morgan had been relieved to find Barclays so eager to poach him. The truth about Band was that he was, at the same time, a popular and seasoned banking professional and a personal wreck.

There is no doubt that he drank to excess. His habit of pouring himself, and gulping down, a four-finger shot of whisky before in-house lunches raised eyebrows at BZW immediately, notably those of the fastidious Rex Cooper. But it did not seem to worry Band that everyone knew he drank. There was nothing furtive about it. Some afternoons, he took a liquid lunch on his own in El Vino's Olde Wine Shades in Martin Lane – where he was to be seen at two o'clock on the Friday before he left for his fatal skiing holiday, downing large gins and eating a slice of pork pie. On other quiet days he could be spotted at the City Brasserie in the now demolished Plantation House in Fenchurch Street – a place priced and designed for expense account entertaining, rather than solitary lunching – where he would sit hunched at the counter in the posture of a man who does not want to be spoken to.

By the time he returned to work after these escapes, his difficulty in stringing coherent sentences together was much more acute than in the morning. But it was still not so bad as it became at evening engagements, when he would habitually reach a state best described as completely blotto.

His marriage was in trouble; he smoked heavily and had a weak heart; he was a lonely man in an intensely pressurized job. Close colleagues liked him and admired his stamina. Some respected his judgement, or at least made a show of praising it. Some were loyal to him. But in the later stages they simply had to manage the organization around him.

None of that was apparent to the wider world, and none of it was predictable from his shining pre-BZW curriculum vitae. The son of an Edinburgh doctor, Band was educated at Rugby and St Edmund Hall, Oxford where he read French and German, before joining Morgan (then styled Morgan Guaranty Trust) in London in 1964. One of his flatmates at that time was Oliver Stocken, later finance director of Barclays, who remembered Band's relentless appetite for nightlife but also the care he took over his grooming. Though still a lowly management trainee, Band kept a full wardrobe of expensive, beautifully laundered Jermyn Street shirts. However demanding his previous night's entertainment may have been, he was never less than immaculate.

Until the end of his life Band retained the physique of a long-distance runner and the leathery tan of a tennis fanatic. At 8.30 a.m. market briefings in BZW's Ebbgate House headquarters he was invariably sharp-eyed, his carefully parted hair still damp from the shower, the day's first pack of Benson & Hedges on the table in front of him. He said little at such meetings, but what he did say showed that he was in touch with the markets. He never looked tired or stressed by the burdens of office.

His polish, and his intelligent handling of clients, was noticed early at Morgan by Dennis (later Sir Dennis) Weatherstone, the British money market specialist who was to become chairman and chief executive of the US bank in 1990. By 1976, when he was thirty-four, Band was head of Morgan's southeast Asian operations in Singapore; from there he moved to Paris as general manager, and then to New York as senior vice-president in charge of international capital market business, combined with geographical responsibility for Europe.

He raised Morgan's profile in the eurobond issuing business, and raised his own profile in the tightknit, big-ego world of top eurobond managers and borrowers. At the same time, he reinforced his late-night reputation: 'Boy, he really partied,' one Wall Street veteran told me, with a sad shake of the head. 'A more dangerous fellow after dark I've never met in my life,' said another banker who had known Band since his Singapore days. 'But he'd go out next morning and play a couple of sets of tennis and be fresh as a daisy. He was incredible.'

But the long-term effects of all that partying had already taken a toll by the time he returned to run J. P. Morgan in London in 1986. Shortly after he joined BZW, it was revealed that he had already had one operation to repair a leaking heart valve, and would have to take time off for another. His weakness for booze also swiftly became apparent.

The story was told of a senior BZW broker of European stocks who had taken Band on an overnight trip to Amsterdam to entertain an important institutional client to dinner. The pair had flown over from London in the early evening, with just enough time to check into their hotel and change. They went on with the client after dinner to a nightclub, where they drank into the small hours.

When they came down to check out early next morning, heading for a breakfast flight back to London, Band looked as sharp as ever. The broker offered, as the junior, to settle both their room bills. His own consisted simply of the room charge; Band's, by contrast, listed most of the contents of the mini-bar refrigerator. This became known, to some of us, as a Band Cocktail: 'Take one hotel washbasin and insert plug; take one mini-bar and empty contents into washbasin. Drink with a straw.'

Booze wasn't the only aspect of the problem. We wondered, in fact, whether Band's cardiologist had advised him to drink like a fish as a desperate measure to suppress the rampant libido which might otherwise kill him. Another unkind theory, that the 'heart surgery' story was merely a cover for an extended drying-out cure, was disproved by Band himself in characteristic fashion: with a group of BZW executives one evening at Chaplin's, a hostess nightclub in Swallow Street near Piccadilly Circus, he took a girl on to the dance floor and promptly ripped his own shirt off. The operation scar was there for all to see.

My own direct experience of him ran true to form. When he came to Hong Kong in early 1989, he said very little about business. He did not tell us about the group's plans elsewhere in the world, or comment in detail on what we were doing in Asia. He might have been listening intently, or he might have been thinking about something else entirely: you just couldn't tell.

To be fair, he must have taken something in. I told him that we were proud of what we had achieved in Hong Kong, keeping close to budget, running a happy ship and building a coherent network of small offices around the region. We were puzzled, I said, that no one from London (including, by implication, himself) ever bothered to comment on any of this. Three weeks later, he sent me a two-line letter telling me, in precisely my own words that we could be proud of what we had achieved.

So much for his management style. But boy, did he party. The first evening, I gave a supper for him and some of the Hong Kong staff in my flat on the Peak. Band reached a trance-like state midway through the meal, but seemed eager to go on. Under instructions from Nick Sibley, BZW's regional chairman, to make sure the chief executive got whatever he desired, we took him — rambling all the while — across to Kowloon-side in the office Mercedes, to the Club de Hong Kong.

This was one of Hong Kong's most famous nightclubs — places, it should be said, where it was common to bump into reputable expatriate and Chinese business leaders, and where many an exciting stock market deal has been cooked up. The most celebrated of them, Club Volvo (wholly unconnected with the Swedish car company, which pursued a series of legal actions to try to reclaim its name), was even scheduled for stock market listing, until the crash of 1987 put paid to the idea. The clubs were run by powerful mama-sans, and staffed by pretty girls who were all available, at a price, to be taken out as 'escorts'.

BZW's senior Chinese brokers, Kinson Hui and Steven Hak, were habitués of one such establishment, the New Tonnochy in Wanchai, and often took me along to meet their circle of young tycoons and deal-fixers. It was here, for instance, that I met a man whose card said he was an assistant general manager of a local bank, but whose real importance in the community derived from the fact that he made a two-way market in New Territories taxi licences.

We referred to these outings, some of the most relaxed evenings I ever spent in Asia, as 'management meetings'. I even kept a whisky bottle with my name on it at the New Tonnochy. My straight-laced successor John Varley told me he was shocked to be offered a shot from it on the first (and, I would guess, only) occasion Kinson took him to Wanchai after my departure.

But having assessed Band's condition on the evening in question, Kinson felt it wise not to take him to our regular haunt, and led us to the Kowloon club instead. We arrived with half a dozen BZW staff, some of them quite junior and eager to make their mark with the big boss from London. Kinson introduced Band in courtly style to the mama-san, and asked for her prettiest girl to join him.

Normal form – including the requirements of Chinese 'face' – might have meant talking and drinking for an hour or so with a selection of hostesses before moving discreetly on. (If a girl assigned to your table did not please, the mama-san would call her away by broadcasting her number on a digital display; another girl would be sent in to bat, and the process repeated until every customer was satisfactorily matched up.) But Band simply eyed the first girl presented to him, asked her if she knew how to rock and roll, and took her straight on to the dance floor.

Within five minutes, he returned to tell us that he and the girl were heading back to his hotel. He was staying at the Mandarin, the territory's grandest and one of the few in Hong Kong which the-oretically did not allow guests to bring in nightclub tarts. If Band was aware of the hotel rule, he ignored it. When Kinson asked him next day (perhaps unwisely) whether he had run into trouble with the doorman, he shrugged blankly, as though he genuinely had no recollection of the evening.

The following night, Sibley gave a more formal dinner party for Band in the Hong Kong Club. Among the guests were a director of Jardine Matheson, a senior Hong Kong government official and a partner of the London solicitors Slaughter & May with an unusually grand wife. Again Band drank deeply. On the way to collect my car after dinner had finished, I dipped into the Captain's Bar on the ground floor of the Mandarin to use the gents. As I came out, Band was heading for the bar.

'Hi,' he greeted me, gesturing unsteadily towards two bar stools. 'Have a drink.'

I thought perhaps at last we would have a serious conversation about the way BZW's Hong Kong business was going. For a minute or two, he seemed to be with me, leaning intently on the bar counter. Then he shifted forward into an uncomfortable posture, staring past me along the bar. For an embarrassed moment, I feared he was about to slump unconscious. Then I realized that he had caught the eye of a tired-looking blonde woman – possibly one of Hong Kong's few European or Australian hookers, who sometimes worked the Captain's Bar – sitting alone on the stool beyond mine.

'Hi,' he said to her, cutting across whatever I was saying. 'Have a drink.' Before I had time to leave the room, he was sliding sideways on to my stool.

In the Far East, we were used to visitors behaving badly: a long way from base, surrounded by forbidden fruit, even the staidest Barclays travellers sometimes let rip. But Band's performances went down much worse closer to home. After one lively trip to Frankfurt, for instance, a furious letter followed him back to head office from the Barclays chief in Germany accusing him of insulting the bank's most important German customers by being so hog-whimperingly drunk. It was really a wonder to those who were not close to the centre of power that Band held on to his job at BZW at all.

But he did so for more than seven years and there were good reasons why. He was by no means useless, after all. He could certainly open doors. He moved in sophisticated social circles, and had partied, in his time, with corporate chiefs and government officials on several continents. The Labour leader John Smith was a family friend. The Conservative trade minister Ian Lang had been at school with him.

He even turned up once at a *Spectator* party – he was a tennis partner and Holland Park neighbour of Luis Dominguez, the magazine's famously smooth, mid-Atlantic publisher. It was the only time I ever saw Band after my departure from BZW, in which he had taken no interest that had communicated itself to me. At the *Spectator*'s overcrowded annual bash, filling every corner of the magazine's narrow Georgian offices and courtyard in Doughty Street, Bloomsbury, there are always dozens of pretty girls from the world of PR and fashionable journalism, but not much room for the niceties of service. As Band arrived, I handed him a large tumbler of whisky. 'Hi, Martin. So this is where you are these days,' he said easily, history forgotten. 'Oh good, a big one.'

But it was easy to forgive David Band his faults. He was a genuine human being. You could not help but like him. People sometimes whispered names of outsiders who might do a better job – Deryck Maugham, the former HM Treasury official who was running Salomon Brothers' branch in Tokyo and later became its chief executive in New York, was a favourite candidate – but if any approaches were made they came to nothing. Within BZW's high councils, Band's inarticulacy was balanced first by the barrister's fluency of Martin Jacomb and later by the Whitehall rigour of Peter Middleton. He rarely interfered in day-to-day divisional management, but the chiefs below him liked it that way. It allowed Ken Sinclair in Markets, Jonathan Davie in Equities, Simon de Zoete in de Zoete & Bevan and Graham Pimlott in Corporate Finance to conduct themselves like feudal barons. In the case of Davie and Pimlott, personal rivalry flavoured all inter-divisional relations – in which I had myself occasionally tried to act as a go-between. They would never have been able to agree on an internal promotion to replace Band, and an external appointment – as the arrival of Bill Harrison after Band's death proved – would only cause unwanted upheaval.

Perhaps more to the point, BZW was performing moderately well – and briefly, very well indeed – throughout the first half of the 1990s, relative to the rest of Barclays which, as we have seen, was grappling with the worst crisis of the century in its domestic and overseas lending businesses. In the bank's *annus horribilis* of 1992, BZW's divisional profits of £241 million represented a 31 per cent return on capital. The power claimed for BZW in international securities markets was at last beginning to show itself to be real: the firm had been global coordinator of a share offering by Remy Cointreau, the French liquor group, and of an issue by Hyundai Motor Co. of Korea. It had acted as adviser and broker in the £958 million domestic take-over of Rank

Hovis McDougall by Tomkins. But still it was the money market dealing activity, imported from the bank in the restructuring at the beginning of the year, which made all the difference to profits. It was not until 1993 that BZW finally came into its own.

This was the year in which favourable markets, genuine improvements in BZW's internal cohesion and some outstandingly clever individual work combined to show what could be achieved by an integrated investment bank with the might of Barclays behind it. Profits reached £234 million for the first half alone and broke through £500 million for the full year, a return of over 40 per cent. Even the Japanese operation, which had been bleeding heavily for two years, broke even. A bull market in bonds made for easy profits in proprietory trading.

Sterling bond issues were lead-managed for Canadian, Swedish and Japanese borrowers. Most importantly, BZW's Equities and Corporate Finance divisions had a huge combined success with their 'enhanced scrip dividend' scheme – an example of the kind of highly technical creativity with which investment bankers sometimes justify their claim to be the élite of the financial world. During the recession years, many UK companies with growing overseas interests and shrinking domestic ones found themselves paying Advance Corporation Tax on their dividends which they could no longer fully offset against corporation tax on their domestic profits – leaving them with mountains of 'unrelieved ACT'. A solution to this problem was invented by two of the cleverest people in BZW, Amir Eilon – a cold, unsmiling market veteran from Morgan Stanley, who once told his staff they should 'learn to sleep quicker' – and Michael Perry, a mercurial, original, amusing young computer wizard who had started out as a BZW graduate trainee.

Their solution is too complex for this book, but essentially involved the companies concerned issuing scrip dividends (dividends in the form of shares) with a cash alternative, underwritten by BZW, for investors who preferred not to take the scrip. What was so clever was the flexibility of the scheme, meeting the needs of several different categories of issuer and institutional investor. British-American Tobacco (a long-standing de Zoete & Bevan client) was the first company to try it out, followed by RTZ and a host of other top names. BZW underwrote nineteen issues during the year, accounting for £2.2 billion worth of new shares. The competition – even Warburgs – was left looking flat-footed. At the end of the year, BZW's 6000 staff shared a £100 million bonus pool, and its seven heaviest hitters, including David Band, received more than £1 million each. Arrangements were put in place (involving offshore trusts) for an even more lucrative long-term incentive scheme.

It was a short burst of glory, however. The deeper truth of the 1993 triumph was that it was achieved not from fees on clever deals but by 'punting the markets', as one senior BZW figure put it to me: dealing profits amounted to £625 million, with all the other parts of BZW contributing a collective loss to reduce the final adjusted profit figure to £532 million. In 1994, conditions became much much more difficult: the US Federal Reserve began raising interest rates and both equity and bond markets suffered reversals. Again, there were some landmark deals to boast about – notably the £1.3 billion financing of Richard Budge's buy-out of British Coal – but BZW's profits halved to £242 million. Again, dealing profits alone exceeded the final net profit figure by more than £100 million, suggesting that significant parts of BZW were incapable of paying for themselves. And Martin Taylor was now in command at Barclays, applying his cool, laser-eyed scrutiny to anything that smacked of hyperbole or disguise from the investment bankers.

But even Taylor would have admitted that, relative to its British competitors, BZW was still an asset with questionmarks over it, rather than a liability. One by one the competition had drawn in its horns or simply ceased to be British. The earliest big name to go had been Morgan Grenfell. Tainted by its involvement in the Guinness scandal and scarred by costly ventures in the securities business, it sold out in 1990 to Deutsche Bank for £950 million – though not before Barclays had tried to buy it in order to bolster BZW with Morgan Grenfell's corporate client list. The fabled arrogance of Morgan Grenfell's senior corporate financiers would not have made this an easy marriage, but Barclays' board finally baulked at the price and the deal fell away.

BZW was by no means alone in suffering set-backs in the difficult markets of 1994, but the real wave of change, sometimes referred to as a second Big Bang, came in the first half of 1995. It began with the collapse of Barings – a leader of the London corporate finance scene and a powerful competitor in Asian equities markets – at the hands of its fraudulent Singapore futures trader, Nick Leeson, at the end of February. After the failure of a brief attempt, co-ordinated by Andrew Buxton, to launch a 'lifeboat' rescue funded by British banks, the firm was bought for £1 by the Dutch financial conglomerate ING, which put up £660 million to cover its losses and £100 million to pay bonuses to keep its staff in place. BZW did not bid for any of the parts of Barings, but gained in reputation from the episode not least because its own systems of risk control in derivatives trading were now recognized to be disciplined and robust, whereas Barings' had turned out to be almost non-existent. The 'flight to quality' which followed brought more securities clients to BZW. The rescued Barings business – though it initially seemed to make a miraculous recovery with ING's backing – gradually withered away.

The Barings crash provoked worries about the capital strength of other independent firms, and next to go was S. G. Warburg, the most powerful British competitor of all. Warburgs had expanded aggressively in London and New York, piling on costs. But it had suffered in the market downturns of 1994, its turnover had shrunk, and it had been shaken by the failure of an attempted merger with Morgan Stanley. In May 1995 it was acquired by Swiss Bank for £860 million, which was only slightly more than its book value. In the following month, Kleinwort Benson fell to Dresdner Bank for £1 billion, and in July, Smith New Court went to Merrill Lynch (with Commerzbank as the underbidder) for £526 million. That left Schroders, Lazards and Rothschilds still operating successfully in traditional merchant banking, but no other British firms trying to be integrated global investment banks.

BZW was now the official national champion. If it was difficult to see what David Band's personal contribution to that victory had been, at least it could be said that he had a strong stomach for market risk, and shared the credit for the successful strategy of 'punting the markets' in 1993. He knew the technicalities of trading better than most people at his level, as was apparent during the Barings collapse, when most other City grandees summoned to the Bank of England were at a loss to understand the details of Leeson's catastrophic dealings.

As for his contribution to BZW's growing reputation in the primary markets, Band knew how to price bond issues, and he knew what clients wanted. He had an encyclopaedic memory for the details of past deals. In internal management, the best that could be said was that he was decisive when he had to be: when he was called upon to exercise the wisdom of Solomon on the splitting of the proceeds of a profitable deal between Equities and Corporate Finance, for example. He did not like personal confrontation, but was prepared to deal with difficult people when necessary. 'Get that arsehole out of here,' was all he said – and all he needed to say to make it happen – on a visit to Tokyo, when an excitable expatriate launched into a tirade of complaint against the management of Mike Connors.

And Band clung tenaciously to the vision of BZW as a global

investment bank, even if he was incapable – at any time of day – of articulating it elegantly, either on a public platform, on paper or at Barclays board meetings. He took lessons in public speaking from an expensive American consultant, whom he frequently recommended to other BZW people, but it made no difference. 'Mr Band came down to talk to us after dinner,' said a fresh-faced trainee who had just passed through BZW's graduate induction course at a hotel on the south coast. 'But to be honest we didn't really understand what he was talking about.' 'The non-executives could never work him out at all,' Sir John Quinton recalled. 'Tom and Martin kept telling us how excellent he was, but he couldn't string a single sentence together.'

Nevertheless Band carried clout on BZW's behalf within the Barclays hierarchy, where senior managers remained in awe of his J. P. Morgan experience, his cosmopolitan langour, his access to corporate chairmen and chief executives, and his performance-related salary deal, which gave him a package of cash and share options in 1995 worth more than £1,300,000.

But ultimately that languid manner was a mask. Deep down, Band was unsure of himself, unhappy, perhaps disgusted with himself: why else would a man in his position, with his advantages, drink alone at lunch-time? A former tutor of mine from Oxford, whom I came across after a 20-year interval in 1993, claimed to be one of Band's few close confidants. Band had recently called him to discuss the possibility that (in the search which eventually led to the appointment of Martin Taylor) he might be promoted to chief executive of the whole Barclays group.

'It was a weird conversation,' my old tutor said. 'The gist of it was that he was absolutely terrified they might give him the job.'

Band had had a nominal deputy since 1991 in the form of John Spencer, a career Barclays manager who had made his name as a dynamic head of the US banking division in New York. In the strange Barclays' way, he was widely believed to have been earmarked for the very top: 'You know who I mean,' a Barclays manager said to me in Tokyo in the mid-eighties, 'That chap in New York who's going to be chairman after Andrew.'

When Treasury activities were moved from the bank to BZW's Markets division, Spencer was brought in as its head. The Treasury move was a particularly difficult one for Barclays die-hards to accept – it led eventually to the resignation of the finance director, Peter Wood – and Spencer's appointment was clearly meant to be seen as a counterbalancing manoeuvre, in which a trusted Barclays commander was taking control of an important piece of BZW territory. But such were the problems and animosities within that territory that Spencer made curiously little impact on BZW as a whole. His star rapidly waned, and in 1994 he left the group.

That made room for the appointment of a more effective deputy, who could make sure that Band's existing job got done properly – though the official word was that Band needed more time for front-line work, pitching for new clients. The choice fell on Donald Brydon, a strongly built, peppery Scotsman who was in fact three years younger than Band, but looked considerably older. Brydon had built the asset management side of BZW (now Barclays Global Investors) into a world leader in quantitative, or passive, fund management. He was not universally liked, and not skilful in forming political alliances, but he was one of the very few senior people in the organization – Oliver Stocken and John Varley are the only other ones who come to mind – who could be described as a seriously disciplined manager. With Band he formed a harmonious working relationship.

By the beginning of 1996, however, Band's time was almost up, in more ways than one. The drinking was becoming even heavier, and he had parted from his wife. 'I don't want to kill you by making you go on in this job,' Taylor told him. Seven years is a long tenure for any chief executive, and Band himself was quite willing to be kicked upstairs to deputy chairman – with the possibility that he would succeed Sir Peter Middleton as chairman in 1998, if he had not been quietly eased out by then. He could rest on his laurels, having held the business together thus far and having driven, with Brydon, the decision (signed in April 1995) to move BZW into spacious new quarters in Canary Wharf. The forthcoming move was both a symbol of the end of an era of growth and a physical confirmation of the commitment to BZW's future.

If there was a cloud on the horizon, it was in the mind of Martin Taylor. He had already shown signs, on several occasions, of exas-peration with the whole BZW project, both because of its hunger for capital at uncertain rates of return and because of continuing personal frictions.

'Do you really want an investment bank?' a senior executive asked Taylor one day in a budget meeting, not for the first time. 'If you sold us now, you'd probably get a couple of billion.'

'Of course I want an investment bank,' Taylor replied, banging the table. 'But his body language said no,' one participant in the meeting recalled. He just wasn't quite at breaking point for such a radical change of strategy. Late in 1995 the Barclays board (prompted by a presentation from Jonathan Davie) pondered the choice of selling up or going on. They decided to go on, so planning for the Canary Wharf move continued, and the search for a successor to Band began. Taylor briefly considered putting himself into the job, but swiftly rejected the idea and decided to look outside.

The man he chose was Bill Harrison, then at Flemings, whom Taylor first contacted in February 1996. An amusing story later went round the markets to the effect that Taylor had consulted his mentor Sir Christopher Hogg as to whom he should recruit, and received the answer: 'The man you want is William Harrison.' But the Harrison that Hogg was referring to was supposedly one William Harrison of Chase Manhattan, who was as tall, smooth and East Coast American as Bill Harrison of Flemings was short, rough and Brummie. Taylor went out and recruited the wrong one. Sadly, the tale holds no water, because Taylor and the Brummie Harrison had done business together before, when they were respectively at Courtaulds and Lehman Brothers.

Harrison had indeed already been approached in 1993 by David Band, to take over the running of BZW's corporate finance activities. Before Band went away on his final holiday, he and Harrison spent some time together, making sure 'all the pieces fitted together and all the key people were onside', as Harrison put it. Insiders might have warned him that the key people were never in fact all going to be onside at the same time: each of them was playing his own game. But Harrison was sufficiently reassured to accept the offer in principle, and negotiations were proceeding as Band left for Val d'Isère.

When the news of Band's death broke, Brydon (who stepped in as acting chief executive) was one of several senior BZW people who spoke to me about him with real warmth and admiration. 'He was like a brother,' he said. In BZW's official history, he added: 'His optimism sometimes took us beyond the bounds of what we thought was possible.' He had no enemies, said another colleague; he was 'a lovely man' and 'a force for good' in the deeply unharmonious working atmosphere of BZW. To most of his staff, Band was a mystery and an embarrassment, but yet he seems with hindsight to have been the kingpin holding the organization together.

After he had gone, there was still plenty of talk of global strategy, but BZW was rapidly descending into a Babel of greed and animosity. Martin Taylor recognized David Band's feel for the business and the loyalty he commanded, but the inarticulacy and the dissolute way of life were not to his liking. Taylor's judgement during his first months at Barclays was that the underlying problem of BZW was not to do with the unsteadiness of markets but the unsteadiness of people like Band. 'We'd like the securities business to be a lot bigger, commensurate with profitability and risk,' he told me in September 1994. 'Barclays can amply supply BZW with all the capital it needs. The constraints on growth in that area are human and managerial rather than financial.'

What he really meant by that remark did not become crystal clear until the 1996 group planning conference, six months after Band's death, when Taylor shocked his audience by remarking that he should have replaced Band two years earlier. By then his views had moved on: he had concluded that Barclays' shareholders could not afford to keep supplying BZW with capital. In fact, he was quietly developing an urge to put an end to BZW altogether. And that urge was encouraged, rather than diminished, by the impact of the man Taylor himself chose to run BZW in preference to Band.

If you encountered Bill Harrison, BZW's fifth and last chief executive (counting the two interim holders of the job, Buxton and Brydon) in an airport departure lounge, it is unlikely that you would place him as a senior investment banker. A top salesman perhaps – the body language and mobile phone technique suggest that instantly – but in something more metallic than financial. There is nothing elegant about him. With his longish hair, curly moustache, big jaw, short legs, swelling paunch and Brummie accent, he might be a retired Aston Villa striker who had made it big in the motor trade.

Actually Harrison supports Arsenal. But what is obvious about him is that he could not care less about elegance, and that what you see is what you get. That is probably why he has such a successful track record with industrial clients, who must find him refreshingly straightforward compared to better-groomed, tighter-lipped conventional City types. He once came top in a Bloomberg News poll as 'the London investment banker you'd most like to meet for a drink'. In the bizarre shenanigans of Barclays and BZW in 1997, Harrison's status as a rough-diamond outsider was particularly useful. He was a scapegoat. The senior executives around him may have been unable to agree on anything else, and barely willing to give each other the time of day, but at least they could agree that Bill Harrison was a disastrous appointment.

Born in 1948, Bill Harrison was brought up by his mother – who worked as a secretary in a Birmingham engineering firm after Bill's father left her – and by his grandparents. He made his way from grammar school, where he captained the soccer team, to the London

School of Economics, where he gained an M.Sc. with distinction in economics. 'I did have a bit of a chip in those day,' he told one interviewer. 'I was pretty intense.'

His background was no barrier to his career, even though it marked him out from the more familiar Home Counties public school type of his City generation. In the early seventies, American banks recruiting in London were able to take advantage of the snobbery of the British merchant banks by grabbing smart graduate recruits who lacked social credentials but (unlike the Oxbridge socialites who were such congenial company, and so good at the *Times* crossword, during my first years at Schroders, for example) showed real hunger to do business. Harrison was exactly that. He began his career at Manufacturers Hanover Bank – where one competitor remembered him as 'an exceptionally aggressive young man' – and proceeded to build an unusually lengthy curriculum vitae.

He moved in 1977 to British National Oil Corporation under Alastair Morton (later, as Sir Alastair, a famously combative Eurotunnel chairman), then to the London office of Lehman Brothers, the New York investment bank, then in 1981 to another oil business, Tricentrol, where he was finance director. In 1983 he became a director of Schroders, but after three years he returned to Lehman for an eight-year stint (by some distance his longest to date) as head of European investment banking.

It was, perhaps, his most successful period: people who worked for him there remember him with real affection and respect. 'Charismatic, incisive, terrific at getting people to work together,' said one. Harrison's celebrated battle-cry – 'A weekend with the family is a missed marketing opportunity' – probably dates from this period. 'He's a real piece of work, a human dynamo with an incredible energy level, a great sense of humour and a very sharp brain,' said another former subordinate, New York mergers and acquisitions specialist Jim Whitcomb.

'A lot of people think he's just an abrasive, hard-driving guy, but he has a very human side,' Whitcomb continued. 'My wife and I had a serious car accident in Gloucestershire in 1991 and we were lying in hospital beds in Cheltenham, all smashed up. In walked this very nice English couple. We didn't know them, but they introduced themselves as Bill's in-laws who lived not far away, and said Bill had asked them to stop by to see us because he couldn't get there himself right away. I've never forgotten that.'

1993 found Harrison resisting BZW's first blandishments, but moving instead to Robert Fleming as head of investment banking.

When he finally accepted Taylor's offer three years later, BZW was his seventh employer in twenty years. Deutsche Morgan Grenfell (now just Deutsche Bank, having absorbed both Morgan Grenfell and Bankers Trust) was in due course to be his eighth, but he stayed there barely a year before announcing that he was moving on again, this time to operate as a solo corporate financier.

In all his appointments with British banks, Harrison had to contend with mixed reactions to – and obsessive press interest in – his non-City persona. At Schroders, one director remembered him as 'a bit of a wild man', superb at winning new business but to be carefully chaperoned when handling established clients – though there is no doubt that Schroders was sorry to lose him. At Flemings, a firm traditionally dominated by deer-stalking Scottish landowners, he attracted headlines such as 'Upstart in the patrician camp', and repeated references to the fact that he had climbed to the top despite his accent. 'It's important to have new blood occasionally,' Flemings' chief executive John Manser told an interviewer, casually reinforcing the prejudice.

Harrison was generally reckoned to have done well for Flemings, extracting new value from the bank's international network and handling major deals such as the Glaxo take-over of Wellcome and ING's rescue of Barings. He favoured a 'transactional' approach, which meant thinking up deals and taking them to companies, rather than relying on an established client list to provide its own deal-flow: it was the ideal approach for BZW, which still lacked a heavyweight corporate finance client list despite its strong connections on the broking side.

'I really enjoyed Flemings and I had a lot of time and respect for them,' Harrison says. 'We did some good business together.' But needless to say – as with David Band and J. P. Morgan – it is not hard to find well-placed people who believe Flemings were relieved to see the back of Bill Harrison. One insider accused him of paying inadequate attention to Flemings' existing client list in his zeal to do deals with more prominent companies: 'a transactional approach just meant a whole lot of ambulance-chasing'; he had also done plenty of hiring and firing. 'When we heard what he was doing at BZW, we just thought, "There goes Bill again." '

When his move to BZW was announced, in June 1996, 'a friend' was quoted in the *Daily Telegraph* likening his appointment to 'making Gazza captain of the England croquet team'. The analogy was odd in one sense, because by comparison with Flemings, BZW was relatively classless. But the firm had a different social aspiration, which was to be more American – 'like Goldman Sachs', David Band had often said, though he never explained how it might get there. The appointment which took it closest to that goal in the post-Band era was not Harrison's, but that of 45-year-old Robert E. Diamond Jr, who joined as head of BZW's Global Markets division (replacing the Vietnam veteran Sam Marrone) shortly before Harrison himself arrived, having approved Diamond's appointment while still officially on gardening leave, on 10 September.

Bob Diamond had been a senior trader at Morgan Stanley and later at Credit Suisse First Boston in London and Tokyo. He was vice-chairman in charge of global fixed income and foreign exchange at CS First Boston, New York, until he resigned in disgust over his 1995 bonus payment – which was widely reported to have been $8 million. His contract with BZW is said to have guaranteed him at least £5 million over the first two years. Bearing a passing resemblance to the actor Christopher Reeve in his heyday as Superman's alter ego Clark Kent, Diamond was known for working out in the gym, eating green salad and making exceedingly complicated demands as to when he should be served coffee with full milk or semi-skimmed or other kinds of beverages during the working day, and with what kind of biscuits. A long memorandum on the subject, confirming negotiations between Diamond's secretary and a BZW catering manager, somehow found its way to several national newspapers.

The physical contrast between Diamond and Harrison was almost comic, and it was Diamond who brought the kind of glamour BZW and Barclays were really looking for. One young manager recalls the launch party for 'the hubris book', Andrew Lorenz's *BZW: The First Ten Years*, held on the anniversary of Big Bang in October 1996 at L'Avenue restaurant in London's St James's Street.

> The old-timers like Jacomb and Camoys were there in their bankerish suits next to this hot-shot newcomer, Bob Diamond, looking casual in his big specs. Everyone wanted to get near him, to touch his golden sleeve. There was a kind of expectation that we were all going to be Americanized, we were all expected to be more like Bob. Peter Middleton made a big speech. Maybe this is just hindsight, but somehow the future already seemed to be more about Peter and Bob and rather less about Bill.

A corporate psychologist, by the way, might have spotted symptoms of deep trouble in some of the design features of Lorenz's otherwise admirable book. Donald Brydon and Graham Pimlott had tried to kill the project at an early stage, rightly anticipating endless trouble if the text gave too little emphasis to the contributions of some of the firm's more inflated egos, or too much to their rivals. In the end – and for precisely that reason, it is said – the book appeared without an index, so that sensitive souls could not easily compare the number of times they were mentioned, and with a plate section of art photographs of cities around the world, rather than selected portraits of BZW heroes.

'On a clear day, from the top of the Canary Wharf tower, you can see for miles,' concludes Lorenz's penultimate chapter, entitled 'Eminence'. 'But not as far as BZW has come, nor as far as it can go.'

It was a nice image, but with hindsight the first association of ideas it provokes is not one of Superman in flight but of the anarchic control tower and the doomed aircraft in the film comedy *Airplane!* As Harrison took over the controls, with Diamond as his co-pilot, they were about to hit serious turbulence.

13

BZW: THE LAST TEN MONTHS

1996–1997: Revolving doors at Ebbgate House – The move to
Canary Wharf – Reassurances from Martin Taylor – No deal
with Smith Barney – Breaking up BZW – The sale runs out of
control – A deal with CSFB

It would be an exaggeration to describe Harrison and Diamond as working in perfect harmony. 'Bob's a hard man to have reporting to you,' said one observer, and reporting arrangements were complicated in any case by the need to refer major credit risk and recruitment decisions up the line to Taylor. But the two BZW chiefs did at least agree that it was Diamond's Markets division which most urgently needed investment and reorganization. They appeared to agree also that no one who worked for a firm like BZW before they got there could by definition be up to the standard they themselves represented and demanded in others. So the revolving doors of Ebbgate House began to spin at dizzying speed.

The first to go was Donald Brydon – a twenty-year Barclays' veteran and the creator, at BZW Asset Management, of one of the group's most successful businesses – whose reward for holding the fort as acting chief executive for six months was to be summarily dispatched by Harrison on his second day in the job. 'Bill doesn't need a deputy,' was the only explanation offered.

It turned out that Diamond did not need one either; he swiftly parted company with Alex von Ungern-Sterberg. Others in Diamond's territory who departed included Yann Gindre, head of debt origination (replaced by Abigail Hofman from Deutsche Morgan Grenfell), Klaus-Peter Moeritz, head of foreign exchange trading (replaced by Paul

Thrush from NationsBank), Nick Carter, head of swaps marketing, Paul Ellis, head of structured products, and Rob Jolliffe and Steve Hones, joint heads of debt syndication. Tony Smith, whose successful sterling bonds team had supposedly been 'ring-fenced' by Diamond as being in no need of radical attention, also left abruptly early in 1997.

To replace this stream of valetudinarians Diamond recruited 140 new people into his division in the first six months. The most senior of them – including Noreen Harrington, former head of Goldman Sachs's emerging-markets bonds business and co-head of the US firm's European fixed income team in London – were on top-of-the-market two-year guaranteed bonus packages running well into seven figures. This in itself caused more internal friction, because the equities side had not been given authority to recruit on such lavish terms and began to suspect a strategic bias towards the debt side: 'The place was suddenly filling up with these million-dollar fruit-eating bond people,' said one disgruntled equity analyst.

All told, some 350 people left BZW in the first months of the Harrison-Diamond era – 50 of them from Markets division in a single day. The average length of service across the firm fell to around two years. This meant that – for all the sincerity of Harrison's urge to yoke people together and at last make BZW work as an integrated house – the instinctive resistance to cross-divisional co-operation within the firm was reinforced by the fact that so many inhabitants of Ebbgate House were complete strangers to each other. 'We really didn't need formal Chinese Walls between divisions,' said one corporate financier. 'Most people just weren't speaking to each other anyway.'

All this contributed to the view that BZW was an incoherent organization with an increasingly unsustainable cost base. Martin Taylor was strongly influenced by institutional shareholders who asked him why he thought he could succeed in the investment banking arena where every other British owner had failed, and his body language continued to communicate his doubts. Almost as soon as Harrison took up his job, he began asking Taylor at regular intervals for reassurance that BZW really had a future with Barclays. He could sense Taylor repeatedly running the numbers and risk equations in his head, and gradually moving to a conclusion.

The annual results for 1996 were not announced until mid-February, in the normal way, but by the end of the year it was clear what sort of pattern they would show. The retail bank was doing relatively well, and group profits as a whole were up 13 per cent to a record £2.36 billion. But within that total, BZW's profits were down by 29 per cent on 1995, to £204 million. BZW costs were up by 18 per cent, driven by a £45 million leap in the remuneration bill – much of that being payoffs to those who had been fired. All of this, Taylor was to say at the results press conference, was 'entirely deliberate', and was giving him more confidence in BZW's future rather than less. The high-profile recruitment campaign for Markets division and the impending move to Canary Wharf were concrete evidence of commitment to the investment banking project. 'I think it's important that people realize that we are doing things to BZW rather than BZW doing things to us.'

But those sentiments were at odds with what he must have really been thinking. By the turn of the year, Taylor was beginning to think about abandoning BZW. The matter came up for discussion at the January board meeting, at which Bill Harrison had been invited to present his plans. It was a bravura Harrison performance. One director recalled him strutting the length of the Lombard Street boardroom, chest puffed like an operatic tenor, as he expatiated about building a world-class investment bank. He and Diamond were already well advanced with the necessary investment on the fixed income and debt side of the business, he said; now he wanted to start investing in the equity side, where distribution was strong but 'origination' (meaning the ability to win mandates for major new issues) was still weak.

Taylor, in the course of his routine monthly commentary later in the meeting, offered an equivocal response to the effect that he was not sure that Barclays could really afford to make a go of BZW. 'Maybe we'll support Bill, maybe we won't,' was the message understood by the non-executives. Though some of them shared Taylor's concern about BZW's profitability and its effect on Barclays' stock market valuation, they were still surprised by Taylor's comment, since Bill had only just been hired by him and the group had committed £200 million to Canary Wharf. Taylor did not press his point further, though he later said that he regretted not doing so. Most unusually, the discussion was not leaked outside the boardroom, so that the senior managers below Harrison were not even aware that it had taken place. The question of major investment in Equities was still hanging in the air, but Harrison emerged with a general mandate to press on.

Or so it seemed, all too briefly. Rumours of sale discussions with Commerzbank, or possibly J. P. Morgan, continued to surface; Taylor himself claimed to have counted the names of fifteen possible buyers in the press during this period. The pace of hiring and firing created a febrile atmosphere. The more uncertain people were about the future, the less willing they were to share client information with their colleagues for the greater good of the firm. And the move to Canary Wharf – which took place in stages between April and June, with Markets division moving on to its spectacular new trading floor ahead of Equities – was creating unhappiness, particularly among the corporate financiers, who felt it was the wrong place for them to be.

None of their clients, or the big City law firms, were there. The powerful international securities firm Credit Suisse First Boston was one of the first Canary Wharf tenants (its former chairman, Michael von Clemm, having been the first promoter of the derelict Docklands site in 1984) but none of BZW's corporate finance peer group in Warburgs and other former British merchant banks were there either. The half-million square feet of new office space offered incomparably better working conditions than Ebbgate House, which everyone agreed was a terrible building. But the Docklands complex was still thought of as the back of beyond, suitable for trading and settlement operations staffed by people from east or south-east London and Essex, for whom it was an acceptable commute.

Approached from the west – with the Jubilee Line tube extension still four years from completion – it involved a change at Bank or Tower Hill station on to the notoriously unreliable Docklands Light Railway, a rattling monument to the Thatcher administration's aversion to investment in public transport. For Chelsea dwellers, driving to work along the crowded Embankment and eastwards past the Tower of London would be the only acceptable option. For commuters into Paddington from west of London, Canary Wharf was a horrendous proposition however you got there.

'The office move became a metaphor for the idea that the seniors did not understand what the people below them really thought about anything,' said one corporate financier. 'The place had a veneer of success at that stage, but underneath it was complete chaos. If you were a psychoanalyst, you might have said it was on the borderline between neurosis and delusion. The neurosis was in this idea that nobody who was already there was good enough, so all the talent had to come from outside. The delusion was that we really were just a couple of breaks away from being Britain's answer to Goldman Sachs.'

But BZW's American dream was getting further away, rather than closer. In early February Morgan Stanley bought, for $10 billion, Dean Witter, a retail broker with 9,000 salesmen and more than 360 branches across the United States, creating a new giant in the market place. Two months later, Bankers Trust bought Alex Brown, one of Wall Street's oldest brokerage firms, for $1.7 billion. These moves were not only reducing the number of possible acquisition or joint venture targets available to BZW, but accelerating the pace of consolidation in a global industry in which inevitably only the very biggest players, or the cleverest niche players with the strongest client relationships and the lowest costs, were likely to survive.

These pressures preyed heavily on Bill Harrison, whose cheer-leading, go-get 'em manner and brilliance in handling clients concealed deep-rooted uneasiness. 'He was all over the place, but never available if you wanted to see him,' said a colleague. 'He'd give you an appoint-ment three days hence, then his secretary would rearrange it twice, then you'd find it cancelled at the last minute.' One ex-BZW manager remembers Harrison in a constant state of high agitation, effing and blinding along Ebbgate House's third floor management corridor while embarrassed senior secretaries dived for cover. Other executives speak of manic phone-calls from Harrison in the early hours, as he reacted angrily to gossip about the firm in first editions of the morning newspapers. 'Never get in a car with Bill,' said one director. 'Within a hundred yards he's yelling at the driver.'

Much of Harrison's perturbation seemed to be provoked by rows with Taylor, both about the need to invest in Equities and about the future of BZW as a whole. But still there was a concerted attempt to paper over the cracks. On the evening of 22 May, after a further bout of rumours about a deal with Commerzbank, Taylor and Harrison put on a show of unity for the assembled staff of the Equities division in the Ebbgate House canteen. Harrison declared that he personally was having 'a whale of a time', that he had found 'nothing but support from Martin' and that the future was 'rosy'. BZW was 'doing very well', Taylor began. He could see 'a huge change for the better' in the three areas which had most concerned him in 1996, which were the weakness of Markets division, the lack of 'client focus' in Corporate Finance, and the 'scratchy, tiresome and partial' relations between BZW and Barclays. 'But for the press,' he said, 'Bill and I would be feeling quite pleased with ourselves.'

And the press were, of course, quite wrong: 'Nothing is going on.' No deal was in the offing. The equities business was not peripheral to Barclays' strategy, but 'central'. 'Debt and equity markets are becoming ever closer. For a financing organization to have an equity franchise is a smart thing to do. I don't expect to lose this bet. I think it's a good one.'

There were hints in Taylor's speech of underlying irritations. He had been given only half an hour's notice that he was expected to address this packed meeting, he pointed out. He had put a considerable amount of his own time and credibility into getting BZW right, including hiring 'a number of very difficult people'. His final message to the restless troops was: 'Calm down and get on with your business.'

The harmonious façade was maintained at least until the first week of August 1997. 'BZW is recovering nicely and its markets business is doing well,' Taylor told the half-year results press conference. 'Over the past six to nine months, we have put the team in place which works well together.' A voice from BZW added: 'Martin is happy now, but we still have a long way to go.'

Martin was not really happy, however, and he had a much shorter distance to go with BZW than his unidentified colleague supposed. When challenged later as to how he squared all his reassuring remarks with what was obviously a growing inner conviction that BZW had to be sold, he offered a fine example of Balliol logic-chopping: he did believe in the future of BZW, he is supposed to have said, but that did not mean that he wanted to own it.

Barclays shares reached a new peak of £14.47 after the announcement of group half-year pre-tax profits up by 8 per cent to £1.33 billion before tax. But the nub of the story was that the good performance was coming from the retail banking side, which was winning almost 24 per cent of new current account business, and from Barclaycard, which had added 370,000 new accounts during the half-year. BZW had produced £124 million, a sharp improvement on the £42 million reported for the previous six months, but still not good enough for Taylor. The result had been knocked back by a £20m loss on derivatives trading (leading to the departure of the deputy head of proprietary trading, Mike Gaeton) following tax changes in the recent Budget. The investment bank was producing a return on capital of only 8 per cent, compared with 34 per cent from retail banking. Smart-alecs could suggest any number of simple bond or stock investments in which Barclays might have invested BZW's capital and gained a trouble-free return of better than 8 per cent.

With wave upon wave of foreign houses trying to buy their way to the front of the London market – Deutsche Morgan Grenfell had been setting the pace, recruiting more than 50 people from Warburgs in the space of a year and forty-four in a single swoop from ING Barings – salary packages for good City traders and corporate financiers were rising at more than 30 per cent per year. And yet 70 per cent of the world's investment banking revenues were generated not in London but in the United States, where BZW had a hopelessly inadequate presence and could not afford a better one. Massive investment would be required to stay in the game at the highest level. 'I really have to believe myself that it is an intelligent thing to do,' Taylor observed at the time. 'And I do not believe it.'

On top of all the analytical reasons not to go on throwing money at BZW, there were more subjective ones. BZW was a gigantic management distraction. To Taylor's irritation, the Barclays' board talked of little else and seemed to him to be in thrall to the idea of owning a global investment bank, whatever the cost. And BZW's people were still monstrously difficult to manage. The firm had some very specialized skills – world-class expertise in the field of electricity privatization, for example, which had won it the mandate for the $11 billion sale of the Spanish state electricity company, Endesa. But it was also accident-prone. There had been two well publicized rows during the winter, one concerning a £250,000 'performance fee' received from Northern Electric during its unsuccessful defence against an American bidder, CE Electric, and another when the electronics distributor Premier Farnell accused BZW of 'mishandling' a profit warning announcement which had had the effect of driving Premier Farnell's share price down by a quarter.

As to internal relations, there were new signs of inter-divisional co-operation among the younger generation of managers, notably Steve Harker in Equities and Charles Stonehill in Investment Banking – brought in from Morgan Stanley to succeed Graham Pimlott (who was now working directly for Taylor on strategy and IT) and generally reckoned to be one of Harrison's best hires. But in other respects relations were still extraordinarily bad. Old animosities between different parts of BZW and between BZW and Barclays were still there.

As well as his troubles with Harrison, Taylor still had a difficult relationship with Jonathan Davie, who had emerged after David Band's death as the nearest thing in BZW to a spiritual leader, but who had been sidelined as deputy chairman when Harker had been brought over from BZW Australia, to run Equities. Davie was market-driven, extrovert and instinctive; Taylor was shareholder-driven, introvert and analytical. It does not require a psychologist to explain why they failed to understand each other. To this nest of tensions had been added an additional layer of trouble: most of BZW's executive committee were uncomfortable working for Bill Harrison, and had said so to Taylor.

Taylor's mind was almost made up, and during August he was already making tentative preparations with his planning staff for a sale. I happened during that month to catch a glimpse of the BZW psyche, six weeks before its death sentence, and a strangely nervous beast it was. On holiday in Asia, I decided to step back briefly into my previous life and call on the firm in Hong Kong and Singapore. In Hong Kong I had to look up BZW in the phone book, because it had moved again, to its third set of expensive offices in ten years; the trading floor was twenty times bigger than the one I had patrolled a decade earlier, but there was almost no one left I knew except the managing director, a young man called Steve Kenny who had once worked for me as a personal assistant. As was often the case with BZW's managing directors, no one seemed to report to him. He sat in his glass box furtively breaking the office 'no smoking' rule and flicking ash into a half-hidden saucer. Hong Kong was a relatively safe haven in BZW these days, he said, because the regional chairman, an ex-Flemings man called Roger Davis, was 'FOB', which stood for Friend of Bill Harrison. Without that protection, he implied, there was no security anywhere.

In Singapore, the office was still where I had left it but there was no one I knew at all on the BZW side. So I asked to say hello to the local partners, Mr Leong and Mr Chua. These charming elderly Chinese gentlemen had sold us a minority stake in their business in 1989, but had never been allowed by the Singapore authorities to sell us the remainder of it and retire. Aged at least eighty, they attended the office every day and did a little share dealing for themselves and their remaining private clients. Mr Chua was notable for the long black hairs which grew straight out of his ears – among Chinese a sign, I always supposed, of the great wisdom which he certainly possessed. They greeted me warmly and we sat down to tea. How was BZW getting along these days, I asked.

'Frankly, we don't know, *lah*,' came the reply, with a characteristic southeast Asian wiggle of the head indicating a subject too delicate to be frank about. 'Always different people coming and going, new people from London, different plans. Really, we don't know what's going on these days.'

Lots of people all over the world did not know what was going on in BZW that month, but some people in London were beginning to get wind of Taylor's intentions. He was still prepared to listen to the alternative case, however, which was to go for double rather than quits and either buy a US investment bank or enter into a large-scale joint venture with one. The candidate favoured by Harrison, as well as by

BZW's New York chief executive Callum McCarthy, was Smith Barney, with which there was already an agreement in place for the sharing of equity research. The names of Lehman Brothers and Donaldson Lufkin & Jenrette were also tossed around as possibilities.

Smith Barney was a subsidiary of the Travelers insurance group – run by one of the titans of Wall Street, Sandy Weill, who also happened to be America's highest paid executive, with a 1997 package of salary, bonus and share options worth $231 million. Smith Barney had a workforce of more than 10,000 stockbrokers across the United States, making it the second largest retail brokerage after Merrill Lynch, but it was less strong internationally and in fixed income products, so the fit was obvious. The approach favoured by McCarthy was not to try to buy Smith Barney (which was not necessarily for sale) but for Barclays to swap the whole of its ownership of BZW for a minority interest in a Smith Barney–BZW merger.

Discussions had taken place with Weill and his deputy, Jamie Dimon, but both the concept and the price were too much for Taylor to swallow. To own 30 per cent of a very large investment bank, with no control over it, seemed to him a worse risk proposition than owning 100 per cent of a smaller one, and he never took the idea to the next stage of discussion at Barclays board level. A last review of possible US expansion plans with Harker and Stonehill in the first half of September merely served to harden his resolve. The longer he waited, he felt, the bigger the risk BZW represented to the rest of Barclays. Out in the Far East, the crisis which had begun in July with the collapse of the Thai baht had spread through the region's currencies and stock markets and was threatening to ripple across the world to Wall Street and London.

Taylor liked to do his thinking at weekends, talking to himself on long walks. (Did he actually talk to himself out loud, one interviewer wanted to know. 'Oh *yes!*' came the reply.) His most radical decisions were then imparted to his colleagues on Monday mornings, and that was the case on Monday 22 September, when he told Buxton, Middleton and Harrison for the first time that he had decided to sell BZW; he then broke the news to Jonathan Davie over lunch, and asked him to take command of the businesses which were to be sold. A full delegation of senior Barclays people was due in Hong Kong at the end of that week for the annual IMF/World Bank meeting, but in the circumstances only Buxton and Middleton set off to hear the highlight of the conference, which was Prime Minister Mahathir Mohamed of Malaysia and billionaire investor George Soros engaging in a vicious exchange of insults over the role of international speculators in emerging markets. Taylor and Harrison stayed in London, locked in heated arguments over the sale plan.

The first questions were how much of BZW Taylor intended to sell, and how much he thought he could get for it. If he had followed his instinct in January rather than September, he believed he might have found an American buyer in search of a European presence which would have been prepared to buy BZW more or less intact, stripped only of those parts of its money market and foreign exchange operations which were essential to Barclays Bank. But those 'plain vanilla' Treasury operations, which would never have been sold, were in fact among the few reliably profitable parts of BZW. So any idea of a price of 'a couple of billion' for BZW was pie-in-the-sky from the start.

Equities and Corporate Finance were obvious candidates to be sold off. Basic money-market dealing was to be kept. But the problem of what to do with the remainder of Bob Diamond's Global Markets division was more complex. Its 'debt capital markets' business (raising bond issues and complex loan deals for large companies) was worth keeping because it was a valuable add-on to Barclays' corporate banking business in a way that (despite what Taylor had said in May) BZW's equity-related corporate finance activity had never been. Its large-scale fixed income trading business was loss-making, but simply to close it down would have involved the costly closing out of large positions in the market. So there was an argument for keeping that too, and gradually scaling it down.

Finally, Diamond himself and the team he had recruited had won the confidence of the senior people at Barclays, including both Middleton and Buxton. Diamond had gained the reputation within the group of being a first-class manager. Given Buxton's attachment to the glamour of investment banking, keeping Bob Diamond was some consolation for losing BZW. So the whole of the debt side of BZW would be kept and renamed Barclays Capital – a name which had been floating around in the ether as a possible alternative to BZW for the best part of a decade, since the earliest days when Barclays had wanted to rein in the de Zoetes faction and show them who was boss.

These considerations were ironed out, in secret, during September. The parts of BZW which were for sale were ring-fenced into a specially created company, and Jonathan Davie was appointed its chairman. One more piece was set aside to be retained: this was the quietly successful 'private equity' subsidiary, which had started life in the early 1980s as Barclays Development Capital, and which had brought a generous

dowry of equity investments into BZW, alongside the National Freight
shareholding; it had been clever enough to remain physically independent of BZW (across the River at Pickford's Wharf, near South-
wark cathedral) all along.

Meanwhile, Taylor swiftly appointed Goldman Sachs to advise on
the sale and asked Graham Pimlott, a take-over lawyer by training, to
take the lead in negotiations on Barclays' behalf. The appointment of
Goldmans was seen afterwards as Taylor's fundamental mistake. 'Never
auction a people business,' observed one veteran corporate financier.
'It's not like real estate.' The only way to have made the deal work
satisfactorily would have been to ask Davie and his colleagues to sell
themselves, but Taylor did not have a working relationship with them
that would have made that possible. Critics also said that he had focused
only on the strategic idea of the sale, and had failed to grasp the
implications of its detailed mechanics. It was obvious that there would
be resentment within BZW at the intrusion of a direct competitor,
Goldman Sachs, demanding confidential client information to pass on
to potential buyers. It was a formula for disaster from the start.

It may be worth noting that, during this crucial decision-making
period, Taylor was doubly distracted by other commitments. Shortly
after the general election on 1 May, he had accepted the chairmanship
of a task force appointed by Gordon Brown to look into the streamlining
of the tax and benefits payment systems; this took up about 10 per cent
of his working time.[1] He was also a non-executive director of W. H.
Smith, the newsagents chain. When he accepted the government role
in May, he felt he could not do both outside jobs and asked Smith's
chairman Jeremy Hardie to release him. But a month later Smith's chief
executive Bill Cockburn suddenly resigned, and Taylor, as chairman of
the board's nominations committee, was obliged to stay on and take an
active role in the search for a replacement for Cockburn. The task was
completed – by the internal appointment of Richard Handover – in
the third week of September, at the height of the internal debate about
the BZW sale.[2]

[1] Rumours in late June said that Taylor had in fact turned down the opportunity to become
Minister for the Welfare State in the House of Lords. He was also understood to have said
no to becoming the head of Tony Blair's Downing Street policy unit. A more speculative
rumour had him turning down the opportunity to succeed Eddie George as Governor of
the Bank of England.
[2] Taylor eventually left the W. H. Smith board in March 1998. He returned to it as non-
executive chairman in November 1999, at a salary of £150,000, which, he said, was 'less
than I normally charge'. In the same press conference he remarked that five years of running
a clearing bank was the equivalent of fifteen years in any other industry.

The peculiar difficulties facing the BZW sale team soon became apparent. First, data prepared for the sale memorandum showed that Equities and Corporate Finance taken together, with what Taylor's planning staff regarded as an appropriate share of BZW's central costs, had never made a profit in any year since the firm was formed in 1986. Secondly, global market upheavals made it a peculiarly bad time to sell a securities business. Thirdly, the major assets of the business which was about to go up for sale were its people, who were difficult to control at the best of times and were highly likely to walk if they did not like what was going on.

But the die was cast, and the rightness of the decision from Taylor's point of view was underlined in the last week of September by the news that Salomon Brothers – the giant Wall Street trading firm, which had suffered its own share of problems over the past five years – had been bought by Sandy Weill's Travelers group for £5.5 billion. It was to be merged with Smith Barney, creating an investment banking powerhouse even bigger than Morgan Stanley Dean Witter. The news reassured Taylor in his belief that BZW could never have hoped to compete at the highest level. John Jay of the *Sunday Times* agreed with him: 'NatWest Markets has already sounded the retreat . . . but BZW is still out there fighting – and bleeding heavily.' Without a big US presence, BZW could not hope to compete, but a purchase on the scale of Salomon would be 'corporate suicide'.

The only good news was the price paid for Salomon, twice the book value of its assets. This misled one City banking analyst into declaring that if, as was now more strongly rumoured than ever, BZW really was for sale, it might command as much as £2.5 billion.

Within BZW itself, a constant round of secret meetings and the summoning back from abroad of senior executives created an atmosphere of deep foreboding. The press were sniffing at the story. Taylor realized it was impossible to proceed without telling BZW staff what was going on. Finally, on Thursday 2 October, the Barclays board heard a presentation from Goldman Sachs and endorsed the sale plan – reluctantly and angrily in the case of some non-executives who felt that they had been presented by Taylor with an ill-conceived *fait accompli*. BZW executives were summoned to a drinks reception to be told the news, which by then also included the resignation of Bill Harrison, a decision he had taken a few days earlier when he saw that Taylor's mind was made up and announced to the board that morning.

'I couldn't preside over the sale of a business that I came in to build,'

Harrison said later. 'In my heart of hearts, I felt that the sale process might go the way it did in the end, and I didn't want people to think I was influential in that process when I wasn't.'

Having lost the argument, Harrison departed with robust dignity. On his last day, he went round the building shaking hands with as many people as he could. 'These things happen,' he told me. 'I'd always had a very open relationship with Martin and with Peter Middleton, but still it was a shock to the system. I tried to conduct myself in a professional way about it, though. I didn't throw my toys out of the cot.'

The blow was perhaps softened for Harrison by the fact that he had earned more than £4m for his turbulent thirteen-month stint with BZW. For 1996 (having signed up in June) he had received, on top of his basic salary, a signing-on fee of £1.5 million as compensation for the bonus he might have received from Flemings, a further guaranteed bonus of £1.25 million and a pension contribution of £110,000. For his nine months' work in 1997, he collected salary of £250,000, compensation for his abrupt departure of £946,000 and a payment of £275,000 towards his pension. He had also been granted more than 132,000 share options at an exercise price of £9.07. With Barclays' share price soaring past £18 on the news of the BZW sale, these were, ironically, worth another million to him.

Harrison certainly knew how to extract a big price, and some people thought it a pity for Barclays shareholders that he did not stay to preside over the sale of BZW. Apart from his skill in selling himself to one bank after another, he was, after all, the man who had sold the collapsed Barings to the Dutch group ING. It is certainly true that he could hardly have got a worse price than the one eventually paid for BZW by Credit Suisse First Boston. But the stock market was glad to see Barclays rid of BZW at any price.

Press reactions were mixed, though all commentators agreed that the sale was a landmark. 'This is a far more important event in Britain's financial history than the collapse of Barings or the sale of S. G. Warburg to Swiss Bank Corporation last year,' wrote Anatole Kaletsky on the op-ed page of *The Times*. 'Barclays, with BZW under its wing, was the last British bank that seemed big enough to have any chance of competing with the great investment houses of Wall Street, or the German, Swiss and Dutch universal banks.'

'I am sorry to announce the demise of the City of London,' said Christopher Fildes in the *Daily Telegraph*, going on to coin a neologism which was rapidly adopted by the rest of the financial press: the sale was 'another game and set in the Wimbledonization of the City, [in which] we stage the tournament but the foreigners are in the finals'. British financiers would henceforth be 'spectators or drones', echoed William Kay in the *Mail on Sunday.* 'This could be the beginning of the end of the City as a leading international financial centre.'

One of the fiercest critics of the sale was Will Hutton, the then editor of the *Observer,* whose best-selling book *The State We're In* had offered the decade's best left-wing critique of the British financial system. To him, Taylor's decision to scrap BZW because it was failing to produce a return on capital of at least 20 per cent – a target 'between a quarter and a third higher' than that of banks in other OECD countries – was a crass example of the short-termism which was 'a menace to the long-term business health of this island'. Other City-watchers were less interested in the underlying philosophy, and more interested in the personalities: 'This is more about Martin Taylor than it is about BZW,' one insider told Neil Bennett of the *Sunday Telegraph.* 'He just doesn't like investment bankers.'

If that was so, he liked them even less after what happened over the next five weeks. Taylor himself has said that his BZW *bêtes noires* were less troublesome than the textile designers he had learned to contend with at Courtaulds, but it is clear that personal relations were by now ice-cold. The resentment towards him was palpable: when he appeared in the trading floor pulpit at Canary Wharf to explain himself, he was received in hostile silence and quickly ushered away by his minders.

'Every profile I've ever read of Martin Taylor starts off by saying he speaks Mandarin Chinese,' one BZW wag said to me. 'But there are a billion people out there who speak Mandarin. Why on earth did we have to pick this one, for Christ's sake?' 'I never thought of Taylor as a colleague, as someone who actually worked in the organization,' one analyst observed. 'He just acted like a rather distant management consultant. It was like the captain of the Titanic, instead of grappling with the helm, summoning the crew on deck and saying, "I have believed for some time that the course you are following is logically inappropriate, and on balance I recommend you put on your lifejack-ets."'

As with the real Titanic, as soon as the bad news broke, the situation became increasingly difficult for the captain to control. The only hope of achieving a successful auction was, obviously enough, to keep several potential bidders in play and to keep each of them in ignorance of the others' final intentions. That called for the strictest possible news management by the Barclays team. What actually happened was that the whole organization, including Barclays board members and senior BZW executives, began leaking information, both true and false, in all directions. Within days, the exercise began to go horribly wrong.

'Goldman Sachs seemed to view BZW as a wasting asset that had to be sold as quickly as possible,' said one participant in the process. 'The person who really picked up the ball and ran with it was Jonathan Davie.'

After his period of quiescence as a deputy chairman, the sale was Davie's opportunity to return to his previous role as the big, back-slapping, ever-present leader of the trading floor. It gave him a huge surge of adrenalin. When he stepped into the pulpit after Taylor to tell his boys that he was there to look after them, he cut a heroic figure. (Corporate Finance people were also invited on to the floor, and it is illustrative of the level of personal recognition across the firm that one young corporate financier recalled the occasion only as 'a rousing speech from a bloke with glasses in Equities'.)

Having assessed the field of possible buyers, the preferred destination of the bloke with glasses was, from an early stage, Credit Suisse First Boston. This was not the easiest idea to sell to his staff, because CSFB had a reputation of being a tough employer and a highly political organization. There were also fears that, since CSFB was a near neighbour in Canary Wharf, a CSFB takeover of BZW might merely be a disguised property deal, enabling CSFB to acquire adjacent, fully equipped trading floors on the cheap, with or without the people to fill them. But in fact CSFB was a good choice both for Davie himself and for his followers, since it was one of the world's most successful investment banks and one of the few in London which was likely to remain unmolested by take-over or consolidation over the next five years. It was a particularly neat fit for BZW because it lacked a significant presence in UK equities or domestic corporate finance, and its physical proximity made the splitting up of back office functions easier to arrange. A first exploratory meeting with Alan Wheat, chairman of CSFB, took place within a week of the sale announcement. Other meetings, involving Davie, Simon de Zoete and Charles Stonehill, took place in New York.

At that stage, however, the press were focusing on other aspects of the story: there was talk of 2,000 BZW redundancies out of 7200 staff worldwide and of an additional bonus pool of £25 million being promised (for payment at the usual bonus time, in March 1998) to those whose stayed with the firm through its transition and did nothing to hinder the sale. City diary columns extracted a laugh from the fact that Sir Peter Middleton had announced the cancellation of two huge cocktail parties, dubbed 'the mother of all opening ceremonies', to celebrate the move to Canary Wharf, for which over a thousand invitations had already been sent out.

More significantly, however, someone from BZW told a Sunday newspaper that he and his colleagues would refuse to give confidential information about their clients to Goldman Sachs, that they would exercise a 'veto' on any buyer they did not like, and that in any event their preference was for an American buyer with a strong Wall Street presence, rather than a European buyer. This latter prejudice was confirmed a few days later when Paribas acknowledged that it had asked Goldman for the BZW information memorandum; the anonymous BZW spokesman immediately let it be known that Paribas was not acceptable.

At the same time Commerzbank, rumoured as a potential buyer at least twice during the preceding year and presumably already in possession of enough information to come to a decision, ruled itself out of the bidding. 'We are not interested in buying BZW or any part of it,' said a Commerzbank spokesman. 'Its earnings just do not compare with our expectations. When we invest in something, we look for a fifteen per cent return on share capital.' Barclays shares dipped 20 pence in response.

Next to rule themselves out were J. P. Morgan and the Dutch group ING, but by Friday, 17 October Goldman's selling prospectus was ready to go out to 'about 20' other firms which were interested enough to sign a legal agreement preventing them from cherry-picking BZW people or business units over the following year. The list was of course secret, but among the names mentioned in the press were Merrill Lynch, Deutsche Morgan Grenfell, Bear Stearns and Donaldson Lufkin & Jenrette (DLJ). CSFB, however, was acknowledged by now to be the front-runner and to be favoured by BZW directors. A 'senior director' of Barclays, meanwhile, let it be known that the bank 'expects to get its price' for BZW, without suggesting what that price might be. Analysts helpfully suggested that it might be between £300 and £500 million. Whatever figure really had been tabled by Goldman Sachs at the 2 October board meeting, there was a growing certainty within Barclays that it had been highly optimistic.

The truth was that only two firms beside CSFB showed any real interest in buying. The first was DLJ: 'We liked the people and the culture,' said one BZW director, 'but they weren't really in a position to do the deal.' 'They spent a long time studying the idea but were really just fantasizing', according to another. The second was Bankers Trust, whose approach was treated with 'derision' by BZW seniors, according to the latter source, but which might have been a serious bidder if it had sensed a warmer reception. By the end of October, Bankers Trust too had pulled out, having transferred its attention to the UK and European equities business of NatWest Markets – a smaller business than BZW's but therefore a less costly one to run – which it duly bought for £129 million a month later.

('The whole BZW sale was an absolutely howling cock-up,' one ex-BZW corporate finance director told me in braying tones at a cocktail party in Sloane Street shortly afterwards. 'The only hope of screwing a reasonable price out of CSFB was to keep Bankers Trust in play. It would have been worth offering them a five million fee just to pretend they were still interested.' That would have been wholly unethical, of course, but a really talented corporate financier might have found a way to get away with it.)

As it was, the Barclays team was left lamely trying to preserve the impression that DLJ might be a bidder, even though DLJ itself had said that – having expanded rapidly in London over the previous nine months, acquiring Phoenix Securities, the corporate finance boutique, and moving into expensive new offices in Bishopsgate – it was 'unlikely' to go for any more major expansion in the near future.

What happened next was never fully reported. Word somehow reached CSFB that it was the only runner in the race. Taking the view that it no longer needed to pay to win, CSFB formally withdrew, leaving no bidders at all and a catastrophic embarrassment for Barclays, where senior people were busy distancing themselves from the débâcle as fast as they could. But CSFB was then cajoled back to the table, with a week's 'exclusivity' to come up with a 'final' offer. CSFB immediately made clear that it was not interested in the Asian and Australasian operations of BZW, and would not even take on its London equity derivatives trading operation. On 7 November, at the last of a series of Friday afternoon meetings on the BZW trading floor – designed to keep staff informed about the sale process and to provide an opportunity for questions to Davie, Harker and Stonehill – the mood turned ugly.

Most people had hoped that the whole worldwide equities business would be sold together, and some were angry that Asia, Australia and other parts would be cut adrift in the CSFB deal. Davie and Simon de Zoete were in a peculiarly awkward position, because as an aside to the final negotiation between Barclays and CSFB they had been told by

CSFB that the deal would only go ahead if they themselves signed up to it first. Having done so, Davie could no longer commend the deal to his colleagues from an objective standpoint. After he had fended off one particularly hostile question, there was silence from the floor, broken by a handful of people who started to jeer.

The deal CSFB finally offered was a miserable one for Barclays. CSFB would pay £100 million – reducing Barclays' embarrassment a little by allowing a nine-figure price for the headlines, but representing only two-thirds of the book value of the UK and European businesses to be taken over. The buyer would take on only 960 staff, of whom the 200 most valued (including, of course, the most senior people) would be offered three-year contracts. Among the other 760, the cost of any redundancies made by CSFB within a specified period would be passed back to Barclays. Barclays would have a one-year management contract to provide back-office support for the transferred businesses, and CSFB would retain de Zoete & Bevan's role as broker to Barclays.

The 'lock-in' contracts offered to the 200 'most valued' people included payments spread over three years – in cash for some and in CSFB shares for others – equivalent to 1997 salary plus the bonus already promised for March 1998. Thus a salesman paid a £100,000 salary and promised a £200,000 bonus would then receive a further £300,000 between 1998 and 2000. All these payments were to be met by Barclays, as a deduction from the £100 million headline figure. The contracts included significant changes (extending notice periods from three months to six, for example) from BZW standard contracts, but the recipients were presented with them at lunch-time on Sunday, 9 November, and given only until 9 a.m. on Monday to sign them. Lawyers who had been made available to advise on any queries in the paperwork offered the opinion that the pressurized timescale for signing did not constitute 'duress', and that 'only a widow or an orphan' really needed advice on such a straightforward contract. With hindsight, a second opinion might have been useful: in at least two cases over the following year, attempts by CSFB to enforce the contract terms, imposing six-month quarantine periods on ex-BZW people leaving to join other firms, were overturned in court.

By this stage Taylor knew he was in for a barrage of criticism, but felt he had got out of BZW as cleanly as he might realistically have hoped. Though BZW's fourth-quarter turnover was shattered by the distractions of the sale, no major clients had been lost, and important deals like the privatization of Telecom Italia, on which BZW was then advising, were able to proceed without interruption. None of the key managers of Barclays Capital had walked out. There had been no 'rogue trading' against the house by disgruntled staff. Though the London stock market fell by 10 per cent in the last part of October, the sale had not been stopped by a tenth anniversary rerun (predicted by some pundits) of the October 1987 crash. The reluctance of senior BZW people to co-operate with the Goldman Sachs sale process was confirmation, to the high-minded Taylor, of what a rotten business BZW was to own in the first place.

As for CSFB's offer, it was, he declared, 'a fair deal and a fair price', a view which could only be supported, as another participant in the negotiation put it, 'if you accepted that a business that was worth about fourpence had actually been sold for fourpence'. Not many people did see it that way, however. The deal was 'two years late and disastrously bungled', said the *Independent*. The minority of commentators who clung to the romantic notion of BZW as the last British champion in global investment banking may have disagreed with the first part of that sentiment. But they were even more emphatic about the second.

The sale price had been deliberately obfuscated in the announcements. The 'lock-in' and redundancy arrangements, and certain other adjustments, made the headline figure of £100 million entirely notional. This gave credence to the version popular in the wine bars of Canary Wharf, that Barclays had 'paid CSFB to take BZW away', though I have found no evidence for Nick Sibley's theory – expounded as we drank champagne in his Riviera swimming pool – that the real price paid by Barclays to do so was as much as £200 million.

Even that would have been modest in relation to the total cost of dismantling BZW. This was revealed in (or rather, had to be ferreted out of the small print of) the 1997 and 1998 annual reports. It consisted of £283 million of staff reduction, property and equipment costs, £140 million of goodwill written off and £49 million of losses on the sale of business assets. Then there were £219 million of operating losses for 1997 in the businesses which had been sold – arising largely in the fourth quarter, trading having come to a virtual halt during the sale process in October and November. Lastly, there were a further £33 million of losses in 1998 from BZW's European, Asian and Australasian businesses before they were sold or closed. That made a grand total of £724 million.

As for BZW's businesses in the rest of the world, the only one that sold well was the only one which was allowed to sell itself. The Australian operation – about one seventh of the size of London – was bought by ABN-Amro for A$177 million (£71 million). CSFB also picked up the Taiwan and Singapore businesses – creating an opportunity, at last, for my elderly friends Mr Chua and Mr Leong to sell out and retire. The rest of BZW's overseas operations were scaled back and rebranded Barclays Capital, or closed down. BZW's Japanese equities business, for the foundation of which I had spent all those months arm-wrestling with the Ministry of Finance, was closed 'with immediate effect' on 28 November 1997.

Ironically, the London acquisition worked extremely well for CSFB, which went on from strength to strength having used BZW to fill several important gaps in its armoury. CSFB's chief economist, Giles Keating, told me it was 'a perfect example of a synergistic acquisition'. The ex-BZW people were certainly better placed there than they would have been if Bankers Trust had been the winning bidder: within a year, Bankers was itself the subject of take-over attention from Deutsche Bank, and when the deal went through six months later, the merger of Bankers' operations in London with Deutsche Morgan Grenfell resulted in hundreds of job losses, much unhappiness and the disappearance of the names of both Bankers Trust and Morgan Grenfell. Of the 900-plus ex-BZW people who did go to CSFB, about 150 left or were made redundant in the first few months; others drifted away later. But two years on, more than 600 were still there and as one of them put it, 'the good ones are thriving mightily'.

The sale to CSFB produced the only outcome which could have held most of the business and its people together, and made them part of a stronger organization. Jonathan Davie and Simon de Zoete may not have endeared themselves to Martin Taylor by the way in which they grasped initiative during the sale, but other senior Barclays people have expressed admiration for what they did. It was, after all, a choice in the end between a deal with CSFB and no deal at all. Davie became a vice-chairman of CSFB and when I last bumped into him in the concourse of Canary Wharf, he was full of bonhomie and full of praise for his new CSFB colleagues' understanding of the securities business. Charles Stonehill became CSFB's deputy global head of investment banking. Steve Harker returned to his native Australia to work for Morgan Stanley. Simon de Zoete, Davie's closest ally, became vice-chairman of CSFB for Europe. I last saw him at York racecourse, watching one of his own horses run and looking immensely pleased with himself. De Zoete has the air of a man who rarely loses, so I put a tenner on his horse. It came nowhere, but I had forgotten to enquire whether he was backing it himself.

14

A SEXIER FUTURE?

1998–1999: No internal candidates – A bout of Californian flu –
The sexiest banker in Canada – Branch banking is going to look
different – And so to judgement.

One of the most obvious tests of the health and self-confidence of large companies is their ability to groom executives for succession to top jobs. Ironically, in the best and most durable companies, the top people often do not seem to be outstandingly brilliant individuals. In Shell, BP or ICI, it often requires energetic PR work to make the next managing director to reach the top of the pyramid sound like an interesting personality to the outside world. Those of recent memory who really were more colourful, like Sir John Harvey-Jones at ICI and Bob Horton at BP, were not best liked by their colleagues. In the banking world, HSBC (post Sir William Purves) is notable for producing a breed of reliable, well-trained bankers and managers capable of running a massive international organization without attracting much attention to themselves as individual strategists and deal-makers. 'They don't have to be brilliant because they've all known each other very well for a long time and they trust each other,' was the simple explanation offered by one competitor.

But Barclays had lost all that. With the departure of Brian Pearse, Peter Wood, Peter Ellwood and others, the thread had been broken. Buxton himself, as chairman, was the last major internal appointment the board had made and the outside world was never happy with him: the conventional wisdom nowadays is that to promote from within is too often to settle for second best. From that time onwards Barclays had to think first every time of external appointments. When it came to looking for a chief executive to replace Martin Taylor in 1998, the jargon phrase was, just as it had been in 1993, 'we need an agent of change', someone with no baggage or preconceptions. The insiders in the competition – John Varley and Chris Lendrum – were clearly at a disadvantage.

Lendrum, fifty-two, the head of corporate banking, was clever, clear thinking and had never made waves, but some insiders thought him not strong enough in temperament for the job. Varley, on the other hand, was generally reckoned an outstandingly able administrator, but was five years too young, had had health problems a few years earlier, and was too recently promoted to his current job to be judged a success in it. Others thought him lacking commercial aggression: 'He may be a first-class chap, but is he going to go straight out and buy a Scottish Widows, like Pitman and Ellwood have just done?' asked one ex-director.

Varley has the disadvantage of being identified (as Sir Jock Pease's son-in-law) as a last vestige of the family system in Barclays. But the system has now been so comprehensively demolished that Varley's connection needs pointing out only as an explanation of why he joined Barclays in the first place, rather than of why he rose to the top of it. It was Rex Cooper, BZW first deputy chief executive (like all de Zoetes men, usually hypercritical of everyone from Barclays) who told me that Varley was 'the best man I've worked with in thirty years in the City'. A solicitor by training, Varley is lawyerish in his precise use of language, has a huge capacity for paperwork, a high moral sense and beautiful manners. His style is impeccably old City, verging on 'young fogey' – good suits, small tortoiseshell spectacle frames, a panama hat in summer, even (an affectation now rarely seen outside the grandest barristers' chambers) stiff, detachable white shirt-collars. It was reassuring to see, when he appeared on television in May 1999 to explain why Barclays was cutting a further 6000 jobs on the retail side, that Barclays image-makers had failed to persuade him into a soft-collared Martin Taylor-ish shirt for the occasion.

In the absence of other leads, the press made more of a race between Varley and Lendrum than was really the case. Most gossips who knew the contenders personally had their money on Varley, but at least one report (by Andrew Garfield in the *Independent*) had Lendrum re-emerging as the front-runner – on the basis that Peter Middleton was 'understood to have decided, after consultation with key board members, that Mr Varley – who has held his current position for barely a year – needs more time before he is considered for the top job'.

But the job was almost certain to go to an outsider from the start. And among the interesting outside candidates were two former insiders who served as reminders of where Barclays had gone wrong a decade and more earlier. The older of these was Malcolm Williamson – who passed sixty in February 1999, but was still five years younger than Sir Peter Middleton. Having become disenchanted with the Bevan regime at Barclays in 1985, Williamson had run Girobank, the Post Office subsidiary, then Standard Chartered, where he was believed to have favoured the idea of merger with Barclays but fallen out with his chairman over it. He left Standard Chartered in June 1998 to run Visa International, the credit card network, dividing his time between London and San Francisco.

Next on the alumni list, and at fifty-five a more obvious prospect than Williamson, was Peter Ellwood, the group chief executive of Lloyds TSB. Like Williamson, Ellwood had risen all the way through Barclays from a junior clerk in the Bristol district to become chief executive of Barclaycard in 1985. But he had then been told, like Williamson, that he could not expect to go higher.

So he looked elsewhere, and was recruited in 1989 to run the retail banking side of the Trustee Savings Bank. When TSB was acquired by Lloyds in 1995, he formed a powerful working partnership with Sir Brian Pitman which drove the merged group to its pre-eminent position, with 15 million customers and 1998 profits of £3.3bn. Though warmer in his manner, Ellwood turned out to be just as tough as Pitman: he chopped 25 per cent of TSB's workforce between 1992 and 1995, and another 10,000 jobs went after the Lloyds merger. For 1998, Lloyds TSB could claim a cost-to-income ratio of 48.4 per cent, compared to 62.4 per cent at Barclays. When his name was floated as a candidate for Taylor's job, Ellwood was said to be 'still very fond of Barclays', but no one could think of any sensible reason why he should want to move back there.

Outside the Barclays old boy network, possible candidates from high street competitors included Peter White, the ambitious chief executive of Alliance & Leicester, Michael Jackson from the Birmingham Midshires building society and Martin Gray, head of retail at NatWest. But the press and the stock market were more interested in the idea of a Scot or an American. The chief executives of the two major Scottish banks, Peter Burt of Bank of Scotland and Sir George Mathewson of Royal Bank of Scotland, both had strong reputations, and both carried with them the possibility of an alliance between their own banks and Barclays.

Discussions with Burt seem to have come to nothing at an early stage in the search, but his name resurfaced after he was blamed for

Bank of Scotland's disastrous flirtation with the American evangelist and entrepreneur Pat Robertson, who was to have been a partner with Bank of Scotland in a US telephone banking venture. When Robertson denounced Scotland to his television viewers as a land which could 'go right back to the darkness' because homosexuals were 'riding high' there, large numbers of customers – including some Scottish local authorities – threatened to withdraw their accounts from Bank of Scotland until the venture was finally abandoned. The fiasco made Burt's position look a little less secure, so brought his name back into the frame, briefly reviving whispers of a Bank of Scotland – Barclays merger.[1]

The forthright Sir George Mathewson of the Royal Bank, on the other hand, was playing from a position of greater strength, and was only prepared to talk about a merger in which he and his young deputy, Fred Goodwin, would take over the running of Barclays from Edinburgh – even though his bank's market capitalization was a mere £12 billion beside Barclays' £30 billion. Mathewson had turned Royal Bank from a fading pillar of the Scottish financial establishment to a lean, aggressive operation for which Scotland looked too small a home territory. But his uncompromising approach met a cold response from Peter Middleton, and the deal looked too big to be achieved on the basis of a hostile bid by Royal Bank.

So Barclays completed its search, and on 11 February the new chief executive was announced: Mike O'Neill, a 52-year-old former US Marine. 'Barclays calls in the Marines' was a useful tag for sub-editors, but not quite as macho as it sounded, since it turned out that O'Neill had served in the Marine intelligence division without going to Vietnam. He had then made most of his 25-year banking career in Continental Illinois, the Chicago bank which had once been regarded as the J. P. Morgan of the mid-West but which had hit the rocks in the mid-1980s and had been taken over by BankAmerica in 1994. He had spent nine years of his career in London. To emphasize his Anglophile credentials, it was revealed that he loved dogs, and that his two red setters were already being prepared for their six-month sentence in British quarantine kennels.

O'Neill had been chief financial officer at Continental and then at BankAmerica, where he had been involved in a rapid expansion of a

---

[1] Burt's recovery from his encounter with Pat Robertson was complete by September 1999, when he launched Bank of Scotland's audacious £25 billion takeover bid for NatWest and was hailed once again as one of Britain's most admired bankers.

network of branches based in supermarkets in California and Chicago, from which the bank rapidly exited again two years later. He went on to play a key role in BankAmerica's merger with NationsBank. But his career had peaked: the aggressive NationsBank boss, Hank McColl, soon sidelined him and his name was in the market for a new job.

But it was by no means a famous name: almost no one in the City seems to have heard of Mike O'Neill before he was picked out by Barclays. During his two periods in London for Continental – as a corporate relationship officer in the 1970s, and briefly as UK country manager in 1984, his profile had not been high – though comments offered by people who had dealings with him in those days were full of praise for his professionalism. In 1984, when Continental was in difficulties and had to be rescued by the Federal Deposit Insurance Corporation, O'Neill took a new job with First Interstate Bancorp, but was seconded back to Continental as part of a rescue team charged with sorting out loan portfolio problems in Europe. He then spent some years as an independent consultant on loan workouts in Asia and the Middle East, before being hired back into Continental in 1989.

All this made O'Neill an experienced banking troubleshooter, said to be tough on cost control, with several rounds of experience of mergers and take-overs: essentially a back-room operator rather than a front man. To the market it was a signal that merger and damage limitation were uppermost in the minds of those who had appointed him. Those who met O'Neill in the course of his recruitment thought him capable of doing more than just delivering Barclays tidily into the hands of a new owner, but that was largely how the media saw him.

There was also some soul-searching as to why no one in Britain measured up to the job. Middleton admitted that it boiled down to 'a question of availability': none of the Brits he had his eye on actually wanted the job. Sir Michael Angus, chairman of Boots and Whitbread, former chairman of Unilever and non-executive director of NatWest, declared in the *Mail on Sunday* that the root of the problem was that the British banking industry rarely produced top-class modern managers because it was still suffering from a legacy of promoting school-leavers who had never worked anywhere else. 'Big UK banks in general, unlike big manufacturers, have suffered by promoting executives who have not spent enough time in the outside world.'

Banking analyst John Tyce of Société Générale added: 'Banking is more competitive and you need sharper people. But in Britain sharp bankers have been regarded as dangerous because they have often tried to over-lend and it has ended in tears. Standing still is not an option any more so you have to go for the exciting candidate. Martin Taylor was perhaps a little too exciting, so they have gone for a career banker with a US edge.'

What was more exciting about O'Neill was his pay package, which set a new benchmark for hired-in British chief executives. He was already rich, having collected some $30 million over the preceding five years from the two American bank mergers, and his BankAmerica contract was said to give him a pension of $2 million a year. But Barclays was willing to make him richer still. He was to receive a starting base salary of £850,000, plus a bonus guaranteed at £850,000 for the first year; he would also receive a package of expatriate benefits worth £175,000 a year and pension contributions of 50 per cent of his base salary. On top of that, he would receive share options worth four times his salary – so £3.4 million – in three years' time, if growth in Barclays earnings per share over the period had beaten inflation by 6 per cent or better. He would invest £5 million of his own money in Barclays shares, and would be awarded another £5 million worth by the bank provided he was still in post in three years' time. Depending on how it is added up, this amounts to some £15 million of remuneration over three years. The package at least had the merit of being transparently performance-related, but still the sheer scale of it caused astonishment in the City.

'Figures are occasionally reported that provoke a suspension of belief in the free enterprise system,' wrote former Conservative MP Sir Ian Lloyd in a letter to the *Financial Times*. 'Can it possibly be suggested that the chief executive of any bank justifies remuneration at least 59 times that of the prime minister . . .' Furthermore, he wrote, the action of the Barclays board in choosing an American implied that 'there is not a single individual in Britain with the requisite skills – an unwarranted slur on the reputation of the City of London'. An even pithier note, and a reminder of how the world had changed, came from Sir Brian Pearse, who pointed out that O'Neill would be paid more in a single year than he had been paid for his entire forty years' service to Martins and Barclays.

Shortly after this, Pearse was also able to calculate that he had earned less in the whole of his distinguished Barclays career than Martin Taylor had been paid for resigning. In the same week that O'Neill was due to start work, it was announced that Taylor had received a £1.6 million pay-off, and would also keep his Barclays' share options. This came on top of base salary of £568,000, bonus of £369,000 and other benefits of £20,000 (a total of £957,000, up from £738,000 in 1997) bringing his total pay for 1998 to £2.5 million. The £1.6 million was in lieu of what he might have earned in 1999, given a projected improvement in profit performance and a rising share price, and set a new benchmark for golden farewells in the financial sector. Happily for Taylor, it also surpassed by a wide margin the £964,000 pay-off for Bill Harrison. 'This type of damages payment is usual for an executive who leaves by mutual consent,' said a Barclays spokesman.

The phrase 'by mutual consent' is important, because it indicates that in legalistic terms Taylor did not simply resign – if he had, he would not have been entitled to any compensation at all. His final departure terms, arrived at by hard negotiation through lawyers, also reflected the fact that in the end he did not actually storm out of 54 Lombard Street on that fateful Thursday, never to return. He made himself available until the end of the year to participate in an orderly hand-over to Middleton, and was then provided with an office and the assistance of his own former secretary in the pleasantly calm sur-roundings of Barclays Private Bank in Grosvenor Street, Mayfair. He operated from there until June 1999. Having signed an agreement (common in the case of such a high-profile departure) which barred him from giving press interviews about his Barclays experience and from disparaging his former colleagues, he disappeared for some months from public view, giving no indication of his next career move.

Friends said that he really had been shaken by the tensions of October and November, and was uncharacteristically unfocused in the early months of 1999. His detractors put it about that after his final per-formance at Barclays he might never be able to work for a major public company again – though his appointment as chairman of W. H. Smith in November 1999 clearly gave the lie to that suggestion. Others speculated that what he was waiting for was a job offer from the Government – perhaps even the revived offer of a peerage and a ministerial appointment. But unluckily for Taylor (according to this theory), the Blair regime had now decided that its policy of recruiting wealthy businessmen straight into government – Lord Simon of High-bury, former chairman of BP, and Lord Sainsbury of Turville from the grocery dynasty being the cases in point – had provoked negative 'focus group' responses, and was not to be repeated for the time being.

Eventually Taylor scotched most of these theories by announcing a portfolio of new jobs in both the private and public sectors. He was helping HM Customs & Excise to formulate proposals to curb the £2 billion annual loss of duty revenues through smuggling of booze and tobacco. He had become a special adviser to Goldman Sachs, the investment bank with which he shared the responsibility for the BZW sale: Goldman would benefit from Taylor's knowledge of Europe and Asia, said an unofficial spokesman, and his understanding of electronic trading would also be an asset. Ex-BZW people were, needless to say, sceptical of the idea of Taylor, having presided over the dismantling of his own investment bank, signing up to work for the one which helped him do so. As well as returning to W. H. Smith, he was also to chair a commission of enquiry into public-private financing of public services and projects. After nine months' break, he looked like a busy and important man again.

But back in the early spring, as Taylor disappeared from sight, the beginning of the O'Neill era was eagerly awaited. It turned out to be a very short era indeed. Bizarrely, O'Neill did not complete a single day's work for Barclays, and did not collect a cent of his massive pay package, though he did buy his £5 million share stake on 23 February and accumulated a substantial profit on it.

At the beginning of March, O'Neill went down with a bout of flu. His Californian doctor performed a battery of tests as American doctors tend to do, however mundane the complaint. A slight heart irregularity was observed, but O'Neill was told it was not significant. On 18 March he flew to London and attended part of a Barclays board meeting. But instead of staying on to take up his post as planned on 26 March, he flew back to San Francisco on 21 March feeling lousy. Barclays then agreed to delay his arrival until 12 April, but on 7 April he suffered a blackout and was told that the heart problem – arrythmia, or a fluttering of the heartbeat – was more serious than the doctor had first thought. Nevertheless he flew to London again, having first briefed Middleton by telephone. An emergency board meeting was set up, and O'Neill was re-examined by Barclays' own doctor – *The Times'* medical columnist Tom Stuttaford, who had passed O'Neill fit in February. Stuttaford confirmed the diagnosis, and O'Neill immediately tendered his resignation – so it was not fair to suggest, as the newspapers gleefully did in their 'Barclays chief quits on first day' headlines, that he had arrived for work and dropped his bombshell resignation in mid-morning. He did indeed attend the office on 12 April, but in a debilitated state and only for the purpose of discussing the unravelling of his contract.

Arrythmia is not an immediately life-threatening condition. It can be brought under control by rest and drugs, and is often treated with mild electric shocks. But it is certainly dangerous to anyone with the stress and responsibilities of a chief executive, even more so if he is coming new to the job and moving half way across the world to do it. Suggestions that the heart trouble story had been cooked up to hide a row between O'Neill and Middleton over their respective responsibilities, or perhaps even a better job offer for O'Neill from another bank, were swiftly crushed. 'I am sure that this is all genuine,' Middleton told one Sunday newspaper. 'Otherwise he would have to be the best actor in the world to pull the wool over the eyes of two distinguished medical teams.'

O'Neill seemed to have been written out of the soap opera after barely half an episode. Middleton was back in charge – and thoroughly enjoying himself by all accounts – taking over the chair as well as the chief executive's office after the annual general meeting the following week. The meeting was Andrew Buxton's last appearance on the platform, but it was a low-key affair which passed off without too much embarrassment. Asked about the possibility of becoming 'the Royal Barclays Bank of Scotland', Buxton replied that if a merger proposal arose which was consistent with Barclays strategy, it would be seriously considered. 'But we are not mesmerised by such thoughts.'

Questions from the floor concentrated on the departure of Taylor: Peter Jarvis, as the non-executive director chairing the bank's remuneration committee, was forced to defend Taylor's £1.6 million payoff as being 'in the best interests of shareholders'. One shareholder, a Mr Carroll, expressed his feelings about the successive departures of Harrison, Taylor and O'Neill: 'Losing one is understandable, to lose the second is just a little careless but to lose a third is unbelievably careless.'

Meanwhile, the head-hunters at Spencer Stuart dusted off their file and went back to work. Perhaps the most unlikely hat to be thrown in the ring, in mid-June, was that of Mike O'Neill, who was reported to be feeling a lot better and interested in reclaiming the job. His American doctors now thought that he might simply have suffered 'an extreme reaction to flu'. The idea of O'Neill returning was 'not impossible' said a Barclays insider, because 'he has proved difficult to benchmark against' in the renewed search. With Middleton putting in such a self-assured performance at the helm, there was no pressure for a quick decision. 'If by August or September the board still has not found anyone, I think it would have to cross their minds to talk to [O'Neill] again.'

All this uncertainty and thinking aloud was not helping Barclays rebuild its image, however. That only became possible when someone more exciting than O'Neill came into the picture. With his carefully coiffed hair and his deep-set eyes, the new candidate even looked more interesting than the blandly bankerish Californian. This was none other than 'Canada's sexiest banker': Matthew 'Matt' Barrett, the flamboyant, 54-year-old, Guinness-drinking, Irish-born ex-chairman of the Bank of Montreal. 'Who says bankers have to be boring?' was one news-paper's reaction, and Barrett certainly provided better copy than any other frontrunner to date for the Barclays' job.

The son of a radio dance-band leader, Barrett was born in Tralee, County Kerry, and educated by Christian Brothers. His ambition was to be a writer, but in 1962 he moved to London and took a job as a clerk in the Waterloo Place branch of Bank of Montreal. Five years later he was sent to Canada as a trainee manager. He rose to become Canada's 'Outstanding CEO of the Year' in 1995. On the way up, he bought Harris Bank, a Chicago retail bank, and made a success of it, built Nesbitt Burns, a leading Canadian investment bank, and launched Canada's first electronic banking system, Mbanx, with an advertising campaign which used Bob Dylan's song 'The times they are a-chan-gin''. He made a salary of more than 3 million Canadian dollars and collected the Canadian equivalent of a knighthood.

Finally, he attempted to crown his 37-year Bank of Montreal career (the last ten years as chief executive, during which the bank's market value quadrupled) by leading it into a £14 billion merger with Royal Bank of Canada. He had planned to lead the merged group for three more years, but when the Canadian government blocked the deal he decided in February to resign – just too late for Barclays to talk to him first time round.

His plan was 'to write a bad book, find my karma and grow a ponytail', with a little consultancy work on the side. But then the head-hunters finally got through to him, and offered him, in Barclays, 'the only financial institution in the world that I could be tempted by'. They also offered him (similar to O'Neill's package) a basic salary of £850,000, a guaranteed first-year bonus of the same amount, £250,000 a year of expatriate allowances and £3.4 million of share options if he hit specified performance targets.

But Barrett had another facet to his life, which prompted the *Sun* – not normally interested in City appointments – to dub him 'the £7 million bonk manager'. Having divorced his wife of twenty-eight years, by whom he had four grown-up children, Barrett had reinvented himself as a flamboyant socialite: 'I want to smell the roses before I fertilize them,' was his own rationale for this. His foray into Canada's high-gloss social scene led him straight into the arms of Anne Marie Sten, a six-foot-tall 44-year-old who had spent her early years as a glamour model for Canada's own tabloid newspapers. Heidi Kingstone, writing in the *Mail on Sunday*, recalled that Anne Marie had once been kept in an apartment in Paris by the Saudi arms dealer Adnan Khashoggi and had described herself as his 'pleasure wife'.

Despite warnings from Barrett's friends that it could not last, the couple were married. According to Kingstone (who claimed to have known Anne Marie for 20 years, since they met on a modelling shoot in the Caribbean), Barrett swiftly discovered just how demanding his new bride could be when she refused to wear a £50,000 emerald necklace he had given her, telling him to give it to his daughter instead. The emeralds had to be replaced by 'a diamond as big as a throat lozenge' before she was satisfied, and it was his new wife's phenomenal running costs which prompted Barrett to contemplate searching for a giant-salaried job abroad. By the time he had found one, however, the marriage was already on the rocks.

In the week that Barrett's Barclays appointment was announced, the Canadian satirical magazine *Frank* – which had been running a contest for its readers to guess how long Matt and Anne Marie would stay married – published on its Internet site some rather dated photographs of Anne Marie naked in a shower, while Barrett himself announced that he was coming to London alone. Anne Marie was reported by Kingstone to have decamped to Monte Carlo, having shipped over the Maserati sports car Barrett had given her and no doubt still wearing that lozenge-sized diamond. She was said to be consoling herself with 'a rich Italian playboy some years her junior'. It was all a far cry from the home life of the average Barclays Bank manager.

But then everything about Barclays is different nowadays. With the results for the first half of 1999, announced shortly after Barrett's appointment, came news of another 1000 job cuts – making 7000 for the year so far – and the closure of up to 50 branches. Sir Peter Middleton felt obliged to say that the closure programme was really designed to improve customer service and would not disadvantage older customers who prefer to deal with a real person over the counter, rather than being forced to resort to telephones, cash machines and e-mail: 'This is not an assault on the elderly,' he said.

Meanwhile HSBC, boosted by a turn-around in Asian markets, had just reported a 10 per cent profit increase; Lloyds TSB came in with a 16 per cent jump in profits to £1.6 billion, with a further 4 per cent cut in the vital cost-to-income ratio; NatWest was up 18 per cent at £1.14 billion, despite rising costs. But poor old Barclays still seemed to be swimming the wrong way, 25 per cent down, with profits reduced from £1.2 billion to £970 million.

The 'incredible shrinking Barclays' laid the blame for another set of bad results on exceptional costs, noted *The Times*. There was a £345 million 'restructuring charge' to pay for job cuts, and a book loss on the sale of Merck Finck in Germany. Exceptional costs certainly seemed to be 'an exceptionally regular feature at Barclays', and there was also an increase in provisions for bad and doubtful debts from £191 million to £320 million.

But there was also some signs of the dawning of a new age. Barrett declared that he would give himself one hundred days – beginning in mid-September 1999 – to come up with a plan to turn Barclays into 'a top-notch wealth management organization'. Meanwhile, new branch layouts were being piloted (in Stockport) which were designed to focus staff on the selling of financial services, while machines and telephone lines dealt with routine transactions. 'It's impossible to contemplate Barclays without branches,' John Varley observed, 'but the feel of branch banking will change.' And rapid progress was reported in converting customers to the idea of Internet banking: Barclays was now Britain's largest Internet bank, with 380,000 customers and a sign-up rate of 10,000 per week.

Sir Peter Middleton offered a comment on this rapid progress which might have been used, in a different sense, as an epitaph for all too many of Barclays' adventures of the past twenty years: 'Any number that you write down is likely to be wrong tomorrow.' And as the calm of Barrett's first hundred days of strategic contemplation was shattered by a hostile take-over bid for NatWest from Bank of Scotland, any prediction of the structure of ownership of British high street banking was also likely to be proved wrong tomorrow or the next day. As Royal Bank of Scotland launched a counter-bid for NatWest, commentators speculated again on how long Barclays could survive without changing its own nature by acquisition or being swallowed by a more aggressive rival.

Which brings us to judgement. Why did so many things go wrong for Barclays in the 1980s and 1990s? Why, in the earlier period covered by this book, did so much go right? Was it simply the workings of historical inevitability, in the sense that all works of human endeavour which achieve greatness tend also to decline into complacency, over-confidence, vanity, fatigue, internal fractiousness, unforced errors, and final humiliation – followed, in happier cases, by renewal and resurgence. It is a pattern which might be applied to English cricket, the Conservative Party, the Soviet Union and Marks & Spencer. It certainly applies to many other banks in the world, including Barclays' most aggressive British competitor in the first half of the twentieth century, the Midland Bank, and its most glamorous role-model in the 1960s and early 1970s, the Bank of America. It will probably happen to many more, including those which today seem so unchallengeably strong and assured.

Indeed, perhaps it will happen to a disproportionate number of large banks, because large banks are peculiarly difficult vessels to steer for any length of time along a straight course. In *Breaking the Bank: The Decline of BankAmerica* Gary Hector wrote:

> One of the most disturbing conclusions others have drawn from BankAmerica's fall is, in effect, that management does not matter much in banking, that it is luck, geography and size that determines a company's fate, not the intelligence and foresight of its leaders. The *New York Times Magazine* intoned in early 1987, 'There are no black hats at Bank of America: it's just that in organizations of a certain size unforeseen problems seem to become unrecognized difficulties and then unmanageable losses. Perhaps ... the time has come to resume the crusade against bigness itself.'

We shall return in a moment to the question of whether there were any 'black hats' at Barclays. But the general point about the unmanageability of fate in banking is one which I made myself, in a slightly different way, in the *Spectator* in May 1992. There is a fundamental reason why banks are more difficult to run than shops like Marks & Spencer, I pointed out. 'At M & S you simply sell someone a pair of trousers: there is an art to it of course, but once it's done, it's done. In a bank you borrow the trousers from one customer and lend them to another; after a lapse of time in which, however cautious your original judgment, more or less anything can happen to the borrower, you have to get them back again and return them to their original owner.'

And, of course, banking on a global scale is a much more complicated proposition than that. Banks are rarely free of trouble, even briefly, I went on, because

> diversity of business, coupled with the complexity of market risks involved and a fatal lack of comprehension between colleagues, is a

recipe for things to go awry. It is a safe piece of advice for a new chairman of an international bank that at any given moment somebody, somewhere in your group, will be doing something utterly disastrous. Your Swiss foreign exchange manager is a fraudster; your general manager has just had lunch with the finance minister of Poland; his deputy has gone to look at a new development in Docklands; half the board want you to bid for Standard Chartered; those smart young men in the investment bank are busy misinterpreting the lawyers' advice on what to do with an unsold rights issue; someone else has just recruited forty equity analysts in New York; and the credit card computer is on fire.

But still we need to ask whether Barclays was especially vulnerable to fate, and if so why. The first observation to make is that, from its origin Barclays was to an unusual degree designed for the comfort and convenience of its own executives, rather than for maximum strategic thrust in its marketplace. 'This is a club,' one newcomer to the group was told frankly by a board director in the late 1970s; and so it was.

'The private character of the banks being thus preserved', by the invention of the local head office system after the 1896 amalgamation, had advantages in terms of the preservation of local knowledge and relationships. But it created the notion of Barclays as a network of fiefdoms, rather than a co-ordinated whole, with an in-built resistance to change. The creation of Barclays (DCO) reinforced that notion, both because DCO was a separate company and a separate breed of people from Barclays Bank, and because the component parts of DCO were themselves distinct entities, run on long reins and slow lines of communication from London. Even in very recent years, a factor to be observed in common between the most turbulent parts of the Barclays empire – such as BZW – and the most successful, such as the Spanish branch network, was that none of them wanted to be told what to do by Lombard Street. Just as the French president Charles de Gaulle once remarked on how hard it was to govern a country which had more than two hundred varieties of cheese, so the ungovernable tendency of Barclays was indicated by at least two hundred designs of 'spread eagle' necktie.

Of course there was, and perhaps buried under the rubble there still is, a generalized pride in being part of Barclays. I felt it myself, even as a front-line officer of BZW in the trench warfare of the late 1980s between BZW and Barclays Bank. But it was remarkable to sense the rising of hackles in encounters between one kind of Barclays man and another: between Barclays Merchant Bank men and provincial branch managers; between International 'pirates' and Limited drones; between authentic DCO 'bush bankers' and correspondent banking managers from the domestic foreign branches: between line bankers everywhere and head office planners and bureaucrats.

Overlaid on all this in the domestic bank was Barclays' unique class structure of the families, the Special List and the rest. As Sir Anthony Tuke once said, if you are going to criticize the family system, 'you have got to be able to say that Barclays has lost out,' and at the time that he said so, in 1981, Barclays had not lost out at all: it had triumphed over its competitors. It is impossible to say whether, if the post-Second World War Barclays had been entirely meritocratic, it would have overtaken Midland even more quickly, or whether – freed from the innate conservatism of family leadership – it would have gone astray earlier than it actually did.

Would Barclays have been a better bank in the 1970s if it had been chaired by the meritocrat Derek Wilde rather than the hereditary Tuke? It might have embarked on fewer foreign ventures which were later regretted, but perhaps it would not have achieved the same level of peer-group recognition as a world leader. Would Deryk Vander Weyer have been a better chairman than Timothy Bevan? Of course I think he would – the reader would not expect me to think otherwise – and so do many other well-informed people. But we cannot know whether a sustained push for growth and innovation throughout the early and mid-1980s, which my father might have delivered, would have produced a safer loan portfolio or a riskier one by the time the economy and the property market turned bad in 1991.

What we can say about the two-tier career structure of Barclays is that it had no justification whatever once the founding partners of 1896 and their immediate offspring had passed on. It was outdated by the 1960s, both in terms of the ownership of Barclays and of the increasingly egalitarian mood of the times, but it was allowed to continue for another generation. It created frustration among talented non-family managers, and it pushed family members to levels of seniority which were beyond their real competence. It contributed, through the survival of the local head office system, to an unwieldy cost-base which took too long to reform and required, in the end, cuts which were deeply destabilizing. It perpetuated the idea that Barclays was not so much a business as a social institution that happened to handle money.

But even so, Barclays was a very well-run club. Until the advent of the Thatcher government's competitive reforms, Barclays enjoyed the benefits of a comfortably protected domestic marketplace. But it did more than just enjoy them; it exploited them with vigour, stealing ground by a series of innovations of which Barclaycard was the first and boldest. Some time after my father died, we found a tape-recording of him addressing Barclays' London Branch Managers Club in January 1982. It is the only recording of his voice that survives, and it captures him at his best, talking fluently, cheerfully, philosophically about the issues facing the bank that winter. Apologizing for the use of a cliché, he talked about 'the management of change ... The way that we shall succeed or not succeed depends on our ability to manage change wisely, not only the ability to see what the market needs but the ability to make the right decisions at the right time, pushing a bit sometimes, moving this great Barclays machine at the pace that customers want and staff can absorb. That ability is of the essence if we are to go on as the successful bank that we are.

'I always put the marketplace first, you have to be driven by what the customer wants,' he went on. 'You cannot get bogged down internally in people's investment in their jobs or their status. On the other hand, it's a great mistake to try to make great leaps into the dark: you're liable to find that no one has come with you, and you have to make a quiet leap backwards again.' Perhaps most importantly for the later parts of this story, he talked about having a general management team 'who trust and admire each other'.

The things he was talking about were the things Barclays lost over the following decade: inner confidence, collegiate trust, the ability to read market signals and to reinvent itself without traumatizing its own people. But the loss of those faculties happened slowly. By the mid-1980s Barclays had lost some of its vigour, but it was still an enormously potent force in world banking. Even in the autumn of 1986, when NatWest took the lead in profitability, most of Barclays' inherent problems seemed to be well under control. The international and domestic banks had merged into one organization, and old loyalties to DCO and Martins had begun to fade into memory. The local head system had been partially reined in. A meritocrat, John Quinton, had been chosen as the next chairman. The long-running problem of what to do with the bank's South African fiefdom had been resolved. For precisely three and a half weeks, between the announcement of Quinton's appointment and the day of Big Bang, it might have been possible to describe Barclays as in harmony with itself and poised on the verge of a new golden era.

But then BZW and the property boom came along and spoiled it all. The culture clash between investment bankers and clearing bankers proved impossible to manage. The idea that BZW people should be paid five or ten times more than their opposite numbers in Barclays caused animosities which interfered with all attempts at internal co-operation. BZW itself was, as I wrote in the *Spectator*, 'the roller-coaster gravy train' which 'never looked anything like the three year plan said it should'. In only one of its eleven years of existence – in 1993 – did it make enough profit to silence its detractors. It made millionaires of many of its employees, but from first to last it probably cost Barclays shareholders the best part of two billion pounds.

And yet BZW was really quite a small aberration in the history of Barclays. Two billion is, after all, less than the total of bad loans written off by the bank in its single worst year, 1992. The recession and property crash of the early 1990s was the trauma from which Barclays never recovered. It turned Barclays from the proud, self-confident institution of a decade earlier into the timid beast of today: restructured for the umpteenth time, incapable of promoting from within, waiting for the next hired-in chief executive, or perhaps the first take-over bidder, to give it new strategic direction.

And the technological revolution of the late 1990s – the phenomenal advance of all forms of e-commerce – is the next threat. It remains to be seen whether Barclays can emerge once more as a leader, or whether it will trail behind until it eventually gives up the race.

Who should we blame? Was the long term decline of Barclays the fault of Bevan for being too cautious, or of Tuke and Quinton for being too expansive? Were Camoys and Jacomb too ambitious, Buxton and Band too weak? Did Taylor simply have his head in the clouds? All of them were well intentioned; all might have been heroes if circumstances had conspired to help them. The only complete answer is that the fate of institutions is as susceptible to change as the societies and markets in which they operate. Whatever is created by the inter-action of time, place, economics and human aspiration is also in the end brought down by it. As my father (talking, as it happened, about the bank's role in financing small businesses) says in his 1982 recording, 'I believe that businesses, like countries and people, continually die and are revived and are born and grow and where you want to be is in the sector that is growing and not dying, even though the risks can be extremely high.'

And in the end it really does not matter whether one form of bank is replaced by another, whether one brand name sinks and others rise, so long as there are satisfied customers, satisfied investors and satisfactory jobs for those who want them. Or does it?

An organization like Barclays is, as I said at the beginning, much more than a business. It has been a part of many people's lives, including my father's and mine, and if it finally disappears it will take part of us with it. For all the harsh things I may have said, I hope Barclays recovers before it's too late. As the old advertising slogans almost said, if there isn't a Barclays, we're probably lost.

BIBLIOGRAPHY

BARCLAYS
Matthews, P. W. & Tuke, A. W. *History of Barclays Bank Limited*, Blades, East & Blades, 1926
—— *A Banking Centenary*, Barclays Bank (DCO) Ltd, 1938
—— *A Bank in Battledress*, Barclays Bank (DCO) Ltd, 1947
—— *The Eagle Looks Back*, The Spread Eagle, 1951
Tuke, A. W. & Gillman, R. J. H. *Barclays Bank Limited 1926–1969*, Barclays Bank Limited, 1972
Crossley, Sir Julian & Blandford, John *The DCO Story*, Barclays Bank International Limited, 1975

BANKING
Gordon, Charles *The Cedar Story*, Sinclair-Stevenson, 1993
Hector, Gary *Breaking the Bank: the Decline of BankAmerica*, Little, Brown, 1988
Holmes, A. R. & Green, Edwin *Midland: 150 years of Banking Business*, Batsford, 1986
Livy, Brian L. (ed.) *Management & People in Banking*, Institute of Bankers, 1980
Nevin, Edward & Davis, E. W. *The London Clearing Banks*, Elek Books, 1970
Reid, Margaret *The Secondary Banking Crisis, 1973–1975*, Macmillan, 1982
Rogers, David *The Future of American Banking*, McGraw-Hill Inc, 1993
Wadsworth, J. E. (ed.) *The Banks & the Monetary System in the UK*, Methuen, 1973

GENERAL
Bower, Tom *Maxwell, The Final Verdict*, HarperCollins, 1995
Carrington, Lord *Reflect on Things Past*, Collins, 1988
Chancellor, Edward *Devil Take the Hindmost*, Macmillan, 1999
Emmott, Bill *The Sun Also Sets*, Simon & Schuster, 1989
Fay, Stephen *The Collapse of Barings*, Richard Cohen Books, 1996

Healey, Denis *The Time of My Life*, Michael Joseph, 1989

Hobson, Dominic *The National Wealth*, HarperCollins, 1999

Hutton, Will *The State We're In*, Jonathan Cape, 1995

Kynaston, David *The City of London: Vol. I: A World of its Own 1815–1890*, Chatto & Windus, 1994

—— *Vol. II: Golden Years 1890–1914*, Chatto & Windus, 1995

—— *Vol. III: Illusions of Gold 1914–1945*, Chatto & Windus, 1999

Lawson, Nigel *The View from No. 11*, Bantam Press, 1992

Sampson, Anthony *Company Man*, HarperCollins, 1995

Young, Hugo *One of Us*, Macmillan, 1989

INDEX

Abbey Life, 163
Abbey National, 12, 24, 200
ABN-Amro, 244
Ackrill, Margaret, 27n., 179
Africa, 53–4, 105–6, 162; see also South
    Africa
African National Congress (ANC), 99,
    101, 102, 103
Airlie, 15th Earl of, 110–11
Akroyd & Smithers, 130
Anglo-Egyptian Bank, 34, 98, 120
Anti-Apartheid Movement, 100–1, 103
Arculus, David, 19
Ardron, Peter, 95
Armstrong, Mr (Helmsley branch
    manager), 201, 202, 205
Ashdown Park, 114
AT&T, 141
Atlantic Computer, 140
Australia, 142, 244
Australia & New Zealand Banking
    Corporation, 34
Ayling, Bob, 20

Backhouse, Jonathan & Co., 29 and n.
Ball, Sir Charles, 63–4
Ball, Chris, 82, 102, 104
Bamford, Tessa, 116
Banco de Valladolid, 86, 197n.
Band, David, 141, 193, 197;
    background and character, 207, 208–
    14, 218; and BZW, 139, 210–21, 223–
    4; death, 207, 209, 220, 232; in Hong
    Kong, 211–13; salary and bonuses,
    215, 218

Bank of America (also Bank America),
    45–6 and n., 48–9, 54, 83, 130, 249–
    50, 251, 258
Bank of China, 12
Bank of England, 14, 28, 30, 32, 80, 87,
    91, 167, 170–1, 190, 191; and bank
    mergers, 50–2; Barings collapse, 194–
    5, 217; Big Bang, 128–9;
    Competition and Credit Control, 58;
    LTCM crisis, 11; and Midland
    Bank's problems, 160, 161; secondary
    banking crisis, 60, 61, 62
Bank of Montreal, 255
Bank of Scotland, 248–9 and n., 257
Bankers' Magazine, 30
Bankers Trust, 85, 223, 229–30, 242,
    245
Banking World, 166
Barber, Anthony, 58, 145
Barclay, Bevan, Tritton & Co., 26, 28–
    9 and n., 61n., 75
Barclay, David, 65n.
Barclay, Joseph Gurney, 108
Barclay, Richard Fenton, 67–8
Barclay, Robert, 28n.
Barclay, Sir Roderick, 108 and n., 110
Barclay, Theodore, 64, 67–9, 68n., 93
Barclaycard, 45–6, 47–8, 122, 158, 231,
    248, 261
Barclays American Corporation, 66
Barclays Asia, 85–6
Barclays Bank: art collection, 70; bad
    debt provisions, 157–8, 159, 167,
    189, 193, 197, 257; Barclays Group
    Values, 202–4; branch closures, 256;

Barclays Bank—*contd*
brand value, 1 and n.; buys Martins Bank, 50–1, 52–3; customer satisfaction, 200, 204–6; dividend cut, 189; eating habits, 67–8, 69–71, 73–4; as family institution, 35, 36, 82–3 and n., 89, 90–3, 95, 260; head office building, 75–6; history, 26–44; Imry loan, 154–6; Internet banking, 257; job losses, 158, 196, 206, 247, 256; leadership crisis, 160, 161–2, 163–8; local head offices, 37, 43, 65 and n.; market share, 89–90, 103, 200; loss of staff morale, 202–4; losses, 189–90; marketing, 48–50, 63; Markets and Investment Banking Division, 158–9; merger rumours, 6–7; 'One Bank' project, 88 and n., 94; operating costs, 199–200, 204; overseas problems, 84–6; 'Premier' banking service, 205; problems of 1998, 5, 7–25; profits, 7, 8, 83, 86, 89, 152, 156, 159, 162, 167, 193–4, 196, 197, 198, 199, 227–8, 231, 257; property lending, 148–9, 152–6, 162; proposed demerger, 13, 17–20, 22; proposed merger with Lloyds, 51–2; in the recession, 157–8, 159, 262; relations with BMB, 259–60; relations with BZW, 137, 161, 171–3, 178, 232, 261–2; relations with Conservative Party, 77–80, 84n.; relations with DCO, 55, 66, 259, 260; reputation, 66; rights issue (1988), 150–2 and n., 156, 199; Saturday opening, 84; secondary banking crisis, 59–62; Senior Directors Committee, 81, 82, 94–5; share buy-backs, 198–9; share prices, 8, 10, 12, 16, 151, 193, 199, 238, 241; and South Africa, 97–106; Special List system, 41–3, 56, 260; sponsorship of sport, 149; student accounts, 100, 103; Taylor's resignation, 22–4, 251–2; Taylor's

successors, 246–51, 253–6; Third World debt, 149; ties, 124 and n.; 'uncles', 67–9, 81; under Taylor, 190–200, 202–6; under Quinton, 148–9; windfall tax, 81; *see also* BZW
Barclays Bank of California, 46n., 129
Barclays Bank (Dominion, Colonial & Overseas, DCO), 108; character of, 53–5; creation of, 34; expansion plans, 56–7; relations with Barclays, 55, 66, 259, 260; restructuring, 54–6; and South Africa, 88, 97–9
Barclays Bank (France) Limited, 107–10
Barclays Capital: creation of, 7, 48, 235, 244, 245; Large and, 14–15; LTCM crisis, 11–12; Russian losses, 9–10; and South Africa, 105; Taylor proposes demerger, 17–19, 22
Barclays Development Capital, 235–6
Barclays Global Investors, 17 and n., 219
Barclays International, 64, 65, 111, 112–13; *see also* Barclays Bank DCO
Barclays (London and International) Limited, 48, 63
Barclays Merchant Bank (BMB): Ball and, 63–4; Camoys and, 64–5; Corporate Services Division (CSD), 115–17; and creation of BZW, 129–35, 139; lunches, 73–4; MVW works for, 113–27; 'off balance sheet lending', 152n.; relations with Barclays, 259–60
Barclays National Bank (South Africa), 98, 101–4, 107
Barclays Unicorn, 79
Barings, 28, 194–5, 216–17, 223, 238
Barrett, Matthew ('Matt'), 255–6, 257
Barrie, Sir James, 38, 49
Bassett, Francis, 29
Baty's Bank, 39
Bear Stearns, 11, 241
Bennett, Barry, 134
Bennett, Neil, 18, 22, 239
Bevan, Emlyn, 67–9, 93, 108

Bevan, Francis Augustus, 29–30, 33
Bevan, Gerard Lee, 129n.
Bevan, Robert Cooper Lee, 30
Bevan, Sir Timothy, 180, 260, appoints
    Camoys, 64; background, 42; and
    BZW, 88, 129, 130, 135, 137; Cedar
    Holdings crisis, 60–1; as chairman,
    2, 69, 81–2, 83, 86–7, 89; in Hong
    Kong, 85; and leadership crisis, 165,
    168; and South Africa, 97, 102–4;
    successor, 90, 93–4, 95
Big Bang (1986), 107, 126–7, 128–9,
    132, 136, 177, 187, 261
Birkin, Sir Derek, 162, 190
Black Monday (October 1987), 138,
    149, 150, 176–7
Bland, Sir Thomas, 75
Blue Arrow, 140 and n., 163
Bolitho, Major Simon, 43
Bolitho, Williams, Foster, Coode,
    Grylls & Co., 31
Bone Oldham, 130
British & Commonwealth group, 140
British Airways, 20, 119, 123
British-American Tobacco, 130, 215
British Telecom, 87, 136, 151, 179, 180
Bromley, Ken, 86
Brown, Alan, 153n., 174
Brown, Alex, 229–30
Brydon, Donald, 219, 224–5, 226
building societies, 84, 200
Burns, Terry, 146
Burt, Peter, 248–9 and n.
Business Week, 66
Buxton, Andrew, 30n., 62, 73; appoints
    Large, 14, 15; background and
    character, 91n., 138; and Barings
    collapse, 194–5, 216; becomes
    managing director, 151; and BZW,
    137–8; as chairman, 2, 165–8, 246;
    and creation of BZW, 131, 132, 134;
    and dismantling of BZW, 235; and
    the Imry loan, 155, 156; as possible
    chairman, 91, 93–5; problems of

1998, 13, 17–20, 21; relations with
    Quinton, 160, 161–2, 163–4;
    relations with Taylor, 7, 197; splits his
    responsibilities, 190, 193, 194; and
    Taylor's resignation, 22–4; threatens
    to retire, 163–4
Buxton, Gervase, 113
Buxton, Lionel Gurney, 108
Buxton, Maurice, 180
Buxton, Thomas Fowell, 91 and n., 104
Byng, Rupert, 176
BZW (Barclays de Zoete Wedd), 4, 103;
    after Band's death, 220–1; attitudes
    to Taylor, 198; autonomy, 136–7; and
    Markets and Investment Banking
    Division, 158; and Barings collapse,
    216–17; Black Monday, 176–7;
    chairmen, 135–6, 144–6; Corporate
    Finance division, 139–42, 144, 215,
    217, 230, 235, 237, 240; creation of,
    88, 107, 126–7, 128–36; David Band
    and, 207, 210–21, 223–4; Ebbgate
    House, 135, 175–6, 229; enhanced
    scrip dividends, 215; Equities
    division, 142–3, 144, 215, 217, 228,
    229, 230, 235, 237, 240; Founders
    Shares, 131–2, 143–4; Global
    Markets division, 235; in Hong
    Kong, 174–5, 177–8, 181; in Japan,
    169, 170–4; job losses, 181–6, 243;
    losses, 149–50; Markets division, 227,
    229, 230; moves to Canary Wharf,
    229; MVW sacked, 157, 182–6;
    name and logo, 132n.; NFC
    investment, 115 and n.; profits, 152,
    162, 189, 193–4, 214–15, 216, 227–
    8, 231, 262; relations with Barclays,
    137, 161, 171–3, 178, 232, 261–2;
    salaries and bonuses, 143, 144, 159,
    162, 174, 177, 188, 215–16, 228, 240,
    243, 262; sale of, 6, 7, 19, 207, 228–
    45; Taylor and, 196; under Bill
    Harrison, 223–5, 227; valuation, 144;
    see also Barclays Capital

BZW Asset Management, 17n.

Cairns, Hon. Andrew, 66n.
Camoys, Tom (Lord Camoys), 82, 95, 184, 207, 224; background and character, 64–5 and n.; Black Monday, 176; and BMB, 116; and BZW, 88, 128–30, 132–4, 135, 136, 137; interviews MVW, 113; suffers stroke, 137, 152
Canary Wharf, 219, 220, 225, 228, 229, 240, 241, 244
Carden, Richard, 130
Carden, Stephen, 130
Carrian, 85–6
Carrington, Lord, 78–9, 80, 101
Carruthers, John, 120–1
Carruthers, Sir William, 120n.
Cazenove & Co., 129–30, 150
Cedar Holdings, 59–60
Chartered Bank, 34
Chartered Institute of Bankers, 166
Chase Manhattan, 83, 102
Chua, Mr, 233, 245
Citibank (Citicorp), 54, 56, 65, 66, 83, 104, 122
Clayton's Case, 113 and n.
Clegg, Sir Cuthbert, 52
Coates, Howard, 142
Colonial Bank, 97, 98, 107
Commerzbank, 217, 228, 230, 241
Connors, Michael, 126, 170, 171–2, 173, 217
Conservative Party, 58, 77–80, 185, 258
Continental Illinois, 121, 249, 250
Cooper, Rex, 133, 137, 138, 176, 209, 247
County Bank, 140 and n.
Courtaulds, 191, 192, 193, 239
Cousins, John, 134, 176
Cowdrey, Colin, 149
Cox & Co. (France), 97, 107–8
Craven, John, 130, 135
credit cards, 45–6, 47–8

Credit Suisse First Boston (CSFB), 15; buys BZW, 6, 140, 238, 240, 241, 242–5; at Canary Wharf, 229, 240
Crocker National Bank, 85, 160
Crossley, Sir Julian, 34, 72, 178
Cummins, Miss F.R., 33

Dai-Ichi Kangyo Bank, 83
Daily Mail, 203
Daily Mirror, 63
Daily Telegraph, 47, 150n., 159, 167, 177, 206, 223, 238
Davie, Jonathan, 134, 185, 220; and Founders Shares, 144; cost-cutting at BZW, 142–3; inter-divisional rivalry, 214; relations with Taylor, 232; and sale of BZW, 234, 235, 236, 240, 242–3, 245
DCO see Barclays Bank DCO
de L'Isle, Viscount, 61 and n.
de Zoete, Simon, 144, 214, 240, 242–3, 245
de Zoete & Bevan, 235; bonuses, 185; creation of BZW, 129, 130–4, 137, 140; Founders Shares, 144; in Hong Kong, 174–5; sale of BZW, 243; Tokyo office, 122, 124; see also BZW
Dean Witter, 229
Deutsche Bank, 83, 216, 223, 245
Deutsche Morgan Grenfell, 231, 241, 245
Deverell, Mark, 156
Diamond, Robert E. Jr, 9–10, 15, 17, 199, 224, 226–7, 235
Dimon, Jamie, 234
Dolling, Frank, 88, 91
Donaldson Lufkin & Jenrette (DLJ), 234, 241–2
Dresdner Bank, 12, 217
Drexel Burnham Lambert, 142, 143
du Cann, Edward, 79–80
Duma, Alex, 117, 119
Dunn, Patti, 17
Durlacher, Dickie, 134

Durlacher, Nick, 134
Durlacher & Co., 130

The Eagle Looks Back, 37–9
Ebbgate House, London, 135, 175–6, 229
The Economist, 59, 60, 112
Eilon, Amir, 142, 182, 215
Ellerton, Sir Cecil, 155n.
Ellerton, Chris, 155 and n.
Ellwood, Peter, 84n., 161, 246, 247, 248
Euromoney, 15, 85, 86, 88
European Banker, 153–4, 167–8
L'Européenne de Banque, 162, 189–90
Evening Standard, 62, 193
Export Credit Guarantee Department (ECGD), 81

Fellowes, Tommy, 133n.
Fildes, Christopher, 150n., 238–9
Financial Times, 8, 16, 82–3, 88, 128, 156, 158, 191, 251
First Direct, 200, 204, 205
First Interstate Bancorp, 250
First National Bank, 104
First-Third Bank, 117–18
Fisher, Edwin ('Tom'), 35n., 41, 70, 92
Fitzherbert, Cuthbert, 41, 42, 43, 90
Fleming, Robert, 8, 222–3, 238
Ford, Dennis, 129
France, 107–10, 189–90, 193, 197
Frank, 256
Freame, John, 28
FTSE 100 index, 176, 252

George, Eddie, 16, 236n.
Germany, 190, 193, 197, 213
Ghana, 54, 56, 105
Gibbs, Major Andrew, 202
Gibson, Tuke & Gibson, 29
Gillam, Patrick, 7
Gillett, Arthur, 97–8
Gillett & Co., 71 and n.
Goldman Sachs, 229, 236, 237, 240, 241, 244, 253

Goodenough, Frederick, 32–4, 38, 44, 54, 82, 92, 98, 179
Goodenough, Roger, 35, 72, 73, 74, 85, 91, 95
Goodenough, Sir William (Will), 34–5, 78n., 92
Goodison, Nicholas, 128
Goodwin, Fred, 249
Gordon, Bill, 19, 197
Gordon, Charles, 60, 61, 67–8, 82
Goslings & Sharpe, 29 and n.
Grant, Sandy, 73, 91n.
Green, Ken, 139
Geer, Peter, 178
Grigsby, Ben, 174
Grove, Simon, 122, 124–6, 132n.
Guardian, 11
Gunner & Company, 32
Gurney, Joseph, 150
Gurney, Quintin, 42
Gurney, Richard, 42
Gurney family, 37 and n., 95
Gurneys, Birkbeck, Barclay & Buxton, 29

Halifax, 7, 17, 22, 24, 200
Hall, Bevan, West & Bevans, 28
Hambling, Sir Herbert, 33, 136
Hamilton, Kirstie, 18
Hankin, Derek, 74, 75, 115
Harker, Steve, 232, 234, 242, 245
Harland, Neil, 114
Harrington, Noreen, 227
Harrison, Bill, 199, 232; background and character, 221–3, 230; pay-off, 252; plans for BZW, 228; resignation, 237–8; and sale of BZW, 233–5, 237–8; staff changes at BZW, 226, 227; takes over at BZW, 214, 220, 223–5
Harvey, Bob, 112–13
'Haslemere Declaration' (1968), 99
Haviland, Christopher, 64, 118–19, 124
Healey, Denis, 63, 145, 147

Henderson, Sir Denys, 19, 95, 162, 163–4, 170, 190
Henderson, Johnnie, 94–5, 103, 130
Heron, 167
Hill Samuel, 140
Hirayama, Mr, 171, 173
Hogg, Sir Christopher, 192, 193, 220
Holden, Sir Edward, 32
Holland-Martin, Sir Deric, 52
Holland-Martin, Edward, 30 and n.
Hollom, Sir Jasper, 60
Hong Kong, 85–6, 174–5, 177–8, 181, 187, 211–13, 233
Hong Kong and Shanghai Banking Corporation (HSBC), 25, 85, 122, 161, 246, 256
Horner, Doug, 60
Howard, Michael, 171
Howe, Geoffrey, 77
Howell, Philip, 104
Hudson, George, 26, 27
Hui, Kinson, 177, 212
Hutton, Will, 78n., 239
Hyundai Motor Co., 214

ICI, 34, 95, 170, 246
Imry Merchant Developers, 154–6, 167, 168, 189
Independent, 179, 244, 247
ING, 216, 217, 223, 231, 238, 241
Institute of Bankers, 82, 113
International Monetary Fund (IMF), 8, 16, 91, 234–5
Italy, 86, 193

Jacomb, Sir Martin, 30n., 69, 70, 115n., 214, 224; appointment of Martin Taylor, 190; at Kleinwort Benson, 131; background and character, 135–6, 144–5; Black Monday, 176–7; BZW's autonomy, 137; chairman of BZW, 91, 103, 135–6, 144–5, 146; in Hong Kong, 175; Markets and Investment Banking Division, 158; at

Marks & Spencer, 21; poor relations between Buxton and Quinton, 162; raids Kleinworts staff, 140; and relations between Barclays and BZW, 172, 178
Japan, 8, 93, 112, 122–7, 133n., 169–74, 215, 245
Jardine Fleming, 125, 126
Jarvis, Peter, 19, 23, 254
Jay, John, 193, 237
Jenkins, Hugh, 162
Jenkins, Huw, 182

Keating, Giles, 245
Kenny, Steve, 233
Kerslake, John, 150n.
Keswick, John, 52
Keyser Ullman, 58, 66, 79–80
Kleinwort Benson, 117, 139, 143; Dresdner Bank buys, 217; Jacomb at, 135–6; Jacomb raids staff, 140; Japanese operations, 123, 125; as possible buyer for de Zoete & Bevan, 130, 131; privatizations, 114, 119; Wedds men defect to, 134
Kynaston, David, 32

Labour Party, 62–3, 77, 78
Lambert, Henry, 35, 42, 82, 88, 93, 112
Large, Sir Andrew, 5, 13–16, 18, 20 and n., 22–4
Latin America, 84, 163
Lawson, Dominic, 168, 185
Lawson, Nigel (Lord Lawson), 3, 19, 77, 80, 81, 116, 136, 145–7, 166
Lazards, 6, 217
Leeson, Nick, 216, 217
Lehman Brothers, 139, 222, 234
Leisk, James, 98
Lendrum, Chris, 18, 22, 23, 247
Leong, Mr, 233, 245
Leslie, Sir Peter, 88, 90, 91, 93–4 and n., 103, 136, 151, 161
Lewis, Michael, 10n., 143, 187

Li, David, 175
Li, Ronald, 175, 177, 186
Lifeboat, secondary banking crisis, 61–2, 80
Linlithgow, Marquess of, 78
Littleboy, Francis, 31
Lloyd, Sir Ian, 251
Lloyds Bank/Lloyds TSB, 24, 62n.; Access card, 48; brand value, 1n.; current accounts, 84; customer satisfaction, 200; international debts, 84–5; market share, 89, 200; and Midland Bank's problems, 160; operating costs, 248; profits, 198, 256–7; proposed merger with Barclays Bank, 51–2; recovery, 163; return of capital, 195
London & Provincial Bank, 107
London & South Western Bank, 107
London Provincial & South Western Bank, 32, 35, 136
Long-Term Capital Management (LTCM), 10–12 and n., 16, 17
Lorenz, Andrew, 128, 131, 138, 141, 224–5
Loudon, John, 209
Lucie, Doug, 100

M & G, 151
McCarthy, Callum, 69, 117, 140, 141, 182, 234
McColl, Hank, 250
McKenna, Reginald, 75, 78
McKinsey & Co., 65, 158
MacLehose, Sir Murray, 85
McMahon, Sir Kit, 135, 160
Mahathir Mohamed, Dr, 121, 234–5
Mail on Sunday, 239, 250, 256
Malaysian Airline System, 13, 119
Malaysian International Merchant Bankers (MIMB), 121–2
Management Today, 195, 200
Mandela, Nelson, 101, 103, 104
Manser, John, 223

Margaret, Princess, 111
Marketchief, 154, 155
Markets and Investment Banking Division (MIB), 158–9
Marks & Spencer, 20–1 and n., 24, 258
Marris, David, 65–6n.
Marrone, Sam, 224
Martinez de Campos, Carlos, 197 and n.
Martins Bank, 36n., 50–1 and n., 52–3, 79
Mathewson, Sir George, 248, 249
Maugham, Deryck, 214
Maxwell, Robert, 152n., 160, 163
Meares & Philips, 142, 144
Mellen, Willie, 134
Merck Finck & Co., 162, 190, 257
Mercury Asset Management, 151
Meriwether, John, 10 and n.
Merrill Lynch, 85, 208, 217, 234, 241
Middleton, Sir Peter, 19, 195, 219, 224, 248; appointment of Martin Taylor, 190, 193; background and character, 145–7, 214; branch closures, 256; chairman of BZW, 145–6; Markets and Investment Banking Division, 158–9; and O'Neill's illness, 254; on Quinton-Buxton regime, 166–7; sale of BZW, 241; and Taylor's resignation, 22–4; and Taylor's successor, 247, 249, 250
Midland Bank, 31, 51, 85, 260; Access card, 48; chairmen, 78; directors, 36; gains market share, 89; headquarters, 75; history, 28, 32; problems, 43, 160–1, 163, 258; profits, 198; sold to HSBC, 25
Miller, Geoff, 88
Ministry of Finance (Japan), 169, 170–1, 172–3, 245
Mobbs, Sir Nigel, 19, 23, 163–4, 190
Monopolies and Mergers Commission, 51–2
Morgan, J.P. & Co., 6, 64, 110, 207–9, 210, 223, 228, 241

Morgan Grenfell, 129, 141, 208, 216, 223, 245
Morgan Stanley, 142, 217, 229, 245
MORI surveys, 200
Morland, Charlie, 47, 72, 113, 122
Morris, Dan, 141
Morse, Sir Jeremy, 81, 91, 163
mortgage lending, 84, 90, 148–9, 152
Mountleigh, 154, 167

National Bank of South Africa, 34, 97–8
National Bus, 139
National Freight Corporation (NFC), 114–15, 144, 236
National Provincial Bank, 50, 51
NationsBank, 250
NatWest/National Westminster Bank, 166; Access card, 48; Bank of Scotland's takeover bid for, 249n., 257; customer satisfaction, 200; gains market share, 89, 90, 103; history, 51; Japanese operations, 123; losses, 163; LTCM crisis, 12; profits, 152, 162–3, 198, 257, 261; rumours of merger with Barclays Bank, 6, 17; secondary banking crisis, 62
Newmarch, Mick, 14, 162
Nicholson, Sir John, 52, 180
Nomura Securities, 85, 123, 169–70
Norman, Montagu, 33, 34
Norrington, Humphrey, 95 and n.
Norwich Union, 7

Oates, Keith, 21 and n.
O'Brien, Leslie (Lord O'Brien of Lothbury), 51, 60
Observer, 239
Office of Fair Trading, 128
Olympia & York, 154, 167
O'Neill, Michael, 2, 249–51, 253–4
Oppenheimer, Harry, 101, 102

Pacific Union, 178

Paget, Howard, 184
Parham, John, 41
Parkinson, Cecil, 87, 128
Parsons, Herbert, 71
Parsons, Thomson & Co., 31, 46
Parsons, Thomson & Parsons, 71
Pearse, Sir Brian, 82, 195; background, 52–3; Lifeboat operation, 62; moves to Midland Bank, 160–1, 246; rights issue, 150, and n.151
Pease, J. & J.W., 31 and n.
Pease, Sir Richard Thorn ('Jock'), 94 and n., 247
Peelen, Jan, 19
Pelly, Derk, 90–1 and n., 95
Percy, Humphrey, 184
Perry, Michael, 215
Phoenix Assurance, 60, 61
Phoenix Securities, 130, 242
Pimlott, Graham, 141, 142, 232; Corporate and International Banking Services, 197, 214; job losses at BZW, 181–2; joins BZW, 69–70, 140, 143; sacks MVW, 183–4, 185; sale of BZW, 236
Pitman, Sir Brian, 163, 195, 197, 247, 248
Plumridge, Philip, 156
Portal of Hungerford, Viscount, 78
Premier Farnell, 232
Prideaux, Sir John, 62
Priestley, Leslie, 89
Prior, Jim, 78 and n.
privatization, 114–15, 116–17, 136, 139, 187, 232
property lending, 148–9, 152–6, 162
Prudential, 7, 151, 190, 205
Puget-Mahé, 142, 144
Purves, Sir William, 161, 175, 195, 246

Quakers, 27 and n., 29, 67, 75
Quinton, Sir John, 74, 146, 179, 180; background, 42; as chairman, 2, 91, 93–6, 96n., 137, 148, 261; on David

Quinton, Sir John—*cont*
  Band, 218; Guinness trial, 151n.;
  heart surgery, 156–7, 159; Pearse
  moves to Midland Bank, 160; and the
  recession, 153–4, 156, 158, 159;
  relations with Buxton, 160, 161–2,
  163–4; retires, 164–5, 167–8; rights
  issue, 150–1, 156; Saturday opening,
  84

Ransom, Bouverie & Co., 28, 61n., 72
Rappoport, Carla, 191–2, 198
Reed, Terry, 180
Reid, Margaret, 58–9, 61
Relly, Gavin, 102
Restrictive Practices Court, 128
Richardson, Gordon, 60, 61, 66
Robertson, Pat, 249 and n.
Robinson, Alastair, 124, 126, 167, 190,
  197
Rogers, Professor David, 208
Ronson, Gerald, 114, 152n., 186
Rosehaugh, 154
Rothschild, Leopold de, 64
Rothschilds, 64, 217
Rouse, Dr Lynda, 116
Rowe & Pitman, 130
Royal Bank of Canada, 255
Royal Bank of Scotland, 48, 51, 248,
  249, 254
RTZ, 81, 130, 215
Rudd, Sir Nigel, 19
Rudge, Tony, 95
Rudloff, Hans-Joerg, 15
Russia, 8–10 and n., 11, 12
Ryder, Charles, 116, 117, 139–40
Ryedale Show, 200–2, 206

Sale, Robert, 95
Salsbury, Peter, 21n.
Samuel Montagu & Co., 63, 139
Schroder Wagg, J. Henry & Co., 110–
  12, 113, 114, 115, 117, 123, 217, 223
Schuster, Sir Felix, 32–3

Scott, Jonathan, 64–5
Scottish Widows, 247
secondary banking crisis, 59–62
Securities and Investment Board, 13, 14,
  136
Seddon, Jeremy, 183–4
Seebohm, Benjamin, 47n.
Seebohm, Frederic (Lord Seebohm),
  46–7, 53, 54, 56, 65, 69, 99–100
Seebohm family, 36–7
Sharples, Tuke, Lucas & Seebohm, 29
Shell, 34, 104, 246
Sibley, Nicholas, 125–7, 142, 211, 213,
  244
Sinclair, Ken, 131–2, 133, 139, 142, 214
Singapore, 119, 120, 122, 178, 184–5,
  233, 245
Smith, Terry, 136–7
Smith, Tony, 227
Smith, W.H., 236 and n., 252, 253
Smith Barney, 234, 237
Smith New Court, 217
Société Financière Européenne, 112
Société Générale, 83, 104
Soros, George, 8, 10, 234–5
South Africa, 54, 88, 89–90, 97–106, 261
Spain, 86, 109–10, 162, 232
Spectator, 165, 168, 185–8, 213–14, 258–
  9, 262
Spencer, John, 184, 218–19
Spread Eagle, 37–9 and n., 47
Staines, Eric, 119–20, 123–4, 126 and n.
Standard Chartered, 6–7, 8, 85, 89, 101,
  122, 163, 190, 194, 248
Sten, Anne Marie, 256
Sterling, Jeffrey (Lord Sterling), 87 and
  n.
Stevens, Colin, 85, 123
Stocken, Oliver, 18, 23, 64, 70, 184,
  197, 207, 210, 219
Stolzenberg, Wolfgang, 154, 155
Stonehill, Charles, 232, 234, 240, 242,
  245
Stuttaford, Tom, 253

Sun, 255
Sun Alliance, 68
Sunday Business, 19
Sunday Telegraph, 18, 22, 83n., 156, 193, 239
Sunday Times, 12, 18, 84n., 237
Swiss Bank Corporation, 13, 14, 18, 217, 238

Takawira, Isaac, 105
Taylor, Martin: background and character, 191–2, 198; and BZW, 216, 219–21, 227–8, 230–9, 243–4; as chief executive, 191, 192–200, 202–6; golden farewell, 251–2; joins Barclays Bank, 5–6; and Large's appointment, 15; merger rumours, 6–7; problems of 1998, 5, 7–12, 16–24; proposes demerger, 13, 17–20, 22; reforms loan book, 195–6; relations with Buxton, 197; resignation, 2, 18, 22–4, 147, 254; sale of BZW, 6, 7, 19, 207; share buy-backs, 198–9; subsequent jobs, 252–3; successor, 246–7; unpopularity, 239
Telecom Italia, 243
telephone banking, 205
Thatcher, Margaret, 77–9, 80, 83–4, 84n., 102, 104, 116, 121, 145, 171, 187
Third World debt, 149
Thomson, Guy, 71
Thomson, Jeffrey, 116–17
Thomson, Sir John, 46–7, 52, 66, 69, 71–2, 92, 179
Thornton, Ronald, 30n.
The Times, 238, 253, 257
Titcomb, Jim, 130, 131, 133
Tokyo, 112, 122–7, 142, 169, 172–3
Tomalin, Michael, 95, 126, 138, 171–2, 174
Travelers insurance group, 234, 237
Treasury Minute (1920), 34, 50
Trenchard, 3rd Viscount, 125

Tress, Mark, 178
Trident, 85
Tritton, Alan, 89, 92–3, 95
Tritton, John Henton, 92 and n.
Trustee Savings Bank (TSB), 248
Tuke, A.W., 30, 31, 33, 34, 41–2, 43, 46 and n.; becomes chairman, 78; family background, 56n.; nickname, 78n.
Tuke, Sir Anthony Favill, 2, 36, 59n., 74, 82–3, 179, 260; and Bevan's successor, 94; as chairman, 69; at DCO, 56, 57; in Japan, 123; retires, 81; and South Africa, 101, 103; US offices, 66
Tuke, Henry, 31
Tuke, W.F., 33–4, 56n.
Tuke family, 29, 36–7

Union Bank of Manchester, 32
United Counties Bank, 32, 35
United States of America: Barclays Bank offices, 66, 85, 86 and n.; Barclays' losses in, 193, 197; BMB in, 116, 117–19; BZW operations in, 141, 142

Vander Weyer, Deryk, 3, 30n., 38n., 66, 147, 201, 260, 261, 262; background, 39–40; and BMB, 64, 115; career in Barclays Bank, 26, 39–41, 44, 59 and n., 66; disillusioned, 87; ill-health and death, 179–81; and introduction of marketing, 48–50; leaves Barclays Bank, 87–8; office, 75; passed over as chairman, 82; reforms local head offices, 65; secondary banking crisis, 61
Vander Weyer, Martin: at BMB, 113–27; BZW's Japanese operations, 169–74; in Hong Kong, 174–5, 177–8, 181, 211–13; sacked from BZW, 157, 181, 182–6; at Schroders, 110–12; works for Barclays in France, 107–10

Varley, John, 142, 143, 182, 184, 212, 219; on Barclay's future, 257; creation of BZW, 131, 134; and demerger proposals, 18; and Taylor's resignation, 22, 23, 247
Visa International, 89, 248

Walters, Sir Peter, 161
Walton, Len, 52
Wanless, Derek, 191
Warburg, S.G., 114, 123, 130, 139, 144, 151, 215, 217, 229, 231, 238
Wathen, Julian, 53–4, 55, 56–7, 66, 85, 119, 124n, 179
Wedd Durlacher Mordaunt, 130–1, 132, 134, 137, 144
Weill, Sandy, 234, 237
Wells, Nick, 140
Wells Fargo Nikko Investment Advisors, 17n.

Westminster Bank, 32, 36; see also NatWest
Wheat, Alan, 240
White, Noel, 47, 201–2
Wilde, Derek, 46, 48, 54, 66, 179, 260
Williams, Charlie Hue, 134
Williams & Glyn, 48
Williamson, Malcolm, 6–7, 8, 89, 94, 190, 248
Wong, Barbara, 175
Wood, Peter, 156, 161, 190, 194, 218, 246
Woodall Hebden & Co., 26, 29
Woodbridge, Cecil, 37
World Bank, 16, 234–5
Wriston, Walter, 66

York Union Banking Company, 26